GOD

THE BESTSELLER

HOW ONE EDITOR

TRANSFORMED

AMERICAN RELIGION

A BOOK AT A TIME

GOD
THE BESTSELLER

Stephen Prothero

HarperOne
An Imprint of HarperCollins*Publishers*

HarperCollins books may be purchased for educational, business, or sales promotional use. For information, please email the Special Markets Department at SPsales@harpercollins.com.

FIRST EDITION

Library of Congress Cataloging-in-Publication Data

Names: Prothero, Stephen R., author.
Title: God the bestseller : how one editor transformed American religion
    a book at a time / Stephen Prothero.
Description: First edition. | San Francisco : HarperOne, an imprint of
    HarperCollinsPublishers, [2023] | Includes bibliographical references.
Identifiers: LCCN 2022041749 (print) | LCCN 2022041750 (ebook) |
    ISBN 9780062464040 | ISBN 9780062464064 (ebook)
Subjects: LCSH: Religious literature—Publishing--United States. |
    Exman, Eugene. | Editors—United States. | United States—Religion. |
    Religious pluralism—United States. | National characteristics, American.
Classification: LCC Z286.R4 P76 2023 (print) | LCC Z286.R4 (ebook) |
    DDC 070.50973—dc23/eng/20221215
LC record available at https://lccn.loc.gov/2022041749
LC ebook record available at https://lccn.loc.gov/2022041750

23 24 25 26 27 LBC 5 4 3 2 1

To the memory of my father,

S. Richard Prothero

Have you ever considered what a sacred thing a book is?

Eugene Exman

Contents

A Graveyard Epiphany

On a warm evening in rural Ohio in the summer of 1916, Eugene Exman approached his old draft horse Nell and started to harness her up. A short and bookish sixteen-year-old, Eugene loved and trusted Nell, who was for him a model of the sort of loyalty, hard work, and silent suffering that were prized and rewarded in his hometown of Blanchester, a small farming town about thirty miles northeast of Cincinnati.[1]

Nell heard things Eugene could not hear. Sensed things he could not see. Whenever it was time to carve a cornfield into rows, Eugene would guide her while his older brother, Harold, would guide the plow. At a young age, Eugene discovered to his delight that Nell knew what to do quite well on her own, so, to his brother's annoyance, he would prop a book on her worn leather collar and bury his imagination in it while she went (mostly) ably up and down the rows on her own.

On this particular evening, the boy and his horse were exhausted from another hot day in the fields. His mother had just fed Eugene a hot supper. He had fed Nell plenty of hay and water. But today there was no rest after dinner, no rocking on the front porch with a cold drink in hand and stories in the air. God called. There was a prayer meeting to attend at Blanchester's First Baptist Church.

A pioneer congregation established in 1845, First Baptist was a product of the Second Great Awakening—a movement of individual and social reinvention that gave birth not only to ecstatic revivals and born-again Christians but also to experimental spiritual and sexual hybrids from celibate Shakers to polygamous Mormons. The Wednesday night prayer meeting was a more staid affair, patronized by a dozen or so elderly folks, almost all women, bent over by rural life in a country still battered by what was then called the Great War. In Eugene's estimation, these patrons of prayer and propriety were good folk, but First Baptist was a fundamentalist church and the church ladies took it as their Christian duty to doggedly decry the sinners in town for their wickedness.

Eugene faithfully attended these prayer meetings because he had been encouraged to do so by his pastor, the Reverend Thomas Wooten, who had rightly identified him as a possible recruit for the ministry. According to the church covenant printed on the back of Eugene's baptismal certificate, First Baptist members affirmed the Bible as God's Word and took it as their "chief business in life" to extend Christ's influence in society. That meant saving souls and abstaining from sin, including "the use and sale of intoxicating beverages." Eugene, who was by his own admission "an insufferably pious adolescent," said amen to all of the above. Raised in a religious home with parents who attended church regularly, Eugene was taught as a child to pray before going to bed. At the age of eleven, at a local revival, he accepted Jesus as his personal savior. He read the Word of God. He believed in miracles. He worried about hellfire and damnation. He did not drink alcohol. He did not have sex. He was stricter than his parents about observing the Sabbath. And he cultivated a secret life of the spirit that was his and his alone.[2]

He also went to church twice on Sundays and met Wooten for an hour one day each week after school to work through Paul's epistles. Eugene thought that his pastor's readings of scripture were dry and the church ladies' Wednesday night testimonies were trite, but he continued to show up. It was his Christian duty.

At First Baptist, Eugene grew not only in faith but also in gossip. For example, he learned that the Reverend Wooten was a kindly but not particularly righteous bachelor who "made it possible for a married lady in his congregation to have a baby." Of course, he made this intervention with the approval of the husband, who, it was said, "had not succeeded in impregnating his wife." The secret came out by degrees. As the baby's face grew into a nearly precise image of the Baptists' minister, the town was scandalized. First Baptist put out a call for a new pastor.

Eugene took his time with the complicated ritual he and Nell had performed for so many years. He gently placed her old leather collar over her head and put on her saddle. He made sure the straps and buckles fit just so. Then he led Nell to the front of the open buggy, hooked her up, and strapped her in. Climbing into the buggy and gently placing his Bible on the seat beside him, he took the reins and pointed Nell toward First Baptist Church.

On the two-mile trek into town, which ran uphill alongside the railroad tracks, he looked back toward home as the sun dipped below the horizon behind him. As the shadows deepened and the sky shape-shifted into yellows, oranges, and pinks, Exman felt as if the wonders of God were being revealed just to him. He felt his body relax as another long day of hard work slipped away.

Just short of town, on a hill on West Main Street right in front of the graveyard where Eugene's parents would later be buried and roughly a quarter mile shy of the modest brick church Blanchester's Baptists had built a few decades earlier, something startled Nell. She reared back and whinnied and stopped short. Suddenly Eugene was surrounded by a great light. He felt a charge move into him. "I was invaded," he later reported. The power moved through his skin and bones and leaped beyond. He felt himself being lifted up and out of his body. He saw the charge reach upward toward the apex of the light.[3]

Preface

At a Labor Day gathering in 2013, an elderly woman with a wide smile and brown hair parted in the middle approached me and asked if I would come to her house to look at her late father's library of religious books. I had gotten similar requests before—many people in New England have a lot of theology books—and I usually ignored them. I ignored this request, too, but for some reason it nagged at me. Her house was in Barnstable Village on Cape Cod just five minutes from mine, and she was an acquaintance of my mother. Why not follow up?

When I finally called, this woman, Judy Kaess, told me that her son had just died unexpectedly, and I should try another day. When I checked back a month or two later, Judy's husband, Dr. Walter Kaess, told me that she had died of cancer. Despite these dual tragedies, Walter called me back a few weeks later and invited me over.

The family home, a large white colonial revival built in 1820, faces Route 6A, otherwise known as Old King's Highway, just a mile west of the Barnstable County courthouse, which marks the center of Barnstable Village. Out back is a large barn and a greenhouse that serves a terraced garden whose grapevines, blueberry bushes, and roses do not suffer for lack of attention. Beyond the backyard a walking path winds through ten acres of woods to Barnstable Harbor. When I finally arrived at the house in the spring of 2014, Walter greeted me with a slight German accent and an easy smile I never could have managed so soon after attending to so much death. A handsome seventy-something retired general surgeon, Walter projected a combination of calm and competence you might well trust with your life. But I was there to see books, and I was hoping to be in and out in one hour max.

Ushering me into a large library fronting Route 6A, Walter invited me to look around. Floor-to-ceiling bookshelves filled two walls, with antique furniture scattered about as an afterthought. I dutifully gravitated to the religion books, expecting to find tomes by dead White men of no interest to me and less interest to booksellers. To my surprise, almost everything was more recent, from a decade or two before or after World War II.

The first book that called out to me was a first edition of *Stride Toward Freedom* (1958) by the Reverend Dr. Martin Luther King Jr. Inside I found a handwritten letter from King's wife, Coretta Scott King, thanking "Mr. Exman" for giving her his own first edition of a later Dr. King book. "I appreciated so much your gracious inscription which brought back pleasant memories of your visit with us many years ago now," she wrote. One shelf down was Mrs. King's autobiography, inscribed to "Eugene Exman, who possesses a beautiful and unselfish spirit, and in appreciation for your contribution to the cause of justice, peace and brotherhood." I felt my heart racing. Who was this Mr. Eugene Exman and how did he come to know the Kings?

The Living of These Days (1956), an autobiography by the renowned liberal Protestant preacher Harry Emerson Fosdick, also caught my eye. I knew Fosdick, who pastored Manhattan's massive Riverside Church in the 1930s and 1940s, from my graduate school studies in US religious history, where my adviser, Professor William Hutchison, specialized in Protestant modernism in the United States. This was another first edition (I checked), and it yielded a handful of signed cards and letters. A Christmas card featured a sepia-tone photo of Fosdick and his wife standing on a dock next to a wooden motorboat with the ocean behind them. In a postcard, Fosdick marveled at the sales of his *On Being a Real Person* (1943): "Am I right in thinking that its distribution is around 250,000 copies? That ought to make good propaganda—if true." Already the visit was more than worth it, and I was kicking myself for not coming sooner.

Alongside translations of *The World of Albert Schweitzer* (1955)—in French, German, Swedish, and Japanese—I found a framed photograph of a man Walter identified as his father-in-law alongside the missionary, organist, and medical doctor Albert Schweitzer, both in suits and ties in Aspen, Colorado. Exman was beaming. Schweitzer was looking more dourly old European, with (I would later learn) a touch of altitude sickness. There were a dozen or so books by the English novelist Aldous Huxley, including *Brave New World* (1932), which made him famous, and *The Perennial Philosophy* (1945), which located a single ancient wisdom tradition underlying all the world's religions. One had a friendly note from Huxley tipped in.

As I was struggling to choose which book to explore next, my eyes fell on a copy of *Alcoholics Anonymous*, more popularly known as the Big Book. It was signed and inscribed by the author, one of AA's cofounders, Bill Wilson: "For Gene—treasured friend whose good works mean so much to me, and to so many. Gratefully, Bill." Next to it, in *Alcoholics Anonymous Comes of Age* (1957), Wilson expressed his "gratitude for all that you have done to make AA what it is."

Who was this extraordinary person—I was already thinking of him as Mr. X-Man—who had somehow befriended not only an AA founder but also one of the most important twentieth-century British novelists, one of the most revered twentieth-century American preachers, and two Nobel Peace Prize winners?

As I sat with these questions, I continued to wonder why I was there. After a few minutes of silence unrelieved by awkward banter, I pulled AA's Big Book off the shelf and told Walter it was rare and important, probably worth at least a few thousand dollars. "We don't want to sell them," he responded firmly. Judy had contacted me, he explained, because her father had been a religion editor in Manhattan for many years, and she wanted to find an appropriate resting place for his books—a university, perhaps, that might keep the collection together to honor his legacy. Now that Judy was gone, Walter said, he felt that responsibility himself. When I asked about his father-in-law's work, Walter explained that he and Judy had met in Vienna a year after Exman retired to the Cape in 1965, so he didn't know much about his career.

As I returned to the books and their enclosed surprises, my historian's instincts kicked in. "Do you have any of his papers?" I asked. Walter rolled his eyes, tipped his head back, and chuckled. "He was a pack rat," he said. "Nobody in the Exman family ever threw anything away."

He led me downstairs.

In a dark, cobwebby corner underneath the creaky basement stairs sat a single filing cabinet, green metal with four drawers. Opening one at random, I found manila file folders organized by year: 1965, 1966, and so on. In one folder I found letters exchanged between Exman and the Episcopal bishop James Pike, who was tried three times for heresy by the Episcopal Church.

It had been hours since the annoyance I had felt as I pulled up to the house was driven out by curiosity and excitement. My time for this visit was over, but I knew I would be back. As I returned the file to its proper drawer, I felt an urgency to learn more about this man whom I had somehow never heard of and to integrate his story into the stories of religion in the United States I had been teaching and writing about for years.

After my short drive home, I took an online crash course on Eugene Exman. On Boston University's website, I found a chapter on him in an award-winning book by the University of Virginia historian Matthew Hedstrom. There I learned that Exman had run the religious book department at Harper & Brothers (later Harper & Row) from 1928 until 1965, and had traveled to Montgomery,

Alabama, early in the civil rights movement to convince King to write his first book. The thousands of books he published over five decades at Harper included both scholarly books in theology and religious studies and more popular books on mysticism and Asian religions. He had a hand in hundreds of bestsellers, including these titles later honored among the "100 Best Spiritual Books of the 20th Century":

Aldous Huxley, *The Perennial Philosophy* (1945)
D. T. Suzuki, *Essays in Zen Buddhism* (1949)
H. Richard Niebuhr, *Christ and Culture* (1951)
Dorothy Day, *The Long Loneliness* (1952)
Huston Smith, *The Religions of Man* (1958)
Pierre Teilhard de Chardin, *The Phenomenon of Man* (1959)
Mircea Eliade, *Cosmos and History: The Myth of the Eternal Return* (1959)
Jiddu Krishnamurti, *Think on These Things* (1964)

I believe little in fate and less in providence, but I felt goose bumps as I realized that I was in the process of uncovering, just five minutes from home, a genealogy of modern American religion— stepping-stones across the stream of American consciousness from Protestantism to pluralism, from dogma to experience, and from institutional religion to personal spirituality. But what truly excited me was the awareness that Exman's books were presenting me with a genealogy of my own professional preoccupations and an invitation to reevaluate them.

I had devoted the prior decade of my professional life to refuting two books on that "100 Best" list: *The Perennial Philosophy* and *The Religions of Man*. Whereas Huxley and Smith were convinced that all the world's religions were essentially the same, I had argued (alongside many other scholars) for irreducible differences among the world's religions. But far from repelling me, this disagreement drew me in. I started to see where the perennialist impulse to downplay religious differences had come from, whom it had captivated, and why. I started to feel Exman's library acting on me, challenging me to enter into the sorts of long and rewarding conversations authors inevitably have with the subjects of their research. Maybe an extended conversation with the remains of Exman's days would teach me something I needed to learn.

I then discovered that my own publisher, HarperOne, was a direct descendant of Exman's religious book department. In 1977, twelve years after Exman retired to Cape Cod, his successors took that department to San Francisco, renaming it HarperSanFrancisco to underscore the fact that they were searching for alternative spiritual wisdom from their new countercultural outpost on America's west coast. "The baseline, the common thing," HarperSanFrancisco publisher Clayton Carlson told the *San Francisco Chronicle* about this new imprint, "is the universal quest." In 2007, HarperSanFrancisco became HarperOne, and ten years after that, on the occasion of the fortieth anniversary of its move west, Carlson wrote on his imprint's website, "We deliberately publish across the entire spectrum of spiritually based movements. We are every tradition's friend and every uncompromising zealot's enemy." After reiterating HarperOne's long-standing opposition to religious absolutism, Carlson returned to the theme of the universal quest. "Because readers have certain backgrounds and concrete life experiences, they need and wish to listen to an author who, in a particular voice, speaks their psycho-spiritual language," he wrote. "Whether that voice is feminist or evangelical, Catholic or Sufi, Buddhist, Taoist or metaphysical in orientation, it is my belief that the common bond is the search."[1]

As I started looking into Exman's story, I learned from Hedstrom's chapter, "Publishing for Seekers," and from a brief mention in a book by the historian of religion Leigh Eric Schmidt, that Exman was a "seeker" himself, committed to "search for reality wherever it may be found." I was coming to see Exman's life as a key link in the emergence of seeker spirituality in the United States—a modern

American chapter in what Carlson had called "the universal quest." How had the United States become a nation of seekers in which spiritual experimentation was something of a national sport, even for self-identified Christians and Jews? Why had *religion* become a bad word for so many, and *spirituality* a good one? How had church-going Protestants like Exman given birth to our nation of religions? And why had personal experience come to play such a crucial role in cultural and religious life in the contemporary United States?[2]

Hunting for Exman's personal papers online, I was delighted to find almost nothing. I learned that, after he retired in 1965, Exman became the in-house archivist for Harper. He was also its in-house chronicler, the author of *The Brothers Harper* (1965) and *The House of Harper* (1967). He gave twenty-eight boxes of his research to Columbia University, but they did not concern the religious and spiritual books I was investigating. There were also scattered letters to and from Exman in various archives across the United States, including a few in the archives of my employer, Boston University. His personal archive was nowhere to be found.

Possessed by some combination of wish fulfillment and intuition, I decided that there was more stuff—a lot more—at Exman's home. The basement filing cabinet had included correspondence only from his 1965 retirement forward. While returning to my car after my first visit to his home, I had glanced at the two-story barn, which seemed to be in unusually good repair for a New England outbuilding. His papers had to be there. I wanted to be the first person to paw through the ephemera of his life, unseen and unread. I called Walter back, and he started digging.

Over the next few years, I visited the Exman house dozens of times. Walter graciously set me up in a dining room where Exman and his wife, Gladys Miller Exman, popularly known as Sunny, had hosted summer retreats for religion authors, including my friend the University of Chicago church historian Martin Marty. Walter now used that room only in the summer when his daughter, son-in-law, and grandchildren were visiting. It became my unofficial office.

I began with books long stored away in closets and the attic, opening a box and placing its contents on the dining room table. With help from my daughter and a family friend, I cataloged them, noting which had inscriptions or ephemera inside or contained Exman's handwritten marginalia.

I learned from one inscription that Exman had been a "cherished friend" of the Yale church historian Jaroslav Pelikan, whose *Jesus through the Centuries* (1985) had inspired my first trade book, *American Jesus* (2003). I learned that Exman was even closer to the civil rights pioneer Howard Thurman, who worked at Boston University as dean of Marsh Chapel while King was doing graduate work there. I learned that Exman had published many of the Hindu swamis I had taught in courses on American Hinduism and that in the early 1940s he had cofounded a retreat center that I had visited in the late 1990s. I also learned that Exman was friends with William Ernest Hocking, the author of *Re-Thinking Missions* (published by Exman in 1932), a book that had obsessed my mentor, William Hutchison.

Things got more interesting when Walter started pulling dozens of boxes of personal and professional papers out of the barn. There were letters to friends and family, but about half the haul comprised letters between Exman and his authors, typically organized by year or author. Other papers concerned his extensive volunteer work with nonprofit civic, religious, and educational groups. There were high school and college papers and report cards, calendars and date books, a dream journal, scrapbooks, readers' reports for book manuscripts, page proofs, and handwritten notes for talks. And there were material objects of the sort that attach themselves to a life and hang on for decades: a Ouija board, a letter opener with a signature etched by Albert Schweitzer, decades of bulletins from Manhattan's iconic Riverside Church, and programs from operas, Broadway plays, and musicals. There were photographs, too: carefully crafted studio headshots and candid photos, including images of an India trip where he encountered a guru he described as "the most compassionate person I've ever met."[3] Walter also uncovered a massive, multigenerational collection of more than a thousand family letters, postcards, and telegrams. One cache of those letters documented Sunny's whirlwind courtship and storybook wedding with Exman, just as he was beginning his career at Harper in the late 1920s. Another comprised condolence letters to his survivors after his death.

As I was making my way through this archive, Walter was cleaning up and clearing out the barn. He took a lot of stuff to the dump—"It doesn't have anything to do with your project," he said when I asked about a pile of plastic bags on the porch. I begged him to let me be the judge of that. In one bag I saved from oblivion, I found Christmas cards from the ethicist H. Richard Niebuhr, the Zen popularizer Alan Watts, and the AA cofounder Bill Wilson and his wife, Lois Wilson.

Walter eventually introduced me to Exman's only living child, Wally, an eighty-something man whom I felt I had already met from the many letters I had read between him and his parents. Weighed down by a difficult childhood and recent months on dialysis, Wally was eager to talk about his father, perhaps because he and his father never talked about much. At our first meeting, he presented me with a paper bag of remarkable material: chapter drafts of his father's uncompleted autobiography, transcripts of Exman's meetings with various psychics, a huge folder on a commune Exman cofounded in Southern California during World War II, and a reel-to-reel audio tape of one of the LSD trips he took as part of a pioneering group investigating the spiritual benefits of psychedelics.

Who was this man who gave birth to hundreds of bestsellers but never finished his autobiography? Who attended a nondenominational Protestant church faithfully every Sunday for decades yet consulted with psychics and meditated for up to three hours a day? Who cofounded a spiritual commune in Southern California in the early 1940s? Who traveled to what is now Gabon in Central Africa to meet Albert Schweitzer in the early 1950s? Who dropped acid in the late 1950s four years before Timothy Leary's notorious experiments with psychedelics? Who traveled to India to take on a Hindu guru seven years before the Beatles did the same? Who had a seemingly happy marriage of close to a half century yet passed down to his son a tantalizing collection of letters from a woman friend and Harper ghostwriter who may have been the most important person in his life? ("Of possible interest if there's to be an EE autobiography," a folder of those letters reads. "Otherwise destroy.")

To wrestle with these questions, I was beginning to see, was to wade across that stream of American consciousness—to discover, in the years from the Roaring Twenties to the countercultural sixties, how the ideas of so many Americans were redirected from thinking to feeling, from ideas to experience.

As the cataloging went on, I consulted with Walter and his daughter, Katherine Kaess Christensen, about how and where to find an institutional home for the growing Exman Archive. In the meantime, Walter and Wally told me I was free to take it all home for my research. As I worked my way through it, I was awed and intimidated by the depth and range of the correspondence, which extended from captains of industry (John D. Rockefeller Jr., J. C. Penney) to politicians (Herbert Hoover, Robert Kennedy) to playwrights (Thornton Wilder) and novelists (Kurt Vonnegut, whose house was just a few blocks down the street).

After close to a decade of research and writing, with boxes piling up in my office, folders strewn across my desk, and Exman-edited books overflowing my bookshelves, I returned one last time to the Exman library on May 1, 2020. It was a century after the Spanish flu had swept through Exman's college, and Walter and I were both wearing masks to be sure we didn't spread or catch COVID-19. I returned to books I had seen many years earlier, beginning again with the Kings. I took photos of inscriptions and of ephemera Exman had secreted inside his most prized books.

This time I stopped to read a carbon copy of a letter Exman had written in 1951 to Harry Emerson Fosdick regarding his autobiography. In this letter, Exman calls out the flaws in Fosdick's story while praising what was praiseworthy. As his suggestions gather steam, he seems to be speaking about his own life as much as Fosdick's. The experiences of any particular individual, if told right, can be read as universal, he tells his old friend. "In a sense your childhood is everyone's childhood and you can help recreate those moods and feelings that affect us all." In words he must have shared with dozens of other authors during his lifetime in books, he advises his friend to "tell the story of your experience." Exman ends the letter with an eloquent charge: to retell his story of a single individual as a story of modern American life: "You will see the book as much more than the story of one man's life. It can be a kind of spring board to telling something of the religious life in America during the last fifty or sixty years. . . . It is a book of your childhood, youth and early manhood in America that is now gone forever."[4]

As I read these words, I felt as if Exman were speaking to some future biographer—to me. Having sat for years with his books and papers, dreams and disappointments, accomplishments and frustrations, I was starting to come to grips with how much his life had already shaped my own since I got that first call from his daughter at summer's end in 2013. I was almost ready to hazard a few conclusions about the role he had played in shaping the spiritual and religious worlds so many Americans inhabit today, and especially his many contributions to what I was coming to understand as the religion of experience.

All I needed was a push, a charge, which I got at the very end of this letter from one editor to his author: "You have lived through one of the most extraordinary and rapidly changing periods of world history and you have shared in its life and history. Make that world come to life, reconstruct it with kindly detachment."

Stephen Prothero
West Barnstable, Massachusetts, 2022

Where God Walks

This book tells the story of a life and an idea. The life was lived by Eugene Exman, who ran the religious book department at Harper & Brothers and then Harper & Row between 1928 and 1965—from the Roaring Twenties through World War II, the civil rights movement, and the sixties. The idea is that religion is about experience, and that experience can be a sort of religion. This is a now popular idea—that life is meant to be lived. It may be a central conviction in contemporary American culture—that what matters when you die isn't the stuff you accumulate but the experiences you've had.

During five decades in publishing, Exman edited thousands of books and hundreds of bestsellers, turning Harper into *the* powerhouse religion publisher in the United States. Exman was present at the creation of the Big Book of Alcoholics Anonymous and AA itself. He traveled to Montgomery, Alabama, early in the civil rights movement to convince the Reverend Dr. Martin Luther King Jr. to write his first book. He brought to American audiences the work of Europeans, including the African missionary Albert Schweitzer, and of Asians, such as the Zen Buddhist expert D. T. Suzuki and the antiguru guru Jiddu Krishnamurti.

Over the course of his long career, the Catholic activist Dorothy Day and the Black Baptist mystic Howard Thurman would thank Exman for editing their books. He would have a hand in publishing two books—Aldous Huxley's *Perennial Philosophy* and Huston Smith's *The Religions of Man*—that spread the good news that the world's religions are different paths to the same mountaintop. He would publish *The Prophets* by the rabbi and civil rights activist Abraham Heschel and a translation of the Hindu classic *The Bhagavad Gita* coedited by the Anglo-American expat Christopher Isherwood and the Hindu leader Swami Prabhavananda. He would also help to make a market for paperbacks of dozens of religious studies classics (many still read today)—from Schleiermacher's *On Religion* to Feuerbach's *The Essence of Christianity* to Eliade's *The Sacred and the Profane*.

Through acts of the creative imagination that doubled as highly profitable business decisions, Exman would exert a profound influence on the course of American religion, helping to challenge understandings of the United States as a Christian nation by popularizing understandings of the country as a nation of religions where religious differences are valued. He would also help transform his country into a nation of seekers in which spiritual experimentation is something of a national sport and searching is valued as much as finding or dwelling. Along the way, he would popularize the religion of experience, which functions in the United States today as an increasingly popular rival to the organized religiosity of churches, synagogues, and mosques.

Exman did more than acquire, edit, and publish bestsellers, however. He also used the convening power afforded him as the dean of religious publishing in the United States to create and sustain a network that would spread the gospel of the religion of experience far and wide. The people he collected and connected would include preachers, priests, rabbis, gurus, philanthropists, captains of industry, university presidents, nonprofit entrepreneurs, and social and political activists. Because most of that network's members were mystics like himself, I refer to it as his mystics club. Core members of this club crisscrossed the borderlands of race, gender, sexual orientation, and religion, but they shared four key characteristics. Each had an uncanny encounter with the divine. Each was a seeker after God. Each heard God's call as a mandate to make the world a better place. And each published with Exman.

Together with his friends and authors, he went on a search for meaning in a world where war had made meaning as elusive as God. He did not always find what he was looking for, but he somehow managed to reshape modern American religion, redirecting the lives of millions of Americans from Protestantism to pluralism, from dogma to feeling, and from organized religion to the religion of experience.

Life in Wartime

Eugene Lester Exman was born on July 1, 1900, to Emmet and Mary Etta (Smith) Exman on their farm in Blanchester, Ohio. His father, the last of nine children, kept a just-the-facts diary, light to the point of weightless on affairs of the heart. For that first day of July in the first year of a new century, his diary read, in full: "Sun. 1. Cool, clear. Went to Blanchester."[1] What Emmet does not say is that he went to town to fetch a doctor to deliver his new son. At least to his busy and practical father, Eugene's birth was literally unremarkable.

Eugene's upbringing was similarly unremarkable, until it wasn't. Like millions of midwestern farm boys of the "Lost Generation," who came of age during World War I, he grew up in a small town at the start of the twentieth century. Then came one of the most remarkable stretches in American history: the Roaring Twenties, the Great Depression, World War II, the postwar economic boom, and the creative tumult of the 1960s. Plus the "search for meaning" that accompanied it all—a search that would preoccupy Eugene's private and professional lives.

The third of four siblings, Eugene arrived after a sister, Helen, and a brother, Harold. His sister Dot was the youngest. The Exman children worked hard on the family farm, raising pigs and growing hay, corn, and oats. They worked after school. They worked on Saturdays (but not Sundays). They worked throughout the summer. And they were never paid. Exman, who stood 5'8" as an adult, used to joke that he would have been tall, like his father, but all the farm work had "worn his legs off."[2]

Eugene must have been at least a competent farm boy, because at the age of sixteen he won a free trip to the Ohio State Fair after raising the best acre of tomatoes in his county in a contest sponsored by the Ohio State Agricultural Bureau. But his real love was books. He read Louisa May Alcott's *Little Women* and *Little Men* as a ten-year-old, acting out his favorite scenes beneath a tree in the pasture. Success in his studies led him from a one-room schoolhouse to local public schools. In a curriculum that included agricultural lessons alongside the three R's, he earned good grades, graduating from Blanchester High School in 1918, one year after the United States declared war on Germany and entered World War I.

In the fall of 1918, Eugene marched off with his brother, Harold, to Denison, a Baptist liberal arts college outside Columbus, in the central Ohio town of Granville. The Exman boys were able to enroll thanks to the Students' Army Training Corps (SATC), which provided shoes, a uniform, and an overcoat, plus room and board, $100 toward tuition, and a salary of a dollar a day. A precursor to today's ROTC, this new War Department program helped the war effort by transforming over one hundred college campuses into training grounds for future officers. It helped colleges by boosting enrollments that had plunged as college-age boys went to war.

The war made the fall of 1918 an unsettling time to begin college. Denison's fraternities were all but closed as men spent most of their time in the barracks and awoke before dawn for basic training. But another battle was lurking. In early October, just as Eugene and Harold were sworn into the army, seven people in Granville became horribly sick. They developed red spots on their cheekbones that quickly turned their whole faces blue. Next came black spots on limbs, nosebleeds, and loss of smell. They had come down with the

Spanish flu, which would eventually infect roughly one-third of the world's population. In the first phase of this global epidemic, most patients developed nothing more serious than sore throats, headaches, and fever. This second phase was far deadlier. Pneumonia typically took those who died, filling their lungs with mucous.

Denison immediately shut down large group meetings, including two of Ohio's most sacred activities: church and football. In October 1918, the student paper *The Denisonian* reported that the school was staying open because it was safer to stay on campus than to return home. Travel is "extremely dangerous," the story read, "since public carriers are the best method of spreading the disease." In late October, administrators shut down get-togethers of any sort, leaving *The Denisonian*'s editors to complain that there wasn't much of anything to write about anymore. Before the year was done, both brothers were hospitalized with the Spanish flu.[3]

Armistice Day—November 11, 1918—further unsettled things. As Germany surrendered, Americans temporarily set aside their fears of infection and partied in the streets to celebrate the end of "the war to end all wars." But the SATC program ended, too, and with it Harold's and Eugene's paychecks.

Harold dropped out and went home. He wanted to be a farmer, and who needed college for that? Eugene stayed. For the remainder of his freshman year he took a job tending to animals at a nearby farm. Later in his college career, he supported himself with various odd jobs, including ringing the college bell between classes. One summer, he rode a bicycle through the Ohio countryside, taking orders for *The People's Home Library* of the R. C. Barnum Company—a self-described practical collection of three books that included medical advice and recipes.

Eugene was a B student. He was not athletic, and he was neither particularly tall nor particularly handsome. In fact, he was as plain as Ohio farmland. But he had an inviting smile and a way with words. He made friends easily and would keep many for life. As an upperclassman, Eugene worked as a reporter and editor for *The Denisonian*.

He was elected to student government. He had an active social life. The Commons Club was particularly important to him. Founded a couple of years before he arrived on campus, it served as an alternative to Greek life for nonfraternity men. Its egalitarianism and inclusivism—it was not expensive, and it was open to any man who wanted to join—appealed to Eugene, who was also active in Christian organizations such as the YMCA and the Baptist Young People's Union.

Through these organizations, thoughts of a career as a Christian missionary snuck up on him. So did doubts about his faith. In his courses, Exman ran into intellectual challenges he was not ready to meet. He had been told that, if he did not believe the whale swallowed Jonah and spit him up on dry land, then he needed to give up the Bible and his Christian faith. "But I could do neither," Exman confessed. He sat up at night with his Christian friends, trying to square what they were learning from their anthropology and zoology professors with what they had been taught by parents and pastors. "We wondered if anyone could, in the 20th century, live out the Sermon on the Mount," he explained. "Or must man have a secular life and a separate religious life? We had no answers."[4]

As graduation neared, Eugene was on the cusp of marrying his college sweetheart, but friends and family warned against it. His spunky aunt Leola told him not to rush into either marriage or seminary, which he was also considering, because he owed it to his parents, and especially to his bedraggled mother, to lift his family out of poverty. Also, young love was suspect. "If we all married our first sweetheart," Aunt Leola wrote, "some of us—most of us— would be in a pretty fix now."[5]

Eugene's college yearbook, which described him as a "genial" young man with "a host of friends," prophesied success in his chosen field of "religious work." His voluntary service with various Christian groups introduced him to missionaries. Letters from Denison classmates working in missions in Burma and China also encouraged that path. When a representative of the American Baptist Foreign

Mission Society (ABFMS) visited Denison in the fall of his senior year, Eugene inquired about a missionary career. An ABFMS official followed up with an encouraging letter urging him to work as a teacher to pay off his student loans before becoming a missionary. "In some respects experience as a teacher is an almost essential part of the proper training for ordained work," the letter read.[6]

As Eugene left Granville and became Mr. Exman in the spring of 1922, he made the sorts of choices that begin to define an adult life. He did not marry his college sweetheart. He did not go straight to seminary. Instead he followed the advice of Aunt Leola and the ABFMS: he got a job for the 1922–23 school year as an English teacher. His $1,300 annual salary (plus room and board) at Elgin Academy in Elgin, Illinois, just west of Chicago, allowed him to pay off his student loans, send money to his family, and save for his future.

While at Elgin, Eugene learned of an opportunity to teach English at Peking University, a Protestant college in the Chinese capital now known as Beijing. He inquired, and in the spring of 1923 he was offered a paid three-year missionary job. The recruiter wrote, "I can think of no privilege greater than that of going to one of our large universities in China to help mold the young Chinese, who will undoubtedly become the leaders of the new China."[7]

As news of this offer spread in Blanchester, First Baptist Church members prayed for Eugene to make the right decision. Harold took a more direct route, telling his younger brother that three years in China would be a "poor move" because then he would never go to seminary. "If God had a great work for a man to do I don't believe he would send him out half trained, but would get him ready first," Harold argued. Eugene's mother also weighed in. "We would rather you would not go to China, [as] there is plenty of work to do here, and maybe we would never meet again," she wrote. "But think well about it and . . . ask the Lord to guide you. I don't want to interfere with his work."[8]

Eugene declined the job, setting his sights on divinity school instead. Denison friends tried to convince him to join them at Crozer Seminary in Upland, Pennsylvania, or Rochester Theological Seminary in upstate New York. Kenneth Latourette, who had taught Eugene at Denison before moving on to Yale Divinity School, made a pitch for Yale. Chicago had its finger on the "pulse of the Midwest," Latourette wrote, but the "intellectual center of the country is still on the eastern seaboard." Another Denison friend told Eugene that the sticker price for Chicago was half that of Yale, its academics were at least as good, and its social life was better. Plus, they could be roommates.[9]

Eugene respected Latourette, who would go on to become a close friend and Harper author, but money was tight and there was still enough of the midwestern farm boy in him to be turned off by claims that the nation revolved around a northeastern university. Moreover, Yale Divinity School was run by Congregationalists, while the University of Chicago had close ties to Baptists. Its Divinity School dean, Shailer Mathews, was a Baptist, as was its university president, Ernest DeWitt Burton, who was also a Denison alumnus. Eugene chose Chicago.

Losing His Religion

When he arrived at the University of Chicago Divinity School in the fall of 1923, Eugene was a Baptist. More specifically, he was a Northern Baptist—a product of the antislavery side of the slavery debate that split that denomination in two in 1845. But what sort of Northern Baptist was he?

Though raised a fundamentalist, Eugene had moved left theologically during college. The divinity schools he had considered were all liberal. The friend who wrote to encourage him to come to Crozer—a seminary Martin Luther King Jr. would later attend—said he was learning the "real message of God, not a distorted, twisted, narrow, old-time conception of God, whittled down to intolerance by ignorance and prejudice."[10] Eugene wanted to learn that message, too.

As he moved in the fall of 1923 from midwestern soil to Chicago asphalt, he found a mentor in Dean Mathews, who was a Baptist of a very different sort from Exman's boyhood pastors. A theologian from Portland, Maine, who was widely regarded as the "dean of American modernists," Mathews championed the social gospel, which defined sin as social rather than individual and insisted that societies needed saving at least as much as souls did. During his quarter century running the University of Chicago Divinity School, he turned that school into a laboratory dedicated to applying social scientific methods to theological problems. "We hope to make the technique of religion as intelligible as arithmetic," Mathews wrote, though his own definition of theological modernism—"the use of scientific, historical, social method in understanding and applying evangelical Christianity to the needs of living persons"—plainly accented reach over clarity.[11]

This "modernist impulse," as church historian William Hutchison called it, provoked an angry backlash in the form of Protestant fundamentalism, and by the early 1920s the so-called fundamentalist/modernist controversy was aflame. Fundamentalists accused Mathews and other University of Chicago faculty of "theological counterfeiting and camouflage." Mathews responded with *The Faith of Modernism* (1924), which sought to find a home in Protestant thought for biblical criticism, evolutionary science, and comparative religion. Mathews also emphasized experiential religion. "Faith in God . . . is not the product of speculation but of experience," he wrote. Vital religion derived from concrete "religious experience" rather than abstract "philosophical affirmation." This emphasis on individual experience commended Mathews to Exman, who had been indelibly imprinted by his Blanchester graveyard experience. But divinity school did not exactly firm up his faith.[12]

His courses taught him to interpret Christian history and the Bible in scientific terms. And the cynicism and materialism of Chicago left him cold and self-centered, uncomfortable around Denison friends he now regarded as "too pious."[13] Whatever searching Exman had been doing for his divine invader he now put on hold, along with any hopes he still harbored for a missionary career.

After earning his seminary degree with a specialization in religious education in June 1925, Exman chose not to become a missionary. He got a job at the University of Chicago Press, where he sold college textbooks, with a few responsibilities in religious books. In February 1928, Exman was visiting a Methodist bookstore in Chicago when the manager there told him that Walter Lewis, who had just started a new religious book department at Harper & Brothers, had died. The manager also told him he would be a natural for the job. Exman laughed it off, certain that the position was "beyond my knowledge or experience."[14] But the idea lingered.

A few days later, he wrote to a Harper sales manager to inquire. A telegram arrived shortly thereafter directing him to track down Harper's trade book editor, Eugene Saxton, at Chicago's Blackstone Hotel. The meeting got off to a rocky start when the younger Eugene refused the older Eugene's offer of a drink. It didn't pick up much after that. Nonetheless, Exman, who was just twenty-seven at the time, received a telegram a week later inviting him to New York for an all-expenses-paid interview. There he met with President Douglas Parmentier, Vice President Henry Hoyns, and Thomas B. Wells, chairman of the board and editor of *Harper's Magazine*. This troika of Harper heavy hitters convinced Exman that Harper was serious about not only him but also the religious book market. The men also gave him a first taste of New York as an intellectual and commercial center, and of publishing as a place he might make his mark.

Back in Chicago, Exman asked himself whether he really wanted the job. "Would I be satisfied with a career as a religious book publisher and be so tagged for the rest of my life?"[15] He knew he wanted more than a paycheck, a family, and a home of his own. He wanted a meaningful life. And though he no longer wanted to be a missionary, he still wanted a mission of some sort, a calling where he could do meaningful work. Was the Lord at work at Harper?

A few days later, on a business trip to Pittsburgh, Exman looked up the Reverend C. Wallace Petty to ask for his advice. The pastor of Pittsburgh's First Baptist Church and a leading Northern Baptist, Petty had impressed Exman during a baccalaureate address he gave at Denison's 1922 commencement. "Take it," Petty said, after hearing Exman out. Religious publishing is in many respects a "more significant and lasting" channel for "the message of religion" than the pulpit, he said. Besides, "there's no better name in publishing and to be getting out books for preachers and laymen to read will give you a tremendous opportunity for influence and service."[16]

Exman, who had still not heard from Harper, sent an overnight letter to Hoyns saying he would soon be on a business trip in Philadelphia if he wanted to talk further. Hoyns called the next morning to offer Exman the job, and after some back-and-forthing the two men came to terms.

It is sometimes said of the supposedly pious Pilgrims that more came to New England to catch fish than to please God. Exman's motivations for his own pilgrimage were similarly practical. He went to New York with the belief, first suggested to him by Petty, that religious publishing could be a Christian calling—that a nation could be shaped by books as surely as by preaching. But he also went for pragmatic reasons. The new job offered more money, more responsibility, and better career prospects.

While still in his twenties, Exman was going to New York to shepherd books into the world by way of one of America's premier publishers—a company, founded by Methodists in 1817, that had published *Moby-Dick* and *Adventures of Huckleberry Finn* as well as those two children's books that had transported him to the frontier of his boyhood imagination: *Little Women* and *Little Men*. He would take it as his mission to expand the popular understanding of the religious book and to stretch its audience far beyond the pews.

A Mission (and a Job)

When Exman accepted the Harper job, the religious book business was booming, with four major trade houses starting religious book departments in the late 1920s. Religious nonfiction was the second-bestselling book genre, trailing only adult fiction. *The Man Nobody Knows* (1925) and *The Book Nobody Knows* (1926), bestsellers about Jesus (the man) and the Bible (the book) by the advertising executive Bruce Barton, had shown that religious nonfiction could sell if it was marketed well. Before 1927 was over, publishers had established a mail-order Religious Book Club and *Publishers' Weekly* had declared a "religious renaissance" in bookselling.[17]

At Harper, Exman would initiate his own revitalization project, which would transform not only the religious book market in the United States but also American religion and American culture. While Exman was at the University of Chicago Press, the overwhelming majority of religious books sold in the United States were either Bibles or parochial projects: collections of Lutheran sermons by Lutheran pastors sold to Lutheran parishioners, or similarly focused books of, by, and for Congregationalists or members of the Disciples of Christ. "Most religious books never reach the great bulk of the reading public," complained Mary Rose Himler of Bobbs-Merrill in an article in *Publishers' Weekly* in 1927, "because most religious books are bigoted and prejudiced" or uninspiring "textbooks for divinity students." Exman worked hard to change all that.

The religious landscape in the United States at the time was largely divided into various sorts of Christians. There were Catholics, of course. But the overwhelming majority were Protestants, who were divided into an astonishing array of denominations: Baptists, Methodists, Lutherans, Episcopalians, and so on. Many of these denominations were themselves divided, by race and into northern and southern White branches who had split over slavery and were now divided over segregation. As an "ecumenical Protestant,"

Exman had no interest in interdenominational battles.[18] His books reflected that stance, downplaying denominational differences and emphasizing the commonalities among Protestants and across Protestant and Catholic lines. Eventually, this inclusive and pluralistic approach would make him a pioneer in publishing trade books about Jews, Muslims, Hindus, and Buddhists. However, this shift from fundamentalist Protestant exclusivism to liberal Protestant inclusivism was just the first part of his project.

The second part was a shift from doctrine to experience. At the University of Chicago, Exman had learned from his mentor Dean Mathews a lesson that Mathews had learned from the philosopher and psychologist William James: that religion is not about the dogmas or rituals of ecclesiastical institutions; it is about personal experience. These twin emphases—on pluralism and experience— were mutually reinforcing. If religion is, as James put it in his bestseller *The Varieties of Religious Experience* (1902), "the feelings, acts, and experiences of individual men in their solitude, so far as they apprehend themselves to stand in relation to whatever they may consider the divine," then there is no way to confine religion to official doctrines, official creeds, and official theologies. If religion is about experience, there is no reason to confine one's religious reading to Baptist or Protestant or even Christian experiences. And what is a *Christian* experience anyway? Had a single encounter with the divine ever come with labels attached? For Exman, a seeker was a seeker was a seeker, no modifiers required. He published books that would help his readers (and himself) in their personal quests for the divine, specializing in writers who could appeal to wide audiences, always in a nondenominational voice and always with one eye on spiritual practices and another on religion in action. His books addressed the day-to-day experiences of ordinary people: war and peace, life and death, depression and happiness. A book by a Protestant laywoman described in one Harper catalog as "a most helpful new approach to the practice of prayer" was said to be "written for the really average person, indifferent or incurious about prayer, but somehow restless and unsatisfied in his search for peace and security."[19]

Exman's books went out into the world at a time before the proliferation of television, the internet, and social media, when books and their authors carried enormous cultural weight. As a result, they were able to do missionary work of their own. The task Exman set his books to doing was to preach to generations of Americans the religion of experience. In the process, they helped create new categories of religious affiliation, from people with multiple religious identities to the "spiritual but not religious" cohort, which is the fastest-growing religious affiliation in the United States today. "The center of interest in religion is passing from theology to life," Mathews had observed in 1924.[20] Exman's books enabled, encouraged, and accelerated that passing.

Exman's work wasn't just a mission, however. It was a job. He knew his job was to make money, and he did that job well. Some have observed a "religious depression," including a sharp decline in religious book sales, that accompanied the Great Depression, which began in October 1929. Exman bucked that trend. Though his first five years at Harper coincided with the end of the Roaring Twenties, the Wall Street crash, and the beginning of the Great Depression, his department's profit-and-loss statements improved every year—from a loss of $13,581 in 1928 to a profit of $19,367 in 1933.[21]

Who was this most intriguing spiritual *and* religious man? As I sorted through decades of papers and photos, and visited various archives, I began to see Exman as a man who remade American religion and culture by remaking himself. In these twin transformations, Exman was influenced by his wife and children, by bosses, editors, and salespeople at Harper, and by friends who became his authors and authors who became his friends. But there were two people who had an especially profound influence on his life: a man who died around the time Exman was born, and a woman, roughly his age, who would become a close friend until his death. The man was a philosopher. The woman was his conscience and his muse.

The Philosopher

Regarding the philosopher, two letters tell the tale.

On February 2, 1958, Exman's daughter, Judy, wrote to her mother, Sunny, from Denison College, where her father was a proud alumnus and her brother Wally was a recent graduate. A second-year student, she was taking, and hating, an introduction to psychology. She hated the lectures, the readings, and her professor's obsession with debunking parapsychology. She especially hated a required book called *Fads and Fallacies in the Name of Science* by the popular science writer Martin Gardner. This "study in human gullibility," as Gardner described it, took aim at dozens of "pseudo-scientists," including more than a few of Judy's father's friends and authors. But Gardner did not target only "medical quacks" and their "cults." He took aim at the publishers and editors who amplified their nonsense.[22]

"The book really upsets me," Judy wrote to her mother. "My professor doesn't believe in ESP, psychokinesis, clairvoyance or prognosis," she explained. "He seems to be teaching the class that his views are correct. It scares me. He seems to say that you must doubt everything unless you can definitely prove it exists or is true." Judy then asked her mother to ask her father to write back with answers.[23]

Exman replied with a long and revealing letter that, after some tried-and-true paternal advice about hard work and determination, made a case for the importance of open-minded parapsychological research. Exman decried the lab-obsessed "rat psychology" that had overtaken academic psychologists in recent years. He also lamented the rise of college classrooms where students were expected to parrot back their professors' views. "In Russia apparently, a student is expected to read and to listen with a minimum of criticism and to give back in class or paper what he has been told to believe," he wrote. Liberal arts colleges should be different. "One important reason for a college education (or for taking a course in psychology) is to develop your own reasoning powers," he continued, "to determine by criticism what seems to be the right answer and the true under-standing, and to check your conclusions with others who want the truth as much as you do." In the absence of this sort of true learning, the United States was at risk of becoming "a society of automata—people who can be made to act by suggestion along the course laid down by a strong leader," as in "Nazi Germany under Hitler."[24]

Exman admitted to Judy that the flying saucers theories of his friend Gerald Heard might well be "off the beam," but he criticized close-minded scientists for failing to look at extrasensory phenom-ena with open minds. "Try not to get emotionally involved in this course," he wrote. "Keep a 'scientific' and detached approach to classroom work and assigned readings."[25]

Finally, Exman alerted his daughter to a philosopher who, more than any other thinker, influenced the trajectory of Exman's personal and professional lives, and to a book that, more than any other book, influenced his publishing career and his own spirituality. "William James taught at Harvard, taught psychology before the days of 'rat psychology,' and his book 'Varieties of Religious Experience' has never been out-dated. It is still a classic treatment of a significant psychological problem," he wrote. "Ask your Professor if you may read 'Varieties' for credit in the course. I'll mail you a copy."[26]

The son of the theologian Henry James Sr. and the brother of the novelist Henry James Jr. and the diarist Alice James, William James was a Harvard professor of psychology and philosophy. He is now widely regarded as a founder of both disciplines. In philosophy he is known as a pragmatist and in psychology as an empiricist, which means that he found evidence for truth in its effects and preferred detailed observations of human behavior to theories about it.

In 1900, the year Exman was born, James was hard at work on the Gifford Lectures he would deliver at the University of Edin-burgh between May 1901 and June 1902. Those lectures reimagined psychology and philosophy by viewing both through the lens of extraordinary religious experiences. The book that grew out of those lectures, *The Varieties of Religious Experience*, exerted a lunar pull on the study and practice of religion in the United States, both in James's lifetime and beyond. That force shaped Exman, who in turn popularized James by channeling his spirit into hundreds of best-sellers, which allowed middlebrow readers across the United States to see religion's varieties through James's eyes. Exman also helped shape a new academic discipline—the study of religion—in the direction of James by publishing authors who, like James, saw truth and beauty in a variety of religious traditions.

James's broad project in *Varieties* was to defend religion among its secular despisers, including his Harvard colleagues. James advanced this project, as he advanced his pragmatic philosophy, by tabling the question of truth and focusing instead on experiences, which he regarded as "the real backbone of the world's religious life." Religious experiences were in his eyes personal and idiosyncratic. They sprang forth not from pulpits and altars but from the uncanny lives of "religious geniuses"—saintly eccentrics who through some combination of temperament and training whittled away at the perceived distance between the self and God in order to achieve (or approach) union with the divine.[27]

Through his exploration of the mysterious experiences of these geniuses (and similarly experiences of his own), James came to see mystical experiences as the most important religious data: "the mother sea and fountain-head of all religion." Everything else, "all theologies, all ecclesiastisms," were to him "secondary growths," secondhand impositions on the original ecstasies of the Buddha, Jesus, and their kin.[28]

Like James, Exman wanted to create a way for people who wanted to be religious to stand among the faithful without slouching with shame. Exman also derived from James many of his core religious impulses: His conviction that religion is good—that "the best fruits of religious experience are the best things that history has to show." His preference for firsthand experiences over secondhand dogma. His disdain for institutionalized religion and his fascination with religious eccentrics. His deep-seated suspicion that ordinary consciousness is not all there is. His commitment to the careful investigation of seemingly outlandish practices such as séances and clairvoyance and mental telepathy and ESP. His principled fuzziness about the divine. His revulsion at the "dull habit" of church pews and prayer books and his attraction to the "acute fever" of those rare religious "geniuses" to whom the "unseen divine" is manifest. His empathy for American religious outsiders, including Buddhists, Hindus, and participants in new religious movements (accompanied by his insistence on viewing them from a Protestant center, which, for him and for James, was always and everywhere assumed). His curiosity about the connection between hallucinogenic drugs and mystical experiences. His allergy to easy certainties. His anti-imperialism, antitribalism, and hostility to war. And, finally, his democratic conviction that real religion is felt rather than thought, and that it can be experienced by anyone, even a sixteen-year-old farm boy.

Both James and Exman were decades ahead of their times. Their work prepared the way for the counterculture of the 1960s and 1970s, and today's culture of experience. What drove them was a search for the extraordinary that transported them out of the day-to-day dullness that was Harvard in the early twentieth century and corporate America in the mid-twentieth century. They were ambitious. They wanted to feel something other than the dull ache of the meaninglessness of so much of modern life. Neither was satisfied with the sorts of cheap thrills that Hollywood and the automobile industry now peddle. They wanted more. They wanted what James called "the great mystic achievement"—the "overcoming of all the usual barriers between the individual and the Absolute."[29]

The religious and cultural historian Matthew Hedstrom is right to observe that Exman "commodified" William James, translating his highbrow lectures into middlebrow bestsellers. As Christian churches were suffering through a Great Depression of their own, it made sense to look to new markets for religion books. And Exman profited handsomely from that strategy, via raises, promotions, and the social status that came with being regarded as *the* leader in his field. Moreover, Exman was a company man concerned—overly concerned, perhaps—with his department's bottom line. But he never fully accepted the view that the business of religion publishing was simply business. "The decision to sell religious books like chewing gum" may have been made by almost every other religious book publisher by the middle of the twentieth century, but the ghost of William James never left Exman's side. He never stopped seeing books as "sacred things" and publishing as a "sacred trust."[30]

The Muse

Exman's conscience and muse was an extraordinary woman named Margueritte Bro. Six years his elder, she came to know him through that old-fashioned technology of the letter. They first corresponded in the summer of 1943 while she was working on a piece for the liberal Protestant magazine, *Christian Century*, on the famed American psychic and clairvoyant Edgar Cayce. They met in person that fall and immediately began a lifelong friendship.

Unlike James, Bro worked largely in obscurity and is unknown today. American publishing in the middle of the twentieth century was a man's world, and the contributions of women to it were (and are) underappreciated and overlooked. Bro and Exman exchanged well over a thousand letters, which appear in the Exman Archive in every dated correspondence folder from the 1940s through the 1970s. Across the cover of one folder dedicated entirely to her, Exman scrawled in bold black pen, "of possible interest if there's to be an EE autobiography otherwise destroy."

Bro was born on August 5, 1894, in David City, Nebraska, into a long line of Disciples of Christ clergy, which included her father, Andrew Harmon, and would eventually extend to six generations, down through her son Harmon Bro and her granddaughter Pamela Bro. A second religion in this family was higher education. Bro's father was president of Cotner College in Nebraska and Transylvania University in Kentucky. Her brother, Henry, and sister, Harriet, also became college presidents.

Margueritte herself graduated from Cotner in 1917. Shortly thereafter, she married Albin Bro, whom she met while she was taking classes at Northland College in upper Wisconsin. By 1919, the same year Exman went off to Denison, she and her new husband were working as educational missionaries in China, where three of their four children were born. They returned to the United States in 1925 to raise money for their mission, but a growing anti-Christian movement in China stymied their return. They never saw their Chinese home again.

Albin shuffled from job to job during the Great Depression, picking up work at Northland College, a religious education association, and a pension fund. For seven years in the 1930s, he worked in sales at the University of Chicago Press. Margueritte earned money in what is now called the gig economy, almost always as a writer or editor. The family's finances improved in 1939, when Albin was hired as president at Frances Shimer College in Mount Carroll, Illinois. There Margueritte looked after their four children and served as a dutiful "first lady" in an era when that uncompensated assignment was more than a full-time job.[31] She also continued to do freelance work, including for Exman at Harper. Beginning in 1950, Albin worked for a few years for the State Department in Seoul, South Korea, with Margueritte at his side. He died of a heart attack in Chicago in 1956. She never remarried.

Bro began writing after returning from China in the 1920s and quickly became an accomplished author. Despite being a dutiful mother and faculty wife, she wrote more than two dozen books under her own name and ghostwrote many more. She wrote half a dozen plays and coauthored a textbook on the theater that went through multiple editions. She wrote pamphlets on topics ranging from social action to pacifism to the Bible. She wrote articles for academic journals and national magazines, contributing regularly to *Christian Century*. She was also a popular speaker who would stop in the middle of an invited lecture to sing a song for popular effect. One of her young adult novels, *Sarah* (1949), is still in print. A coming-of-age story, it takes off when Sarah's dying father devotes his last words to predicting that she is going to be a great artist. Unfortunately, marriage gets in the way.

Though a devoted member of the Disciples of Christ, Bro was also attracted to what the historian of religions Catherine Albanese has referred to as "metaphysical religion." This tradition affirmed, among other things, the power of the mind to heal both the body and the world. As she saw it, psychics and mystics understood far better than ministers and theologians the subtle correspondences between the physical and spiritual planes. Like James, who turned to a spiritualist medium in 1885 after the death of his son Herman, Bro was captivated by the possibility of communication with the dead. She believed in reincarnation. In fact, she was drawn to the long menu of uncanny experiences James once cataloged as "conversations with the unseen, voices and visions, responses to prayer, changes of heart, deliverances from fear, inflowings of help, [and] assurances of support."[32]

Bro and Exman were both members of the Lost Generation, which came of age during World War I and entered middle age during World War II. The shipwreck of belief in progress on the shoals of those wars—a belief that had profoundly shaped the modern world since the Enlightenment—deeply unsettled them. What was happening to the United States and the world? Where was God when American airmen dropped atomic bombs on Hiroshima and Nagasaki? As pacifists, both saw the modern world—its nationalism, its militarism, and its secularism—as a threat to meaningful human life. They saw themselves as seekers after meaning. And they sought to find that meaning in God. Specifically, they found meaning in mystical encounters of the human and the divine, and in techniques such as prayer and meditation that fostered those encounters.

But it wasn't just meaning they were seeking. They were seeking an antidote to the illness of modern materialism and militarism. And they found it in religion. Without religion, they reasoned, the world blows up.

Shortly after they began corresponding in the summer of 1943, Bro started doing freelance editorial work for Exman. She continued that work for many years, both as a freelancer and on staff. She helped acquire authors and books. She evaluated manuscripts and wrote reader's reports. She criticized Exman for not reading manuscripts carefully (or at all) and for possessing "a certain innocence" about their faults. She copyedited. She suggested book titles. She wrote catalog copy and jacket copy and weighed in on book designs. She helped promote books. She suggested places to advertise them. She also ghostwrote many books on Exman's list, often under the bylines of men. She navigated these tasks with grace, stroking egos when necessary but always insisting on writing that made sense, both at the sentence level and in its overall argument and design.[33]

It is hard to overstate the impact Bro had on Exman's life. Exman's son Wally, who fondly remembered listening to jazz music with Bro in his father's study, described her in an interview as "Dad's peer and therefore someone to listen to and be reckoned with." She was, Wally added, "a strong influence on his life." In fact, Exman was more intimate with Bro than he was with anyone else. He saw their friendship as "a gift of God." The many letters they exchanged, sometimes multiple times a day, were personal and professional, attending to the challenges of books and to their shared hopes and dreams, beliefs and doubts. Exman trusted Bro's editorial judgment. Regarding his personal life, she was his closest confidante and his most influential sounding board. He told her things he barely was able to tell himself—about his family, his work, and his ongoing quest for God.[34]

A Collector of Mystics

Exman was not the first American pilgrim to wander from institutional to individual religion—from the dogma and rituals of the one true church to the "blooming buzzing confusion" (James's phrase) of the varieties of religious experience. There was James before him and Bro beside him, and Emerson, Thoreau, and other Transcendentalists before them all. In their own ways, Puritans in the colonial period and Methodists in the early republic also redirected religious folk toward the drama of individual experience, not least the transformational act of conversion. So did Quakers, who harkened to the Inner Light of the divine. But Exman was the first to combine the resources of a major American publishing house with the tactics of a savvy editor, the support of a smart collaborator, and the missionary spirit of a philosopher who doubled as an evangelist for the religion of experience.[35]

All this work began with a single moment in Exman's life. That moment was not the start of his first day at Harper or the time he met Margueritte Bro or the moment he heard he had his first bestseller. His life turned on the events of that warm summer evening as a teenager. Just short of town, roughly a quarter mile shy of Blanchester's First Baptist Church, something startled Nell. She reared back and whinnied and stopped up short.

When it comes to describing what happened next, words fail. Exman experienced a combination of a lack of understanding and a craving to understand that often accompanies such moments. Later, he would report that he was surrounded by a "great light." He was filled with "immense joy." He said, "I was lifted from my body into unimagined and indescribable glory. I was invaded by a power that obviously my body could sustain only for a brief time."[36]

This graveyard experience was momentary, and it could easily have been forgotten. Uncanny experiences of this sort are more common than most of us imagine; almost all human beings have them at some point in their lives. All too often, we shake our heads and explain them away. We had too much to drink, perhaps, or not enough to eat. We had a fever, or maybe stress had gotten the best of us. There are all sorts of ways to forget events like this, but Eugene did not walk in those ways. He chose to remember this moment. And he chose to retell it. In ensuing years, he would characterize what happened as a "blinding moment," a "divine invasion," a "kind of lightning stroke," and an "'out-of-the-body' experience." He would interpret it as "a foretaste of the ecstasy the soul may enjoy after the death of the body," a glimpse of "the Eternal Now." He also drew on a metaphor that is often close at hand for teenage boys: "The experience is best described as that which comes to man and wife at the climax of intercourse when at orgasm each is lifted momentarily out of self-hood into a transcending union."[37]

Exman's later retellings differ in some details but converge on three important points. First, it was an experience of joy, not terror. Second, it was an experience of the divine, "a real experience, I suppose a mystical experience." Third, it was so powerful that it left him convinced he would never doubt God again.

As the divine receded behind its customary cloak of invisibility, and as Nell, now calm, began to slouch toward town, Eugene exclaimed, "Oh, God, I never again need doubt that you are!" Like most other prophecies and promises of the young, this one turns out to be incorrect. He would doubt. In divinity school, he later confessed, "I began to think that my experience was possibly the result of unsatisfied sexual yearnings or possibly a glandular disturbance." When asked in one course to write his religious autobiography, he let that moment pass, perhaps because he was ashamed to relate it: "I did not mention that God was once my burning bush beside an Ohio roadside."

As an adult, Exman returned to this Blanchester graveyard experience repeatedly, like a lucky stone you pick up and turn over and examine from time to time, recalling where you found it and why you still treasure it, begging it to speak. The silence that followed he filled with words of his own, recording at least a half dozen versions of his graveyard epiphany—in letters to friends, in handwritten drafts of his unpublished autobiography, in talks, and in conference proceedings.

After this key moment in his life, Exman became not so much a true believer as a seeker after invisible things. His vision, like that of most seekers, was clear from time to time, but often foggy. The boy who doubted and then believed became a man who believed and then doubted. But he would never forget his encounter with what William James called the "unseen divine." From his mystical moment forward, he would continue to chase after that first "transcending union," that original orgasm with the divine. Like any other addict, he craved that high from the first shot forward. And when he could not find that high on his own, when his divine lover went missing (as gods and goddesses tend to do), he would seek it out in the lives of others. He became, in his own words, "a collector of mystics."

When we think of seekers nowadays, we tend to think of people who either don't really know what they are looking for or value searching for its own sake. The term conjures up uncommitted types who flit from one spiritual fad to another in search of the "Real Thing." Seekers try on yoga and tai chi for style before taking off for a weeklong mindfulness retreat. Their search is for community. Or identity. Or both. Restlessness drives them.[38]

But Exman knew what he was searching for, because he had already found it. He was searching for the not-always-unseen divine of the Blanchester graveyard. More than anything else, he wanted to return to that primordial mystery: the encounter of the human and the divine. He wanted to be struck again by a bolt of lightning. To mumble, "God is."

In his concluding remarks at a 1967 retreat, Exman returned once again to his adolescence in Blanchester. He had been a teenage boy raised in a pious home that stressed bedtime prayers and church attendance and Bible reading, he said, but nothing ever really clicked:

I tried awfully hard . . . in this evangelical, fundamentalist community, to find out what the experience of Christ was. The preachers
who exhorted us to be converted and to change our ways and
to come to Christ, seemed to know that there was an experience
which could be had. But it did not come to me when I "went
forward" as was customary in those evangelical churches. It did
not come to me when I was baptized as I thought it might.

Then one Wednesday evening, Exman continued, "I was driving a
horse and buggy, into town, and I can take you to the place today:
where, on a hillside, I suddenly had an experience which I knew was
it. It was a lifting out of myself, it was a kind of lightning strike, a
sudden awareness that I was—I suppose I was praying—a sudden
awareness that God is."[39]

As he doubted in divinity school and as he suffered through the
"dark nights of the soul" known to trouble even people of strong
faith, he would take himself back to that moment when he was
graced with "a real experience . . . a mystical experience . . . [an]
inward experience of the presence of God." Memories of such experiences, he told his fellow travelers at that retreat, assure us in dark
times "that we have been where God walks."[40]

But Exman was not content merely to remember that moment.
He inhabited a world in which militarism and materialism threatened
to obliterate the possibility of a meaningful life. He responded to
that threat by seeking to return to the presence of God that had
upended him as a teenager on the road to Blanchester. This search
was experiential. It was also experimental. He tested all sorts of
techniques—from prayer to meditation to "cell group" meetings to
communal living to LSD—that might somehow seduce the divine
into invading him again.

During this quest, Exman sought out mystics, God seekers, and
spiritual experimentalists who might help him find what he was
seeking. "I have a hobby," he once confessed, "of collecting and
cataloging saints."[41] When he found them, he befriended them and

prayed with them and enrolled them in his unofficial mystics club. He also worked with them and corresponded with them and published them, amplifying their voices (and his own). The books they made together made more readers, more books, and more seekers after the divine.

If you think of the books that Exman published at Harper from the 1920s into the 1960s as one massive anthology of religious experiences, a Book of Books, it is hard not to see its similarities to James's *Varieties of Religious Experience*. Rejecting the authority of religious institutions, leaders, and scriptures, it locates the beating heart of the sacred in individual experiences without forgetting that experience is always social, too. And it is preoccupied above all with mystics and saints. Whereas James the philosopher cited Buddhists and Hindus and Sufi poets and medieval Catholic and modern Quaker mystics in his classic, Exman the editor published all of the above. In fact, almost all of the most popular and enduring books on Exman's list are records of religious experiences: autobiographies by Harry Emerson Fosdick and Dorothy Day, biographical accounts of Albert Schweitzer, King's reminiscences of the Montgomery bus boycott, and so on. Other books he helped bring into being, including Huxley's *The Perennial Philosophy* and the Big Book of AA, follow precisely the autobiographical method James pioneered in *Varieties*.

The book that follows is a close reading of that Book of Books, which was edited by Exman, informed by James, and inspired (and in some cases written) by Bro. It is also a story about that most intriguing man who ushered them into the world: An Ohio fundamentalist who remade himself and American religion by championing religious diversity without ever quite shaking his Protestant upbringing. A pacifist who jumpstarted the culture wars by making plain that the political landscape in the United States was deeply divided between a religious right and a religious left. A mystic whose unrequited longing to see God led him to befriend and publish other mystics. A Christian who went to India in search of a Hindu guru. A company man and a countercultural man who sat on boards of directors during the week and dropped acid on the weekend. Exman helped reimagine and remake American religion, bending the arc of US history toward an interfaith America where religious boundaries are blurred and religious variety is valued.

This is a story of a collector of mystics who founded a club for mystics who went in search of God and of meaning, together and alone. It is also a story of American culture on a quest of its own — a search, born of two world wars, for some resolution of its still unresolved identity as a nation of Christians *and* a nation of religions. It is a story of the emergence of the religion of experience as an American religion, perhaps *the* American religion, and of the emergence of a broader culture of experience that continues to shape a nation today.

CHAPTER ONE

America's Pastor
Harry Emerson Fosdick and the
Religion of Experience

As Eugene Exman was preparing to quit Chicago for New York and his new job at Harper & Brothers in the spring of 1928, he tracked down his University of Chicago mentor, Dean Shailer Mathews, to say thank you and goodbye. Mathews, a fellow Baptist, offered to smooth his former student's transition with a letter of introduction to another Baptist: the Reverend Harry Emerson Fosdick.

Three years earlier, Fosdick had been featured on the cover of *TIME* magazine as "the least hated and best loved heretic that ever lived." When Exman arrived in New York, Fosdick was the pastor of Park Avenue Baptist Church in Manhattan and a professor at Union Theological Seminary. He was also a bestselling author who attracted millions of listeners a week on NBC's *National Vespers* radio program. The *New York Times* printed his sermons, and his writing appeared in magazines as distinct as *Atlantic Monthly* and *Ladies' Home Journal*. In his spare time, Fosdick composed popular hymns and drew on his abundant social capital to amplify pacifists and civil rights activists. For all these efforts, Martin Luther King Jr. lauded him as one of "the foremost prophets of our generation."[1]

Fosdick would go on to become a leading author for Exman,

who would publish seventeen of his books, including many best-sellers. They would also become close friends, meeting regularly for lunch and exchanging letters. In time, Fosdick would flatter Exman as "a grand publisher," and Exman would describe Fosdick as not only "a friend, pastor, adviser, author" but also "the most unforgettable character I've met."[2]

When Exman arrived in New York in the spring of 1928, he did as Mathews suggested. He looked up Fosdick and joined his Baptist church. In his early years in New York, Fosdick was a relatively minor player in Exman's life. Exman was too embarrassed to approach his pastor about publishing for Harper, and he wasn't all that interested in church, even if it was led by a man who was coming to be regarded as America's pastor. Though Exman enjoyed Fosdick's sermons and loved the music, faith remained for him a foreign country. Then a minister from far away introduced him to something he could believe in.

On the last weekend in January 1929, Exman went to Pittsburgh on a business trip to ask the Reverend Petty about writing a book for Harper. Less than a year into the job Petty had encouraged him to take, Exman was twenty-eight years old and living alone in a Gramercy Park apartment. When he arrived in Pittsburgh, Petty and his staff set him up with Petty's administrative assistant Gladys Miller, who had graduated from Denison two years before him. Because of her cheerful disposition, Gladys was known to her friends as Sunny.

She and Exman hang out with a few of those friends over the course of a weekend. They see a movie. They go out for dinner and dancing. Exman and Sunny steal away for a kiss. They also fall head over heels for one another.

In the 1920s equivalent of texting obsessively, they exchange letters almost daily after he reluctantly returns to New York. Exman stays up late to write of his love and longing, sometimes rushing to the mailbox in time for the overnight train to Pittsburgh. He can't stop thinking and dreaming about Sunny. He finds it hard to work. It's expensive to talk on the phone, but Exman pays for it. In the first letter he sends to her, on his first full day back in New York, he declares his love for her. He's not sure he believes in soulmates, but he is convinced that they have been brought together by a power greater than themselves. He is desperate to see Sunny again so they can see if the feelings they have for one another are true love. The next day he begs her in a letter to come to New York so they can have some time alone and away from the friends who chaperoned them around Pittsburgh. He includes a sketch of a train arriving in Penn Station with him sitting alone on a bench pining away for her. In other letters from the first week after their first weekend, he describes their relationship in spiritual terms. It is a "holy experience," part of a "divine plan," he says. "The spirit which is you and the spirit which is I have found one another." On the Saturday one week after they met—their anniversary, Exman says—he calls Sunny his "little Sunbeam."[3]

Sunny does come to New York on the following weekend. Now Exman at least is certain that they are meant to be married. Even as he is working to bring out a book called *Beyond Agnosticism*, his relationship with Sunny—a "spiritual communion," in his words—is rekindling the faith he lost in divinity school. "I can't disbelieve in God when I think of our love," he tells her. He thanks Sunny for breaking through his years of lonely self-reliance and making him vulnerable. He rhapsodizes about their relationship in words that will find echoes in his later writing about mystical union with the divine. He feels with Sunny a heaven-sent spiritual oneness he expects to intensify over time, especially after they are married and are able to consummate their union. He fantasizes about making love with her and about the simple pleasures of everyday life in New York City, including going to the theater, going to church, and wandering around Manhattan.[4]

The only child of Frederick and Minnie (Farner) Miller, Gladys is, like Exman, a farm kid, though her family farm is in Perrysburg in northern Ohio, just southwest of Toledo and Lake Erie. Her family life is troubled, however. Her father is a "cussed and grouchy man" who inflicts verbal and emotional abuse on Sunny's mother, who in turn leans on Sunny for support.[5] Sunny and Exman are determined to make a very different life for themselves, and to start as soon as possible. In a telephone call on Valentine's Day, less than three weeks after their introduction, Sunny agrees to marry him at the beginning of the summer. Two days later, he sends her a card with holes in it so she can size her finger for a ring from Tiffany & Co.

Exman and Sunny were married by Petty at Pittsburgh's First Baptist Church on June 6, 1929, and honeymooned in Europe, where Exman did some Harper work to help pay for the trip. They lived for a short time in Exman's Gramercy Park apartment. In the long term, they would move to the suburbs in Scarsdale, New York, as they raised a family that included a son, Wally, a daughter, Judy, and an adopted son, Frank. In the short term, however, they moved to an apartment near Fosdick's new church on Riverside Drive and 115th Street, just west of Columbia University. That church would take its name neither from a Protestant denomination nor from an author of a New Testament gospel but from its location on Riverside Drive.

Harry Emerson Fosdick and Riverside Church

Harry Emerson Fosdick was born in Buffalo, New York, one generation before Exman, in 1878. Like Exman, he was raised in a conservative Baptist home, but because his hometown had no Baptist church, he attended a Presbyterian Sunday school and a Methodist youth group. He, too, was exposed as a child to traumatic fire-and-brimstone sermons, which left him "weeping at night for fear of going to hell, with my mystified and baffled mother trying to comfort me."[6] Economically, Fosdick's family fared better than the Exmans did on their farm. His father's work as a high school teacher and principal afforded his family a comfortable middle-class existence, with enough money to attend summer sessions at the Chautauqua Institution, a revival meeting of sorts that featured learned lectures rather than come-to-Jesus altar calls. All was not well at home, however. Fosdick's mother was chronically depressed, and both she and her husband suffered nervous breakdowns. Fosdick responded by digging into his textbooks, graduating from Colgate University (in 1900) and Union Theological Seminary (in 1904, after one year at Hamilton Theological Seminary).

Whereas Exman's crisis of faith would come during divinity school, Fosdick's came after his first year of college, when, in his words, his "somewhat childish and unsophisticated Christian ideas [ran] headlong into oncoming science" and "shook my faith to pieces." As he accepted evolution and rejected biblical infallibility, he later reported, "I no longer believed the old stuff I had been taught. Moreover, I no longer merely doubted it. I rose in indignant revolt against it." He asked himself, "How could a man be intelligent and still be a Christian?" That question sat unanswered until his senior year, when his Hamilton Theological Seminary professor William Newton Clarke restored his faith in God. Clarke taught Fosdick to put experience first—to understand theology as a distant echo of the primary personal experiences that form the true foundation of all real religion. Of Clarke, whom he lauded as his "spiritual godfather," Fosdick wrote, "I used to say to myself, 'Now, there's an honest man with a great intellect, and he can be a Christian. Why can't I?'"[7]

Clarke learned the gospel of the religion of experience from William James, who saw religion as fundamentally personal, interpreted Christianity as one religion among many, and understood life-changing experiences such as conversion and mystical encounters as the crux of the religious life. Clarke, in turn, commended James and experiential religion to Fosdick. "I vividly recall the thrill of pioneering books, such as James's *The Varieties of Religious Experience*," Fosdick later wrote, adding that James "inspired my generation as few men did."[8]

Fosdick graduated first in his class from Union in 1904 and was ordained as a Baptist minister. That same year he accepted a call from the well-heeled parishioners of the First Baptist Church of Montclair,

New Jersey. After more than a decade there, he left in 1918 to become an associate pastor at First Presbyterian Church in Manhattan's Greenwich Village neighborhood. During this first phase of his ministerial career, Fosdick authored a trilogy of books on the meaning of the Christian life—*The Meaning of Prayer* (1915), *The Meaning of Faith* (1917), and *The Meaning of Service* (1920)—which brought him wealth and fame as an author of devotional classics.

Fittingly, Exman discovered Fosdick through these "meaning" books. During his junior year, while he and his friends were trying, and failing, to reconcile their Christian faith with what they were learning, Exman picked up Fosdick's *The Meaning of Prayer*. There he encountered "a man who did have some answers, who was to orient and inspire me for years to come."[9] He also began to learn how to pray.

While Fosdick was writing devotional books and Exman was reading them, American Protestantism split into two factions, one on the left and the other on the right, that continue to define the fault lines of religion and politics in the United States. Taking their marching orders from a series of pamphlets called *The Fundamentals* (1910–15), conservatives rejected the liberal ideas Fosdick and Exman had learned in college, including biblical criticism, evolutionary science, and comparative religion. Convinced that Christianity was a belief system, "fundamentalists," as this group came to be known, emphasized five doctrines that were in their view "fundamental" to the Christian faith:

- *the inerrancy of the Bible*

- *the imminent Second Coming of Jesus*

- *the Virgin Birth*

- *the bodily resurrection*

- *the atonement, or reconciliation of God and humans, through the death of Jesus on the cross*

Fundamentalists insisted that these doctrines needed to be interpreted "literally," through their commonsense meanings, rather than allegorically or metaphorically. In this respect, they weren't all that different from evangelicals, a broader group of traditionalists who had been around since at least the early nineteenth century. What distinguished fundamentalists from evangelicals was their militancy. As the church historian George Marsden put it, "A fundamentalist is an evangelical who is angry about something."[10]

In the early 1920s, liberals struck back, led by Fosdick, who on May 21, 1922, delivered a sermon that made fundamentalists even angrier. It also opened the second stage of his career—as an anti-fundamentalist crusader.

For those who love a good story, it is tempting to describe Fosdick's most famous sermon, "Shall the Fundamentalists Win?," as a challenge to a duel. But Fosdick, who saw himself as an evangelical *and* a liberal (and an "evangelical liberal"), was more a lover than a fighter. If what came to be called the fundamentalist-modernist controversy was, as one historian argued, a "family fight," Fosdick was the kid trying to keep his parents out of divorce court.[11]

The liberal Protestant project the fundamentalists loved to hate was at its heart an effort to carve out a space where it was possible to be both Christian and modern. Charting a "third way" between godlessness and dogmatism had been from the Civil War onward the task of liberal Protestant thinkers, including James, who had labored to reconcile academic life and Christian faith by convincing his Harvard friends that Christianity was compatible with reason, science, and the modern world. Although Fosdick's answer to the question he posed in his sermon title—"Shall the Fundamentalists Win?"—was plainly no, it wasn't fundamentalism's defeat he was after. His goal was something more like a tie—a church big enough for fundamentalists and liberals alike. When read backward through the pandemic of polarization in US politics today, his sermon comes across as strikingly moderate. Fundamentalists were at liberty to believe what they wanted about the Virgin Birth and the Second Coming, he argued, but they should not infringe on the liberty of other churchgoers by insisting that everyone else ape their interpretations. "Is not the Christian Church large enough to hold within her hospitable fellowship people who differ on points like this and agree to differ until the fuller truth be manifested?" he asked.[12]

Fosdick claimed that he had no intention of starting a religious war, describing his most famous sermon years later as a "plea for tolerance, not likely to be misunderstood except by people who persist in misunderstanding it." But the text does invite readers to interpret it as something more prickly than an olive branch. Fosdick denounced his antagonists as "illiberal and intolerant" and likened them to Roman Catholics: "If they had their way, within the church, they would set up in Protestantism a doctrinal tribunal more rigid than the pope's." These were fighting words at a time when immigration and anti-Catholicism were surging, and Fosdick surely meant to land a punch, perhaps even a low blow. Without calling into question Fosdick's intentions, it seems reasonable to conclude that he was possessed that late spring day in 1922 by two competing spirits, one conciliatory and one militant, which would battle for supremacy in his own mind (and in American society) for decades to come. "Shall the Fundamentalists Win?" was nonetheless interpreted, in the moment and forevermore, as a call to war. "If ever a sermon failed to achieve its object, mine did," Fosdick later observed. "What came of it was an explosion of ill will."[13]

That explosion was not solely Fosdick's doing, however. The fuse was set and lit by competing oil men, who represented "sparring spirits of capitalism" inspired by very different Christian models of making money and giving it away. In the West, "wildcat Christians" bankrolled the publication and distribution of some three million copies of *The Fundamentals*. In the East, John D. Rockefeller of Standard Oil worked through his PR guru Ivy Lee to print and ship "Shall the Fundamentalists Win?" to some 130,000 ministers across the country. As news of Fosdick's sermon spread like oil on water, the angry letters that arrived in his mailbox seemed to anticipate the dehumanizing vitriol of twenty-first-century social media. One letter writer called Fosdick a "syphilitic louse"—an "indescribable Thing-in-human form . . . spewed up by Satan from the slimy depths of Hell."[14]

As fundamentalists and modernists tussled, the General Assembly of the Presbyterian Church in the United States pressured Fosdick to step down from First Presbyterian Church. Fosdick offered to resign in May 1923, but his congregation refused to accept it. When it became clear that he would likely face a heresy trial if he lingered any longer, he again offered his resignation in October 1924. This time it was accepted. On March 1, 1925, just as Exman was finishing his divinity school studies, Fosdick preached his farewell sermon and left for a sabbatical in the Holy Land.

Amid this drama, John D. Rockefeller Jr. was working to land a major acquisition. The most powerful philanthropist in the world was recruiting the most powerful preacher in the country to lead his Park Avenue Baptist Church congregation as it transitioned to a much larger, nondenominational church in the Morningside Heights neighborhood near Columbia University. Fosdick said no, telling Rockefeller he did not want to be seen as a personal pastor to America's wealthiest man. Rockefeller replied, "Do you think that more people will criticize you on account of my wealth, than will criticize me on account of your theology?"[15]

Fosdick kept the talks open because he was drawn to Rockefeller's vision of an inclusive community church set amid one of the country's largest student populations. He also shared a lot with Rockefeller. Both were "ecumenical Protestants" allergic to denominational infighting. Though by no means anticapital, they were both social gospelers who believed that Christians should focus more on caring for the poor than on punching their own tickets to heaven. They were also the two most important figures in America's informal liberal Protestant establishment. While Fosdick held forth in books, on the radio, and from the pulpit, Rockefeller provided the capital to amplify his message.

On April 17, 1925, in a letter to the chairman of the Board of Trustees of Park Avenue Baptist, Fosdick laid out a series of conditions that would need to be met before he would agree to join Park Avenue Baptist Church as it made its pilgrimage to Riverside Drive. Membership would need to be open to "all disciples of Jesus Christ," and anyone desiring baptism or any similar rite of initiation into the faith would be "immersed, sprinkled, or (if Quaker scruples are present) welcomed on verbal confession, as each individually might choose."[16] Ministers would be chosen without regard to denomination. And the church itself should not carry any denominational identifier. Finally, he insisted that his annual salary never exceed $5,000. Members of the Park Avenue Baptist Church voted on May 22, 1925, to call Fosdick as their preacher. Three days later, he agreed.

Fosdick preached his first sermon as pastor-elect of his new congregation on May 31, 1925, right around the time of Exman's University of Chicago commencement. Fosdick cast shade on an American Christianity that had become "vast and complicated, organized, creedalized and ritualized." Then, drawing on two of his intellectual heroes, he challenged his parishioners to join him in a "vital reformation" that would discard "second-hand religion" for firsthand experience (as the Transcendentalist Ralph Waldo Emerson had done) and turn their church into something Abraham Lincoln might have joined.[17]

On October 3, 1926, fresh off a sabbatical in Europe, Fosdick preached his first sermon as the official pastor of Park Avenue Baptist Church, where Exman would join him a year and a half later. He promised to focus not on the "barnacles" of creeds and rituals that had glommed on to religious institutions but on "religion itself, revealed in the spirit of Jesus as a vital, saving and sustaining power in human experience." It was by all accounts another Fosdick tour de force, preached again to an overflowing crowd. Construction of Riverside Church began in 1927, and its first worship service took place on October 5, 1930. The Exmans were in the congregation.[18]

Middlebrow Religion

In the summer of 1929, Exman and Sunny settled into their new life in "the Big Apple," as a sportswriter had recently dubbed New York City. This was the tail end of the Roaring Twenties, an era of mass production and mass consumption, of electricity and cars and radios and movies. Women, who had earned the right to vote in 1920, asserted their rights to dress, smoke, and drink as they pleased, though the right to drink ran headlong into Prohibition, which began in 1920 and would last until it drowned in its own self-righteousness in 1933. Culturally, the twenties hosted the Jazz Age and the Harlem Renaissance. The year 1929 alone saw the publication of Ernest Hemingway's *A Farewell to Arms*, Virginia Woolf's *A Room of One's Own*, and Thomas Wolfe's *Look Homeward, Angel*.

The Wall Street crash in the fall of 1929 was around the corner and so was the Great Depression. But a "religious depression" had already arrived, at least for liberal Protestants, whose victory over the fundamentalists opened onto a period of persistent losses— in missionary energy at home and abroad, in ministerial prestige, in church attendance, and in church giving.[19] It wasn't yet clear to anyone, and certainly not to a twentysomething Ohio farm boy about to become a bigshot editor in New York City, but the Protestant establishment of which he was a part was beginning a long decline, losing church members, donations, and cultural authority.

Still, it was a strangely good time to get into religious publishing. And for a young man to renew his faith.

The religious book business was booming, thanks to authors and publishers who seized the opportunity to make meaning out of the vertigo so many Americans were feeling as they rode the wake of World War I into the Great Depression. In 1925, *The Man Nobody Knows* by the advertising executive Bruce Barton had helped turn Jesus into a celebrity rivaling the Yankees' Babe

Ruth and Hollywood's Charlie Chaplin. That same year, Harper had started its religious book department. In 1927, the Religious Book Club launched, with Fosdick on its editorial board. Like the Book-of-the-Month Club, which had shipped its first books one year earlier, it offered a curated selection of books to a middlebrow public eager to outsource to experts the burden of deciding which books merited their attention.

The word *middlebrow* was first used shortly after World War I as a term of derision by elite defenders of great art and literature against whoever might dare to mix what should not be mixed: the "highbrow" culture of the intelligentsia and the "lowbrow" culture of the masses. For dumbing down the classics, for cutting away nuance and complexity, for vulgarizing all that is true and beautiful, these tasteless makers and marketers of middlebrow culture deserved nothing but disdain—or so said their critics. Exman, who made a living shooting the gap between "highbrow" and "lowbrow," took it as his mission to bring big ideas to ordinary people, translating work by "the best and the brightest" into language an expanding American middle class could understand.[20]

Exman's books shared a few key features with other middlebrow literature. First, they addressed the many rather than the few, promising to bring insights from thought leaders to general readers. Second, they offered practical solutions to the problems of everyday life. Third, they focused on persons and personality, offering "a picture of the world that, for all its modern chaos, domination by abstract and incomprehensible forces and worries about standardization, was still the home of idiosyncratic, individual selves." His bestsellers ran toward biography and autobiography, genres in which agency could flourish alongside emotion, and personality and empathy were developed and extolled.[21]

More importantly, Exman's books were the offspring of an arranged marriage between commerce and culture. He wanted to make money for Harper and earn capital (cultural and otherwise) for himself. As a missionary for religion, he also wanted to bring into the world books that were excellent and meaningful. He was convinced that the world was in crisis, held captive by materialism and militarism. He was also convinced that religion books had a role to play in saving that world, by redirecting readers' lives from themselves to God and from God to others. In articles and speeches and at spiritual retreats, Exman argued not only for reading and talking about devotional books but also for owning them, for having and holding them so you could return to them over and over and mark them up (as he did) along the way.

"Fortuna's Wheel"

When Exman arrived in New York, Fosdick was a Macmillan author. That is not surprising, because Macmillan, which had just published the first book of the ethicist and rising theological star Reinhold Niebuhr, was at the time the leading name in religion books in the United States. Shailer Mathews was also a Macmillan author and a frequent outside reader of its manuscripts. Despite this success, Macmillan's religion editor was fired shortly after Exman joined Harper and was not immediately replaced. As Exman later recalled in his unfinished autobiography, he felt as if "Fortuna's wheel stopped almost in front of me." Here was an opportunity to poach key authors from Macmillan, just as he was starting his new job. Or, as he put it more delicately, "I saw no reason why I would not make an occasional and discreet inquiry to find out if, missing an old editor, an author might be interested in signing up with a young one."[22] Exman swung and missed at the now popular Christian apologist C. S. Lewis, but hit a home run with Fosdick, who went on to publish seventeen books with Exman between 1932 and 1961, many of them bestsellers and Religious Book Club selections. Winning over Fosdick was no easy task, however.

Exman had first heard Fosdick preach in January 1925 from high in the bleachers in Chicago's Orchestra Hall, where Fosdick's "inflections of voice, animation of face and body, and gestures of hands" combined with exciting ideas to produce what Exman called "the greatest preaching I had ever heard." After joining Fosdick's church, Exman came to regard him with awe and respect. Gradually, the two became friends. Both loved classical music. Both had been raised in conservative Baptist homes. Both were loyal to their liberal arts colleges, eventually serving on their boards of trustees. Both went to seminary and on to some combination of preaching and publishing, with Fosdick writing books on the side and Exman giving talks and sermons and leading retreats in his spare time. Still, Exman was hesitant to approach Fosdick about coming over to Harper. "To commercialize on this spiritual and pastoral experience," Exman later wrote, "was for me, a shy fellow any way, a most difficult undertaking."[23]

Exman's stock-in-trade in his early years at Harper was the sermon collection. He sought out famous and not-so-famous preachers, and then he and his colleagues edited their manuscripts in keeping with Harper's standards and Exman's vision. Exman was keen to publish a collection by his own pastor, whose sermons had been broadcast to millions since he joined the Sunday afternoon NBC radio program *National Vespers* in October 1927. As a faithful presence at Riverside Church—he and Sunny saved hundreds of bulletins from its services—Exman knew the power of Fosdick's sermons. He also knew that Fosdick's personal approach translated better onto the page than sermons that were satisfied with simply interpreting scripture. Exman's son Wally preferred football to church on Sundays, but judged Fosdick to be a "great orator." "When he was giving a sermon, man, you paid attention," he recalled.[24]

When Exman finally raised the possibility of a sermon collection, Fosdick responded with a curt "no." Exman, gently pushing back, noted that Fosdick's sermons were already being printed in Riverside's *Church Monthly* and that pamphlets of his sermons were "going out by the thousands." "Such should suffice," Fosdick replied.[25]

With a sermon collection off the table (for now), Exman approached Fosdick about doing a collection of essays. The result was Fosdick's first book with Exman and a big bestseller: *As I See Religion* (1932), a collection of six previously published magazine articles that, better than any other single source, sets down Fosdick's mature thinking.

The decision to include the term *religion* in this title is notable. The book might have been called "As I See Protestantism" or "As I See Christianity," but Fosdick and Exman were aiming for a broader audience, and they wanted to use broader terms. They didn't want readers to think they needed to convert to Christianity or Protestantism to learn from what Fosdick had to say. On the book's first page, Fosdick presented an inclusive and pluralistic vision of religion that embraced religious founders such as "Christ and Buddha" alongside the Protestant revivalist Billy Sunday and the Hindu-born Indian revolutionary Mohandas Gandhi. It was not yet time for the perennialism later championed by Exman and so many of his authors, however. Fosdick rejected the temptation to seek "some irreducible minimum that, like carbon in sweet sugar and in bitter strychnine, makes one substance of all faiths from Shintoism to Christian Science." To argue that all religions "at heart mean one thing," Fosdick continued, was to assert "an identity which does not exist." It was also to deny religious diversity, given the fact that "the various religions are really various," with each religious tradition speaking its own language in its own ways.[26]

What is striking about these assertions, and this book, is how faithful they were to William James on religion. It was as if James had come back from the dead and was given a massive church in Manhattan and a flair for popular preaching. What would James say? What would he do? "William James understood religion; he knew its native speech," Fosdick wrote, and then he went and did likewise, describing religion as a matter of personal experience, celebrating its varieties, and interpreting them in psychological terms. "Religion at its fountainhead is an individual, psychological experience," Fosdick wrote. "It is primarily concerned not with formal creed and church but with inner experience."[27]

Antiwar Prophet

Exman never learned what caused his pastor to reconsider the sermon book, but in the spring of 1933 Fosdick called to say he would look over his sermons that summer to see whether there might be a book in them. That book, *The Hope of the World*, appeared on November 10, 1933, though not without "some misgiving," as Fosdick noted in the book's foreword, "for the essential nature of a sermon as an intimate, conversational message from soul to soul makes it impossible for printing to reproduce preaching and, unlike the traditional child, sermons should be heard and not seen." That book's success led to eight more collections of Fosdick's sermons, all published by Exman. Together these books further popularized Fosdick's thinking, not only among readers but also with parishioners whose preachers, including Martin Luther King Jr., borrowed heavily from his sermons.[28]

"Shall the Fundamentalists Win?" was Fosdick's most famous sermon, but "The Unknown Soldier" was a close second. It was delivered from the pulpit of Riverside Church, likely with Exman in attendance, on November 12, 1933, one day after Armistice Day (now Veterans Day) and just days after *The Hope of the World* appeared. There Fosdick offered one of the most stirring rebukes in American history to the god of war. He also disavowed his own warmongering past.

When Americans were itching to intervene in World War I, Fosdick had scratched that itch, urging his fellow citizens not to forget "how to die for a holy cause." He defended the war in his bestselling book *The Challenge of the Present Crisis* (1918), and applauded US soldiers in a magazine article as "strapping Samsons, aflame for a fight." He also visited troops in Europe as a cheer-leader chaplain with the YMCA.[29]

That tour changed his life, transforming him into a pacifist and antiwar activist. In 1922, he coauthored "The Churches' Plea Against War and the War System," which was signed by 150 Protestant and Catholic leaders. A year later, he denounced war as "the most co-lossal social sin . . . absolutely, irrevocably un-christian." Fosdick's experience in Europe also led him to reject the "dogma of national-ism," which he termed "the most dangerous rival of Christian prin-ciples on earth." Now an internationalist, he addressed the League of Nations in Geneva in 1925. "War is suicidal," he said. "If mankind does not end war, war will end mankind."[30]

On Armistice Day 1933, a day also set to commemorate tombs of the Unknown Soldier across the globe, Fosdick distilled more than a decade of antiwar activism into a deeply personal plea for peace. Standing in a Riverside pulpit carved with images of Old Testament prophets, he began by confessing sins he had committed while visiting European battlefields during World War I. "I have an account to settle between my soul and the Unknown Soldier," he said. "I, too, was persuaded that it was the war to end war. I, too, was a gullible fool and thought that modern war could somehow make the world safe for democracy." He confessed that he had exploited the youth-ful idealism of the soldiers he met, seducing them to march to their deaths. Then he made a personal pledge to do war no more:

> I renounce war because of what it does to our own men. . . .
> I renounce war because of what it compels us to do to our ene-mies, bombing their mothers in villages, starving their children by blockades, laughing over our coffee cups about every damnable thing we have been able to do to them. I renounce war . . . for the lies it lives on and propagates, for the undying hatreds it arouses, for the dictatorships it puts in place of democracy, for the starva-tion that stalks after it. I renounce war and never again, directly or indirectly, will I sanction or support another![31]

"The Unknown Soldier" was a sensation, covered and reprinted in newspapers and magazines across the country, placed into the *Congressional Record*, condensed in *Reader's Digest*, and published by Exman in Fosdick's second book of sermons, *The Secret of Victorious Living* (1934). It confirmed Fosdick's place as one of the most influential antiwar activists in the United States in the interwar years, and added a strong pacifist voice to Exman's Book of Books.

When Exman joined Fosdick and became a pacifist is not clear. He seems to have come to that position during the late 1920s or early 1930s, and he never wavered from it. Like Fosdick, he joined the Peace Pledge Union (PPU), a pacifist organization inspired by Fosdick's sermon. Also signing this pledge were the English writers Aldous Huxley and Gerald Heard, future Exman authors and friends who gave lectures and wrote manifestos on behalf of the PPU.

Over the course of his career, Exman would become not only the most important publisher of religion books in the United States but also a leading publisher of pacifists. His Book of Books would come to include writing by or about such leading war resisters as Huxley, Heard, Albert Schweitzer, Dorothy Day, Howard Thurman, Martin Luther King Jr., and Fosdick himself.

Varieties of Religious Liberals

The collaborations of Fosdick and Exman were perhaps as consequential as the joint ventures of Fosdick and Rockefeller. Neither Rockefeller nor Exman played a role in the first phase of Fosdick's career—as a devotional writer in the 1910s. Rockefeller played a key role in Fosdick's second phase—as modernist spokesperson in the 1920s—by bankrolling the rollout of "Shall the Fundamentalists Win?" and by offering him (after the fallout) a soft landing at what became Riverside Church. However, during the final and longest phase of Fosdick's career—when he took a turn toward the therapeutic beginning in the early 1930s—it was his Harper books that made his reputation as a popularizer of the sort of experiential spirituality that now commands a huge share of the spiritual marketplace in the United States.

Exman and Fosdick were close collaborators who shared a common identity as liberal Protestants, but they also differed in important ways. Fosdick, like his mentors at Colgate and Union, is best understood as an "evangelical liberal." He had experiences in his youth that can be categorized as mystical: "hours of mystical insight, vague but moving compulsions of the spirit, at times involuntary and surprising, at time consciously sought in solitude." He was also heavily influenced by the Quaker mystic and pacifist Rufus Jones, so much so that he considered becoming a Quaker and edited an anthology of Jones's work late in his life. But Fosdick fits best in the gospel-centered evangelical liberal camp. He wrote a bestselling book about Jesus and another about the Bible, which he knew well and cited often. "If I did not consider myself an evangelical Christian," he said to his critics while at First Presbyterian Church, "I surely should not be preaching in an evangelical pulpit."[32]

Unlike Fosdick and other evangelical liberals, Exman rarely prayed to Jesus. He read more eagerly and widely in Buddhism than his pastor did, and he was better integrated into networks of Hindu leaders. Fosdick's declaration that "Jesus will never be surpassed" would not have made sense to Exman, who saw Jesus as one mystic among many.[33] His Blanchester graveyard experience was the defining moment of his spiritual life. It led him to become a collector and publisher of mystics and a seeker after God. For all these reasons, he is best understood as a mystical liberal.

These differences should not be overstated, however. Both Fosdick and Exman saw individual spiritual experience as the essence of the religious life, even as they insisted that prayer and meditation fostered and in fact required social action. Exman wrote a pamphlet called *The Escapists* that took aim at the stereotype of mystics as apolitical navel-gazers solely concerned with their own spiritual rewards. As has been noted, both men were pacifists. Both served in leadership roles for the Fellowship of Reconciliation and lent their names to statements against nuclear weapons by the Committee for a Sane Nuclear Policy. As an icon of liberal Protestantism, Fosdick was rightly criticized for his naïveté about human sin and social progress, and for his refusal to rage against economic inequality or racism as he did against war. However, after his youthful warmongering, Fosdick never confused faith in God with the sort of nation worship that continues to bedevil American society today. In fact, he and Exman were wary of both "denomination first" and "America first" thinking. Fosdick stumped for the League of Nations while most American leaders were still opposed to it, and Exman, who was actively involved in outreach to the United Nations, wrote an interreligious prayer for use in the UN Prayer Room (now known as the UN Meditation Room).

Though both were friendly to the social gospel, each rejected Christian socialism and downplayed class struggle, perhaps because of their many close connections with businessmen and the well-to-do. Both were members of the Century Club, which catered largely to writers and artists but also included in its rolls Rockefellers, Vanderbilts, Astors, and other captains of industry. And though both opposed racial segregation and were personally close to Martin Luther King Jr., neither practiced anything like what in the twenty-first century would come to be called antiracism.

In keeping with their shared middlebrow mission, neither Exman nor Fosdick was an innovator. "No one today need read him or probably does read him for a single theological insight," the otherwise appreciative church historian Martin Marty wrote of Fosdick.[34] The idea that organized Christianity is an impediment to the Christian life did not start with him. Neither did the emphasis on religion as experience.

Exman and Fosdick were brilliant popularizers. They understood the needs and aspirations of ordinary Americans because they had grown up in Blanchester and Buffalo. They knew how to speak to Americans who hadn't gone to fancy schools. They knew how to cast complicated ideas out into the wider world. And they did that best through books, which shaped a nationwide conversation about religion in modern America.

A Therapeutic Turn

After crusading during the second phase of his career against fundamentalism and then against war, Fosdick devoted himself in his career's third phase to the fusion of therapy and spirituality that would secure his reputation as perhaps the greatest liberal Protestant preacher in the United States in the twentieth century. This fusion was influenced by his deep investment in the ideas of William James and by broader psychological currents in the United States during and after World War II. More personal experiences were also at play.

As a boy of seven, Fosdick had what he described as "a definite experience of conversion." As a teenager, his struggles with doubt were relieved by mystical moments—"indubitable experiences of spiritual reality."[35] These events offered Fosdick a firm foundation for his later conviction that religion is built on experiences. But the defining event in his youth was a frightful encounter with his personal demons in the fall of 1901. This encounter almost led him to take his own life, but without it he never would have found himself on the leading edge of the therapeutic turn in mid-twentieth-century American spirituality that is still playing out today.

Fosdick had been engaged in the summer of 1900 to Florence Whitney, a recent Smith College graduate whom he had met while at Colgate. The next fall he found himself alone in New York City with a heavy load of graduate courses in theology at Union and philosophy at Columbia. He was also working at the Mission at Mariners' Temple in the Bowery on Manhattan's Lower East Side, where he was confronted by the fragility of day-to-day life for New York City's poor, and by his own inability to reckon with it. He couldn't sleep. His stomach swirled. His vision blurred. Thoughts

of suicide gripped him and would not let go. So he ran away, first, to
Worcester to see his fiancée and, then, to Buffalo to see his family.

After his father caught him with a razor at his throat, he landed,
humiliated, in a sanitarium in upstate New York. It was, Fosdick
later wrote, "the most hideous experience of my life." It was also the
most generative. "For the first time in my life, I faced, at my wit's
end, a situation too much for me to handle," Fosdick wrote. That
situation threw him to his knees. "I learned to pray," he explained,
"because I desperately needed help from a Power greater than my
own." Without that experience, he never would have written *The
Meaning of Prayer*, which introduced millions of readers (Exman
included) to prayer as a form of meditation.[36]

"Neurotic agony" (his words) also fired Fosdick's interest in the
psychology of religion, transforming its obsessions into his own.
Whereas Exman was a collector of mystics, Fosdick was a collector
of the nervous, the anxious, and the depressed—"sick souls," James
called them—who shared the experience of finding oneself in a pit
with no way out. This obsession directed Fosdick to the work of
James, who had also suffered a nervous breakdown that almost led
him to take his own life. When Fosdick returned to Union to re-
sume his studies, he discovered that Union did not offer courses in
the new hybrid field of psychology of religion, so he read James on
his own, including *Varieties*, which had just been published in June
1902. He graduated from Union in May 1904 and married Florence
Whitney that summer.[37]

Many years later, while he was still at First Presbyterian in
the early 1920s, Fosdick decided to open up a "confessional" of
sorts for individual counseling sessions with his parishioners. First
in line was a young gay man and, to his credit Fosdick, who had
"never knowingly . . . met a homosexual," immediately realized he
was in over his head. He reached out to Dr. Thomas W. Salmon,
a professor of psychiatry at Columbia, who became his guide and
confidant through recent revolutions in the field of psychology and
psychotherapy. These counseling sessions, which Fosdick brought

to Park Avenue Baptist and then Riverside Church, revitalized his career. And his life. "Here I saw Christian faith, implemented by psychological insight, actually work," he wrote. "Here religion was not simply a set of ideas, but a living force substituting faith for fear, strength for weakness, hope for despair."[38]

The postwar era would see a rush of interest in the new field of psychology, and a series of bestselling books on religion and personal peace—*Peace of Mind, Peace of Soul, Peace with God*—followed. Also popular were two books by the prosperity gospel pioneer Norman Vincent Peale: *A Guide to Confident Living* and *The Power of Positive Thinking*. But Fosdick's *On Being a Real Person* (1943) beat them all to the bookstore. Fosdick's "big book," as Exman called it, pioneered this postwar genre of spiritual reassurance and established Fosdick as *the* popular voice in therapeutic spirituality.[39]

On Being a Real Person is and is not a war book. The battles it discusses are personal rather than global, spiritual rather than military. But it appeared during World War II and took aim at the loss of meaning that arrived as a second global conflict further undercut faith in progress, faith in reason, and faith in faith. The Harper religious books catalog for spring 1943 pitched the book as an "inspirational" and "self-help" offering—a "heart-to-heart talk" by "a physician of the soul." Lest that pitch be read as shallow, the ad copy (vetted as always by Exman) took pains to add that there was "nothing superficial or artificial" about *On Being a Real Person*.[40]

A middlebrow hit, the book was condensed in *Reader's Digest* and featured by the Book-of-the-Month Club. A special Armed Services Edition made it widely available to soldiers. It hit first place on nonfiction bestseller lists, sold at least three hundred thousand hardcover copies, and is still in print today. According to Exman, it became Fosdick's most popular book because it "revealed the real Fosdick—the sympathetic Christian counselor who found time in an impossibly busy schedule to sit down with folks and talk over their personal problems."[41]

The central problem Fosdick took up in the book—"the greatest single tragedy in the world"—was an ongoing epidemic of incomplete, disintegrated, and unhappy people. "Wars come and go," he observed, and the weight of economic depressions, natural catastrophes, and social inequalities fall on different people in different ways. But "in mansion and hovel, war and peace, wealth and penury, domestic felicity and discord, among the uneducated and in university faculties, an omnipresent calamity is found." Everywhere you look, people are miserable.[42]

What to do?

It is often thought that religious traditions are a sort of alchemy, magically spinning ordinary human beings into saints or immortals or perhaps even gods. For much of his life, Exman struggled to make himself into a saint through prayer, meditation, and other contemplative disciplines. But the world's religions are far more likely to challenge us to become truly human. *On Being a Real Person* did just that.

Like James in *Varieties*, Fosdick focused in this book on individual cases. Though he diverged from James (who gravitated toward extreme cases) by focusing on "those who pass for normal or near normal," Fosdick, too, organized his parishioners (and readers) into various categories of experience, reckoning with individuals who struggled with self-acceptance, egocentricity, anxiety, and depression. His book also dealt frankly with sexual desire, which it described as "natural and right." And, though it presumed heterosexual monogamy as the sexual ideal, it was, according to religious studies scholar Heather Rachelle White, "the first text in a burgeoning new genre of spiritual self-help to speak of homosexuality."[43]

"The primary command of our being is, get yourself together, and the fundamental sin is to be chaotic and unfocused," Fosdick wrote, though the word *sin* here was ill chosen, because his approach was therapeutic rather than moralistic. "Moralism deals with symptoms and condemns results; psychotherapy diagnoses causes and is concerned with cure," he wrote. To the chagrin of conservative Christians who stressed the depths of human sinfulness, the arc of

Fosdick's cases bent not from sin to salvation but from sickness to health, depression to happiness. But how?[44]

Given Fosdick's contributions to therapeutic spirituality, it is important to note what his book did *not* do. Fosdick was not preaching "the power of positive thinking" that Norman Vincent Peale would popularize nearly a decade later. Neither was he selling "the prosperity gospel," which emphasizes becoming rich in Christ's name. Repeatedly, he recognized the power that heredity and environment have over us. In fact, he described those factors as two of the three building blocks of personality. The third (and most important) was personal response. Throughout his bestseller, Fosdick offered examples of people such as Helen Keller who, refusing to become "helpless victims," overcame hereditary and environmental challenges to become integrated people.[45]

Many reviewers remarked on the surprising lack of religion in *On Being a Real Person*. And the book, if read on a case-by-case basis, does seem to consist primarily of homespun wisdom and pull quotes from what is now the therapeutic consensus: accept yourself (including your sexual desires), conquer egocentricity, shoulder responsibility, and deal with your fears and anxieties. However, a closer reading reveals a book shot through with religious references, concerns, and arguments. Jesus exemplifies real personhood. The minister's office is the room where it happens. And underlying every page is the author's core conviction that Freud was wrong and Jung was right. No, religion does not cause neurosis, as Freud claimed. As Jung perceived, religion resolves it.

On Being a Real Person is best understood as a spiritual solution to the modern malaise. Its driving question is: How do we extricate ourselves from our collective calamity of unhappiness? It begins to answer this question by observing that the crisis brought on by two world wars and an economic depression is fundamentally a crisis of meaning. For this crisis, the solution is faith. Here Fosdick makes an argument for faith that echoes James's pragmatic argument for the same: it works, and it is true because it works. Faith yields positive "psychological effects," not least the integrated personality itself. It "awakens listless minds, expels negative moods, releases dormant energy, breaks through the isolating walls of lonely selves, and creates in insecure souls a basis for steadiness and poise."[46] Crucially, a spiritual outlook makes meaning in what might otherwise appear to be a meaningless world, and that meaning in turn helps us find our truest selves.

Making Meaning

In May 1959, more than a decade after Fosdick stepped down from Riverside Church and not long before Exman would himself retire, Exman and Fosdick appeared together on an NBC television special series titled *Wisdom*. NBC introduced Fosdick as the "minister emeritus of America" and Exman as "his longtime friend and editor." Exman then interviewed Fosdick about his life and his faith.

The interview concluded with a discussion of the Buddha. Exman, who had immersed himself in Asian religions in ways Fosdick never would, paraphrased the Buddha's last words, in which he instructs his followers to rely on themselves and not external authority. "I don't rely simply upon myself," Fosdick responded. "It seems to me that when we reach ourselves at our deepest we discover there the divine invasion." In that discovery lie answers to the big questions that confront all human beings: "Does life really have a basic meaning? Did it come from somewhere? Does it have purpose running through it? Does it have a destiny ahead of it?"[47]

It is easy to imagine that what we now refer to as the "search for meaning" is a perennial human endeavor. Surely, the Buddha was searching for meaning when he left his family's palace and began his life of wandering. And didn't that same search animate the wandering of Abraham and Jesus? Not exactly. At least in the English language, the "search for meaning" wasn't a thing until World War I. The phrase began to catch on around 1920, the year the Irish poet W. B. Yeats wrote (in his poem "The Second Coming"): "Things fall apart; the centre cannot hold." There Yeats tied the arrival of global war to a global loss of innocence and haltingly gestured toward a new faith, with a newborn savior (or demon?) who would come to replace the remains of the old order. Between 1940 and 1950, a "search for meaning" commenced in earnest in a modern world that seemed to be pulling up the anchors of meaning that had secured Western civilization for two millennia. Usage of the phrase *search for meaning* and related terms began a sharp upward ascent and have continued to hit new highs in recent years.[48]

Fosdick and Exman were obsessed with this search, and with the crisis in meaning that precipitated it. Exman published books on the topic. He wrote an article called "Search for Meaning" that also appeared as a pamphlet.[49] His seeking did not lead him to give up church on Sunday, but it did lead him to look for alternatives. Like Fosdick, Exman was convinced that the materialism and militarism of modern life had brought on a crisis of meaninglessness, which would be resolved by religion (or spirituality) alone. But of what sort?

Americans have long been "a nation of joiners." And churches are among the organizations they have long joined. However, from the slave spirituals of the early 1600s to the Great Awakening of the early 1700s to the Transcendentalist musings of the early 1800s to the Pentecostal revivals of the early 1900s, Americans have exhibited a profound ambivalence about organized religion. Colonial and early national revivals dug channels of religious authority that bypassed local ministers and local churches. Thoreau found the divine in the ripples on Walden Pond. Emerson—his words appear more than forty times in Fosdick's diaries—urged Harvard Divinity School's class of 1838 to refuse to accept their faith "at second hand," to "cast behind you all conformity, and acquaint men at first hand with Deity." For Frederick Douglass and many other abolitionists, to love the "pure, peaceable, and impartial Christianity of Christ" was to hate the "corrupt, slaveholding, women-whipping, cradle-plundering, partial and hypocritical Christianity of this land." When William James found the heart and soul of religion in personal religious experience, reckoning the dogmas, rituals, and creeds of religious institutions as thin veneers over the solidity of solitary souls underneath, he was in good company.[50]

Fosdick, as the pastor of America's most iconic church, surely believed in the importance of at least one Christian institution. Exman wasn't so sure. He and Sunny went to Riverside Church faithfully on Sundays. But Exman was always looking for more intimate ways to find God. The analogy is imperfect, but he related to institutional Christianity like President Ronald Reagan would later relate to the federal government: he didn't particularly like it and, if pressed, would have agreed it was part of the problem rather than part of the solution. Every church is "an institution absorbed with the concerns that occupy the time and attention of any secular grouping," Exman observed. That's why there wasn't much difference "between a meeting of the Board of Directors of my publishing firm and a meeting of the Board of Deacons of my church."[51] In Exman's view, God was far more likely to show up at weekend retreats and in small prayer groups.

Though fundamentalists criticized him for continuing to search for something they had already found, Fosdick wasn't much of a seeker. The focus of his career did shift over the years—from devotionalism to antifundamentalism to therapeutic spirituality—but his understandings of God, Jesus, the Bible, and religion were strikingly stable. He was a person who had wrestled with the illness of depression and found its cure in "the religion of personality." Rather than a seeker, Fosdick was a "dweller."[52]

Exman was different. Forever seeking yet another encounter with God, he was not content to rest in the knowledge that he was becoming a real person. Neither was he content to wrest happiness out of unhappiness. In the end, Exman inclined more toward James's mysticism than his pragmatism. What he wanted most was to join the ranks of the theonauts of James's *Varieties*. He wanted to be a mystic and a saint. He wanted to see God's face—to feel once again the jolt of that spiritual current that had coursed through him as a teenager in front of the Blanchester graveyard.

In the final line in his "Search for Meaning" essay, Exman seems almost literally to be looking back to the "divine invasion" he experienced atop his horse Nell that night. "There does seem to be evidence that life can be made more meaningful," he concludes, "if we remove the blinkers from the work-horses of science and give fuller rein to the race-horses of the spirit."[53] Happily, Exman did not run that race alone. Among the many friends who ran it with him were two writers from England who were engaged in a similar search. Their quest took them from London to New York to Los Angeles in the late 1930s. In the early 1940s, Exman's joined them in founding a coeducational spiritual commune devoted to experimenting with various techniques for encountering the divine. Would three hours a day meditating in a pitch-black room do the trick? Would the California desert do them in? And would the money run out? Exman and his friends were determined to find out.

CHAPTER TWO

Collecting Mystics
in a California Commune

On July 4, 1941, Exman took a cab to Pennsylvania Station and boarded a westbound train. His destination was Southern California, but he wasn't going on vacation. He was declaring his spiritual independence.

Exman was now more than a decade into his Harper career, and though he prided himself on his cosmopolitanism, the overwhelming majority of his books were still by and for Christians. The broad categories he employed in his catalogs—Introduction to Religion, Bible, History of Christianity, Theology, Comparative Religion— read like a catalog of the courses the University of Chicago Divinity School had offered when he enrolled there two decades earlier. He was now good enough at his job to be bored by its routine: inbox, outbox, manuscripts, meetings.

His religious life also suffered from repetition. The crisis of meaning brought on by World War I and intensified by World War II had done what the climate crisis would do to future generations. It left a pit in the stomach of many, and led at least some small vanguard to address the crisis with direct action. In the face of the wartime crisis of meaning, many left their churches on grounds of irrelevance. Exman remained at Riverside. In fact, he and Sunny were fixtures there, serving on committees and teaching Sunday school. But churchgoing wasn't doing anything to help him revisit his Blanchester graveyard experience. In fact, it was now compelling him to look for God in new places. As he saw it, organized religion had not only failed to prevent these wars; it had fueled them. Instead of contributing to a cosmopolitan order in which all human beings are respected as children of God, it had led adherents of rival religions to beseech their gods to murder and maim one another.

In January 1941, just days after entering his fifth decade on earth and a few months before stepping onto that westbound train, Exman had told his author and friend Thomas Kelly that he was looking to stir things up in the God department. "I've been [led] recently to enlarge my own spirituality," he wrote in a letter, adding that he and a few friends had begun meeting regularly in New York City as "a kind of 'Beloved Community.'"[1] Exman organized that community, which met on Monday nights to meditate, share a meal, and discuss devotional literature. He cultivated friendships with East Coast Quakers such as Kelly, who combined opposition to war with contemplative prayer. And then he headed west.

After disembarking at LA's Union Station, he found his way to a small Baptist college in La Verne, a citrus town nestled in the foothills of the San Gabriel Mountains along iconic Route 66. There a couple dozen would-be saints and mystics were gathering for a monthlong seminar titled "The Life of the Spirit." World War II was taking human lives by the millions in Europe, Africa, and Asia, and the La Verne Seminar, as this gathering came to be called, was in many respects an antiwar project. It was sponsored by the American Friends Service Committee (AFSC), a pacifist organization of the peace church known as the Quakers, or Friends. It was organized by Philadelphia-area Quakers. And it grew out of similar meetings Exman had attended at Pendle Hill, a Quaker conference center outside Philadelphia. But Exman hadn't come to California to talk politics. He had come to experiment with spiritual practices, to see which, if any, might reconnect him with the divine.

The La Verne Seminar, which met in a modest dormitory, was

populated by "cultural creatives"—writers, editors, clerics, activists, schoolteachers, and college students and professors.[2] The English expatriate author Christopher Isherwood was there with his cousin Felix Greene and his friend Denny Fouts. Greene, a pacifist who according to Exman possessed "considerable executive ability and the charm of good looks," handled the event's administrative details. Fouts, a make-love-not-war conscientious objector and high-price prostitute later memorialized by the writer Truman Capote as the "Best-Kept Boy in the World," had recently moved in with Isherwood and was trying (and sometimes succeeding) to trade in his sex, drugs, and alcohol for meditation. The Hollywood-based Congregationalist minister and activist Allan Hunter attended with his wife, Elizabeth Hunter, whom Isherwood judged to be "spiritually . . . the most adult member of the group." Other participants included Exman's New York City friend Denver Lindley, who edited *Collier's*, a popular weekly with a national circulation topping two million. The roster of Quaker participants included the convener Harold Chance, who had served the AFSC in various leadership roles, and Rachel Davis DuBois, a pioneer in intercultural dialogue and a future civil rights activist and Exman author. Half a dozen college students also attended, but the sun around whom the La Verne Seminar orbited was the British expat, historian, philosopher, author, and lecturer Gerald Heard, who would dazzle the participants (Exman included) with his brilliance, his learning, and his Christlike red beard. He would quickly become the most important spiritual influence in Exman's life.[3]

The British Mystical Expats

Born in London in 1889, Gerald Heard, the son of a Church of England priest, wanted to follow in his father's footsteps until he lost his faith as a teenager. After graduating with honors in history from Cambridge University in 1911, he suffered a mental breakdown in his early twenties, brought on in part by his inability to accept his homosexuality in a society where such acceptance was hard won. For a decade beginning in 1919, he worked for former member of Parliament Sir Horace Plunkett. Interactions with Plunkett's friends earned Heard a reputation as a brilliant conversationalist. He made a name for himself as a popular science writer in the late 1920s and a BBC science commentator in the early 1930s. Of his work at the BBC, where he sneaked in episodes on telepathy, ghosts, and after-life survival, the science fiction writer H. G. Wells wrote, "Heard is the only man I ever listen to on the wireless. He makes human life come alive." According to the English novelist E. M. Forster, Heard possessed one of the "most penetrating minds in England."[4]

As it became plain that the war to end all wars had failed to live up to its name, Heard became a pacifist in 1934. The next year he convinced his friend Aldous Huxley, who had just published his blockbuster novel *Brave New World* (1932), to join the Fosdick-inspired Peace Pledge Union.[5] Over the next few years, these two men experimented with meditation techniques—to recharge their pacifist activism and find a solution to the problem of the modern malaise. Much as AA's Bill Wilson would come to believe that an experience of God was required for alcoholics to recover, they were convinced that a religious experience was required for social recovery. Neither Heard nor Huxley was interested in secondhand religion. Both wanted "direct experience of eternal life." By the spring of 1937, they were convinced that the place to find it was the United States.[6]

On April 7 of that year, with the world still stuck in the Great Depression, Heard and Huxley left Southampton, England, on an ocean liner in the company of Huxley's wife and son, Maria and Matthew Huxley, and Heard's longtime partner, the socialite Christopher Wood. Exman had been trying to woo Heard to Harper at least since 1936, and shortly after his arrival in New York City, Heard stopped by Exman's office to meet him. They talked books and ideas, and Exman later remembered the hour they spent together as "one of the most stimulating I had ever experienced." With *The Source of Civilization* (1937), Heard inaugurated a prolific career writing for Harper's trade and religious book departments. Under the name H. F. Heard, he authored science fiction and detective novels for Harper and other publishers. As B. D. Vest, he contributed to *ONE*, an openly gay magazine, where he presented homosexuality as "a potent spiritual force that might have some important role in the evolution of human consciousness."[7]

Later in 1937, a cross-country trek in a Ford sedan deposited Heard and the Huxleys in the Los Angeles area, where they formed—with Isherwood, who joined them in 1939—a potent trinity of spiritually restive British writers.

Maria Huxley saw Heard and her husband as a Mutt and Jeff duo, with "Aldous so slow and calm and passive, Gerald vehement and busy and coercive." Heard was slim, about five-foot-nine with auburn hair. When Isherwood last saw him in England, he was "exaggeratedly clean-shaven—barbered and tailored, with a sort of fastidious understatement—carefully unemphatic, witty, catty, chatty, sly." The "new Gerald" was, in Isherwood's words, "disconcertingly, almost theatrically Christlike, with his beautiful little pointed beard, which tilted the entire face to an upward, heaven-seeking thrust; artistically, even dramatically shabby, in a sort of blue painter's smock, washed-out blue jeans and sneakers." Huxley, who compensated for his near blindness with a prodigious memory, also presented as an unkempt scholar, though in his case the uniform was a baggy suit and a wandering tie. But, physically, they couldn't have been more different. Huxley's sturdy, six-foot-four-and-a-half-inch frame was topped by a massive head bent over by weight and custom, as poor eyesight had for decades required him to employ a magnifying glass simply to read. Isherwood was shorter than either Huxley or Heard but more conventionally attractive, with a round face and a broad, easy smile that would keep him boyishly handsome well into his seventies.[8]

Huxley was straight. Heard and Isherwood were gay, though for

Heard homosexuality meant a titanic clash between spirit and matter that he took up with all the martial spirit of early Christians. Michael Murphy, who was later inspired by Heard and Huxley to establish Esalen, a spiritual retreat center in California's Big Sur, saw in Heard "a peculiar mixture of wild and inhibited. Wild in his ideas and inhibited in his (homo) sexuality." According to Exman, Heard was "sexually indulgent" until he commenced a program to beat back his sexual urges. "He would sit in ice-cold bath water. He would go out into the cold ('ten degrees below frost') dressed below the waist only in very thin trousers, thin socks and shoes," Exman wrote. "His doctor advised against it and said he would do damage to his sanity. But he persisted," living as a celibate from 1934 forward.[9]

As pacifists, Heard, Huxley, and Isherwood were repelled by warrior politics in England. As seekers, they were attracted to the spiritual ferment of the United States, eager to experiment with psychic phenomena and (in time) psychedelic flights to the divine. Exman joined them in their search for God, and popularized them in turn, seeing into print writing by all three men that helped to make midcentury American society increasingly open to the wisdom of Asian religions and the varieties of spiritual experience.

Though the other two persons in this expat trinity have now obscured Heard almost to the point of invisibility, Heard, who has been described as the "godfather of the New Age movement," was a major figure in mid-twentieth-century Anglo-American religious thought.[10] Critics complained about his clunky prose, which never measured up to his conversational gifts and never much improved. (Exman and Bro edited it heavily.) But it is hard not to see those critiques as protests by proper British atheists against a man who not only was God-besotted himself but also had the gall to convert the celebrated author of *Brave New World* into a preachy pacifist. Their collective spiritual turn made Heard and Huxley pariahs in British literary circles, where faith was at the time a sign of intellectual leprosy. To get away from the sniffing may have been one reason they decamped to California, whose desert winds and sea breezes seemed intelligently designed to muffle the noise from London's paragons of all that was right and all that was good.

As if to prove that he would continue to be a bad influence, Heard sought out two Indian intellectuals (both of whom would go on to write for Exman) and introduced them to his English friends. Swami Prabhavananda was a spiritual descendant of the pioneering Hindu missionary Swami Vivekananda, who had dazzled audiences at Chicago's World's Parliament of Religions in 1893 and formed the Vedanta Society in New York City one year later. Vivekananda was a follower of the Hindu reformer Ramakrishna, whose experiences of God-realization through many different religious paths had convinced him of the unity of the world's religions. The Indian philosopher Jiddu Krishnamurti is harder to describe. In 1909, at the age of fourteen, he was recruited by leaders of the Theosophical Society, an international organization in Madras (now Chennai) dedicated to spreading the truths of Asian wisdom in the West. They groomed him to be a messianic figure called the new World Teacher, but Krishnamurti, after moving to Ojai, California, in his midtwenties, refused that role. "I do not want followers," he said. "The moment you follow someone you cease to follow Truth."[11]

In February 1938, Heard met Krishnamurti in Ojai. Two months later he returned with Huxley. The next year, Heard met Swami Prabhavananda and introduced him to Huxley and Isherwood. Of this Anglo-American trinity — "The British Mystical Expatriates of Southern California," in the words of the Zen popularizer and Harper author Alan Watts — only Isherwood became a card-carrying Vedantist, memorializing Prabhavananda decades later in his bestselling memoir, *My Guru and His Disciple* (1980). Heard lectured at the swami's temple and wrote for his magazine, but broke with him early in 1941 over the swami's "minor luxuries" (Isherwood's words): tea parties, cigarette smoking, fast cars, all quite incompatible with Heard's otherworldly asceticism. Huxley followed Prabhavananda for a time, but he warmed more enduringly to Krishnamurti, with whom he shared a disdain for the rituals and hierarchies so important to Prabhavananda's organization. Huxley would go on to write a foreword for Krishnamurti's Harper bestseller, *The First and Last Freedom* (1954), praising the author for saying no, no, no, no, and no to scriptures, dogmas, gurus, rituals, and prayer. Isherwood, who said yes to all of the above, was unimpressed, though he did praise Krishnamurti for what he saw as a singular accomplishment: "He had done what no other man alive today has done: he had refused to become a god."[12]

"Be the Hyphens"

In October 1940, Exman met with Heard in Southern California. *The Creed of Christ*, which Harper would publish later that year, was in page proofs, and Exman wanted to discuss how to publicize it and what Heard might write next. Heard said he didn't know anything about publicity, and he hadn't any idea about what to write next. Exman was devastated. He had crossed the country largely to see Heard, and their meeting seemed over before it had begun.

In an effort to keep the conversation going, Exman said that he had just read Heard's lectures on the Lord's Prayer and had been moved by them. He had long felt that churches demanded very little from their members and delivered even less, he told Heard. He was sometimes stirred by Fosdick's sermons, but they gave him "no spiritual direction and no challenge to disciplined living." "I want to know more about prayer," he said. "I want God to be more real."[13]

"In that case, I do want to see you again," Heard replied.

They met at Heard's house the next day for tea and biscuits, and later for a walk-and-talk with Huxley and Isherwood. Heard talked about Jesus and the Buddha and spiritual discipline. "Renunciation was the key word," Exman later remembered. Another key word was "anonymity." Heard suggested that Exman try to spend a short time each day in meditation—"To place myself in the light of God" and to discern "who, what and where I was."

In letters Heard sent to Exman just before the La Verne Seminar, Heard described Exman and himself as bridge builders toward a "new syncretism" largely derived from Hindu and Catholic mystics. "We have to be the hyphens," he said. Heard envisioned the spiritual evolution of human consciousness as *the* project of the age. Humans were the result of billions of years of evolution, but their spiritual development had been arrested, and this new East-West combination would spark new advances. Heard's working hypothesis was deceptively simple: God exists, and the purpose of human life is to encounter God. Exman shared this view. The question for both men was how. What sort of training would equip seekers to find God?[14]

The training program at the La Verne Seminar featured three-times-a-day meditation sessions, shared meals, and lots of silence. The schedule, designed by Heard, who functioned as the event's unofficial spiritual adviser, looked like this:

- 5:00. Get up.   5:30–6:30. Meditation.   7:00. Breakfast.
- 9:00–10:30. Discussion period.   11:30–12:00. Meditation.
- 12:30. Lunch.   4:00–5:30. Discussion.   6:00–7:00. Meditation.
- 7:30. Supper.

During lunch and dinner, someone read from a spiritual classic. Nine o'clock was lights out, and following the Benedictines, the Catholic order that observes the rules of Saint Benedict, participants were to be silent from that time until after breakfast the next day.[15]

In an effort to focus on the eternal over the temporal, participants banned newspapers and magazines. They did not eat meat. They meditated, mostly in silence, in a dark room in a dormitory basement. Their discussions, held in a dormitory lounge, took up big questions at the intersection of contemplation and social action:

- *Is the life of prayer a form of escapism, or is it, perhaps, the most direct form of action?*

- *Granted that the present order of things is in a state of collapse, what could be the structure and sanctions of a new order of society?*

- *Can we construct a utopia which is truly theocentric?*[16]

As they wrestled with these questions, they formed two groups: "actives" (the Quaker contingent), who wanted to change the world; and "contemplatives" (Heard's friends, including Isherwood and Exman), who wanted to change humanity (and thereby change the world). The actives were suspicious of Heard's flirtation with Asian wisdom and his commitment to celibacy. The contemplatives were suspicious of the Quaker tendency to prioritize politics over spirituality.[17]

Isherwood served up biting character sketches of the participants in his diary. He described Allan Hunter, the Congregationalist minister from Hollywood, as "a lean sunburnt man with thin fair hair and a gaunt, deeply lined boyish face" who took Christ as "his personal leader—as real to him as Roosevelt." Hunter wanted nothing to do with celibacy, but he "could never have enough of Gerald's talk," Isherwood added. "'A little more on that, Gerald, please—' he would say, as though asking for a second helping."[18]

As for Exman, here is how Isherwood portrayed "Gerald's publisher":

He was a short, pale, fair-haired man whom one could easily imagine in a monk's robe with tonsure and rosary. His serious plumpish white face with the rimless glasses might, superficially, have appeared merely goody-goody—he had something of Disney's Three Little Pigs—but his eyes were mature and calmly alert . . . Also, there was a suggestion of worldly-wise humor; he was, as they say, nobody's fool. In the course of his business life he had met and sized up plenty of cranks, lunatics and crooks; and his approval was worth having. He had always been devout. Devotion came easily to him, and this made him seem unctuous to those, like Denny, whose stomachs were sensitive.[19]

Much of the work of the La Verne Seminar followed ideas outlined in two short *Training for the Life of the Spirit* pamphlets published by Exman in 1941 and 1942 and jointly written by Heard, Exman, and the *Collier's* editor Denver Lindley. Like these pamphlets, the seminar challenged participants to contribute to the ongoing evolution of human consciousness by evolving spiritually themselves. It trained them in contemplative techniques that were said to alter conduct, character, and then consciousness. While experimenting with these techniques, they would find themselves walking "the true path of evolution" taken by "epoch-making saints" who had proved by personal experience that "the road to the top of the mountain is open."[20]

Alongside prayer and meditation, the seminar emphasized two additional techniques for training in the life of the spirit. One was action in the world. "The life of the spirit is not . . . a life of retreat," a report prepared after the seminar read. Contemplation is not withdrawal from this world but training for effective action in it. Exman would make a similar point later in a pamphlet of his own called *The Escapists*, where he speaks of prayer as a flight *into* reality rather than a flight *from* it. Nonetheless, Heard and Exman insisted that, because the ills of modern society were more spiritual than material, curing them had to begin with the individual.

A second spiritual practice stressed at La Verne was the deep reading of devotional books. But which books? Heard answered that question with a "bibliography of the life of the spirit" that highlighted core texts in mysticism and Asian religions, including the Hindu Upanishads and the Daoist scripture the Daodejing. In this way, the seminar advanced Exman's project of creating a new canon of spiritual texts for seekers, with a decidedly Jamesian emphasis on the mountaintop of individual spiritual experience: the mystical encounter.[21]

Heard also plugged a perennial favorite by the Roman Catholic priest Thomas à Kempis—"A new edition of *The Imitation of Christ* . . . being brought out by Harper's"—even as he warned against books that were either "too specifically Catholic" or "too evangelical." Here Heard was following the model of Exman's evolving Book of Books, by insisting on "nonsectarian" classics that could be read by religious folks of many varieties. Simultaneously, he proved that, for him at least, "nonsectarianism" had its limits.[22]

The La Verne experiment ended on August 3, 1941, when most of the participants packed up and headed home. Exman returned sadder and wiser. While railroading west, he had been so excited that he felt selfish about coming. "You aren't neglecting your family," Sunny reassured him. "For Heaven's sake enjoy yourself." But he did not enjoy himself. In the blazing dust bowl that was summertime La Verne, God seemed for the first time in Exman's adult life to be almost defiantly distant. While those around him seemed to be growing in "the Practice of the Presence," he was experiencing the Presence of the Absence.[23]

But Exman soldiered on. Over the next year, as he collaborated with Heard, Huxley, Isherwood, and Felix Greene on the "Beloved Community" they were imagining into being, he and Heard grew increasingly friendly. Heard appreciated Exman's social and administrative skills. Exman appreciated Heard's intelligence and learning—his "brilliance as a speaker, his vast knowledge, his broad sympathies, his common sense, his lack of smugness, his humor and modesty." They corresponded regularly about the books they were editing and writing. Heard reviewed manuscripts for Exman. He even lent Exman $11,000 to buy a house, while Exman handled some of his investments.[24]

The hundreds of letters they exchanged in the early 1940s went beyond mutual regard to something like the tenderness Heard described as the proper alternative to sexual striving. Heard referred to Exman as his "spiritual companion" and to themselves as "fellow seekers." "I thank God for helping me by sending you along," Heard wrote. "I think of you with joy and affection and class you in my mind with my dear and intensely valuable" West Coast friends, he said, adding, "I don't know anyone who intellectually . . . holds quite the key central position you hold" in their emerging community. By the end of 1941, Heard was telling Exman that he was disinclined to publish with anyone else.[25]

An Experimental College

"Focus" was the working name for the project Heard had been hatching for years. Its genesis can be traced to Heard's *Ascent of Humanity* (1929), which had promoted small intentional communities as a way to break down the modern obsession with the individual. By 1940, Heard and Huxley were sharing plans with Exman for "a new kind of Quaker college or seminary" but "something smaller and more exploratory"—a group of perhaps a half dozen sincere seekers after the divine.[26] This experiment got going when Heard committed about $100,000, which included a substantial inheritance he received after the death of his former employer Sir Horace Plunkett. Heard asked Exman to open and oversee a trust fund for the project and to sit on its Board of Trustees. Exman agreed, and the plans advanced quickly for a community of seekers and pacifists intent on redeeming a warring world through the shared practices of silent meditation, prayer, and devotional reading.

On December 10, 1941, just three days after the Japanese bombed Pearl Harbor, Greene reported that he was negotiating with the owner of a three-hundred-acre desert ranch in Trabuco Canyon in the Santa Ana Mountains, roughly sixty miles southeast of Los Angeles. The price was a little more than $40,000—over budget—but, in what would become a pattern, Greene was able to convince

Heard to go bigger, in this case by convincing an anonymous donor to put up an additional $25,000. War shortages presented additional obstacles, but Greene was an administrative savant who managed to wrangle not only the financing but also an architect, builders, and supplies. He also did a lot of the manual labor himself, working throughout that winter with "superhuman energy."[27]

On the last day of February 1942, less than three months after Pearl Harbor Day, the footings for the buildings were poured. In March, the walls started to go up, and the site took on the appearance, in Heard's words, of "a mining town at the dawn of a boom."[28] That summer, a rough facsimile of an Italian monastery, complete with redbrick walls and walks, tile roofs and floors, cloisters and court-yards, and heavy beams carved from local live oaks, had emerged from the rugged foothills of the Santa Ana Mountains.

There would be no electricity until after the war, but there was a bell tower, a dining hall, and a kitchen, plus bedrooms in the main structure for singles and in outbuildings for married couples. A library, stocked by Exman, included an extraordinary collection in compar-ative religion, mysticism, and prayer. But the soul of the place was the Oratory, a windowless circular structure topped with a dome and dug down into the earth, where seekers gathered three times a day for "shared silence." Given its height and depth, it seemed in the darkness to have no roof, and its shape made it "a whispering gallery" that all but commanded the sort of inward turning the place was meant to cultivate. Though set at the northern edge of the complex, the Oratory was, in Huxley's words, "psychologically central."[29]

As their project went forward, the founders brainstormed a proper name for what they had been calling "the Centre" and "the Ranch." What to name a place meant to function as a prayer lab, a commune, an agricultural cooperative, and a refuge for consci-entious objectors? Isherwood, after joking that it should be called the "Southern California Branch of the Non-Sectarian Society for the Practice and Study of Mysticism," pushed for a place name and nothing else. Heard wanted to call it a college, by which he meant a *collegium*: a "community" and "'a clearinghouse' for individual religious experiences and ideas."[30] Exman and others pointed out that *college* did not mean that in the American context, but the trustees deferred to Heard and the place became the Trabuco College of Prayer, which was quickly shortened in practice to Trabuco College.

This "experimental college," as Exman described it in his unpublished autobiography, was up and running just in time to hold its first summer seminar from July 15 to August 4, 1942. As at La Verne, Heard lorded over the gathering, while Greene ran the trains. Exman, who offered Heard curricular suggestions, again crossed the country to attend. Huxley, who had not been at La Verne, also came. In letters home, Exman marveled at the fifteen-mile views and the beauty of the place, including the first cactus bloom he had ever seen. The twenty-five seminarians were "more unified and better" than the La Verne group, in his judgment, and possessed by "a fine spirit of unity and fellowship."[31]

The schedule largely followed the La Verne script, with three-times-a-day group meditation, mealtime readings from mystical classics, discussions, and lots of silence. Exman found the silent sessions in the darkness of the Oratory alternately comforting and frightening. "On rare occasions it was deeply joyous, even ecstatic," he said.[32] Seminar members again combined communal living with manual labor (Huxley washed the dishes), all infused with an experimental spirit, the urgency of wartime, and more than a touch of the megalomania of a bodhisattva intent on saving all sentient beings from suffering. Would civilization survive this war? The answer somehow depended on what a couple dozen seekers might discover in four weeks together in the desert.

This gathering distinguished itself from La Verne by its careful attention to non-Christian religions. Exman's handwritten notes from the proceedings refer to Christianity sparingly. (A rare reference reads, "Protestantism is a dying religion.") Exman refers in those notes to Hinduism, Buddhism, Jainism, Shintoism, Confucianism, and Daoism, and observes that many participants believed that

Hinduism and Buddhism had the most to contribute to "a common religion of today."[33]

A week into the seminar, Jesus came up. Huxley argued the Vedantist position that God incarnated many times, while the Christ followers asked, "Is not Jesus the greatest?" According to the unpublished and "strictly confidential" official report of the seminar, Exman channeled his inner James by directing his fellow participants away from theology and toward "the path of practical, experiential religion, i.e. mysticism." Huxley agreed. "We should start with a psychology," he said—with "direct experience" and "the mystic insight."[34]

After Exman returned home, he and Heard continued to write regularly about their approach/avoidance relationship with Christianity. As a churchgoer and church leader, Exman still had two feet firmly planted in the Christian tradition, but that world was shaking under his feet, as Heard, who was increasingly disinclined to describe himself as a Christian, pushed him beyond "Jesocentric theology" to a more inclusive and expansive spirituality.[35]

In August 1942, days after the Trabuco seminar had ended, Exman took stock of his life in a revealing autobiographical letter to Heard. Now in his early forties and officially in middle age, Exman was proud of his professional accomplishments, which had provided a comfortable living for his wife and three children. His religious life had been marked by times of doubt and "complete secular absorption," but he had stood by the church "and left the cardinal sins to others." The problem was that he did not know God. Financial security, social status, and material comforts had distracted him from his search, turning him by degrees into a functional atheist. However, he was now coming to see his prior goals—"fortune and fame and pleasant indulgence"—as "mediocre and unworthy." He was determined to recapture the "momentary exaltation of spirit" he had experienced on the road to Blanchester—to rededicate himself to knowing God "as an inner experience."[36]

After Trabuco, Exman was also increasingly inclined to see

egotism as a barrier to his spiritual growth. And he was coming to see contemplative prayer as the answer. Fosdick and Heard had both taught him that prayer wasn't about asking for and receiving something. It was about trying to sit silently in the presence of the divine. Cultivating this new prayer discipline had not changed things overnight. "I'm lazy, and selfish and often resentful," Exman confessed to Heard. "I'm lustful when I want to be loving." But he could feel change coming.[37]

"A Club for Mystics"

American history is full of communal experiments, spiritual and otherwise. The Transcendentalists' Brook Farm lasted six years and was not particularly religious. The clearly religious Mormons are coming up on two centuries. Some of these experiments were led by charismatic leaders. Others were not. Most operated on a small scale, with communities of a few dozen, who often came and went. Trabuco was by design a modest effort. But it was historically significant, out in front of Allen Ginsberg, Jack Kerouac, and other Beat Generation authors who "discovered" Buddhism in the 1950s, and of the Beatles and John Coltrane and others who flocked to various forms of Hinduism in the 1960s. It was farther out in front of the sharp rise in interest in Asian religions that followed the opening up of Asian immigration (and the immigration of Asian religious teachers) by the US Congress in 1965.

In September 1942, just after the first seminar was over, a short leaflet called *Trabuco* summed up what this experiment was all about. Though published anonymously, it was coauthored by Heard and Huxley with Isherwood's help. It reads like a manifesto. "Humanity is failing," it states, before connecting the dots between that failure and the wartime crisis of meaning: "We are starving—many of us physically, all of us spiritually—in the midst of plenty. Our shame and our failure are being blatantly advertised, every minute of every day, by the crash of explosives and the flare of burning towns. We admit this. We are not proud of our handiwork. We know that we have, somehow, taken the wrong road. Many, even now before the shooting stops, are wondering how to find the way out." To this problem, a new political or economic ideology was not the answer. Neither was a new international organization. Why? Because "the will to destruction is within ourselves." There- fore, the way forward was for individuals to find "the way back to God." That way was neither quick nor easy. In fact, it involved "a slow hard lifetime of study, prayer and disciplined, ascetic living." As a coeducational, not-for-profit, and "un-denominational" col- lege, Trabuco was founded to offer training in that way of life. To that end, it was dedicated to three objectives: researching prayer and meditation techniques, experimenting with those techniques to see which work best, and integrating the techniques that work best for each individual into their daily lives.[38]

The long-term goal was to turn Trabuco into "a modern version of the mediaeval university," complete with students, "masters" to teach them, and "doctors" to bring their discoveries to the wider world. In the meantime, it would function as a "self-subsisting" cooperative hosting students and a few permanent residents. The diet would be simple and the fees moderate.

The Hindu tradition that deeply influenced Heard, Huxley, and Isherwood had long recognized four life stages—students, house- holders, retirees, and renouncers—each with different duties. There was a time for education and another to work and raise a family. There was also a time to retire and, for a lucky few, a time to re- nounce work and family obligations in order to devote oneself 24/7 to achieving spiritual liberation. Trabuco blurred these stages, offer- ing a mix of householder and monastic life—a taste of renunciation for nonrenouncers. There were college students as well as single and married folks at Trabuco. But Heard drew the line at children. When asked by a visitor when children might be welcome, Heard replied,

"Later, later perhaps." When a friend asked what that meant, Heard said, "After my death."[39]

Another leaflet called "Some First Steps in Meditation" revealed an ongoing challenge with visitors and free riders: outsiders help pay the bills, but they also threaten to distract the community from its core purpose. Isherwood's solution was one "essential" rule: "No passengers. . . . In a place like Trabuco, which isn't a monastery and admits both the sexes, you will find your most earnest members bringing their lukewarm wives, husbands, or friends along . . . 'for the ride.' And before you know it, there'll be children too!"[40]

After church groups came knocking with plans for weekend retreats, a handout called "The Way of Life at Trabuco" made a similar point. Trabuco was "not a hostel." Neither was it just a school. It was a research "laboratory" whose central "experiment" was "to restore an essential contact that has been lost—contact with the spiritual world." Its "chief technique" was "deep continuous attention," cultivated in group meditation, walking, silence, and reading alone at meals.

One easy way to keep out the free riders was to ratchet up what Heard referred to as the "athleticism": a strict meditation schedule, silence, simple meals, and abstention from sex, meat, and cigarettes. Another hard practice was anonymity, which had emerged as a key value, likely in conversation with participants in Alcoholics Anonymous. At Trabuco, that meant not attaching your name to things and otherwise working to keep the ego at bay.

The most intriguing leaflet offered four perspectives, all edited by Exman, on the Trabuco experience. Greene's contribution is lost, but the gospels according to Heard, Isherwood, and Huxley survive in the Exman Archive. Heard presented Trabuco as a chapter inside an expansive social and religious history of the perennial quest for "the religion of direct experience." Isherwood offered a natural history of the place, setting it geographically between the Santa Ana Mountains and the Pacific Ocean. Huxley narrowed the focus, homing in on what he saw as "the reason for Trabuco's existence"—group meditation in the Oratory: "Trabuco provides people who live 'in the world' . . . with an opportunity of becoming acquainted with the experience of shared silence, of spiritual work in common."[41]

While Trabuco moved away from its original identity as a college, its leaders struggled to reclassify it. Then Heard and Isherwood hit on the phrase "a club for mystics." Isherwood observed that "'monastery' is misleading because it implies authority, celibacy, a dogma, and vows," whereas Trabuco is "organically democratic." At Trabuco, "you are among colleagues, not masters and disciples," he explained. Heard then tracked the development of "group intentional living" in Western civilization—from the monastery to the college to the club. "The monastery is hierarchic, the college academic, the club liberal," he explained. "It is not confined by dogma nor divided up into specialized faculties." Then, marrying two seemingly incompatible terms (*mystic* and *club*), he located their common ground in the search: "Full freedom to search has led to the club; utter devotion to the search results in the mystic."[42]

Celibacy and Otherwise

Rumors swirled around Trabuco Canyon that the new residents were running "a nudist colony," but celibacy was actually the ideal. The second *Training for the Life of the Spirit* pamphlet commended "a way of effortless sublimation whereby animal passion, the sheer drive of crude sex, may be mastered." It also commended "tenderness" as an alternative to sex. This tenderness was there in the affections many women residents had for Heard, and he for them. It was there in the Heard/Exman correspondence. Not everyone at Trabuco was content with tenderness, however. Felix Greene fell in love with Elena Lindeman, a Mexican American actress with green eyes and long braids who was one of Heard's "prize pupils." They decided to marry. Greene asked for Heard's approval, which Heard refused.

They married anyway, in the winter of 1944–45, at the Mt. Hollywood Congregational Church of Allan and Elizabeth Hunter.[43]

Bro, who had met Exman in person in 1943 and was now reviewing and editing manuscripts (including Heard's) for Exman, arrived at Trabuco just after the wedding. She had wanted to go for years, but her way had been blocked by finances, ill health, and a husband who expected her to be available to host college social events. She finally made it in February 1945, thanks to her friend Myrtle Walgreen (the wife of the drugstore chain founder), who took Bro as her guest. "I'm here!" she wrote Exman. "I have felt so desperate about coming—as if I could never go on and find my way unless I could get here—as if this were the one path to God. . . . When are you coming?" In a later letter, Bro confided to Exman that she sensed "something unhealthy" about the Greene-Lindeman marriage. "He has a sad record of broken homes and hearts, of instability in many aspects," she wrote, while fearing that Lindeman—"the poor lamb"—didn't know the half of it. There was karma at play, and sex, which Bro described as "the stuff of the creative life." Greene and Lindeman left shortly after their wedding, leaving some to remark that "Heard's chief monk had run off with his chief nun."[44]

It was a huge loss. Greene and Heard had been Trabuco's dynamic duo, with Greene playing the administrative genius to Heard's unofficial guru. Heard had been the lead "contemplative," but Greene's departure—for Krishnamurti's ashram in Ojai—meant that the lead "active" had gone missing. Interim managers came and went, but no one could replace Greene when it came to making repairs and smoothing over the sharp edges of Heard's leadership style, which somehow managed to demand allegiance while refusing responsibility.

Bro, a Heard aficionado, blamed Greene, while rightly recognizing that the scandal signaled a tectonic shift in the place. Almost as soon as she arrived, she was fearing that it might crack. "For good or ill, it seems to me this is G.H.'s venture," she wrote regarding Heard. "He made it; on the authority of his life it rests. As director, he should have a free hand. When he fails, it fails. Until he fails, it deserves unqualified support." A book Heard authored around this time contained a similar hint of Trabuco's coming demise. "Here lies the basic reason for the continual frustrant efforts of men to live group-dedicated lives," he wrote, "a wonderful promise at the start, and a disappointment and indeed a scandal at the close."[45]

By the beginning of 1947, Trabuco's doors were close to closing. Heard let his friends know that his financial and emotional resources had been shot. He told Exman he needed a sabbatical, and when he stepped down later that year it took more than faith to hope he was coming back.

There was the sort of flailing that goes on at the end of such things—new visions laid over old ones like two pairs of glasses with different prescriptions, efforts at clarification that only make things more difficult to see. There was talk of a children's school, a retreat center, and a publishing venture. Old board members (Exman included) stepped down. New ones signed on.

Exman worked harder than anyone to keep things going. In the spring of 1947, he wrote Heard, offering to raise $10,000 a year from "friends of Trabuco": "Would $500.00 a month beginning right away ease the situation?" That summer, he dispatched his friend and colleague John Chambers to Trabuco. In September, he came out with Sunny and his kids, who stayed at a nearby cottage. Exman brainstormed with Charles Dana, a philosopher and a new trustee, about bringing in families to make Trabuco more economically sustainable. He proposed that Bro's son Harmon Bro and his wife, June, manage the place during an "interim period" before Heard's hoped-for return.[46]

None of that worked. A last-gasp effort by the new trustees to turn Trabuco into a pay-to-pray retreat center rankled Heard, who wasn't in it for the money and didn't want to see the place turned into a religious theme park. He moved out in October 1947.

Exman continued to hope against hope that Heard's sabbatical was just a sabbatical. In March 1949, he returned to Trabuco to troubleshoot one last time, but the place had been vacant for months and there was nothing to be done. Heard was already working to hand it over to Swami Prabhavananda and the Vedanta Society. After a series of contentious trustee meetings, it was finally agreed on May 3, 1949, to do just that. The Methodist minister Albert Day, another new trustee, told Exman he had done all he could to stop the takeover. "Certainly Vedantism in America will always be a fringe cult," he wrote. "I tried to get Gerald to see that," but Heard had already gone over to "the Hindu zone."[47]

Why Trabuco Failed (and How It Didn't)

There is no shortage of theories regarding why Trabuco failed. In a self-serving analysis, the Vedanta Society of Southern California concluded that it failed because it was coeducational and was not affiliated with a religious order. Swami Yogeshananda, a convert to Vedanta who spent time at Trabuco in 1945, said it was "insufficiently austere," with "three ample meals a day plus fairly high 'tea.'" A more plausible theory is that it was too strict. There just weren't enough Americans in the 1940s willing to meditate three times a day, keep silent at night, abstain from sex, and wring their sustenance out of desert sand.[48]

Others pinned the blame on Heard. The historian and armchair psychoanalyst Laurence Veysey concluded that Trabuco failed because Heard was psychologically warped. "Ever since boyhood he had lacked something crucial in terms of self-acceptance," Veysey wrote. At Trabuco, he was "inwardly torn," wanting to play the spiritual director but paralyzed by an "aloof shyness in his make-up, a tendency to retreat into isolation, which suggested that he was fundamentally ill suited to group living." As a result, "life at Trabuco became a form of solitary confinement."[49]

Maria Huxley also blamed Heard, minus the psychoanalysis. "Gerald really made a mess of the whole thing" by setting himself up as a guru, she wrote. He "was even more of an autocrat than we had thought," always forgetting that "God and Gerald were not the same thing."[50]

Heard *was* a peculiar man, and there were people who left Trabuco because of his peculiarities. But dozens of letters in the Exman Archive testify that Heard was the main draw. The actress Margaret Gage praised his "heroic, unselfish effort" at Trabuco. Rachel Davis DuBois, who would go on to work for Martin Luther King Jr. at the Southern Christian Leadership Conference, regarded Heard as a major force in her life. "What a brain!" she said. Franklin Zahn, a Caltech engineer and conscientious objector, rejected any suggestion that Heard was an autocrat. "He was far too much a liberal to accept total submission of one person to another, or even to an institution," he insisted, describing Heard as a humble crusader against pride whose commitment to ego deflation was the "most important contribution to my own spiritual life."[51]

Bro and Exman were also Heard loyalists. Letters between Exman and Heard continued to be affectionate throughout Trabuco's downfall, with Heard often expressing his gratitude for Exman's friendship and his ongoing commitment to their shared search. "He remains the one man in my life," Bro told Exman. "Literally he is the one person I could least well do without. And I feel sure you would say the same thing."[52]

One overlooked theory regarding Trabuco's failure is that intentional communities almost always fail. From this perspective, Trabuco just did what such places do, albeit on its own time and for its own reasons. Among those reasons, three were paramount. It ran out of energy. It ran out of money. And Heard ran out of both.

Another contributing factor to Trabuco's demise was the end of World War II. Trabuco was built in the aftermath of Pearl Harbor and began to collapse not long after atomic bombs obliterated Hiroshima and Nagasaki on August 6 and 9, 1945. The original vision had anticipated a core crew of residents whose prayers, labor, and money would keep the place going while a steady stream of paying visitors dropped in for seminars. Out of this core, some saints might emerge. But residents were hard to recruit and harder to keep, and the big influx of young pacifists and seekers expected after the war never materialized. Heard had staked his reputation on the proposition that spiritual training in small groups was the cure to modern materialism. The world said otherwise.

The United States did see a postwar religious revival that brought new bodies and souls into places of worship and spiked religious book sales. But readers of many of the most popular religion books of that period—Rabbi Joshua Liebman's *Peace of Mind* (1946), Bishop Fulton Sheen's *Peace of Soul* (1949), and Billy Graham's *Peace with God* (1953)—showed little interest in hard work. Resting in the easy comforts of Norman Vincent Peale's *The Power of Positive Thinking* (1952), they were more devoted to thinking their way toward a new car or a new house than to praying their way toward God. They were also keen on marriage and children, leaving little room, even on weekends, for the ascetic disciplines of the desert.

Harold Winchester, an East Coast businessman who witnessed Trabuco's last days firsthand, offered a bottom-up theory regarding Trabuco's failure to reboot. Winchester was an "active," and what he saw at Trabuco was the inability of "idea purveyors" to pull their weight. There are just too many people here, he wrote in a letter to Exman as the Vedantists were taking over, "who think because they have said something that they have already done it." He then mused about California bringing out "the coocoo in people." "The idea of eternal sunshine is an escape philosophy anyway and this country down here is full of escapists who do not wish to battle either spiritual or physical weather." They are forever rushing here and there "after every new prophet or idea or fad."[53]

In retrospect, it is clear that Trabuco's fortunes hung too heavily on the charisma of two extraordinary men. When Greene left—he became one of the first Western journalists to report from North Vietnam during the 1960s and then a documentary filmmaker in

China and Cuba—all the work he had been doing to keep the place going became evident. When Heard left, Trabuco was done.

The Vedanta Society of Southern California did not pay for the property, but it did assume its debts. It also paid to return the neglected physical plant to something of its former glory. At a dedication ceremony on September 7, 1949, Trabuco College officially became the Ramakrishna Monastery, a name it retains today. One of the first things its new owners did was to put up an altar to Hindu gods that made Heard and Huxley go pale.

A Literary Legacy

If judged by its own lofty aims—to research and teach the life of the spirit, to produce saints, and to advance the evolution of human consciousness—Trabuco was not particularly successful. It trained only a few hundred people, and none, Heard included, seem to have become saints. A quick glance at CNN.com will confirm that it did not succeed in advancing the evolution of consciousness, though the founders of the Big Sur retreat center Esalen have long credited Trabuco as a major inspiration for their efforts to advance human potential. Unlike Esalen, which celebrated its sixtieth year in 2022, Trabuco also failed on the longevity front. As it was coming into being, Greene told Exman that, while secular intentional communities typically expire after a few years, religious ones last a generation on average. Trabuco made it six or seven years, depending on how you do the counting.

When it comes to research and publications, however, Trabuco was a major success. It didn't yield the breakthroughs on prayer that Heard wanted, but it attracted an extraordinary group of writers and intellectuals whose work was shaped by their experiences there. Timothy Miller, who made a career of documenting the half-lives of American utopias, argued that Trabuco's "positive influence on those who benefited from their experience there continues to resonate through our society."[54] That influence was felt by a long line of visitors who meditated in the Oratory, weeded the garden, and walked the grounds in conversation with Heard, Huxley, and Exman. These visitors included W. Y. Evans-Wentz, an early translator of the Tibetan Book of the Dead; the poet Ezra Pound; the Zen scholar-practitioner D. T. Suzuki; the AA cofounder Bill Wilson; and the author of *The Religions of Man*, Huston Smith. Heard, Huxley, and others also used the Trabuco library to produce an impressive array of articles and books, including many published by Exman at Harper.

The two *Training for the Life of the Spirit* pamphlets, collaborations by some combination of Heard, Huxley, Isherwood, Greene, and Exman, were published by Exman as Trabuco was coming into its own. Another joint project, *Prayers and Meditations* (1949), which Heard described as "imprints left by an attempt at group religious life," also grew out of Trabuco. Exman signed up authors during his California visits, and when his right-hand man, John Chambers, visited Trabuco in the summer of 1947, he reported, "There seems to be a manuscript hanging from the limb of every tree here!"[55]

Many of the Hindu books Exman published in the late 1940s and early 1950s involved Huxley, Isherwood, and Swami Prabhavananda in various combinations. Huxley contributed a foreword to a book on the Vedanta movement founder called *Ramakrishna: Prophet of New India* (1948). Isherwood and Prabhavananda collaborated on two translations: *The Song of God: Bhagavad-Gita* (1951, with a Huxley introduction) and *How to Know God: The Yoga Aphorisms of Patanjali* (1953). Isherwood also produced an edited volume with contributions by Heard and Huxley called *Vedanta for Modern Man* (1951), and when Exman published Krishnamurti's bestseller, *The First and Last Freedom* (1954), Huxley wrote a glowing ten-page foreword. Exman also brought out three translations of Hindu scriptures by the Indian philosopher and statesman Sarvepalli Radhakrishnan, who would eventually serve as India's president.

Strengthening the case for his emerging status as an East-West "hyphen," Exman gave a prominent place in his catalogs to

Buddhism as well. One important contributor was the Japanese author D. T. Suzuki, who met and influenced the Beat Generation writers during a five-year sojourn as a Columbia professor in the mid-1950s. Three of Suzuki's books made their way into Exman's catalogs, beginning with *Essays in Zen Buddhism: First Series* (1949).

Exman also planned a survey of the world's religions by Margueritte Bro, who corresponded with him about that project as early as 1945. In November 1946, after meeting with Bro in Chicago on his way to Trabuco, Chambers gave a thumbs-up to her comparative religion book. In March 1947, Exman used his expense account to buy Bro a long list of Hindu, Buddhist, Confucian, and Daoist books from the Psychic Book Center in Manhattan. In June 1947 Bro wrote Exman with a pithy description of the project that accented the search. "It's still objective but it's more of an inside job," she wrote. "I want the essential thing in each religion to shine out. Not just a history of things people have thought about the world and God but the feeling of a moving search with roads drawing nearer and nearer together as the searchers approach Him." The book never happened. Bro took on other writing and editing projects, and when her husband left Francis Shimer College and went overseas with the State Department, she joined him. But Huston Smith filled the gap with a book that read like a line-by-line fulfillment of the promise of Bro's proposal. With 3.5 million copies sold, *The Religions of Man* (1958)—now *The World's Religions*—is the most widely read book ever in religious studies. In a different world, its royalties, and its byline, might have gone to Margueritte Bro.[56]

The Perennial Philosophy

The most important books to come out of the Trabuco experiment were twinned projects that pioneered now-popular thinking about the unity of the world's religions. Both Heard's *Eternal Gospel* and Huxley's *The Perennial Philosophy* were published by Harper.

Huxley's came out of the trade department and Heard's out of religion, but both were promoted by Exman, advertised in his catalogs, and merchandised by his salesmen, who visited religious bookstores nationwide to hand-sell his books. Heard and Huxley developed their arguments in conversation with each other and researched them in the Exman-stocked Trabuco library. Each argued, in his own way, for what would come to be called perennialism, which Heard defined in a 1943 article as the view that "the essentials" of the world's religions "are one."[57]

Although Heard had been drawn to Asian religions while in England—as early as 1934 he read a translation of the Daodejing by his friend Arthur Waley—most of his pre-Trabuco religious writing for Exman was explicitly Christian: books on the Lord's Prayer (*The Creed of Christ*, 1940), the Beatitudes (*The Code of Christ*, 1941), and the temptations of Jesus (*A Dialogue in the Desert*, 1942). Heard took a small step in a post-Christian direction with *The Gospel According to Gamaliel* (1945), which, by examining early Christianity through the eyes of a rabbi, aimed to build bridges across the Jewish-Christian divide. In *The Eternal Gospel* (1946), Heard further widened his aperture to explore what he referred to as "the Everlasting Gospel" and "the Perennial Wisdom." "All religion is one," he argued, adding in classic Jamesian fashion that "the common denominator and working factor in all the great religions" is experiential.[58]

The Eternal Gospel might have made a fine starting place for the modern revival of the perennial philosophy, but Huxley was a much better writer than Heard, and Heard seemed compelled in his book to return, like the choruses in his father's Church of England hymnal, to Christian themes. Huxley, by contrast, found his home ground in Hindu philosophy. In this way, Heard and Huxley demonstrated that, while religions may be one, there are many perennial philosophies. More than Heard's Protestant version, it is Huxley's Hindu-derived version that is remembered today.

The Perennial Philosophy was an odd candidate for a multigenerational bestseller. It is a challenging book, pitched quite high for middlebrow readers. And it is basically an anthology. Like James's *Varieties*, which presents long first-person accounts of the extraordinary religious experiences of ordinary people (some go on for pages), it presents snippets (typically shorter than James's) from the spiritual and theological insights of mystics, with a voiceover of sorts from a bestselling British novelist. *The Perennial Philosophy* overcame these obstacles by presenting a clear and consistent argument that provided hope for readers ravaged by war. Instead of imagining no religion, as John Lennon would do, Huxley imagined a shared religion that would undercut theological incentives for war. Huxley also helped chart a path from religion to spirituality, preparing the way for those who describe themselves today as "spiritual but not religious." To be precise, Huxley modeled how to be religious in one way (the personal way of mystical experience) without being religious in another way (the institutional way of churches, clergy, dogmas, creeds, and rituals). At the heart of his version of perennialism was the claim that the world's religions all derive from universal teachings about the mystical encounter with the divine. In that regard, they are different manifestations of one shared wisdom tradition. In the immediate aftermath of World War II and amid echoes of the Great War that preceded it, this was to many a welcome argument.

Huxley devoted *The Perennial Philosophy* to the sorts of mystical geniuses James called saints: Laozi and Zhuangzi of early Daoism; medieval Catholic mystics such as Saint Teresa and Meister Eckhart; Quakers and other modern Protestant pacifists; and Rumi the Muslim Sufi poet. Huxley also drew on Hindu texts such as the Upanishads and the Bhagavad Gita and Buddhist scriptures from the Dhammapada to the Tibetan Book of the Dead. Together this cloud of witnesses converged on the "Highest Common Factor" in the world's religions. Huxley did not claim that this factor was in all religions. He claimed only that it was perennial, continually appearing and disappearing, buried here and uncovered there, in purer and more bastardized forms, throughout world history. Huxley found more of this secret sauce in earlier than later Buddhism, and more in medieval Catholic mystics than in modern Protestants. As he offered these comparisons, Huxley equated beliefs and practices that scholars of religion now see as distinct, presenting Christian "salvation" and Buddhist "enlightenment," for example, as basically the same.[59]

Though *The Perennial Philosophy* is now widely revered as a mystical classic, it is oddly sectarian, slanted against Christianity and toward Hinduism of the Vedantist type—a bug (or feature) Christian reviewers did not fail to notice. The perennial philosophy could be found in Christianity, Huxley conceded, but only if you were willing to dig beneath centuries of encrusted beliefs and corrupt practices of the "priestly caste." In his telling, institutional Christianity was a runway of decadence of a different sort, showcasing "persecution, simony, power politics, secret diplomacy, high finance and collaboration with despots." Christian nations, he argued in a strikingly prescient passage, "have ceased to be Christian in anything but name, and the only religion they profess is some brand of local idolatry, such as nationalism, state-worship, boss-worship and revolutionism."[60]

Dissenting from Heard's evolutionary perspective, in which superconsciousness was just around the corner, Huxley told his story of the world's religions as a narrative of decline—from firsthand experiences of founders to the hearsay of their followers. "The Christ of the Gospels," he wrote, "speaks against vain repetitions . . . insists on the supreme importance of private worship . . . has no use for sacrifices and not much use for the Temple." But then "historic Christianity" piled on the public rituals and sacraments. A similar development took place in Buddhism. The Buddha of the early Buddhist scriptures denounced ritual as a roadblock to liberation. But that did not prevent the religion he founded from making full use of ceremonies and "vain repetitions."[61]

Like so many of his contemporaries, Huxley was deeply scarred by the rat-tat-tatting of two world wars. While more secular thinkers in his generation interrogated "the crisis of man," Huxley joined

Heard and Exman in preoccupying himself with the crisis of meaning and the search for God. In *The Perennial Philosophy*, that search began with a withering critique of the modern world and its hyphenated idolatries—"Church-worship, state-worship, revolutionary future-worship, humanistic self-worship"—which together compelled modern people to hate and to kill, with hand grenades, rocket launchers, and (in the case of American believers in "hell-fire faith") atomic bombs. As always, Huxley cast his withering eye on pious hypocrites who "begin by putting haloes on the heads of the people who do most to make wars and revolutions, then go on, rather plaintively, to wonder why the world should be in such a mess."[62]

Huxley also attacked the "organized lovelessness" of environmental exploitation. "We waste the earth's mineral resources, ruin its soil, ravage its forests, pour filth into its rivers and poisonous fumes into its air," he wrote, nearly two decades before Rachel Carson's landmark environmental publication *Silent Spring*. Huxley denounced anti-Semitism and anti-Catholicism as well as the "contempt and exploitation of coloured minorities living among white majorities, or of coloured majorities governed by minorities of white imperialists."[63]

Though Huxley talked a good game when it came to religious experience, he had little interest himself in contemplative practice. He presented the perennial philosophy preeminently as a way of knowledge. Humankind's final end, he wrote in the book's first sentence, is "the knowledge of the immanent and transcendent Ground of all being." He devoted the first chapter to the Hindu doctrine that the essence of God and the essence of the human are one. And though he acknowledged that the goal of the perennial philosophy is experiential and mystical—divine-human union—he repeatedly described that union as a kind of knowing. "The aim and purpose of human life," he concluded, "is the unitive knowledge of God."[64]

The Perennial Philosophy was widely reviewed in Christian periodicals and leading newspapers and magazines. Reviews were extreme in both directions. Those who hated the book branded

Huxley an intolerant scold and a dilettante. In a rant that might have made Exman smile, the conservative Jewish magazine *Commentary* objected to the book's "popular tone, its vulgar appeal to the lending-library public." The *Christian Century* editor W. E. Garrison served up the most predictable review, wherein a defender of Christian truths attacked the book for attacking Christian truths. Reflecting on that review, Bro, who wrote regularly for Garrison and knew him well, told Exman that Garrison seemed like one of those "unhappy Mystics and not-quite-hatched saints" who are drawn to mystical experience but, having failed to pursue it, look back on the lost opportunity with yearning and annoyance.[65]

Alfred Kazin, a precocious literary critic who had recently won the first of what would be four Guggenheims, presented his most unusual review in the form of a prayer. "Lord, Lord, you who know that my unworthiness to review this breviary of mystical touchstones is almost as great as Aldous Huxley's striving to reach you by texts [and] precepts . . . Lord, hear out my complaint against this book," he began, "yet let me praise first the passion, the scope, the image of an ideal, with which it has been made." What followed is difficult to paraphrase, as this "prayer" continued over four *New Republic* pages, but the complaint amounted to a Jewish refusal of Huxley's Greek-style mistrust of this world, sex, and the body. "He thinks you are above time, history, suffering," wrote Kazin. "Lord, what else are you if you do not rise out of these?"[66]

Though Kazin wrote the best review, the one that really mattered came from the Danish writer Signe Toksvig. "It is the masterpiece of all anthologies," she wrote in the *New York Times Book Review*. And then she dressed up *The Perennial Philosophy* with superlatives like so many rose petals on a wedding bed. After moving lovingly through Huxley's understanding of mystical knowing of the "divine Ground," Toksvig turned to his social ethics. Is Huxley not right to view "theological imperialism" as "a menace to world peace"? To roll his eyes at the "blandly bumptious provincialism" of Christians who know nothing of the sacred books of the East? To those who have ears to hear, she concluded, Huxley has written "the most needed book in the world."[67]

Because of the influence of *The Perennial Philosophy*, many now assume that Huxley invented perennialism. Huxley himself traced perennialism to the German philosopher Leibniz, who wrote into the early eighteenth century, and scholars today credit the sixteenth-century Vatican librarian Agostino Steuco, who used the term in the title of a treatise published in Latin in 1540.[68] But it was Huxley who popularized the perennial philosophy, carrying it outside theological libraries and departments of philosophy into ordinary homes and everyday conversations. And it was Exman who sold it, alongside hundreds of complementary entries in his Book of Books, which kept the drumbeat of perennialism going into the twenty-first century.

Thanks to Huxley, Heard, Exman, Trabuco, and Harper, *The Perennial Philosophy* became a huge bestseller, and perennialisms of various sorts became the most popular alternative to Christian exclusivism in the United States in the 1950s, 1960s, and beyond.

A Club of His Own

Trabuco also had a profound effect on Exman, whose identity began to shift as soon as he got off the train in Los Angeles in the summer of 1941 and looked out over breaking waves toward China, Japan, and India. He never ceased to be a Christian, a Protestant, and a Baptist, but those identities yielded to his new identity as a seeker. Convinced by William James and others that religion was about experience, and inspired by Heard to seek it out, Exman rededicated himself in the early 1940s to his search for God. Now in his forties himself, he turned increasingly to new texts and teachers. If the life of the spirit is about experience, why confine your studies or your seeking to the experiences of Christians alone?

As Exman read more widely and eagerly in Asian religions, he peppered his letters with references to Hindu and Buddhist beliefs and practices such as karma, reincarnation, and nirvana. He also began a long-standing practice of meditating multiple times a day and kept charts of his progress. (This discipline annoyed his son Wally, who complained in multiple interviews about his father insisting on not being bothered during his meditation time.) Exman continued to meet weekly on Monday evenings with his small "cell group" to meditate in silence, share a meal, and discuss devotional books.

By the time the Trabuco experiment came to a close, this man who had lost his "club for mystics" in Southern California had created a new one for himself in Manhattan. After his Blanchester graveyard experience, Exman had begun a quest for God that would wax and wane. He had lost his faith at the University of Chicago. He had found it again in Sunny's arms. In California, his spiritual circle expanded to include Hindu gurus and their disciples. After Trabuco failed, he started his own mystics club centered around his office and the Quaker meetinghouse off Gramercy Park where his Monday night cell group met. Like the earlier Metaphysical Club of William James and his philosopher friends in and around Cambridge, Massachusetts, this was more a conversation than an organization, and its members were never clearly defined. But the question at hand was plain: How to find God?

Populated by authors who became his friends and friends who became his authors, Exman's mystics club proved to be a boon to his personal search and his professional success. By dramatically expanding his network of fellow seekers, it gave him new conversation partners in his ongoing quest for God. It also gave him new authors and new audiences for his department's books.

Before Trabuco, Exman was a successful publisher of mostly Protestant books written overwhelmingly by White liberal Protestant men. Religious diversity meant little more to him than publishing clergymen of various Protestant denominations and cajoling them to write for general readers. People of color were few and far between in Exman's catalogs, and women were only slightly more visible. During the Trabuco experiment, Exman continued to befriend and publish White liberal Protestant men, but his circle of friends and authors expanded to include Black activists and intellectuals, Hindu swamis and Zen masters.

Meanwhile, books on Hinduism and Buddhism began popping up in his catalogs. As early as 1950, books on Asian religions were coming so fast and furious that buyers for Christian booksellers were complaining to Exman's salesmen of theological whiplash. In January of that year, Fred Becker, one of Exman's favorite sales-men, reported that a Lutheran bookstore had objected to an over-abundance of Harper books on Asian religions. Exman apologized. Given that his key dealers were "middle of the road booksellers," he admitted, "it was a mistake in publishing judgment to bring out several Hindu books at one time," and then to pile Suzuki's *Essays in Zen Buddhism* on top of them. But the books on Asian spirituality did not stop. As Exman explained to Becker, "We ideally publish the books today which are going to be increasingly referred to in the tomorrows."[69]

All this personal and professional development was aided and abetted by Huxley, Heard, and other Trabuco associates. But a woman he met during the Trabuco years was at least as influential. She pushed him well beyond experiments in prayer to experiments in the paranormal, bringing new spiritual interests to his personal life and new authors to his Book of Books. She also opened the doors of his mystics club wider than ever before, and made a place for herself in that network, and in Exman's life and work.

CHAPTER THREE

Margueritte Bro, Strange Spirituality, and the Ethics of Publishing

In the early 1940s, the sick, the dying, and the curious converged on Virginia Beach, Virginia, to see a man who was offering an unusual approach to physical and spiritual healing. Most came for "medical readings" offering diagnoses of their ailments and suggestions for cures. Others came for "life readings" that might reveal to them long-lost episodes in their past lives or offer answers to spiritual and religious questions that perplexed them in this one.

Margueritte Bro was never at a loss for penetrating questions, and she struggled throughout her life with physical ailments. But when she came to Virginia Beach in the spring of 1943, she came as a writer on assignment for *Christian Century*, the flagship liberal Protestant weekly where she had been a regular contributor for over a decade. Her editor, W. E. Garrison, had asked her to review a biography of Edgar Cayce, "The Sleeping Prophet" of Virginia Beach. The author was Thomas Sugrue, an Irish Catholic writer who was unable to walk when he went to see Cayce in 1939 and left on his own feet two years later. Still in print, *There Is a River: The Story of Edgar Cayce* is sold today as the life story of "a medical clairvoyant, psychic, and Christian mystic," who became "the grandfather of the New Age." It tells the tale of Cayce's discovery of his clairvoyant abilities as a teenager in the 1890s and the founding of his

Association for Research and Enlightenment (ARE) in 1931. It also details those medical and life readings that Bro went down to observe. Her obsession with Cayce would lead her to Eugene Exman and a relationship that would define both of their lives for the next four decades.

When Bro arrived in Virginia Beach, Cayce's Tuesday evening Bible study was about to begin. She sat in, and she and Cayce immediately hit it off. He had been born in Kentucky, and she went to college there. They were both Disciples of Christ members. They were deeply interested in prayer and meditation, yet equally convinced, as Bro later wrote, that "spiritual growth has to go hand in hand with service."[1] Cayce, after learning that Bro had been a missionary in China, seemed keener on learning about her mission than on talking about his psychic gifts.

Bro spent three days in Virginia Beach reading Cayce's case records and observing him as he went into a trance to give his various readings. She became convinced that Cayce was the real deal: "a genuine psychic . . . as honest as daylight, simple, humorous and religious in an entirely unaffected way." In her June 1943 book review, she was more cautious about the content of Cayce's readings than the content of his character, calling for "scientific investigation which might prove or disprove the usefulness" of his diagnoses and treatments. To that end, she suggested an investigative committee composed of a medical doctor, a psychologist, a minister, someone adept in things of the spirit, and, for some strange reason, an editor as well.[2]

Bro next pitched an account of her pilgrimage to *Coronet*, a digest-size national magazine owned by *Esquire*. "Miracle Man of Virginia Beach," which *Coronet* published in September 1943, opened with a story of a skeptic named Steve who went to see Cayce in one last, desperate attempt to save his new wife, Betty, from a life-threatening degenerative disease. Cayce lay down on his couch. After his wife gave him Betty's full name and address, he said, "Yes, we have the body," before launching into his diagnosis and suggestions for a cure. Steve wanted to know how it all worked.

Cayce told him he had no idea. But the reading saved Betty nonetheless. Bro then told tales of other converted skeptics, herself included.

"I once was blind but now I see" is an old trope in the history of the metaphysical tradition, which attends to such hard-to-believe matters as past life memories, precognition, out-of-body experiences, spiritualist communications with the dead, extrasensory perception, after-death survival, and psychic healing of the Cayce sort. Like mystical experiences, the reality of such things cannot be proven to outsiders. It can only be suggested through accounts of personal experiences. And who better to make the case than converts? In this tradition, unbelievers who became believers have long played the role filled centuries earlier by Saul, that alleged persecutor of Christians who became a Christian himself (and took the name Paul) after seeing the risen Christ on the road to Damascus. In "Miracle Man of Virginia Beach," Bro confessed her own tendency to explain things away, only to explain why in this case she simply could not. Bro gave the last words of her feature to a telegraph operator who for fifteen years had been routing wires to Cayce. "That many people can't be crazy," he said.[3]

Bro's *Coronet* feature did for Cayce in 1943 what a *Saturday Evening Post* had done two years earlier for Alcoholics Anonymous. "The first mail stacked up taller than I," Bro reported, and Cayce had to hire fistfuls of people just to handle it.[4] Two of them were Bro's son Harmon and his wife, June. Harmon would go on to devote his life to writing about Cayce, beginning with a controversial 1955 doctoral dissertation at the University of Chicago. He and June would later cofound the Cape Cod–based Pilgrim Institute, a center for the study of spirituality devoted to exploring Cayce's legacy.

"Dear Mr. Exman"

On June 16, 1943, just two weeks after Bro's *Christian Century* book review appeared, Gerald Heard wrote Exman from Trabuco.

"Do you know a woman named Margueritte Bro?" he asked. She had written Heard about *There Is a River*, which he and Huxley already had been reading, because she was "anxious that someone scientific should test the man's diagnostic powers and try, if possible, to understand the method." In August, as she was writing the *Coronet* piece, she wrote Exman about Cayce, likely at Heard's suggestion. Exman responded with an appreciative note. "We have only a kindergartner's understanding of Mr. Cayce's reach of the mind, and I don't think he could sustain these gifts if he wasn't focused on the needs of the world," he wrote. Unfortunately, that letter has survived only in a Bro letter quoting it. Other letters that kicked off their four decades of correspondence have also gone missing.[5]

The first of the hundreds of Exman-Bro letters now in the Exman Archive dates back to August 27, 1943, and picks up in the middle of things, as Bro tries to convince Exman to travel to Virginia Beach to see Cayce for himself. It is postmarked from Cable, Wisconsin, in the lakes region of the northern part of that state, where Bro and her family would go during the summer. What is striking about this letter is the ease with which she engages Exman both intellectually and spiritually. "Do you think there might be some significant material for experimentation in gathering the suggested treatment for certain diseases and having the treatment tested by medical authorities?" she asks. She tells Exman she wants to do more articles on "Mr. Cayce's 'gift,'" and reports that she has just pitched one to Frederick Allen, editor in chief at *Harper's Magazine*. She also attempts to gauge Exman's interest in "a modest book" on Cayce. Finally, she suggests that she and Exman meet in New York in September, after all her get-back-to-school obligations are over at Shimer College, where her husband is president. That book never materialized, but the correspondence it opened continued until Exman's death in 1975.[6]

The two didn't meet in New York City, but sometime in September, Exman visited her in Chicago. Shortly thereafter, Exman wrote to Heard to share what Heard paraphrased as a "vivid experience." Exman seemed to be concerned that he had done something wrong.

"I feel sure there's no ground for misgiving," Heard reassured his friend, even as he urged him to sublimate his sexual urges (as Heard himself was trying to do). "We must remember that we are returning to a Franciscan possibility of happiness," he wrote, "when the feeling that someone else also loves God gives suddenly a freedom, release, and mutual delight which is different from all the other affections a man may feel." Heard alerted Exman to the work of the Scottish psychiatrist Ian Suttie, who in a rebuttal to Freud had emphasized love over sex and tender regard for the mother over Oedipal competition with the father. Heard then made his case for tenderness. "There has been throughout the Western world of gentlefolk such an ungentle repression of all affection—outside a very small family group and even in that—that we had arrived at what he wisely calls 'The Taboo on Tenderness,'" Heard wrote. To be a man nowadays is to repress tenderness. The solution is to resist the all-too-human tendency to "clutch and cling" and to give and receive tender affection instead.[7]

Like her prior letter to Exman, the second letter in the Exman Archive is addressed formally—"Dear Mr. Exman"—but already the writing is more familiar. "All last night and today I was excited about having found you—but depressed, too, because you live so far away," Bro wrote on October 9, 1943, shortly after he had visited her in Chicago. Apparently Exman had come to her home for dinner while her husband, Albin, was away. Bro is thrilled to have met Exman because he seems to understand her, whereas her husband does not. "[I am] wondering why—why—I can't apparently get a thing across to the people I'm nearest to," she writes, referring to Albin. "It's like feeling a bright light burning within but a thick opaque chimney shutting the light from those who need to see." Then, turning to their visit, she writes, "But there is this to console one. If I had more outside help, I might shoot the works physically because the charge is mighty when it does come in, isn't it!" It's an exuberant letter, and in the end she asks for more: "Please do have a free hour while I'm in New York. I'd even get up early!"[8]

As of October 22, 1943, Bro (now writing from Virginia Beach) is addressing Exman as Eugene or Gene, and urging him to join her in Virginia Beach to see Cayce for himself and get his own "physical" and "life" readings. On the back of the letter, Exman writes, "Do I have heart trouble?" It is not clear whether he is speaking literally or metaphorically, but on October 25 he takes a night train to Virginia Beach and spends two days with Cayce.[9]

Almost immediately, the pattern of Bro's letters to Exman is established. The language is smart, fun, and often funny. There is attention to the personal and the professional. There is an ongoing back-and-forth over books and other matters of the spirit. Mutual affection is expressed. Family is discussed. (Her son Harmon, for example, appears in one letter as a "sensitive, keen-minded chap" who, though recently ordained, "doesn't know whether he is an agnostic, a humanist or a whose-it.") And there are at the end (and often the beginning) reveries regarding the created world that border on nature mysticism:

> Today I thought of you. It was dusk and I lay down for an evening meditation. Looking out at the stark bare maple which was so gorgeous when you were here, I was freshly swept with wonder at a tree's acquiescence to the ways of God. The long wait without a single stirring of life. The acceptance of the elements. We would have all our roots torn out in a frenzy of waiting. And yet I seem to recollect how it was to be a tree. No wonder [the seventeenth-century French mystic] Brother Lawrence laid his conversion to the mere sight of a winter tree.[10]

Before 1943 was out, Exman and Bro had met in Virginia Beach, and Bro was spending a fair chunk of Christmas Day at her typewriter composing a letter to her new friend. That letter ran three single-space typed pages plus three additional pages of postscripts. Bro opened with a confession. The letter she just received from him "gave me the double dithers," she wrote. "I practically hugged you by remote control because I do like my men smart."[11]

In the body of this letter, Bro praised Exman for seeing the precise problem she had pinpointed in a manuscript she was editing, adding that the two of them were among the one in a hundred who could look at a book and spot its central flaw. "It's a pity I'm not in the editing business because I was born with a gift for it," she wrote, "and my gifts are so few and far between that sometimes I feel sorry I didn't follow one and cultivate it." She then promised to send Exman a manuscript of her own someday and gave him a few details about a book she was writing for Doubleday and a novel she was just getting going. "Why don't you live near enough so I can talk with you about it?" she asked.[12]

In one P.S. to this letter, Bro complained about her endless first-lady work at Shimer, including the prospect of hosting "a damn silly tea" and then jabbering at an engagement party with "people who have too much money and never an idea." Bro conceded the theoretical importance of "a good school for good girls" but, in practice, she wrote, "I hate it to hell and if I knew any more cuss words I would work them in." After threatening to "WALK OFF from the whole works" someday, she signed off: "Hoping you are in a sweeter mood and that none of your husbands gives teas."[13]

Bro's Cayce book never materialized, but Exman became convinced of at least some of Cayce's gifts, and he and Bro became close friends and colleagues. Bro began freelancing for Exman almost immediately after they met in the fall of 1943, juggling nearly as many responsibilities as she had at home. Exman's career, while successful in the twenties and thirties, took off after that. Together they formed a publishing team that helped to reimagine and reshape twentieth-century American religion and culture.

The Attraction of Like Minds

Bro's life in publishing produced an extraordinary body of work that, according to her son Andy, stretched all the way back to her years in

China, where she honed her writing skills with long letters to friends penned in a "breezy journalistic style which made it easier to read."[14] In addition to plays, textbooks, pamphlets, and articles, Bro wrote dozens of books, both fiction and nonfiction, for children and adults, and contributed introductions and chapters to many others.

Bro had a hand in almost everything Exman was doing at Harper, acquiring, evaluating, editing, and promoting books. She edited sermon collections, which she despised, because so many preachers were in her experience dreadful writers. But she also worked as an editor on projects by some of the most important religion authors of her time, including Reinhold Niebuhr, Harry Emerson Fosdick, Gerald Heard, Howard Thurman, and Dorothy Day.

She authored at least six fiction and nonfiction books for Harper's juvenile book and religious book departments. Three of her books were "as told to" projects, including an autobiography by the medium Arthur Ford. Like Ford, who channeled the words of others while disclaiming them as his own, Bro also worked as a ghostwriter for dozens of magazine articles and books. She also coauthored many books (one in Japanese).

Her own book topics ranged widely. *Indonesia: Land of Challenge*, one of the half dozen books she wrote for Harper, won critical acclaim. She was especially drawn to religious topics, with books on prayer, the church, and the Old Testament. Her first single-author book, *When Children Ask* (1940), about parenting, appeared before she met Exman. Her last, *The Book You Always Meant to Read: The Old Testament* (1974), appeared in her eightieth year. Many of Bro's books were widely read and reviewed—in academic outlets such as the *Journal of the American Academy of Religion*, in national magazines such as *Harper's*, and in major newspapers, including the *New York Times*, *The Washington Post*, and the *Chicago Tribune*.

In an era before personal computers, she did her writing on a typewriter. The sounds of the carriage return and of keys thwacking paper offered a comforting background to her children's household lives. "We all grew up with that sound," Andy said in an interview. It reminded her children that "she was nearby."[15]

Bro was very good at what she did. She was good because she was smart and savvy. She excelled both at seeing a book manuscript as a whole and at fixing it part by part. She had strong opinions and was not afraid to voice them, even when her authors (and her boss) were powerful men, such as the esteemed Yale church historian Kenneth Latourette, whose manuscript she described like this: "It is a MESS. Triter writing would be hard to dream up. Which wouldn't be so bad if he said anything but he doesn't. . . . I just don't see that we are obligated to accept such a corny book, even if he is a long-time author. A major opus may be worth the editing but why every ad interim potboiler? And why so fast?"[16]

Long before she met Exman, Bro worked in various capacities at the Chicago-based *Christian Century*, where she wrote the book review that led her to Exman. There she regularly locked horns with Paul Hutchinson and W. E. Garrison, both editors there. In 1943, in an argument with them about Cayce, she insisted that they were "not true empiricists or they wouldn't scoff [at] an experience they never tried."[17] At Harper, she often disagreed with Exman, and he and his authors benefited from the exchanges. Bro was also Exman's most important personal editor for just about everything he wrote for publication. In this capacity, she deftly combined cheerleading and criticism. She did the same when it came to Exman the man, whom she criticized for falling short of "right livelihood" and for failing to put in the spiritual work necessary for what they agreed was the real task of human life: growing closer to God.

During the forties and fifties, when she did the bulk of her work at Harper, it was not uncommon for Exman to take on authors who knew very little about how to write and even less about writing a book. Bro was often the unsung ghostwriter who did that work for them. She traveled to her authors' homes, often working with them for days at a time, convincing them to cut this or add that, and in many cases writing large chunks of their books alone at her type-writer. In this role, she was the uncredited primary author of dozens of additional contributions to Exman's Book of Books and an un-acknowledged collaborator in Exman's success at Harper.

Amid all this editorial work, Bro and Exman were able to find time to see each other. They saw each other at the presidential home at Shimer, and at the nearby Hazelwood estate of her friend Myrtle Walgreen. They saw each other in Chicago and New York. Those visits never seemed to be enough. They wrote about longing to see one another, including in this June 1949 letter from Bro: "I bet if we were holy enough there would be a way to waken on a crisp summer morning such as this one and say to the mountain of frus-tration imposed by space when we want to talk with someone miles away, 'Mountain, be thou cast into the sea' and presto! The sense of separation would be removed."[18]

The attraction between Exman and Bro was certainly physical. One of Bro's grandchildren, who has seen family photographs of her, reports that "she was a knockout as a young lady," with piercing blue eyes. Later in life, she was "very slender," with "brilliant white hair." Another grandchild adds that, despite her small stature, "when she came into a room she would just light it up." Exman was neither tall, nor dark, nor conventionally handsome, but he dressed well, almost always in a proper suit and tie with a fashionable hat and ele-gant glasses. He spoke in a pleasing baritone and often surprised new acquaintances with how warm and approachable he was, given his eminence in his field. As his daughter-in-law Linda Cohen observed in an interview, publishing has a lot of pretentious people, and he stood out as "a gentle, modest personality" with "no pretention."[19]

Bro and Exman noticed these things in one another, but their mutual attraction was also a meeting of hearts and minds. Their relationship was intense because they shared so much spiritually and intellectually and were able to write (and talk) to each other about all of it.

Exman was attracted to people who were both intellectuals

and spiritual seekers. He wanted to learn more about spiritual experience—by reading and publishing books by medieval Catholic mystics, by experimenting (alone and in small groups) with contemplative techniques, by engaging in conversations with fellow seekers about the same, and by gathering like-minded friends and authors into his mystics club. He rarely talked with Sunny about any of this. "You had to be a certain intellectual person to be able to communicate with him," Wally said of his father. "He certainly didn't have that with my mother." Neither did he talk with her about his spiritual experiences or experiments. Regarding his "straight-laced" mother, Wally explained, "She liked what she could see in front of her. And that was going to church every Sunday and meeting with people after church. . . . This business of Indian philosophies and Virginia Beach people—she didn't want to deal with it." When asked who was eager to talk with him about his intellectual and spiritual pursuits, the first person Wally named was Margueritte Bro.[20]

Exman and Bro saw books as "sacred things" and themselves as "book-souls." Exman once speculated that the reason he was so immersed in books was that "in my former life I was careless about or perhaps callous to books and literature." Bro may have been even more book-happy. "Nothing in all I've ever read," she confided to Exman, "gives me the shock I get from Saint John of the Cross when he voluntarily gave up all his books lest occupation with them shut him from direct contact with God." Exman and Bro also shared an understanding of "the ministry of publishing" as a "sacred trust" and of their relationship as divinely ordained. "I think we were brought together professionally for two purposes," Bro told Exman. "I was needed to get out certain books we would not otherwise have taken on, and we were intended to help each other."[21]

These two friends shared as well a long list of beliefs, practices, attitudes, and sensibilities. Born just a few years apart, they were both members of the Lost Generation, which went searching for meaning in the years between the world wars. Theologically, they were liberal Protestant churchgoers who believed in science and evolution, read the Bible historically and allegorically rather than literally, and saw the beauty and wisdom in non-Christian religions. While living in Chicago, Bro sent her children to a local Reform Jewish temple so they could learn about the Hebrew Bible. When she traveled throughout Asia with her son Andy she took him into several Buddhist temples. "Anywhere you would see a figure of Buddha there was always a pause and she would talk about it," Andy said. "I could see it meant a great deal to her."[22] Because of her years in China, Bro's Asian religious interests gravitated toward Confucianism, Daoism, and Buddhism. Exman, because of his association with Trabuco, inclined more toward Hinduism.

Like Exman, Bro was both religious *and* spiritual—a regular churchgoer with a deep distrust of how most Christians went about their Father's business. Bro and her husband were both ordained Disciples of Christ ministers. She and her family went to church just about every Sunday, and she preached on occasion. She also prayed frequently and read the Bible. She dated her letters in keeping with the liturgical calendar ("Easter Day," "All Saints Day"). Exman was a similarly faithful parishioner and volunteer at Riverside Church, and like Bro he was inclined to modify nouns such as "creeds," "dogmas," and "ritual" with adjectives such as "empty." What mattered in religion, they both believed, were internal realities, not external performances. What mattered in life was encountering God.

Though Exman and Bro devoted their professional lives to the written and spoken word, both were convinced that true religion was about experiences rather than explanations, first-person encounters rather than secondhand theology. Bro's son Andy recalls his mother emphasizing the virtues of silence during their visits to the Bahá'í temple in nearby Wilmette, Illinois. "Christian pastors have logorrhea. They just have to talk themselves to death. There's not enough internal life going on," he remembers her telling him.[23] But she was sufficiently self-aware to admit she was afflicted with that disease herself, as she was continually either writing down her own words or editing the words of others.

In their letters, Exman and Bro lamented their own busyness. They worked too hard and played too little, missing out on spiritual growth in the process. "Why must we always dash about when all the truly exciting things happen in quietness and stillness," Bro asked in one letter. "There was Martha with her opportunity to sit right down by Jesus and talk—and she left to iron the company dinner napkins," she wrote in another. "I'm sure we are all the time missing out on Something Significant because we drive so hard."[24]

Each believed that God had a plan for their lives, that the purpose of life was seeking after God, and that the searching involved experimenting with various spiritual practices, ideally in conversation with fellow seekers in small groups. In this shared search, they sought out saints and mystics as guides.

Bro and Exman also believed that their efforts to imitate these spiritual exemplars should produce not only spiritual growth but also progressive action. Bro stood with suffragettes who won the vote for women in 1920. She wrote about the conversion of her children to the "dry" cause in Christian Century in 1930 and addressed a Woman's Christian Temperance Union convention in 1934. She was out in front of many White liberal Protestants in her early support for civil rights. She also denounced anti-Semitism, even as she criticized the State of Israel for what she saw as its illegal occupation of Arab lands. In a chapter titled "Religion and Social Action" in an edited volume from 1942, she drew on the language of the Protestant social gospel, including "social sin" and "social salvation," to argue for "economic justice and interracial brotherhood" and "equality of opportunity for all in matters of health, housing and education." Of the twenty-three contributors to this volume, Bro was the only woman.[25]

Like almost all of Exman's most important authors, Bro was a committed pacifist. She and Exman were active in the leadership in the Fellowship of Reconciliation and opposed to war in any form. They praised Schweitzer's ethic of Reverence for Life and Gandhi's ethic of nonviolent resistance. They were also committed internationalists, supportive of the work of the United Nations. At a time when antigay bigotry was almost universal, they both had queer friends and were by all accounts fully accepting of them. Gerald Heard, who was openly gay, was a major influence on both. "I look to him as a seven story pagoda," Bro wrote.[26]

Despite these commonalities, Bro and Exman disagreed, often fiercely. Though they were both "seeking souls," they were not soulmates, if by that term one means two pieces of a split human being that, when reunited, fit together seamlessly.[27]

Bro was somehow both more attuned to the difficulties of life on earth and more upbeat than Exman. She struggled throughout her life with physical ailments and she carried far heavier burdens than he did at home. "What I need is a good wife," she told him in more than one letter. "Or a husband who [is] a combination errand-runner, plumber, tree transplanter, painter and cook," she wrote in another. But she was an idealist and a dreamer who allowed herself the flights of fancy necessary to write good fiction. Repeatedly she wrote to Exman about how happy and hopeful she felt. "One day discloses so much to defeat the spirit. And at the same time, so much elation!" she wrote in the midst of the horrors of World War II. "The beautiful spring is all about us and one nearly bursts with joy in it—even while the world is drenched in blood and heartache." Nearly a decade later, she wrote, "I like life better and better don't you? Continually it has more meaning and more amazement. The unseen manifests ever more clearly."[28]

One place the unseen manifested for Bro was in the Book of Nature, whose beauty, she believed, was "the soul's true catharsis." Often her letters began or ended with hymns of praise to the "glory" (a favorite word of hers in these exclamations) of the natural world—odes to the joys of fresh fallen snow, the deep woods, the colors of fall leaves. "The Dear God, or maybe Mrs. God is spilling color over the trees again," she wrote to Exman one autumn. "Fall is early although not cold. I go around in a state of mild ecstasy."[29]

Thanks to his steady paycheck from Harper (with raises along the way), Exman had a comfortable life financially by the time he met Bro, but he was weighed down by his job's responsibilities. Bro was constrained by the financial and time pressures of her household. When her husband was a college president, she had very little time. When he was unemployed or underemployed, she had to work to pay the bills. Her letters to Exman refer repeatedly to her financial straits.

Exman was also more closely knit into circles of power and influence. He was friends with some of the most powerful businessmen in the world, including John D. Rockefeller Jr. and Henry Luce (who once offered him a job at *Life* magazine). He was also closely connected with not only university professors but also academic administrators, including deans at Harvard and the University of Chicago. Bro was also well connected. She spent a lot of time at the Hazelwood retreat of her friend Myrtle Walgreen, for example. But she moved in less heady social circles than Exman did. The institution of higher learning she knew best was Shimer College, a junior college for women where she was tasked primarily with entertaining students, faculty, and visitors in the presidential home.

Bro was also more single-mindedly committed to their shared search for one more glimpse of the divine. "I . . . always want another revelation," Bro said, in words Exman might have written. In fact, he wanted another revelation desperately. But his willpower was weak. He did not have the discipline for sainthood that Bro did. After the sudden death of the Cayce biographer Thomas Sugrue, who had become a close friend of Bro, Exman, and their friend John Chambers, she wrote a bitter letter to Exman and Chambers complaining about their collective inability to do what was really required for proper training in the life of the spirit. "We're a lot of word-mouthing mouldy saints," she complained. Exman took the criticism in stride, perhaps because he knew himself to be a man up to his neck in the preoccupations of this world. "What you are scolding us for is not being saints when we should be," he responded. "Well, we are far from sainthood and that station is probably well beyond us in this life." Bro fired back: "Of course I'm accusing you and John of not being saints. And accusing myself most of all. There is no good reason we should not be saints and I do not think it presumptuous to know it."[30]

Given their shared obsessions with work and spirituality, it should not be surprising that Bro's and Exman's children complained on occasion about their shortcomings as parents. Bro's children remember her as a loving mother who "alienated her children" by trying to micromanage their lives.[31] Exman's son Wally had the opposite complaint about his father, whom he described as preoccupied with work and with meditation, leaving him with just a handful of memories of times when he and his dad really connected.

Ghostwriting for Mediums

Something else that Bro and Exman shared was a deep curiosity about what William James called the "More." American religious life has always been infused with a metaphysical impulse, which captured the imagination of both Bro and Exman. In fact, it was their shared interest in the psychic Edgar Cayce that brought them together in 1943. They both believed in reincarnation. They both consulted with mediums. For Exman, the modern scientific worldview was unable to account for mystical moments like his road to Blanchester experience. For Bro, medical materialism could not account for what she, with her own eyes, saw Cayce do. Here again, both followed the example of William James.

Shortly after their infant son Herman died from complications of whooping cough in July 1885, James and his wife began visiting the Boston-based medium Leonora Piper. That same year, James cofounded the American Society for Psychical Research (ASPR), which investigated scientific claims of experiences—telepathy, clairvoyance, mediumship, and apparitions—that seemed to defy scientific understanding. The next year, he famously defended Piper in his ASPR presidential address, saying, "If you wish to upset the law that all crows are black . . . it is enough if you prove one single crow to be white. My own white-crow is Mrs. Piper." Piper convinced James of telepathy, but he had "not the glimmer of an explanatory suggestion to make" regarding how she came to know what she knew.[32]

The philosopher Ralph Barton Perry, James's student and biographer, observed that "James's interest in 'psychical research' was not one of his vagaries, but was central and typical." It was also long lasting, stretching over four decades. James ultimately concluded that there was lots of evidence for "really supernormal knowledge" but not enough to convince him of the possibility of communicating with the dead. On that matter, he wrote, in true empiricist fashion, "I remain uncertain and await more facts."[33]

This empirical approach to the paranormal is yet another way that James haunted Exman's religious book department. Like James, Exman and Bro knew that some so-called psychics and mediums were frauds, and that some of the stuff legitimate psychics and mediums did was fraudulent. That is why they took pains not to publish "pseudo-stuff" in this field. Nonetheless, both were convinced of the reality of the unseen world and the capacity of spiritual geniuses to tap into it.[34]

Bro had two feet firmly planted in the world of the metaphysical, however, whereas Exman had only one. According to her daughter-in-law June Bro, Bro was "religious in a psychic sense" and "completely in tune with what people call New Age." Cayce told her in one of her readings that she had been a friend of Mary the mother of Jesus and had attended the wedding where Jesus performed his first miracle. "She loved to talk about it like she was there," her granddaughter Pamela Bro reported, but "she was too smart and too well read" to believe everything Cayce told her.[35]

Karma and reincarnation come up routinely in Bro's letters to Exman, and from her earliest letters to him, she was an advocate of paranormal investigations. She also worked hard to normalize the paranormal. "The reader[s] I'd like to reach," she told Exman, are "women and men whose experiences in prayer outrun their explanations and who feel 'queer' for having vivid experiences of 'leading' or of a sense of the presence of a loved one."[36] That sentence could have been written by William James.

Exman was sympathetic but more circumspect. He had his Harper overseers and their profits to consider, as well as the unwritten rules of propriety in polite society. As a result, he never went quite far enough into the paranormal to satisfy Bro. That said, he had multiple sittings with Cayce and other mediums, who convinced him that something genuine was being communicated to him by the spirits of the dead. He also took his children to see these seers. Wally reports that all he got out of these visits was confusion, but Exman was able to pass his metaphysical interests along to his daughter, Judy, who passed them on to her daughter, Katherine. Bro was even more successful in bequeathing these interests. Her son Harmon Bro wrote multiple books about Cayce, and his daughter Pamela Bro moved to Virginia Beach, which she calls her extended family's "spiritual home."[37]

Strange Spirits

Of the three as-told-to autobiographies Bro wrote, two were about mediums. *In the One Spirit* told the story of Harrie Vernette Rhodes, a relatively unknown woman from Minnesota who specialized in spiritual healing. Rhodes also exercised other spiritual gifts, channeling spirits of the dead and writing down poems and even books dictated to her from "the other side." In explaining these gifts, Rhodes contrasted her own passivity with God's activity. The healer is "empty and ready," she said. "The treatment comes from God; the power flows through Him."[38]

Another as-told-to autobiography by Bro, titled *Nothing So*

Strange and published in 1958, concerned the trance medium Arthur Ford, who became famous in 1929 when he claimed to contact the great magician (and skeptic) Harry Houdini from the other side. Ford attended Transylvania University in Kentucky, where Bro's father was later president, and like so many in Bro's family, he was ordained and served as a minister in the Disciples of Christ. Ford became aware of his psychic powers—he allegedly heard (and reported) the names of soldiers days before they died—while serving in the army during World War I. After the war, he made his living as a traveling trance medium channeling the words of a spirit guide (or "control") he called Fletcher. He then founded the First Spiritualist Church, which gathered in New York City's Carnegie Hall. At Bro's urging, Exman had multiple sittings with Ford, and in 1955 he worked with the Bros to bring Ford to Wainwright House in Rye, New York, where he spoke at an evening meeting. This retreat center was largely populated by liberal Protestants, and many objected to ceding their podium to a psychic. But Ford won them over, and soon he was speaking at Protestant churches nationwide.

Bro would later credit Exman with bringing Ford "to Protestant respectability" and making possible the Spiritual Frontiers Fellowship (SFF), a group of about seventy-five mostly Protestant clergy dedicated to exploring unusual spiritual experiences and reporting their findings to the churches. The SFF was established in 1956 by Ford, the Methodist minister Paul Higgins, and Albin Bro. That same year, Ford, who early in his career got into trouble in spiritualist circles for affirming reincarnation, got a lift from a reincarnation craze brought on by *The Search for Bridey Murphy* (1956), a book turned into a movie about a housewife who recalled her past lives.[39]

Bro was friendly with Ford, who read at her husband's memorial service. She sat for many readings with him, and she introduced him to Exman and Chambers, who had their own readings. After Chambers's death in August 1955, Bro said that sessions with Ford and his spirit guide Fletcher allowed her to continue to communicate with Chambers. In fact, Bro described Chambers in her letters to Exman as an active contributor to the religious book department long after his death. In a December 1955 letter, she reported that the spirit of Chambers had told Exman to "get help right away," adding that two new editors were needed after his death, not one. Chambers also urged Bro to stick with her Harper job, as Exman needed the help and there was important work yet to do. "Whatever you do, don't you leave," he allegedly told her from the beyond.[40]

Ford did almost nothing for *Nothing So Strange*. "I got four typed pages from him, period," Bro complained after it was done. So Bro wrote it from introduction to dust jacket, and she was proud of her work. "A whale of a good tale," she called it, "an assurance to the reader that the gap no longer exists . . . between science and these excursions of the spirit we know as prayer and meditation."[41]

Catalog copy promoted the book as a story of one man's experiments into "the increasingly recognized sphere of extrasensory perception" and "an adventure into a little-explored realm of the human spirit." When it appeared in the summer of 1958, ads underscored Ford's democratic conviction that "everyone has psychic endowment" while playing up his friendships with the rich and the famous, including the Sherlock Holmes writer Arthur Conan Doyle, who hailed a Ford demonstration he attended in London as "one of the most amazing things I had ever seen in forty-one years of psychic experience." *Nothing So Strange* also benefited from a blurb by the novelist Upton Sinclair, who called it "an extraordinary book by an extraordinary man." A private endorsement came in a letter from the philosopher W. E. Hocking, Exman's friend and James's former student. "I am immediately engrossed in his story, as an important comment on the marginal inklings of beyond-ness that happen to all of us at odd moments," he wrote.[42]

Norma Lee Browning, a reporter and columnist for the *Chicago Daily Tribune*, was less impressed. Her review emphasized the "fine living" Ford made by allowing Fletcher to inhabit his body before "a paying audience." Browning's eye rolling stirred things up on the

Tribune's letters-to-the-editor page, so much so that one of many letters on the review carried the headline, "That Book Again." Higgins, the Methodist cofounder of the Spiritual Frontiers Fellowship, called the "flippancy" of Browning "inexcusable," given the persistence of "spiritual phenomena" in "the main stream of the Christian tradition from Jesus and Paul to Swedenborg and Wesley," not to mention the importance of the subject to "some of the world's best known clergymen, educators, and scientists." Another reader placed Ford in a broader litany of the saints, running back to "nonconformists like Socrates, Jesus, or Gandhi [who] have been crucified in more ways than one by . . . dull, commonplace and unimaginative minds."[43]

The book itself, written "in collaboration with" Bro, channels her voice as Ford channeled Fletcher's. It affirms Bro's commitments to interracial churches. It affirms her conviction that "the future of the Protestant faith is in the hands of people who can blend mysticism with the social gospel which together make up the whole program of Christianity." It describes prayer as Bro understood it—as "going into the Presence" rather than asking for a car. And it refers to Edgar Cayce as "the most gifted man, psychically, whom I have ever known."[44]

Nothing So Strange also credits James with introducing Ford to ESP, via a Transylvania University psychology professor who loaned him a copy of *Varieties*, told him about the American Society for Psychical Research (and its London-based counterpart, the Society for Psychical Research), and shared with him books on mystical experiences and surviving bodily death. The book also invokes James in arguing that psychic phenomena are surprisingly common: "Lately everyone is psychic."[45]

The book borrows from *In the One Spirit* by setting its protagonist's spiritual exploits against the day-to-day dramas of a human life, including Ford's struggles with alcoholism, which would introduce him to AA, to Bill Wilson, and to the reality of "the Power greater than myself." The book then proceeds largely anecdotally, with stories of Ford's sittings with various clients, including Exman himself, who is advised to "do more publishing in the psychic field . . . and not so much sweetness and light."[46]

One distinguishing feature of *Nothing So Strange* is its religious pluralism. As Bro describes him, Ford was baptized in the Episcopal Church at the request of his "ardent non-church-attending" father, yet raised a Baptist by his mother. Because of his not-so-biblical interests in Catholic saints and Unitarian ideas, Ford was excommunicated from his Baptist church at sixteen. As he came into his psychic powers, he cast about for a teacher and found one in Swami Paramhansa Yogananda, who came to Boston from India in 1920 for an interreligious congress and then stayed on to form the Self-Realization Fellowship. Yogananda was almost blasé about Ford's gifts, which he claimed to possess himself, as he believed psychic abilities were far less important than deepening one's awareness of God. *Nothing So Strange* also delves into Ford's perennialism, which by the time the book appeared was being taught not only in Huxley's *Perennial Philosophy* but also in Huston Smith's *The Religions of Man*. As Ford spoke with Yogananda and listened to him lecture, he "learned that truth belongs to neither East nor West, but is a universal thing, which only seems different when one does not look beneath its varying cultural expressions."[47]

Another characteristic of *Nothing So Strange* is its willingness to acknowledge the reality of psychic frauds and hoaxes. "Any control who issues orders and attempts to substitute for the free will of the sitters, or who tries to direct the minutiae of their lives, should be suspected of pretending to be other than he is," Ford (and Bro) wrote.[48]

"Right Livelihood"

One of the most important things Bro did for Exman was to challenge him like no one else could. Her children and in-laws

remember her as a kind yet "bossy" mother whose high expectations for her children often made them feel inadequate. "You
should have been better," she was always telling them. "You could
have been more." Her defense was that "we live in this world to
help other people grow." And she pushed, pushed, pushed her
children to do just that. In this respect, at least, Exman appears to
have been family.[49]

Bro and Exman met as they were both entering mid-life, just
months after Exman had written that long autobiographical letter
to Gerald Heard, honestly summing up his accomplishments and
failures and recommitting himself to the hard work of coming to
"know God as an inner experience."[50] Bro joined this effort to push
Exman toward his better angels. Praising him lavishly and criticizing
him harshly, she challenged him to be a better publisher, a better
person, and a more committed seeker after God. During the first
decade of their relationship, as Bro observed Exman's interactions
with Heard during the 1940s and with Schweitzer in the early 1950s,
she became increasingly convinced that Exman had all the makings
of a great man, a saint perhaps.

Professionally, she challenged him to stay true to his original
conception of his Harper job as a religious mission akin to the foreign missions Bro and many of Exman's college friends had under-
taken. She challenged him to take on better books and to turn down
lesser projects that might make money but wouldn't do anything
to improve readers' lives or elevate public conversations. She urged
him to be more of a force for good in the causes they shared, to
be more forthcoming in print and in the office about his own faith
commitments and spiritual experiences. She also challenged him on
the ethics of publishing, criticizing him for failing to treat his writers
and employees (Bro included) with the attention "right livelihood"
required.

Regarding his personal life, she urged him to slow down, to
say no to more things so he could recharge his body and spirit. In

addition to his work schedule, which eased up during the summer but required lots of travel and long days the rest of the year, he always had a full slate of volunteer activities—at Riverside and Denison, especially, but also with his local school board and a long list of nonprofit groups. Bro argued that Exman's tendency (one she shared) to say yes to all of the above made him susceptible to the sorts of health problems that vexed her. That same tendency brought down the quality of the books he was publishing.

Exman ran a very successful department and, when necessary, was able to make the-buck-stops-here decisions. But in his personal life, and not infrequently in the office, he was a surprisingly passive person. Like his friend the AA founder Bill Wilson, he believed that humans act best when they are led by something greater than themselves. As Exman saw it, we wait on God's leading too little and are often too confident about the rightness of our actions. Repeatedly in his letters, writings, and speeches, Exman preached the importance of what AA came to refer to as "letting go and letting God." "It is not what we think important that necessarily is important; it is always what we are truly led to do, often against our own protests, that turns out to be of real significance," he told a friend in October 1946. "We have got to lose this surface egotistical will which leads to things which 'I' must do to 'make my contribution' or 'live the full life.'" A month later he told Bro in a letter that we must "keep remembering that it is not we who work but God who works in us."[51]

Exman made plain his views on the hierarchy of divine and human activity in a series of letters he wrote advising young men how to respond to World War II and the draft. "It is not man's doing but God's doing . . . to bridge the chasm" between "where we are now and . . . where we ought to be tomorrow," he wrote to a correspondent who had asked him how to respond to the horrors of a world in which the US government had exploded atomic bombs. Exman explained his position like this:

Part of the whole trouble of the world is [that] everyone, to a greater or lesser degree, thinks the progress ahead can come only through our own striving. Actually the mess we are in ought to be sufficient proof that man working by himself is incompetent to achieve worthy ends. Thus we come back to the fundamental principle that what we can do and are certainly asked first of all to do is to make of ourselves the kinds of persons we ought to be and ought to become. This is the job closest to the hand and hardest to do.[52]

Although this might sound like an excuse to withdraw from politics and even from individual action itself, it did not do that for Exman, who was active in pacifist groups such as the Fellowship of Reconciliation and the Committee for a Sane Nuclear Policy. But it did make him more of a hands-off manager of his religious book department than Bro would have liked, and more passive in his spiritual life and lax in his spiritual discipline.

A Cooperative Venture

As Bro challenged her friend to change his life, Exman listened and responded. While still in the early years of their relationship, they began to dream about a way to resolve what they saw as their most pressing personal and professional challenge: how to craft lives that would allow them to search for God while also doing important work in publishing. In the late 1940s, this dream turned into an escape plan. Exman approached Heard about it while Trabuco was failing during the summer of 1947, and in many respects it now reads like a revision of that communal experiment.

The plan went like this: Exman would quit Harper and leave New York. He would join Bro somewhere in the Midwest, where they would start their own publishing cooperative, surrounded by a few trusted colleagues and unconstrained by the logic of capitalism. By unleashing the full force of their collective energies, this venture would change not only their lives but also the lives of individual readers and the society in which they lived. This plan came with considerable risks, however, especially for Exman.

Exman was very good at his job, perhaps too good. He made Harper a lot of money, but only by publishing books he and Bro knew to be subpar and by turning down some potentially important books unlikely to be big sellers. Bro and Exman knew that this is not what the Buddha was talking about when he told his followers to practice "right livelihood." It was not what Heard was talking about when he urged Bro and Exman to become modern saints for whom prayer was more important than profit. If Exman could extricate himself from Harper and uproot himself from the rat race of Manhattan, they would have more freedom, more fun, and a better work-life balance. They would also be doing something that Exman had wanted to do from the time the Reverend Petty had first told him to take the Harper job: engage in meaningful work that was both a religious mission and a personal calling. They would publish only authors and books they loved. They would bring their faith commitments more explicitly into their work. In their new head-quarters, staff meetings could open with silent prayer. Imagine having a business with "its own little chapel for meditation," Bro wrote to Exman in October 1947. "Every book you contemplate publishing should lie there in state for twenty-four hours. The book itself will cast a vibration."[53]

Early in 1948, Bro made another pitch for this collaborative venture. "I think one of the things you have to do in this incarnation is to venture and risk. Not be tied to security," she told her friend. Chicago would make sense as a headquarters because "the life current is strongest and freshest" in the Midwest, and because she could commute from Shimer, where her husband was serving as president. Bro suggested that their business could include a magazine edited by Heard. As for the books, "Plenty of books would come your way," Bro wrote. "You wouldn't need to publish any but the best. . . . Each author would feel the cooperative enterprise."[54]

Discussion of this idea picked up just after Albin Bro retired from Shimer on October 18, 1949. Later that month, Bro sent a long single-spaced letter to Exman pushing hard to make this venture happen. For some time she had been editing a Harper book she hated about a mystic she loved. It was starting to feel like prostitution, she confessed, before launching into a detailed plea to stop talking about their publishing venture and to act instead. "Why on earth don't we seriously go after this business?" she asked. She told Exman of land she had found in Savanna, Illinois, a small town west of Chicago on the Mississippi River with a population of about five thousand. "I bet we could find someone to finance the venture," she wrote. "Some of us could have homes there— including a common dining room with dishwashing done! At least a one-meal-a-day dining room." They could publish a magazine and a library of twenty-five-cent spiritual classics, and send free books to missionaries. "Heck, I don't want to have a safe job all my life," she said, addressing herself to Exman's risk aversion. "Better to venture. Then we'd never have to take on a [book] we didn't believe in." She finished with one more reason to take on this project: "We could help each other to fuller life."[55]

Bro was the prime mover here, but Exman had plenty of reasons to come along. One day, he took out a piece of scrap paper and wrote down the pros and cons of leaving Harper and starting up his own shop with Bro. He listed eighteen reasons to go and three to stay. The "go" list included these reasons:

- *Harper's "too big"*

- *Job now done there*

- *[Harper] will not decentralize*

- *If move is made, it must be made before I am much older*

- *Authors are available to get business started*

- *Business set-up on coop basis a step in right direction. Selfish capitalism is on way out*

- *[Staff people] to work in getting the enterprise under way are available*

- *Move from NY would relieve me of involvement in Riverside Ch*

- *Good time now to sell Scarsdale house*

- *If we believe that evol. of consciousness requires venturing into the unknown, turning away from the soft and easy course, then this direction toward the new, the more sensitive is right*

- *Now must pub. at Harpers a considerable number of unimportant books*

The much shorter "stay" list included these three reasons:

- *Business cycle: if deflation comes soon the new enterprise might fail*

- *Sunny would prefer to keep security of Harper position*

- *Financial security (if it is a good thing) more likely with Harper: important for educating children, etc.*

Exman shared these notes with Bro, who annotated them in her own hand. "I'm not sure that Scarsdale and Winnetka [a Chicago suburb where she was then renting] are Christian places to live," she wrote. "I have a feeling that people need to be stripped down recurrently—to risk—to travel with light baggage, to have a sense of mission to which financial security is dedicated."

Bro also offered three rejoinders to Exman's three reasons to stand pat:

- *If it is right it will survive*

- *The move may provide a new experience for [Sunny]*

- *[Financial security] is not important really*[56]

One factor that neither party mentioned was what would happen to their marriages. Would Sunny really move to the Midwest so her husband could become business partners with Bro? Wasn't the Exman-Bro friendship a big part of this venture's attraction? If so, what would living and working in such proximity augur for that relationship, for good or for ill?

Serious discussion of this plan continued into the early 1950s. Bro asked Exman to "try to hold your mind open as to whether you might leave Scarsdale," but Exman found it impossible to act.[57] He was risk averse by temperament, so financial security *was* important to him. He wasn't as troubled as Bro was by the subpar books he felt pressure to publish. He also found it hard to shake the prestige that Harper offered.

Exman did not just remain at Harper, however. He became more entangled there. The longer he stayed, the more the money and the status piled up. Stock options supplemented his rising salary and lavish expense account.

After years of lamenting the distance between them, Bro and Exman finally found a way to live near one another in the spring of 1954. Albin landed a job (with Exman's help) as associate director of Wainwright House in Rye, New York, and the Bros moved just a few miles away from the Exmans' Scarsdale home. Established a few years earlier as a retreat center for internationalists and pacifists— Exman was on the board—Wainwright House operated under the auspices of the Laymen's Movement, a nonsectarian effort that worked with businessmen to integrate spirituality and ethics into American life and with the United Nations to foster world peace.

This could have been a perfect time for Exman and Bro to settle into a new stage in their relationship, and Bro was game. She was convinced that writing and editing books was a calling worthy of the full attention of a human life. She loved Exman and wanted to spend time with him. She worried that he worked too hard and that his busyness threatened his health. It also compromised his moral life, by diverting his attention from the needs of his employees and freelancers (Bro included) and by crowding out the attention required to make bad books good and good books great. It threatened his spiritual life, too, by sapping the creative energies he might otherwise have devoted to the search. But Bro also worried that her friend was becoming a company man overly enamored of his power lunches at the Century Club and his seat on the Harper Board of Directors. She worried that he was conforming his interests too readily to Harper's interests—that her voice in his head and the voice of what the Quakers called the Inner Light were being increasingly drowned out by the clicking and clacking of adding machines. "I suspect this is a testing time in your life," she told him in his mid-fifties. "Treat yourself like a great man, one of 'God's men,' and you will be a great man. You will be God's man. . . . I shall pray for you to have discrimination."[58]

Those prayers, and any plans Bro and Exman might have been making, were interrupted in the mid-1950s by two sudden deaths. Midmorning on August 17, 1955, John Chambers, Bro's close friend and Exman's beloved associate director, collapsed from a heart attack on the southwest corner of Park Avenue and Thirty-Sixth Street. Because Chambers was walking just a few blocks to get something from his apartment he hadn't brought his wallet. When he collapsed he was taken as a John Doe to Bellevue Hospital, which served the poorest of the poor. Seven or eight hours elapsed before Exman was able to track his body down and identify him to authorities.

The death hit Exman and Bro hard. Chambers was just forty-five years old. He wasn't married, and Bro had been urging him for years to take better care of himself. Exman was perhaps his dearest friend. He and Chambers shared, as Chambers put it, an "undeclared awareness and singleness of purpose" that meant "more to me than any other association in my life." Exman put off a planned European trip to handle the funeral arrangements, which included a memorial service conducted by Howard Thurman, who was also close to Chambers.[59]

Exman would eventually replace Chambers (at Bro's suggestion) with Mel Arnold, who would go on to succeed Exman after his retirement in 1965. But within days of Chambers's death, Exman was also negotiating with Bro to ease the transition by coming to work with him at Harper's headquarters. Soon she was commuting from Wainwright House to work for him full-time. Exman did not see Bro as a candidate for his new associate director. We do not know how Bro felt about that, but she was bold and bitter enough to suggest that, if she had XY chromosomes and fewer wrinkles, she might have been in line for the job. "Too bad I'm not young and male. I'd probably do you proud," she said.[60]

Early in 1956, Albin Bro left Wainwright House for medical reasons, and in March 1956 he, too, died of a heart attack. Bro was distressed. She was in her early sixties, with four grown children and more than a dozen grandchildren. Exman was shaken, too. He and Sunny had been friendly with the Bros as a couple. They shared meals on occasion, and Bro addressed the letters she sent to the Exman home to both Sunny and Eugene. But her husband's death opened all sorts of new opportunities for Bro. And for Exman. If the two of them were ever going to start up their own publishing venture, that would have been the time. But Exman, who had been promoted to vice president at Harper in 1955, let that time pass.

An Affair?

In the eight years I sifted through the ephemera of Exman's life, one question kept nagging at me: Did Exman and Bro have an affair? Obviously, they had an affair of the heart. They loved one another. They were more intimate in many ways with one another than they were with their spouses. But did that relationship ever move from the writing of letters and the editing of books into the bedroom? It is difficult to know how to answer this question, and what to make of its import, if any. However, it seems worth the effort to accumulate the evidence.

Very few Bro letters were made available to me by the Bro family. I learned from various family members that there were letters saved here and there, and I knew from the Exman Archive that Bro had fantasized about writing a book called "Letters from an Editor," which would focus on Exman's letters to her. So I held out hope that those letters might surface. However, all I was able to track down through the Bro family were a few letters she sent home from abroad.

As for the Exman Archive, there is no way of knowing how, if at all, it was curated by Exman or his heirs. Were selected documents secreted away by the family? Was some of the correspondence destroyed? There is that folder of Exman-Bro letters from the late 1950s with that note in Exman's hand: "of possible interest if there's to be an EE autobiography otherwise destroy." That folder was not destroyed, and it was handed over to me with letters inside, but the note testifies to the fact that Exman considered destroying documents for posterity's sake. This folder covered a period when Exman and Bro had a falling-out over a book they were publishing by Martin Luther King Jr. Is that why Exman considered these letters to be potentially toxic? Did he remove letters from that folder? Finally, there are definitely letters that Bro wrote to Exman during the early months of their relationship that have not survived. Did Exman throw them away? He sifted through his archive at some point in the 1960s or 1970s, annotating documents as he went. Did he remove anything then?

Archival matters aside, there is testimony from people who knew Exman well. Christopher Isherwood reports in his published diaries that, as of July 1941, a little over two years before he met Bro, Exman, then forty-one years old, "wasn't any longer having relations with his wife." His source is Gerald Heard, who, according to Isherwood, "knew all our secrets."[61]

Exman's son Wally, whose relationship with his father was fraught and unresolved even at his own death in 2021, was not an entirely trustworthy narrator, but he, too, painted a picture of a marriage between his father and mother without much physical intimacy. He and his sister, Judy, "had always been suspicious" of their father when it came to extramarital sex, he said, and they talked at length about their parents' relationship. "We never saw our parents hug," he said, and they saw "how difficult it was in terms of the sexuality part of it." According to Wally, "she did not particularly care for sex . . . and Dad was . . . I think he enjoyed sex a great deal." Exman's closest relationships were with women, added Wally, who believed that some of those relationships became sexual. "I know his sex life with my mother was not terrific," he said. "He had to have some outlet." As for Sunny, Wally said, "she was supportive in the sense that she let him do it. She never got in the way of it. She knew it was important to him. . . . She understood that that was who he was. . . . Maintaining the marriage was of utmost importance." Again according to Wally, Sunny even joked at times about "all of Dad's girlfriends." Bro herself joked in a letter to Exman about how Sunny "should be glad that it is us old ladies who are so frank about appreciating her husband," only to add, "Of course, you may also have a young string which you keep in another stable."[62]

Letters Bro and Exman exchanged are flirty at times. "My dreams all run to beds and sleep (note the sleep; it haint what you and Cassanova think)," Bro wrote. "You stay away from any other boy friends . . . and we will manage perfectly," Exman wrote to her.[63]

In multiple letters, Bro confided in Exman about difficulties she was having with her husband. In one of the first Bro letters in the Exman Archive, she tells Exman that she just "can't get across to" her husband. She can't talk with Albin like she talks with him. And Albin doesn't understand her like he does. Bro also raises the possibility of moving on. "I love my family but sometimes I think of leaving permanently," she tells him.[64]

This evidence amply supports the conclusion that Exman and Bro had an emotional affair. They confided in one another. They reveled in the camaraderie born of the books they read and the authors they knew. They wrestled over the books they edited. They prayed and meditated together. They sought to move into the Presence together. They gently held each other's hopes and dreams.

Given this evidence, it seems reasonable to conclude that Exman did not confine his sexual experiences after his marriage to Sunny alone. His life was devoted to seeking spiritual experiences without much regard for traditional religion. Given Wally's testimony, it does not seem too much of a leap to imagine that he would have been open to seeking unconventional sexual experiences as well, especially if his marriage was as empty of joy in that regard as his church was bereft of opportunities to encounter God.

That said, there is not enough evidence in the Exman Archive to demonstrate that the Exman-Bro relationship advanced beyond emotional to sexual intimacy. Neither is there even a hint of the sort of guilt that might be expected from two churchgoers having an affair in midcentury America. Moreover, the Bros and the Exmans seem to have been friendly as couples. Margueritte addressed many of her letters to both Exman and Sunny, and the Bros and Exmans had dinner together on many occasions.

When I raised the matter of Exman's alleged affairs with his son-in-law, Walter Kaess, Walter responded, "Who cares?" There is wisdom in that response. It is important to observe, however, that Exman's most intimate relationship was not with Sunny. It was with Margueritte Bro. That relationship involved overlapping spiritual journeys. It also involved unequal and hierarchical workplace dynamics that would ultimately bring their publishing relationship to an end. That said, Bro shaped Exman's life, and his life's work, like no one else.

CHAPTER FOUR

Catholic Activism, Anti-Catholicism, and *The Long Loneliness* of Dorothy Day

Dorothy Day was on a mission when she marched into Exman's office late in 1949. It had been sixteen years since she had published the first issue of the *Catholic Worker* on May 1, 1933. Since then she had taken up many new projects while rarely putting down an old one. Already a countercultural icon and a Roman Catholic saint in the making, she had marched and rallied and picketed and protested. She had been jailed for the privilege, followed for years by the FBI, and denounced as un-American even by many of her fellow Catholics. Meanwhile, she had transformed her penny-a-copy paper from a monthly into a movement, with dozens of houses of hospitality and farm communes across the country. Though lauded and damned as a pacifist, Day was best known for her life of voluntary poverty and for her personal acts of mercy to the poor, the hungry, and the homeless. However, on this particular day, she was on a mission for mammon. She had just returned from Staten Island, where she had once fallen in love with a man. This time a farm was the object of her desire. The down payment was $1,000. And she was determined to get it from Exman.

In the 1930s, Exman had seen into print a few books by and

about Catholics and Jews. There was a series of books by the Chicago-based Conservative rabbi Solomon Goldman, a biography of the Roman Catholic cardinal John Henry Newman (written by a Protestant minister), and a collection of the writings of the medieval Catholic mystic Saint John of the Cross (by a Catholic priest).[1] The Trabuco experiment introduced Exman to Hindu authors and prodded him to publish widely in Asian religions in the 1940s. The African American mystic and civil rights pioneer Howard Thurman also found a place on Exman's list, beginning with *The Negro Spiritual Speaks of Life and Death* (1947). So did an increasing number of women. But these cracks in the White, male, Protestant wall did not precipitate a flood of books by authors who checked other boxes. Then came the Cold War, which challenged Exman to diversify his Book of Books in the direction of Judaism and Catholicism. His response to this challenge led to a golden age in the Harper religious book department in the 1950s.

After the United States dropped atomic bombs on Hiroshima and Nagasaki in August 1945, and as the World War II battles at Midway and Iwo Jima faded from memory, America's politicians preoccupied themselves with battling the specter of communism. In the hot war recently concluded, the Axis powers (Germany, Italy, and Japan) had fought the Allied powers (Great Britain, France, the Soviet Union, and the United States). Next came the Cold War, which featured Americans and Russians in a battle that pitted allegedly theistic capitalism against atheistic communism. This battle also produced a hunt for communists at home and new conceptions of American religion.

During the 1930s, American Jewish writers had coined a new term, "Judeo-Christianity," and employed it in the information war against Hitler and Nazism. This "Judeo-Christian idea," in the words of the Jewish novelist Sholem Asch, was both a rebuke to Christian anti-Semitism and an invocation of a new world order in which Christians and Jews would stand shoulder to shoulder against religious bigotry. It spread rapidly during the early 1940s, as the horrors of Nazi anti-Semitism became increasingly clear. After World War II, the Judeo-Christian tradition emerged as a key concept in American life, though it was now deployed by politicians, preachers, and publishers against godless communists rather than Nazi theologians.[2]

The invention of the Judeo-Christian tradition helped spark a religious revival in postwar America that in turn reinforced Judeo-Christian ideals. Attendance at religious services swelled. More Americans identified as religious, and more people understood religion as something that came in a variety of flavors. Meanwhile, sales of religious books skyrocketed, turning rabbis, priests, and ministers into bestselling authors. Rabbi Joshua Liebman, Bishop Fulton Sheen, and Billy Graham hit bestseller lists with their own spins on what is now called "positive psychology." The sociologist Will Herberg, in his landmark book *Protestant-Catholic-Jew* (1955), reimagined Judeo-Christianity as a party of three, welcoming Catholics and Jews into a national household previously occupied by Protestants alone. According to Herberg, Protestantism, Catholicism, and Judaism were now three branches of one democratic faith, which worshipped one God and stood strong against communism.[3]

During World War II, Harper had been a member of the Council on Books in Wartime. The council's logo, which appeared in Exman's catalogs, depicted a bald eagle, its wings outstretched, taking flight from a stack of books. Encircling these symbols of American power and the power of learning was the council's all-caps logo: "BOOKS ARE WEAPONS IN THE WAR OF IDEAS." Exman contributed to that war with new books by Catholics and Jews.[4]

Two of those books became Catholic Book Club selections in 1946: *Whereon to Stand*, "a layman's explanation" of Catholic Church teachings by the Catholic poet John Gilland Brunini; and *Tales of the Twain*, a "prejudice-shattering" novel by Catholic author and Exman friend Sam Constantino. Building on the devotional classic *The Imitation of Christ*, which he published in translation in 1941, Exman produced translations of classics by other medieval

Catholic mystics, including Saint Francis de Sales's *Introduction to the Devout Life* (1950), which Exman's catalog billed as a "devotional classic . . . among Catholics and Protestants alike."[5]

Postwar Jewish additions to Exman's Book of Books included a series of volumes on the Bible by Solomon Goldman, but the most important Jewish newcomer was Martin Buber—"the greatest living Jewish philosopher," in Reinhold Niebuhr's estimation—whose books showed up in rapid succession in Exman's catalogs, beginning with *Eclipse of God* (1952) and *The Legend of the Baal-Shem* (1955).[6]

Exman's quintessential Cold War book and a staple on bestseller lists across the country was *American Spiritual Autobiographies: Fifteen Self-Portraits* (1948). This multireligious collection was edited by Louis Finkelstein, chancellor of the Jewish Theological Seminary (near Riverside Church) and a leading figure in Conservative Judaism in the United States. Like Fosdick, Finkelstein was a multimedia religious personality with radio and television shows to his credit. As the founder of an institute that convened multireligious conversations, he also had top-notch interfaith credentials. Finkelstein introduced his Protestant, Catholic, and Jewish authors as "a cross section of America," and two women and two African Americans were included. In the opening essay, M. L. Wilson, a Unitarian who served under two presidents in the Department of Agriculture and identified as "a convert to the religion of William James," offered homespun stories of rural America during the Cold War. In one of those stories, his father presided over three prayers at the dinner table: a Jewish blessing in Hebrew by a peddler passing through his Iowa farm, a Catholic blessing by a resident farmhand, and a silent Quaker grace led by his wife. When Wilson closed with a "credo of my faith," he began by affirming the "Judeo-Christian, democratic" ideal of "tolerance."[7]

Amid this Judeo-Christian vogue, Exman drafted a mission statement for his religious book department. It appeared for the first time on his catalogs in 1952 and remained beyond his retirement in 1965. Rather than presenting his department's work as Jewish and

Christian, however, Exman presented it as religiously pluralistic and religion-friendly. The mission statement read: "It is the policy of the Religious Book Department at Harper & Brothers to publish books that represent important religious groupings, express well-articulated thought, combine intellectual competence and felicitous style, add to the wealth of religious literature irrespective of creedal origin, and aid in the cause of religion without proselyting for any particular sect."[8]

This commitment put Harper on record as religiously pluralistic. But it could not erase the centuries of Protestant-derived anti-Catholic bias that continued to inform Exman, Harper's corporate culture, and American society.

Boom

As the postwar religious revival continued and the religious book market boomed, observers struggled to make sense of it all. In "Reading, Writing, and Religion," which ran in *Harper's Magazine* in May 1953, Exman weighed in, arguing that religious book sales were actually stronger than estimated, because narrow federal rules for what constituted that genre excluded many books clearly "animated by a religious spirit." Novels, for example, didn't count as religious books, even when they depicted the life of Jesus. And non-fiction books by Aldous Huxley, including *The Perennial Philosophy*, didn't count, because he was considered a novelist. Regarding Rabbi Liebman's *Peace of Mind*, Exman observed that its author was "a religious man" who "wrote the book for religious reasons," yet the six hundred thousand copies it sold in its first two years counted as "inspirational" rather than "religious" sales. Exman himself counted as "religious" books that trafficked in subtler religion, including AA's Big Book, which he called "the best modern testimony I know of the power of religion to save sinners."[9]

How to account for this book boom? Alongside "fear of war,"

Exman pointed to a loss of faith in science accompanied by increased interest in religion among psychologists. He also credited the demise of "dogmatic religion" and the rise of "'one-world' consciousness." "We are aware now, as mankind never before has been, of our close proximity to other races and religions," Exman wrote. "We are learning from them and absorbing some of their faith." Crucially, he wasn't talking any more about Baptists, Methodists, and Episcopalians. He was talking about "the Hindus and the Moslems and the Buddhists," who "are viewed with lessening antagonism and heightening appreciation" and whose "saints and seers are read for more than 'comparative' interest."[10]

This religious cosmopolitanism will register with many readers today as admirably tolerant. But the pluralism that Exman, his co-workers, and authors were constructing in the middle of the twentieth century was neither as diverse nor as inclusive as it might sound. It was a decidedly Protestant pluralism with anti-Catholic reflexes passed down from European Reformers who recoiled at priests and sacraments, New England Puritans who sought to purge worship of all vestiges of priestly privilege, Baptists dead set against creeds, and Transcendentalists hostile to rituals. In this Protestant pluralism, there was lots of room for Hindus. For Catholics? Not so much.

There was some room, however. As has been noted, Exman was friendly to the writings of medieval Catholic mystics. And he had drawn into his mystics club a small yet influential coterie of Catholic friends who shared his interest in uncanny experiences and his conviction that true mysticism was not escapist. Exman devoted nearly a quarter of his *Harper's* article to the boom in books of, by, and for Roman Catholics. He noted that Harper's trade-book editor Eugene Saxton had observed fifteen years prior that "there was little demand for Roman Catholic books except Missals and devotional books." Nowadays, "Roman Catholic books are printed and bound, packaged and promoted, as any trade book would be," Exman wrote, and "are better written, better edited, and often published by big trade houses."[11]

As this article shows, Exman ventured out of his comfort zone during the Cold War, meeting, publishing, and in many cases befriending rabbis, Zen masters, and Catholic priests. All these authors stretched his understanding of what religion was, but no one did that more than Dorothy Day.

A Disreputable Saint

Day and Exman first met at a gathering on religion and publishing held from December 30, 1948, to January 3, 1949, at Pendle Hill, a Quaker retreat center outside Philadelphia.[12] Then in her early fifties, Day was well on her way to becoming an icon of the American Catholic Left. A whisper campaign to canonize her as a Roman Catholic saint was also underway. As a college dropout and a Catholic laywoman, Day was not an obvious candidate for Exman's religious books list. Whereas he was a political and theological liberal, she was a political radical and a theological traditionalist, left of many leftists on capitalism and in lockstep with the Vatican in opposing birth control and abortion. Exman and Day led very different social lives as well. He was at home in the world of America's rising middle class, with a seemingly stable family life and comfortable connections to a vast network of power players in business, education, government, entertainment, and religion. Day was at home with powerless players, at odds in nearly every way with Exman's bourgeois world of Harper stock options and Century Club luncheons. She was, in the words of her friend the Catholic activist Daniel Berrigan, "a lonely woman, alone in the church, in the culture, in the acculturated church." In fact, she was ill at ease everywhere this side of heaven, viewing life on Earth as something we are passing through. "Life is but a night spent in an uncomfortable inn," she often said, quoting Saint Teresa of Ávila.[13]

Exman and Day had a lot in common, however. Both were born right around the turn of the twentieth century. After childhoods undisturbed by war, they saw the innocence and optimism of their Lost Generation sacrificed on the altars of two global conflicts. Their ensuing search for meaning was complicated by the destitution of the Great Depression and by an unnamed yet acute affliction that went by many names: "Alienation, anxiety, dread, a sense of being askew, off-center, lost in a void."[14]

Exman and Day were also mystics, convinced by William James (whom Day read with intriguing reverence) that the heart knows what it wants and what it wants is religious experience. Both regularly attended spiritual retreats. Exman led many, and toward the end of her life Day was working on a Harper book (never published) about her retreat experiences, including a mystical moment when she was graced with "a vision of the transcendent destiny of all life."[15] Neither Exman nor Day had any interest in mystical escape, however, vowing instead to do good in the world by combining contemplation with efforts to help "the least of these." Day lived and worked among the disinherited. For Exman, such work was at arm's length. He did his protesting with his pen rather than his body, and while he worked his connections to get conscientious objectors (and alleged communists) out of jail, he was never jailed himself.

Day was raised outside the church and Exman inside it, but each embarked on a spiritual journey that eventually found them in their respective pews (Day, daily; Exman, weekly). Both believed that human life continued beyond the grave, and that human society included the living and the dead. Though deferential to her local priests and bishops, Day was convinced, as was Exman, that organized Christianity had scandalously diverged from the religion of Jesus and the spirit of his Sermon on the Mount. As a result, both sought out primary spiritual communities in smaller groups than church congregations—Day in her houses of hospitality and Exman in his Monday evening cell group. Crucially, Day also shared with Exman a long-standing commitment to absolute pacifism that had brought them into conversation with Quakers and to that Pendle

Hill retreat. (Even after Japanese airmen bombed Pearl Harbor on December 7, 1941, both opposed the US entry into World War II.)

For all these reasons, it should not be surprising that, when Day came into Exman's office a few months after they met at Pendle Hill, she left with a $1,000 advance. Exman was at the time widely respected, though he didn't always respect himself. He was a long-standing member of Denison's Board of Trustees, and his growing résumé included nonprofit service at his local school board, Riverside Church, the American Bible Society, and the Fellowship of Reconciliation. With hundreds of bestsellers to his credit, he had long been regarded as the "dean of religion publishing."[16] Yet he was unable to shake a nagging perception that he was falling short of the sainthood to which Heard and Bro had called him. Day had a more formidable reputation, though she had made it by being disreputable.

Today she is an official candidate for canonization as a Roman Catholic saint, lauded by Pope Francis as a "servant of God." Back in 1949, she was more likely to be described as a servant of Stalin. In fact, since 1940 the FBI had been accumulating a file on her. In that file, agents described her as "a very erratic and irresponsible person" who was "consciously or unconsciously being used by Communist groups." FBI Director J. Edgar Hoover personally ordered her "custodial detention in the event of a national emergency." Unlike Exman, a civic-minded man who voted, signed petitions, and wrote to members of Congress, Day neither voted nor paid taxes. Mistrustful of big government, she had zero interest in the New Deal programs Exman applauded.[17]

Exman respected Day, both for the sacrifices she was making on behalf of the poor and for the giant steps she was taking toward saintliness—actions Exman lacked the willpower to take himself. In Day's political life, the gap between conviction and action was admirably slim. She seemed to Exman to be able to practice the presence of God far more easily and consistently than he. Her life was in many respects an indictment of his own, and unlike Hoover,

Exman was a good enough man to applaud her for it, not least with an agreement to publish what would become one of the classic spiritual autobiographies in American history.

"The First Hippie"

Dorothy Day was born on November 8, 1897, into a nominally Protestant family in Brooklyn, New York. Her mother was a home-maker. Her father was a sportswriter with a weakness for race horses. Together John and Grace Day would have five children, with Dorothy in the middle. As her father lost and found newspaper work (and won and lost bets), the family shuttled between middle-class comforts and fears of impoverishment. They moved from New York to the San Francisco Bay Area, where they lost everything in the earthquake of 1906, and Dorothy witnessed the outpouring of grace to the destitute that would later come to characterize her ministry. "While the crisis lasted," she later wrote, "people loved each other."[18] The next stop was Chicago, where Dorothy gradu-ated from high school as a precocious sixteen-year-old. In 1916, after two years at the University of Illinois, she dropped out to fol-low her family back to New York City. When her father objected to her work as a journalist, she found a room of her own on the Lower East Side and a place among Greenwich Village bohemians and radicals.

Sixties icon Abbie Hoffman would later anoint Day "the first hippie," and she played the part in her late teens and early twenties. In an era when good women were expected to marry and raise children, she wrote for a series of radical periodicals. She marched against the draft. She went to jail for agitating for women's suffrage. She smoked and cursed and hung out with avant-garde artists. She was also an ac-complished drinker who, according to her friend the author Malcolm Cowley, was admired by gangsters "because she could drink them under the table."[19]

Day had a series of ill-fated romances with writers, including the communist Mike Gold, who reveled in Tolstoy's churchless religion, and the playwright Eugene O'Neill, who urged her to read Augustine's *Confessions*. "The life of the flesh called to me," she later wrote of these not-so-saintly years. "The satisfied flesh has its own law."[20] Another relationship, with a volatile newspaperman named Lionel Moise, led to a pregnancy, an abortion, and two suicide attempts. A short-lived marriage to Berkeley Greene Tobey, an older (and wealthier) man, took her to Italy, where she worked on an autobiographical novel.

Politics was her passion in these passionate times, but, at least as she told the tale, faith gestated in her from a very early age. She attended a Methodist church with a girlfriend as a young child and was baptized as an Episcopalian, at her own request, when she was twelve. "I was filled with lofty ambitions to be a saint, a natural striving, a thrilling recognition of the possibilities of spiritual adventure," she later wrote. She abruptly gave up those ambitions in her teens. In college, she reports, "I rejected religion."[21]

In her early twenties in New York, Day, now a "dedicated atheist," found herself slipping into churches. When offered a book to read in jail after her arrest in Washington, DC, she asked for a Bible. In Chicago, she received her first rosary from a friend. In Saint Louis Cathedral in New Orleans, she learned how to pray it. Day also credited Eugene O'Neill, a God-haunted ex-Catholic, for her gradual religious awakening. Despite his atheism, Day wrote, "he brought to me such a consciousness of God . . . an intensification of the religious sense that was in me."[22]

The Eleventh Virgin, the autobiographical novel Day began in Italy, was greeted unkindly when it appeared in 1924, including in the *Oakland Tribune*, which called it a filthy story of "a young female moron who is inordinately proud of the fact that she remains a virgin after having reached the age of reason." Warner Brothers executives were less nauseated by the novel (and the sex), optioning it for $5,000. Day used her portion of that windfall to buy a fisherman's shack on Staten Island that would become her personal spiritual retreat.[23]

There, on the island's south shore facing Raritan Bay, she entered a transitional phase between the bohemianism of her youth and the austerity of her adulthood. As she left city streets behind, setting her days by the rhythms of the tides, she found new friends, including a fisherman named Lefty, who lived in a nearby shack gloriously apart from the evils of the market economy (he always had a chair overlooking the water for his friend). She also pursued the most fraught and fulfilling romantic relationship of her life—with Forster Batterham, an anarchist and atheist whose mistrust of the institution of marriage and institutional religion bordered on loathing. Forster would provoke a crisis in her life that she would resolve only by leaving him and becoming a Roman Catholic.

Personal Religion

This personal crisis is the subject of much writing about Day, including her own *From Union Square to Rome* (1938), and on the whys and wherefores of her conversion there is no agreement. The natural delights that surrounded her on Staten Island surely played a role, awakening in her the sort of nature mysticism that also stirred Howard Thurman and Margueritte Bro. "The beauty of nature which includes the sounds of waves, the sounds of insects, the cicadas in the trees—all were part of my joy in nature that brought me to the Church," she wrote. Also drawing her churchward was her desire for structure in what had been a chaotic life. "We all crave order," she observed.[24]

Day saw becoming Catholic as a way to stand in solidarity with the poor. After World War II and the GI Bill, Catholics would move rapidly into elite colleges and the middle class, but the Catholics she encountered in the 1920s were poor and working class, often Irish and Italian. She wanted to be one of them, but being with them would suffice. To do otherwise would be to betray "the class to which I belonged, the workers, the poor of the world, with whom Christ spent His life."[25]

Because Day was a reader and writer, there were many literary influences as well, including Saint Augustine, Dostoyevsky, and William James. In Augustine's *Confessions*, she found a genre (spiritual autobiography) and a narrative arc—from sin to conversion—that she made her own. In Dostoyevsky, Tolstoy, and other Russian novelists, she found thick descriptions of everyday Christians striving to imitate Christ. But James was particularly important to her conversion. "Reading William James' *Varieties of Religious Experience* had acquainted me with the saints," she explained.[26]

In *Varieties*—a book that according to one biographer "meant the world to Dorothy Day"—James addressed the postreligious types who would surround Day in Greenwich Village.[27] While his friends were making modernist arguments against religion—as ancient superstition rooted in ignorance and fear—James made a religious case against modern materialism. There is more to life than meets the eye, he argued, and he referred to that unseen presence as the "More." Those who glimpsed that presence, however fleetingly, he beheld with envy and awe. He encouraged his readers to do the same.

Though James had no delusions about the efficacy of gimme prayers for good weather, he insisted that "inward communion or conversation with the power recognized as divine" was "no vain exercise of words." In fact, he saw prayer of that sort as "the very soul and essence of religion." Regarding Catholics, James was respectful. No fan of ritual or doctrine, he criticized the "fixed definitions of man" and "positive dogmas about God" advanced by Catholic theologians. But he applauded Catholic saints and mystics as exemplars of "living religion."[28]

Famously defining religion as "the feelings, acts, and experiences of individual men in their solitude, so far as they apprehend themselves to stand in relation to whatever they may consider divine," James focused in *Varieties* on the concrete over the abstract, individuals over institutions, personal experiences over collective beliefs. Among those experiences, James devoted special attention to mysticism and conversion. His focus on "personal religion" resonated with Day, whose friends had long decried the evils of organized religion. And his descriptions of the encounters of individual humans with the "More" helped her make sense of the confusing tug she felt while sitting in a pew or holding a rosary.[29]

In a passage from a letter Day would regularly cite—she copied it into her journal in 1973—James made a case against "big religion" that also influenced Exman, Fosdick, and King:

> I am against bigness and greatness in all their forms, and with the invisible molecular moral forces that work from individual to individual, stealing in through the crannies of the world like so many soft rootlets, or like the capillary oozing of water, and yet rending the hardest monuments of man's pride, if you give them time. The bigger the unit you deal with, the hollower, the more brutal, the more mendacious is the life displayed. So I am against all big organizations as such, national ones first and foremost; against all big successes and big results; and in favor of the eternal forces of truth which always work in the individual and immediately unsuccessful way, under-dogs always, till history comes, after they are long dead, and puts them on the top.[30]

As Day read James on conversion and underdogs, she began to read her own life as a journey from sin to redemption to service to others. She also began to interpret her soul-sickness as a necessary precursor to conversion. James's *Varieties* introduced her to the lives of the saints (Catholics and otherwise), including her beloved Teresa of Ávila—the "expert of experts" among the mystical saints, in James's words, and "one of the ablest women, in many respects, of whose life we have the record." In James, Day encountered an author, raised like her amid Protestants, who not only saw "the value of saintliness"—the egolessness, charity, and voluntary poverty—but also seemed to ache for it, as for something he knew he could never attain.[31]

In another passage Day wrote down and recited—she read it aloud to her friend Lefty on the Staten Island shore—James lauded the poverty of saints even as he lamented the impoverishment of the modern world. "Poverty *is* indeed the strenuous life—without brass bands or uniforms or hysteric popular applause or lies or circumlocutions; and when one sees the way in which wealth-getting enters as an ideal into the very bone and marrow of our generation, one wonders whether a revival of the belief that poverty is a worthy religious vocation may not be . . . the spiritual reform which our time stands most in need of," he wrote. "We have grown literally afraid to be poor. We despise any one who elects to be poor in order to simplify and save his inner life." What was now most needed was to learn to sing "the praises of poverty once again"—to liberate ourselves from material things, to reacquaint ourselves with "the unbribed soul."[32]

Of all the reasons for her conversion to Catholicism, Day emphasized her experience of having and holding a child, which put her in search of a vessel large enough to contain her overflowing gratitude. The "natural happiness" Day experienced upon the birth of her daughter, Tamar Teresa, on March 4, 1926, made her ache for "greater happiness," a combination of nature and the supernatural as mysterious as the Catholic Mass itself. She found that something extra in the divine: "Forster had made the physical world come alive for me and had awakened in my heart a flood of gratitude. The final object of this love and gratitude was God. No human creature could receive or contain so vast a flood of love and joy as I often felt after the birth of my child. With this came the need to worship, to adore."[33]

Day desperately wanted to baptize her baby as a Catholic and to become a Catholic herself. But she also wanted Forster, who refused to subject himself to the institution of marriage or to pretend he did not find her growing interest in religion revolting. "In every way" she loved him, she wrote in lines that, should she become canonized, must rank among the sexiest passages ever penned by a Catholic saint: "I loved him for all he knew and pitied him for all he didn't know. I loved him for the odds and ends I had to fish out of his sweater pockets and for the sand and shells he brought in with his fishing. I loved his lean cold body as he got into bed smelling of the sea and I loved his integrity and stubborn pride."[34]

And so the "natural happiness" she experienced with Forster warred with the supernatural happiness she was experiencing as an almost Catholic. All this warring within herself, and with Forster, who continued to denounce religion (as "morbid escapism") and baptism (as "mumbo jumbo, the fuss and fury peculiar to women") wore Day down. She started to have what we would now refer to as panic attacks. "I became so oppressed I could not breathe and I awoke in the night choking," she wrote. Her time for choosing had come, and she chose the church.[35]

She presented Tamar for baptism at Our Lady Help of Christians on Staten Island in July 1927. Forster refused to come, and tortured times followed. Day remained desperately in love. She could not stop herself from hoping that Foster would marry her, but Forster remained resolute. This impasse produced the sort of crisis that James had identified as a necessary prerequisite to conversion. She told Forster to move out, and in December 1927 Day herself was baptized. "It had seemed like death, at the time, to become a Catholic," Day later wrote.[36] But it was not a clear break. She continued to see (and sleep with) Forster on occasion.

On December 8, 1932, while in Washington, DC, reporting on the National Hunger March, Day went during the Feast of the Immaculate Conception to the National Shrine of the Immaculate Conception at Catholic University to see if she might find guidance regarding the future course of her life. "I offered up a special prayer," she later wrote, "that some way would open up for me to use what talents I possessed for my fellow workers, for the poor."

The next day, a knock at the door of her apartment announced the presence of an odd man with a French accent and a Niagara of ideas. His name was Peter Maurin.

The day after that, she wrote Forster a final, tortured good-bye letter. In subsequent weeks, as Maurin talked and Day listened, she knew they would make a formidable team, and the second half of her life turned with all the conviction of the tides off Staten Island.

Peter Maurin and the *Catholic Worker*

Peter Maurin was a French-born Catholic social theorist, twenty years older than Day, who wanted no part in either communism or capitalism. He spread his ideas—houses of hospitality for the poor, roundtable discussions to foster "clarification of thought," and agronomic universities—by wandering from place to place and delivering in simple verse his "Easy Essays." He picked up whatever manual labor he could along the way, but "troubadour for God" was his real calling and talking was his full-time job.[37] In his partnership with Day, he played the theorist and she played the activist. Maurin had been unable to translate into action his utopian interpretations of Catholic social teachings. Day became his translator, transforming his ideas into concrete "acts of mercy" on behalf of the poor, the hungry, and the homeless.

One of Maurin's proposals was a Catholic newspaper, which, thanks to Day, debuted on May 1, 1933, as the *Catholic Worker*. The front page featured two of Maurin's "Easy Essays" plus stories about the exploitation of child laborers in the neighborhood, Black laborers in Mississippi, and women garment workers nationwide. A short notice dedicated this inaugural issue to New York City police officers, and a note titled "To Our Readers" explained that the newspaper was meant to show the homeless and the hopeless "that the Catholic Church has a social program . . . [and] that there are men of god who are working not only for their spiritual, but for their material welfare."[38]

Maurin, who thought the paper should stick to his philosophy of work, objected to all the wage and labor talk. ("Strikes don't strike me!" he said.[39]) But Day persisted, writing about unions and strikes and women and race. After a Black reader objected to the inaugural edition's masthead, which featured two White workers, one with a pick and the other with a shovel, an artist got to work, producing a new design featuring two laborers, one Black and one White, joining hands, with Jesus between them, his arms around each. An eight-page monthly, the *Catholic Worker* sold for a penny a copy, just what it sells for today. By the end of 1933, monthly circulation had topped a hundred thousand copies.

Day actualized another of Maurin's ideas the following winter when she turned her apartment into a house of hospitality. Maurin's model, which called for "a group of men living under a priest," conflicted with Day's lay sensibilities, so her next two Catholic Worker houses were an apartment house for women and another for men, neither with priestly supervision.[40] By 1936 there were thirty-three houses of hospitality nationwide. Next came a series of farming communes—on Staten Island, in Easton, Pennsylvania, and in upstate New York. In this way, the Catholic Worker developed over the course of the 1930s from a newspaper into a movement devoted to seeing Christ in all people, including (and especially) the homeless and the poor.

That movement was buoyed by the Great Depression, which brought in volunteers and stretched its bread and soup lines, but World War II was a challenge. Houses of hospitality lost many of their workers to the draft and to conscientious objector camps. Day's pacifism, which she shared with Exman and many of his authors, was also a challenge. During the Spanish Civil War of the late 1930s, she had refused to side with either the Catholic Church, which supported the Fascist Francisco Franco, or the many communists, socialists, and anarchists who opposed him. During World War II, she sided with conscientious objectors and draft protesters. Exman took a similar position, supporting dozens of young men who refused to register for the draft. This shared commitment brought together Day and Exman at the end of 1948 at Pendle Hill.

Later that winter, Day went to Princeton to visit a friend. She ran into another friend, Malcolm Cowley, who told her he was revising his autobiography. Day, who would go on to enjoy a long correspondence with the Catholic convert, Trappist monk, and author Thomas Merton, was already aware of the huge readership that was greeting Merton's autobiographical *Seven Storey Mountain* (1948). She, too, had new things to say. The Catholic Worker movement was sixteen years old. Tamar was now married with a daughter of her own. And Peter Maurin was on his deathbed. Might it be time to revisit *her* autobiography?

Day had fallen in love with a twenty-two-acre farm that had just gone on the market on Staten Island. The price was $16,000, but the down payment was just $1,000. "A way to pay for the farm presented itself," writes one of her biographers.[41] So she got down on her knees and prayed. Then she marched into Exman's office and marched out with a $1,000 advance, just enough to reserve what would come to be called Peter Maurin Farm. But it wasn't just the farm Day wanted. She wanted to retell her story from the perspective of a more mature faith—as a confession along the lines of Augustine and a conversion story worthy of William James.

The Long Loneliness

If Day's lay Catholicism was a stretch for Exman's religious books list, her autobiography fit in as neatly as Fosdick in his Riverside pulpit. Like many other Exman bestsellers, *The Long Loneliness* narrated a series of personal experiences without losing sight of the importance of religious community and the imperative of social and political action.

Exman assigned John Chambers to take the lead on this book, with Jim Shaw doing the copyediting. Day got along well with both men. ("Jim Shaw made wonderful suggestions all through," Day wrote in her diary. "Nothing like a good editor who knows what you are writing about.") After an early manuscript review, Shaw offered, in a February 1951 letter to Chambers (who forwarded excerpts to Day), an astute three-part abstract of Day's spiritual journey:

> There was a
> > GROWING UP
> > into
> > RADICAL ACTIVITIES
> (pt 1)
>
> Followed by
> > HUMAN HAPPINESS
> > Which led to God and
> > SPIRITUAL CONFLICT
> > With a literal
> > CHOICE BETWEEN MAN AND GOD
> > Which brought on a
> > RESTLESS INTERLUDE
> (pt 2)
>
> Before
> > PETER MAURIN AND THE CATHOLIC WORKER
> (pt 3)[42]

A couple of days later, Chambers wrote Day again, enclosing additional notes from Shaw, whose synopsis of a key chapter (written in Day's voice) nudged Day to raise the stakes of her "harrowing choice between God and man," church and Forster:

My child is baptized and the question of my own baptism faced.
I face the loss of the one person I do not want to lose, a person I
know to be good. I face separation from radical social activities
I never want to give up, activities I know to be good. I join a
Church which I know has often taken the side of the rich and
powerful to the neglect of the causes of the poor. The moment of
reception leaves me cold, barren of consolation, empty.[43]

As she revised *The Long Loneliness* with these notes in mind,
Day set down the key moments and themes that are now staples of
Dorothy Day life stories, even as she insisted that the book wasn't an
autobiography. "I hate my *Long Loneliness* being called an autobiography. It is more the story of a conversion," she later wrote. "I tried
to write only of those things which brought about my conversion to
the faith."[44]

In the book's prologue, Day wrote, "All my life I have been
haunted by God." Then she set about documenting that haunting.
She was attracted at various times to Methodism, Episcopalianism,
and Catholicism, and repulsed at other times by all of the above. She
cast the angst that led to her final decision for Catholicism inside a
narrative that arced, as if by God's hand, toward faith. The effect is
a sense of inevitability about the whole thing—a precociously pious
Protestant girl who becomes a young atheist marching inexorably
toward the Holy Mother Church. Day marches godward not because
she listens to the beat of her own drummer but because she is human, and "it is a psychological necessity of human nature" to glory in
God and to commune with others who do the same—"to reverence,
to worship, to adore."[45]

There are sins along the way, of course—it wouldn't be a conversion story without them—but Day does more telling than showing,
and not much telling either, glossing over details slathered across the
pages of *The Eleventh Virgin* and excising any mention of her abortion. As a result, the reader is often left wondering what all the fuss
is about: How much sin is there, really, to confess?

The "long loneliness" Day explores in the book is both shared and intensely personal. All human beings know such loneliness, Day says. It is there in the suffering and death we must all face. But we all experience the long loneliness differently. Day feels that loneliness when she leaves her baby brother to go to college, and in her twentieth year in New York when she has "no friends . . . no work." She feels it in her alienation from radical friends who had hoped her Catholic piety was a passing fling. She feels it at the Catholic Worker, where the easy grace she displays with sinners and saints, the down-and-out and the up-and-coming, cannot stave off the loneliness she feels as she works to help the poor in a society ruled by the wealthy. She feels it as well in her relationship with Forster, who, Day writes, "lived with me as though he were living alone."[46]

The only solution to this shared yet singular loneliness, Day concludes in a postscript to *The Long Loneliness*, is the love found in community. It is community—the shared work, the shared conversation—that banishes the long loneliness. So "the final word is love," she says. It is only because we love and are loved that we are able to say "we are not alone any more."[47]

Day didn't address *The Long Loneliness* to her fellow Catholics. "She wrote the book for the general reader, not just the Catholic reader," a biographer observes, "and everything about it suggests her desire to reach beyond the small circle of her admirers."[48] If so, she was on this rare occasion following orders. The "general reader" was the Great White Whale of Exman's department, and writing for a broad audience was a mantra he and his coworkers chanted repeatedly to their authors, Day included.

The two-page splash announcing *The Long Loneliness* in the Harper religious books catalog for Winter 1951–52 kept looping back to this middlebrow mantra. The author's "self-revelation of a St. Francis of the city streets" (the catalog never called her a Catholic) would "hearten and shame everyone of whatever race and religion who reads it." Two quotes by Exman's friends and authors made a similarly ecumenical point. The Catholic author Thomas Sugrue called the book "an inspiration for everyone," and the Quaker philosopher Douglas Steere called it "most welcome news to her many friends in all confessions." In a final effort to underscore the appeal of the book to non-Catholics, the "market" section at the end of this catalog copy promised "it will interest everyone who desires social justice" before noting that even the *Catholic Worker* wasn't just for Catholics, because its circulation was "one third Protestant."[49]

When *The Long Loneliness* was published in January 1952, an ad Exman placed in the *New York Times* read, "There never was a life story like this one . . . a tender-tough, sweet-salty, always engrossing account of a St. Francis of the city streets." Reviews were generally positive, though less fawning. *Kirkus Reviews* called Day "a writer of experience and competence" and her book "absorbing." *Newsweek* said the book was "bright and clearly written." *The Washington Post* described it as "an impassioned cry for justice for the poor and disposed" and "the glowing story of an inspired life." The *Chicago Daily Tribune* called the writing "frank and humble" and the book "engrossing." *The Long Loneliness* "has wit, humility, and humanity," the *New Yorker* concluded, "and is a good cut above the run of inspirational literature."[50]

The liberal Catholic magazine *Commonweal* ran an odd review that disappointed Day and angered her friends. "I am not going to say much about *The Long Loneliness*," the Catholic priest H. A. Reinhold wrote, before admitting that he hadn't read the *Catholic Worker* "for many years" and had never cracked any of Day's previous books. None of that prevented him from taking a whack at this one: "To me it sounds a bit weary, disenchanted, repetitious, rather too meditative; somehow the picture is painted by a faint hand and the colors are wan with sadness."[51]

Sales also disappointed Day, in part because she had already given away the royalties. In the first six months of 1952, the book sold a respectable 9,500 copies, which easily covered her $1,000 advance. Proceeds from her first royalty check went to Tamar and the Peter Maurin Farm. Almost all of the rest went to repay debts.[52]

A two-part *New Yorker* profile occasioned by *The Long Lone-liness* boosted sales and buoyed Day's profile after it appeared in October 1952. "Many people think that Dorothy Day is a saint and that she will someday be canonized," wrote Dwight Macdonald, though the case he made for Day's greatness ran through the hallowed halls of US history rather than the memory palaces of the Vatican. While reckoning with seeming contradictions in Day's character, Macdonald rightly saw that Catholic Workers themselves defied standard political classifications. "They are for the poor and against the rich, so the capitalists call them Communists; they believe in private property and don't believe in class struggle, so the Communists call them capitalists; and they are hostile to war and to the State, so both capitalists and Communists consider them crackpots," Macdonald wrote, rightly perceiving how Day was crafting an identity for herself and her followers that disregarded traditional political and religious binaries.[53]

At the *Catholic Worker*, readers were of many minds about all this attention in a Midtown Manhattan magazine that advertised Lockheed aircraft, Cartier rings, and Gigolo perfume. Its editors judged the Macdonald *New Yorker* profile to be "pretty fair." Other Catholic Workers said it had been "a terrible mistake to have allowed ourselves to be entangled with that magazine which is an outstanding source of nourishment for the bourgeoise mind." Some on the left who were not yet affiliated with the *Catholic Worker* responded by signing up. "If the Catholic Church can produce a Dorothy Day," one man said, "then that's for me."[54]

"Good Catholics Are Too Catholic"

At least since 1951, while she was still working on *The Long Lone-liness*, Day had been researching a biography of Saint Thérèse of Lisieux (1873–97), a popular French Carmelite nun who died the year Day was born, at the age of twenty-four. Known affectionately as "the Little Flower," she was revered by many Catholics for her simple faith and her pursuit of the "little way," which gloried in the small over the big, the everyday over the extraordinary, the simple act over the hero's quest. For her humility, Thérèse was deemed great—by Pope Pius X, who called her "the greatest saint of modern times," and by Mother Teresa of Calcutta, who borrowed her own name from Saint Thérèse of Lisieux. But she had her detractors, too, who described her as "the dullest of saints." "The sophisticates don't like her," Day told the *New Yorker*. "They think she is flowery and sentimental. But the common people like her, and so do I."[55]

Day's Thérèse book presented Exman with a challenge. Earlier in the 1950s he had published two biographies of Catholic nuns by a Minneapolis-based educator named Anne Cawley Boardman. Neither sold well, and Exman and Bro, who was Harper's hired fixer for both Boardman books, had struggled to shape them for general readers.

In a lengthy letter about the first biography, Bro pushed Boardman to write for a broader audience. Her book about the founder of the Dominican Sisters of the Sick Poor would be "a natural" for people interested in that sisterhood, Bro wrote, "but it ought also to be of general interest to Catholics and further to a great many Protestants."

Bro also urged Boardman to finesse the way she spoke of prayer to her "general audience," an audience Bro conflated with "the Protestant reader":

> If you can have Sister Mary's quoted prayers addressed to God or to Jesus and leave out the Infant Jesus, readers will follow along much more happily with you. I don't know what difference it makes but most Protestants are horrified at the idea of going around talking to the Baby Jesus; I guess they feel that he grew up and they would rather converse with an adult. If that isn't anthropomorphism I don't know what is, but the fact exists very strongly. Actually, most Protestants don't pray to Jesus at

all but to God in the name of Jesus. Whenever you can so express yourself as to carry the Protestant reader along with you in a devotional and highly appreciative frame of mind without in any way doing violence to your own material or to your own convictions, I think it would be a great service.[56]

Boardman's second book also frustrated Bro. "The Boardman is a terrific headache! I tell you, good Catholics are just TOO Catholic," she told Exman in a February 1954 manuscript report, adding that she had just written to Boardman "about keeping an eye on her mixed audience and trying, for goodness sake, to have a more ecumenical point of view." A month later, writing from a convent where she and Boardman were collaborating, Bro promised, "I'm not going to take my fingers off the manuscript until I feel it will be fittin' for Protestant readers as well as Catholic. What a job it is to keep a book from being too Catholic. Such uphill work!"[57]

Day sent a partial manuscript of her Thérèse book to Harper in November 1955. Exman, who found the draft wanting, called her to suggest she go to Thérèse's hometown of Lisieux to do additional research. Day refused. Exman pushed back with unusual forcefulness. I have "a very strong conviction that this is what you must do—that it is what you are meant to do," he wrote in a letter that made his case in moral, literary, and artistic terms. "There is no doubt that you can turn out a much superior piece of work if you go to the places where Marie Therese was, studying the records, reading the letters, and talking to people still living that knew her," he wrote. "You have a spiritual responsibility to Catholics and non-Catholics alike, and to Americans in particular, to interpret this saint of modern times through the eyes of an American." He then employed God's providence, Day's character, Harper's bankroll, and his own intuition in a final effort to win Day over. "If it is God's will that you go, and if it is Dorothy Day's characteristic determination to overcome obstacles, then Harper's will make it financially possible," he wrote. Day, who was not in the habit of acquiescing to institutional men without collars, refused again.[58]

In June 1956, Jim Shaw, the editor who had worked on *The Long Loneliness*, wrote Exman from Peter Maurin Farm on Staten Island, where he was working with Day on the Thérèse book. Pronouncing the manuscript "satisfactory," Shaw explained why he had left her unusual "prose style" and "thought structure" both "virtually untouched." Her "loose-jointed sentences, the omission of 'ands' where one might expect them and their use where one might prefer a new sentence, are due neither to carelessness nor haste," he wrote. "They are part of a deliberate effect and a long-standing habit of writing." As for her love of parentheticals, Shaw loved them, too. "I think that this habit, much as it may drive a logical man's mind mad, has a distinctive artistic effect. It does with thought much the same thing as Imagist poets do with images."[59]

Bro thought otherwise. In a report to Exman, she blasted the manuscript and the author in unusually hard-hitting language that oozed anti-Catholic bias. "I gather we are not discussing whether to publish but only how," given that "you are probably under an understandable spell about her," she began, before going on to register her strong dissent. "Although it has an element of soul searching it seems religiously psychotic to me," Bro said of the manuscript, before turning to the writing, which she deemed "adequate . . . but not inspired," with "no grace of phrase and no particular insight."[60]

Bro then addressed Exman, both familiarly and urgently—there was in her view more than one book at stake here—in a floridly anti-Catholic passage worth quoting at length:

> Gene, why should we promote a way of thought which counteracts the dignity of man in the eyes of God? It is really pernicious to build up a "saint" who accepts the most outlandish and preventable misery because she is "Jesus' little ball, his plaything" on whom he can try out his sadistic whims. Why should we extoll a

nun who finds out that she is haemorrhaging from [tuberculosis] of the lungs and begs her to say nothing about it so that she can go through with the severe penance of Lent, ignoring the commonsense claims of the body? This is psychopathic mortification. And it is not ancient history; much of this story happened since 1900. I just rebel at magnifying subversion of human worth even if a laudable and romantic selflessness was achieved. Hells bells, if we did all emulate the Little Flower we would have a generation of emotionally chastened nincompoops. . . . I still think I'd let the [Roman Catholics] promulgate their own doctrine while we try to develop an equally selfless personality which does not do violence to God's creation.[61]

There is no record of what Exman thought of this characterization of devotional Catholicism as sadistic, pathological, immature, and idiotic. But it did not stop him from forging ahead with the book. After Day had reworked it on and off for two years, she resubmitted it in October 1958. Exman initially received it with "pleasure and excitement." However, after showing it to new readers, he told Day in person in his office two months later that he could not publish it. "The intellectual Catholic readers were against it," Day reported in her diary, and a competing biography on Saint Thérèse was coming out at Pantheon. The book was "just not good enough," she told a friend in a letter. "Not my style, according to them." Exman, who desperately wanted to keep Day as a Harper author, suggested that she publish it privately through the *Catholic Worker* (for $1.50 instead of Harper's expected $5) and offered to help make that happen by advancing money to print it and absorbing the costs of Shaw's editorial work. The book finally appeared as *Therese* with Fides Press in 1960.[62]

It is hard to know what role Bro's anti-Catholicism played in killing the book. Day aficionados largely agree that *Therese* is not a good book, and it *was* a hard project to spin to general readers. But Bro did have Exman's ear, and though he did not always follow her advice, it is hard to imagine that her characterization of Saint Thérèse's piety as "sadistic" and "psychopathic" had no effect.

Loaves and Fishes

Exman and Day pressed ahead with another project, and by the spring of 1960 he was offering her a contract for a book telling the story of the Catholic Worker movement. Her working title was *The Last Eleven Years.* Harper lobbied for *The Cost of Love.* It appeared in 1963 as *Loaves and Fishes.*[63]

Thomas Merton, whose *Seven Storey Mountain* had made him a literary star well beyond Catholic circles, called *Loaves and Fishes* " a serious book about matters of life and death, not only for a few people, but for everybody." The Christian socialist Norman Thomas characterized it as a "sequel to the beloved autobiography of this 'patron saint of Skid Row.'" But it isn't exactly a sequel and it wasn't for everybody. It reprised roughly the last third of *The Long Loneliness*, from the arrival of Peter Maurin in 1932 to his death in 1949, while shifting the focus from Day to her Catholic Workers.[64]

There are chapters that amount to mini essays, including one on poverty as a scourge and a vocation. There are observations on the touchpoints of Day's thought and action, including her keyword of *love* and her disdain for the cult of consumption. Day also narrates the conflicts that arose out of her decision to open Catholic Worker farms and houses of hospitality to everyone, including racists and anti-Semites who at any moment might turn any one of them into "a house of hostility." Such is the "cost of love," Day shrugs, an unfortunate by-product of the Catholic Worker policy of radical inclusion.[65]

What is most striking about *Loaves and Fishes* is its heavy reliance on compact character sketches of hundreds of people who moved in and out of her houses of hospitality, farms, and newspaper offices. These portraits are affectionate yet honest, confessions of the sins and shortfalls of Day and her Catholic Workers. They also amount to her own personalist manifesto.

The chapter on Peter Maurin begins, "We loved him dearly, this Peter of ours, and revered him as a saint, but we neglected him, too. He asked nothing for himself, so he got nothing." Later, Day admits that Maurin, though certainly a saint, wasn't easy to like. "He was twenty years older than I," she explained. "He spoke with an accent so thick it was hard to penetrate to the thought beneath, he had a one-track mind, he did not like music, he did not read Dickens or Dostoevski, and he did not bathe."[66]

In the Hindu tradition, devotees who go to temples to encounter their chosen gods engage in *darshan*, or sacred seeing. In this intimate practice, the heart of Hindu devotionalism, devotees look into the eyes of their chosen divinity and that god or goddess looks back. Day and other Catholic Workers did something similar, but instead of seeing Christ in a wood carving they saw him in the poor, and in one another. These intimate encounters were social, political, and ethical. They were also mystical—opportunities to encounter the divine mystery up close and personal in other human beings.

The Second Vatican Council (1962–65), a global gathering of Roman Catholic bishops also known as Vatican II, was meeting in Rome when *Loaves and Fishes* appeared. At this council, bishops declared that their church was its people, not its hierarchy. Day made that same point in *Loaves and Fishes* and in her life: The Catholic Worker is not its newspaper or its farms or its houses of hospitality. It is neither Day nor Maurin. It is everyone who chooses poverty in order to love the poor, and it is the poor themselves. Some of these people are likable. Others, not so much. But to Day they all offer an opportunity—*the* opportunity: to love the god in everyone you encounter, through tangible acts of mercy.

Day, who praised Saint Francis as a "great personalist," is often referred to as a personalist herself. This vague term is hard to define, because it has been put to very different uses in philosophy, in theology, and in ordinary language. Martin Luther King Jr. was influenced by the Boston Personalists of Boston University who believed that personality was the fundamental fact about both divine and human life. Day got her personalism from Maurin and the Catholic social justice tradition. "We are Personalists because we believe that man, a person, a creature of body and soul, is greater than the State," she wrote. "We are Personalists because we oppose the vesting of all authority in the hands of the state instead of in the hands of Christ the King."[67]

Insofar as *personalist* refers to someone who values persons over institutions, and who thinks of religion in personal rather than social terms, it applies as well to Exman and to his Book of Books, which emphasized the personal voice and the biographical and autobiographical genres. Exman's central unit of analysis was neither nation nor society nor community nor family. It was the person. That is why he wrote so many articles, gave so many talks, and published so many books, including Day's *Long Loneliness*, about the lives of saints. Characteristically, Exman did not understand this term narrowly. To him a saint was anyone who lived a life characterized by a persistent and disciplined effort to search for God and to make the world a more just and equitable place.

In her autobiographical writing, Day demonstrated the power of individuals who seek to imitate Christ. Her key actors were neither churches nor nation-states. They were persons who help. Who love. Who look into the faces of the poor, the hungry, and the homeless and respond as if to Christ. This was the "personalist revolution" for which Day labored.[68]

She waged that revolution on every page of *Loaves and Fishes*, which is less a history of the Catholic Worker movement than a series of lovingly drawn portraits. As she describes Peter Maurin Farm, she focuses on the farm's "family": "Today there is an old newspaperman who has come to stay with us while he recovers from a long illness; a pretty young girl who is pregnant, and whose family doesn't know it; a man who sits quietly in a corner trying to get over a spree on the Bowery; a Negro girl from the south and her two little children." Elsewhere in *Loaves and Fishes* readers encounter Jack English, who came to the Catholic Worker from a POW camp in Romania and left to become a Trappist priest in Conyers, Georgia; "Dan, who sold the paper on the streets; Slim Borne, who washes dishes"; and Stanley Vishnewski, a "cradle Catholic" who, despite his conviction that converts like Day were "rash and reckless" anarchists, had been with the Catholic Worker for twenty-seven years. Many of these people get a few sentences, or even just a part of one. Then an exquisite short chapter pops up—"What Has Become of Anna?"—a prose poem almost, about an enigmatic woman who came by a Catholic Worker house warily and then gratefully, only to meet a tragic end.[69]

The book's closing chapter ends with a gift to that elusive "everybody" to whom Merton commended the book, and especially the Protestants Exman and Day hoped would buy it. It reprises a typical day in the life of the Catholic Worker, and on the last page there is a psalm and a hymn. But there is also the sort of labor that doubles as prayer, freely offered by "Marie, who is a Protestant." When the singing is over, "Marie picks up her broom and begins to sweep. Readying the room for tomorrow is her last act of today," Day writes. "She is always the last to leave. When her work is done, she pauses near the door, and then, with a little look-around of satisfaction, departs."[70]

Anti-Catholic Bias

More persistently than any other observer of American Catholicism, the Northwestern professor Robert Orsi has pointed out how anti-Catholic bias, which dismisses Catholic practice as "something of the past, not the present," has operated inside liberal Protestant and other groups widely believed to be tolerant, inclusive, and pluralistic. Today "spiritual but not religious" is widely thought to signal a broad-minded cohort that, among other things, prefers personal spirituality over organized religion. But what does this phrase mean? Orsi writes: "It means my religion is interior, self-determined, individual, free of authority; my religion is about ethics and not about bizarre events, and my ethics are a matter of personal choice, not of law; I take orders from no one. In the context of Western history, this means, 'I am not Catholic.'"[71] Exman does not exactly fit this description. He was obsessed with "bizarre events," which he featured in his Book of Books, where readers encountered volumes by and about mediums who channeled spirits of the dead, plus a hall of fame of medieval Catholic mystics. But the norms of Protestantism were normal to Exman and most of his authors. So it should not be surprising to learn that Bro thought Day odd, and that Day felt at odds at times with Exman and his coworkers.

Day had an interior spiritual life and ethical religion that Exman and his Protestant readers could easily recognize. And her agonizing conversion was a matter of personal choice and willpower. But she did not believe her life was entirely self-determined. The way she narrated both *The Long Loneliness* and *Loaves and Fishes* made room for divine providence (as Exman did in his own autobiographical reflections). In her telling, the germs of her adult faith were planted in her by God and nurtured by friends who gave her rosaries and took her to Mass. And for all her professed anarchism, she was willing to take orders from Catholic bishops.

In her diaries and letters, Day writes that she felt at odds with Harper in various ways, but she seems to have agreed with Exman that, to write successful trade books, she would need to navigate with care the Protestant/Catholic divide that she had crossed when she left Forster and became a Catholic. While working on *The Long Loneliness*, she admitted to a friend that her columns were slapdash in comparison with a carefully produced book. "When writing in haste in the *Worker* one gets away with murder," she wrote. "But when you are working for the *New Yorker* or for Harper's you must be very slick and sophisticated, also grammatical!"[72]

Day's disagreements with Harper employees were more about

substance than style, including the substance of the godly life. Regarding prayers addressed to the baby Jesus, Bro had cajoled Boardman to rewrite them in order to "carry the Protestant reader along" without, of course, "doing violence" to her own convictions. But therein lay the rub, and as a person of conviction Day saw it plainly. She was on board with writing in ways that non-Catholics could understand and with reaching more people (and getting more royalties) in the process. But she rightly resented how Exman and his coworkers worked to recast her story in the image of Protestantism.

Just after *The Long Loneliness* appeared, and while Dwight Macdonald was interviewing her for the *New Yorker,* Day wrote a letter to a friend expressing her resentment of the anti-Catholic uses to which the folks in New York were putting her words and work. "I hate being used as a club to beat the Church and the hierarchy over the head with. I am a loyal Catholic and please God intend to remain one to the end of my days," she wrote, adding, "I have no reservations when I say I mean obedient Catholic."[73]

There were also points of doctrine that coarsened Day's relationship with Exman. As a mystic, he was convinced of the reality of the mysterious and unseen things that many of his fellow Protestants wrote off as metaphors. He believed in mystical encounters with the divine, including his own that night on the road to Blanchester. He believed in a saintliness that surpasses all human understanding. But as Day worked on *The Long Loneliness,* she kept bumping heads with "liberals like Harpers, Sugrue, Macdonald" about her unapologetic affirmation of traditional Catholic doctrine. "I believe that Christ's body and blood are present in the sacrament and that I partake of it as truly as I partook of my mother's milk," she wrote of the Catholic doctrine of transubstantiation. But those liberals kept imagining that she "took it as a symbol." Not so, Day wrote. "I literally believe. Lord help my unbelief."[74]

These tensions surfaced not only with the Saint Thérèse manuscript but also with *Loaves and Fishes.* Just after Christmas 1962, as *Loaves* was about to go to press, Day wrote a pointed letter to

Exman. Her copyeditor, Edward Sammis, had made last-minute changes "which do not convey my meaning," Day protested, and had substituted his views for hers in a chapter he had written entirely on his own. "This is nonsense," she told Exman. "The thing is a hodge-podge now and I must register my complete dissatisfaction" until it "is restored to some measure of its former meaning." Exman wrote back immediately, reassuring her that all would be well. "You must be satisfied with the book," he told her.[75]

Exman understood Day's complaints because he felt at odds himself with Harper corporate culture and with modern American life, particularly on the Eastern Seaboard. He believed in the divine Presence. He refused to reduce his deepest religious experiences to metaphor. When he encountered something new and strange in the world of religion, his reflex was to affirm rather than to deny. Yet when it came to working with Day, he and his coworkers found it impossible to reckon with her on equal terms. She was sadistic, Bro said. She needed to ditch the dogma so Protestants could say amen to what she had to say. Day, to her credit, was humble enough to wonder whether the fault was partly, even largely, hers. "I am a journalist, not a biographer, not a *book* writer," she confessed in *The Long Loneliness*. But she saw the big picture clearly. She understood that she and Harper were engaged in a clash of civilizations. A clash between the rich and the poor, yes. (Harper, she wrote, was a "big bourgeois firm.") But also a clash between Catholic and Protestant worlds—a clash Exman typically "won," but not without revealing the fault lines in his Protestant pluralism, its intolerance in the face of real religious difference.[76]

Despite their love songs to pluralism, liberal Protestants in the United States have rarely found their way to doing anything kindlier with Roman Catholics than agreeing to follow Jesus's commandment to "love your enemies." This should not be surprising, as Protestantism originated in sixteenth-century Europe with a series of protests against Roman Catholic popes, priests, and practices. Later Protestants continued to identify themselves, as their forebears had during the Reformation, over against Roman Catholics, emphasizing their greater (and superior) emphasis on the Bible, their more egalitarian attitudes toward ministers, and their elimination of many Catholic sacraments. Of all the religious antagonisms that have bubbled up and boiled over during the course of United States history, anti-Catholicism has been the most persistent. Groups such as the Transcendentalists and the Theosophists, who found it impossible not to love the ancient wisdom of Asian scriptures, found it impossible to love much of anything about modern Catholicism, which was for them *the* model of the "organized religion" they loved to hate.

Day's ascent as an American icon—she was the face of pacifism in the 1960s and beyond—demonstrates the strides Roman Catholics made in the United States during the Cold War. Alongside President Kennedy, who in 1960 became the first Catholic elected president, she demonstrates that the anti-Catholicism she experienced at Harper, while hurtful, was of a very different order from the anti-Catholicism that saw churches burned and dozens of Catholics killed a century earlier.

By the time *Loaves and Fishes* appeared, Dorothy Day had become the voice of American Catholic conscience as surely as Martin Luther King Jr. had become the voice of American Protestant conscience—an advocate on behalf of the poor in a world where capitalism seemed to be impoverishing more people every day, and on behalf of peace at a time when the military-industrial complex was inventing not only new sorts of bombs but also new reasons to drop them. Like King, however, Day put her body on the line. She was arrested a dozen times, the last alongside Cesar Chavez and the United Farm Workers in 1973, just two years before Exman's death. When she died on November 29, 1980, the *New York Times* remembered her as "a nonviolent social radical of luminous personality." David O'Brien, a historian of American Catholicism, eulogized her as "the most significant, interesting, and influential person in the history of American Catholicism." On November 4, 2022, as Roman Catholic authorities continued to weigh her case for sainthood, New York City Mayor Eric Adams commissioned a new vessel for the Staten Island Ferry in her name: the *Dorothy Day*.[77]

Unlike almost all of Exman's bestselling authors, Dorothy Day never became his friend. He took her side in many in-house Harper discussions. He visited her at one of her houses of hospitality. He showed up at retreats where she was speaking. He sent her kind letters and encouraging postcards. He recommended her for things, including a seat on the board of the World Parliament of Religions in 1952. That same year, he referred to Day in a letter as one of Gerald Heard's "peers," alongside AA founder Bill Wilson and others.[78] This would have heartened Day, who admired Heard, whom she had known through pacifist circles since the 1930s. But she and Exman were never buddies. Exman helped raise thousands of dollars for a college founded in Naples by his Catholic friend Bruno Scott James, but the only record we have of him assisting the *Catholic Worker* is a ten-dollar check he wrote to Day's fall appeal in 1960.

Why? Gender is part of the answer. Publishing was even more of a man's world in Exman's lifetime than it is today. Another factor was economic class. Though born poor on a family farm, Exman had become a bourgeois editor at a bourgeois firm, and Day's voluntary poverty both thrilled and shamed him. Yet another factor was religion. Yes, Exman published Catholics eagerly during the Cold War. In the 1950s, his catalogs began to include lists of "books by Catholics, or of special interest to Catholics," and by the spring of 1960 he was publishing separate catalogs of "Harper's Books of Special Interest to Catholics." Beginning with *The Phenomenon of Man*, which became a runaway bestseller in 1959, he brought the French Catholic philosopher and scientist Pierre Teilhard de Chardin (posthumously) to the attention of American readers. Exman also had plenty of Catholic friends, but they were all liberal Catholics who were on board with his criticisms of dogma and ritual and "organized religion."

The inclusion of *The Long Loneliness* and *Loaves and Fishes* in Exman's Book of Books was part of the slow march toward inclusion, diversity, and cosmopolitanism in American religious life at the middle of the twentieth century. So was Day's emergence as a countercultural icon. However, her difficulties at Harper, and with Exman, demonstrate that this pluralism came with Protestant strings attached. Other Catholic authors on Exman's list had fewer troubles in editorial meetings than Day did. That was in part because they were liberals, in part because they were men, and in part because they were respectable members of society. But it was also because Day had more conviction than they did, because she was less motivated by money, and because she had the willpower (and the power) to push back.

CHAPTER FIVE

African Missions, Colonialism, and *The World of Albert Schweitzer*

On September 12, 1950, Eugene Exman boarded the S.S. *Ile de France* in New York City and headed for Plymouth, England. It was the first leg of a long pilgrimage to Lambaréné, a small Central African village on the banks of the Ogowe River, some 125 miles from the coast of French Equatorial Africa (now Gabon). A hurricane had just passed along the Eastern Seaboard, so his luxury liner cut through big waves and rolled to the rhythms of long swells as it crossed the Atlantic. For a few hours each morning during the seven-day crossing, Exman edited a manuscript of Gerald Heard's novel *The Black Fox*. He meditated daily, kept a diary of his voyage, and drafted letters. He also marveled at the meals prepared by the French chefs, including snails at lunch ("Out of this world," he told Sunny), caviar at dinner, and at least one ten-course "Captain's Dinner." He also reflected in his diary on the meaning of the "blue-block impersonality" of the ocean. "We take the large tracts of land for granted and we savage them by dividing states into countries," he wrote, as if channeling Henry David Thoreau. "But the sea is vaster really; and seems much more so because it can't be sectioned off."[1]

Pilgrims typically set off for a sacred place—Mecca, Jerusalem,

Vatican City. Some go in search of holy people. Exman's pilgrimage was of the latter sort. He was seeking out a man he would later list alongside Fosdick, Thurman, and King as the greatest influences on his life. Exman's mother had died fewer than two weeks before he shipped out, and he was conflicted about leaving his family behind during a two-month journey that would find him in England, France, Germany, Switzerland, Portugal, and Africa. But he took comfort in marking his adopted son Frank's first day at Cornell and thinking of Wally rushing fraternities at Denison. He was comforted as well by the belief that providence was favoring his journey to the celebrated theologian, philosopher, musician, doctor, humanitarian, and mystic Albert Schweitzer. "I must continue my faith that God has a plan in which my little effort plays some part," he wrote in his ship diary.[2]

Regarding Schweitzer, Exman was an early adopter. By the time Exman left for Africa in the fall of 1950, Schweitzer had achieved fame in Europe and the United States. He had appeared on the cover of *TIME*, and *Life* had called him "the greatest man in the world." Gerald Heard was only slightly more measured. "I'm glad that Schweitzer's philosophic outlook appeals to you," he wrote to Exman in the summer of 1949. "Now that Gandhi is gone he probably represents best the ideal of the world citizen whose outlook is based on religion." As for Exman, he had been publishing books about Schweitzer since 1944, including two biographies by his friend the Anglican clergyman George Seaver, who interpreted Schweitzer as a "Christian revolutionary." Exman saw Schweitzer as a fellow mystic with whom he shared the conviction that mysticism and ethics were two sides of one coin.[3]

In 1949, during Schweitzer's only United States visit, Exman had accompanied him on a round-trip train ride from New York City to a festival in Aspen, Colorado. That trip was for business and pleasure. Schweitzer was reportedly working on his theological magnum opus, and Exman was determined to sign it up. To do so would be a coup comparable to signing Barack or Michelle Obama today. However, with the demise of Trabuco earlier that year, Exman was also looking for a new spiritual exemplar, perhaps one who embodied this-worldly sacrifice more than the otherworldly Heard could ever muster. He wanted to sit at the feet of a living saint, to learn what Schweitzer had to teach.

Schweitzer was widely known as a modern-day renunciant. After making a reputation as a philosopher, theologian, author, and musician, and accumulating doctoral degrees along the way, he traded it all in to become a village doctor in Africa. He traveled fourth-class by rail. He carried his own bags. And he wore his clothes for decades, with appropriate repairs along the way. These commitments had turned him into one of the most intriguing people in the world. Why had this extraordinary man given up so much for so little? And would his reputation as a medical miracle man turn as African colonies gained their independence?

On his way to Africa, Exman spent a month in Europe that again mixed work and play. He made no effort there to observe a Schweitzer-like path of voluntary poverty. After docking in Plymouth, he continued on to London, where he met with Schweitzer's wife, Helene, and then with writers and publishers, running into his own author Anson Phelps Stokes on an elevator at the five-star Connaught Hotel, where they were both staying. Exman went on a shopping spree at Harrods department store with the Boston-based Beacon Press editor Mel Arnold (whom he would soon lure to Harper), purchasing socks and sweaters for himself and Chanel perfume and linen tablecloths and napkins for Sunny. He saw John Gielgud play a senile King Lear at the Shakespeare Memorial Theatre in Stratford-upon-Avon. He toured the Lake District. With Emmy Martin, Schweitzer's close friend and adviser, he toured Schweitzer's birthplace in Kaysersberg and his headquarters in Gunsbach (now both in France). Though charmed by roads "crowded with ox carts carrying loads of grapes" destined to be transformed into dry Alsatian wine, he was saddened by "signs of demolition" in villages "shelled and nearly destroyed by our troops." From nearby

Strasbourg, he took the Orient Express to Stuttgart, Germany. He bought a beret outside Paris. As his European adventures wound down, he flew from Paris to Lisbon, staying in the lavish Palace Hotel in Estoril, twenty miles west of Portugal's capital city.[4]

Another flight, this time on a modest, forty-five-passenger clipper plane, made three stops before depositing him some twenty-two hours and 3,450 miles later in Leopoldville, now Kinshasa in the Democratic Republic of the Congo. It was Exman's first long plane trip, and he warded off anxiety by recalling his spiritual goals. "I must not be hurried or anxious. There is a reason for my coming here and I have often been reminded of God's providence and care," he wrote in his diary. "Here I should try more and more to live for the day that now is—for what it gives—and not . . . be anxious about what is to come."[5]

During the remaining six hundred miles of his journey, Exman roughed it by train, truck, and dugout canoe. A thirty-two-hour trip on a "leisurely, French-owned, native-manned, fourth-class train" from Leopoldville to Dolisie offered him an opportunity to test his patience. Excruciatingly slow—it averaged six-and-a-half miles an hour—the wood-and-coal-fired steam train had to stop every fifteen miles or so to load wood and gather steam, and there were nineteen stations where passengers and freight had to be loaded and unloaded, plus various rest stops for the crew. Exman counted "more than two hundred of us—I the only white person" on the train, where he did his best to communicate in "halting French."[6]

Next came a bone-crushing drive in a Dodge truck along a gravel road from Dolisie to Lambaréné. At one stop in a small village, Exman noticed a boy staring at him and recalled his earlier self. "I look into his eyes and see, all of a sudden, another boy, not in Gabon, but in Ohio," he wrote. "A farm boy, in town with his parents for Saturday afternoon shopping, has slipped away to the railway station to see the Baltimore and Ohio Capitol Limited go through." Unlike this young Eugene, who is astonished by the train, this boy (at least in Exman's imagining) is astonished to see that human skin can be "so colorless."[7]

The last stretch of Exman's journey took him four miles by dugout canoe upriver to Schweitzer's hospital, where he arrived at 5 p.m. on October 15, 1950, right at the start of spring and just at the end of tea time. Exman shared news of Schweitzer's family and friends in Europe, and soon the two men were laughing and recalling the misadventures of their cross-country trip together a year earlier. As the "shaggy philosopher-theologian-musician-surgeon" showed him around, Exman thought to himself, "This is it!"[8]

Intellectual Wandering

Albert Schweitzer was born on January 14, 1875, in Kaysersberg in Alsace, a contested borderland that long alternated between French and German rule. Though Alsace lies today in northeastern France, where the Vosges Mountains slope down to meet the Rhine River, almost all of it was ceded to Germany in 1871, so Schweitzer grew up speaking German, French, and the Alsatian German dialect. He wrote most of his books in German, which he considered his native tongue, but his family spoke Alsatian and wrote in French. (Schweitzer's many letters to Exman were typically written in French.) During Schweitzer's lifetime, the French never quite accepted him. Many Germans embraced him as an honorary German. Schweitzer saw himself as an Alsatian and a citizen of the world. When asked about his competing loyalties to the countries that had long contested for his native land, and for a share in his reputation, Schweitzer replied (in neither French nor German), "*Homo sum*": "I am a human being."[9]

His father, Louis Schweitzer, was a Lutheran minister, as was the father of his mother, Adele Schillinger Schweitzer. The famed American socialist of the early twentieth century Eugene Debs and the French existentialist and playwright Jean-Paul Sartre were both cousins. Albert's parents moved months after his birth to Gunsbach, ten miles from Kaysersberg, where Louis pastored a church for fifty years, until his death in 1925. Albert's uncle was also a minister—at the Church of Saint Nicholas in nearby Strasbourg, a position Schweitzer himself would later occupy.

Schweitzer grew up with the stories of the New Testament gospels, the cadences of his father's liberal Protestant sermons, and the sounds of music. His mother's father built organs, three of his uncles played the organ, and by the age of nine he was a substitute organist at his father's church. Away from the organ, Schweitzer was a mediocre student. In the summer of 1893, when he was eighteen years old, one of his uncles arranged for him to go to Paris to study with Charles-Marie Widor, a world-famous organist who set him on a path to becoming a world-famous interpreter of the composer Johann Sebastian Bach. Along that path, Schweitzer juggled his commitment to music with commitments to theology and philosophy, which he began studying in the fall of 1893 at the University of Strasbourg. Though his studies were interrupted by a year of required military service, he did well enough to go on to graduate work in Paris, Berlin, and Strasbourg.

A strong inclination toward intellectual wandering—from the life of Jesus to the philosophy of Kant to the compositions of Bach— did nothing to arrest his academic progress. At the University of Strasbourg, he finished his doctoral thesis on Kant in March 1899, earning his philosophy doctorate four months later. He then wrote two theological theses, both on the life of Jesus. The first earned him a doctoral degree in theology in 1900. The second, a postdoctoral "habilitation" degree completed in 1902, credentialed him to work as a professor in German higher education. That same year, Schweitzer was hired as a lecturer in theology at the University of Strasbourg. In 1903, he was appointed principal of its Theological College of Saint Thomas. Building on his New Testament research, he later published two different editions of *The Quest of the Historical Jesus*

(1906 and 1913), which earned him an international reputation in New Testament studies that endures to this day.

Somehow Schweitzer also managed to find time to study the philosophies and religions of India and China. Years later, he would publish those findings as *Christianity and the Religions of the World* (1923) and *Indian Thought and Its Development* (1935). Though a Protestant thinker, Schweitzer was an empathetic reader of Indian scriptures. His graduate school faculties offered no courses on Indian thought, but he read independently in Indian ethics and was drawn to Hindu theories of karma. The Indian principle of ahimsa, or nonviolence, which would play a major role in Gandhi's nonviolent resistance strategy (and, through Gandhi, in the civil rights strategies of Martin Luther King Jr.), also informed Schweitzer's ethics, as did the tendency in Indian ethics to think in terms of "sentient beings" rather than humans alone.

Schweitzer supported himself during his doctoral studies by working as an assistant minister at the Church of Saint Nicholas and by giving organ concerts across Europe. According to a Bach scholar, those concerts made him "the world's best-known organist . . . far better known than Bach had ever been."[10] Meanwhile, his wax cylinder recordings introduced Bach to listeners outside of churches and concert halls, and his biography of Bach, published in French in 1905, established him as a bona fide Bach scholar.

Schweitzer also found time to pursue a relationship with Helene Bresslau, the daughter of Jewish parents who had tried to shield her from growing anti-Semitism by baptizing her as a child. There was talk of marriage, but Schweitzer warned her (correctly, it turned out) that a marriage between them would not work out well.

Into the Congo

As a biographer, Schweitzer homed in on moments when his subjects—Jesus, Paul, Bach, Kant—made key decisions, acted on them, and changed the courses of their lives (and human history). He did the same in narrating his own life story.

His first key moment came in 1896 at the age of twenty-one while he was studying in Gunsbach. Immersed in his studies in philosophy, theology, and music, he was at the time a contented young man, so much so that his contentment troubled him. "It struck me as incomprehensible that I should be allowed to lead such a happy life, while I saw so many people around me wrestling with care and suffering," he later wrote. "I resolved to devote my life till I was thirty to the office of preacher, to science, and to music." Thereafter, he would dedicate himself to the "direct service of humanity." But where? And how? Schweitzer worked for a time with orphans, released prisoners, and the homeless. Nothing clicked.[11]

His grand plan crystallized in a second key moment in the fall of 1904. Opening a copy of a French missionary journal, his eye fixed on an article pleading for missionaries to go to the Congo with the Paris Missionary Society. By the time he finished the article, he had decided to serve humanity in Africa. "My search was over," he later said.[12]

Schweitzer wanted to go to Africa as a missionary, but because of his liberal theology and his controversial views on the historical Jesus, the Paris Missionary Society turned him down. In the fall of 1905, to the disappointment of his family, his professors, his university colleagues, his organ teacher, and millions of fans of his music, he announced his plan to go to Africa as a doctor. Resigning from the Theological College of Saint Thomas, he enrolled in medical school. "It was for me a spiritual experience," Schweitzer later said of his seven-year medical education, which fatigued him more than anything he had ever done.[13] Nonetheless, he managed to publish during those hard years his two books on the quest for the historical Jesus; an expanded, two-volume German edition of his Bach biography (in 1908); and *Paul and His Interpreters* (1911). He also got married, in June 1912, to the previously mentioned Helene Bresslau, who, with an eye on helping her husband in Africa, became proficient in general nursing and anesthesia. In 1913, he earned his third doctorate, in medicine. Unable to kick his New Testament studies habit, he wrote a doctoral thesis titled "The Psychiatric Study of Jesus."

As he was preparing for his new life in Africa, he and the Paris Missionary Society arrived at a compromise. Schweitzer would stick to medical rather than missionary work, remaining "as mute as a fish" when it came to theology. He would also finance his hospital himself, through proceeds from his writing and organ playing, via donations from European friends, and by going into debt. Schweitzer further promised that his work would be "undenominational and international." Any good he and Helene might do, they would do as a human beings and "not members of any particular nation or religious body."[14]

On Good Friday, March 21, 1913, Schweitzer and Helene stepped onto a train in Gunsbach and set out for a new life. After sailing down the European and African coasts, they disembarked at Cape Lopez, once a major port in the slave trade to the Americas. A paddleboat steamer took them up the Ogowe River, arriving at Lambaréné on April 16. One final hour-long stretch by canoe landed them at the missionary station, where they were to build their hospital, 40 miles south of the equator and 125 miles from the Atlantic coast.

The Schweitzers bootstrapped their operation by working with leaders of two nearby tribes, the Fang and the Galoa, who helped build, maintain, and staff it. The Schweitzers and their assistants treated two thousand patients in their first nine months, with Schweitzer operating on hernias and attending to "skin and elephantiasis ulcers, leprosy, sleeping sickness, scabies, dysentery, malaria, heart disease, venereal disease, toothache, and broken bones."[15]

In 1914, just a year after the Schweitzers arrived in Lambaréné, World War I broke out. As holders of German passports, they were placed under house arrest as enemy aliens. It was difficult to bring food, medical supplies, and money to Lambaréné, and the Schweitzers suffered from anemia. Schweitzer had written earlier of the demise of Western civilization, but like so many others of his generation, his Christian faith was shaken by the war. He spent his downtime trying out ethical and mystical ideas that would eventually lead him to develop and refine his signature ideal: Reverence for Life.

Schweitzer had experimented with this concept a few years earlier in his Strasbourg classroom, describing the divine mystery that lies at the core of all life as the source of this universal ethical ideal, which he saw as an ethic of radical care, visible in all cultures and somehow animating even those atheists who alter their gait to avoid stepping on a worm. For years Schweitzer continued to turn this concept over in his head, without ever fully formulating it. When that formulation finally came, it arrived, Schweitzer said, as an "unexpected discovery, like a revelation in the midst of intense thought."[16]

This third key moment in his life occurred in September 1915. Helene had contracted tuberculosis shortly after the Schweitzers arrived in Africa, and it had now worsened. She and her husband had decamped to Cape Lopez in an effort to nurse her back to health. Schweitzer was on a barge moving up the Ogowe River in search of an ailing missionary's wife. It was slow going, and he was "lost in thought" as he struggled "to find the elementary and universal conception of the ethical" he was seeking. For months he had been working to no avail on this ideal. "I was wandering about in a thicket in which no path was to be found. I was leaning with all my might against an iron door which would not yield," he wrote. Then a new thought came to him with the shock of revelation:

Late on the third day, at the very moment when, at sunset, we were making our way through a herd of hippopotamuses, there flashed upon my mind, unforeseen and unthought, the phrase Reverence for Life. The iron door had yielded: the path in the thicket had become visible. Now I had found my way to the idea in which world- and life-affirmation and ethics are contained side by side! Now I knew that the world view of ethical world- and life-affirmation together with its ideals of civilization is founded in thought.[17]

This perennial moral principle emerged out of Schweitzer's reflections on Eastern and Western thought—from Kant's efforts to find a universal morality to Schopenhauer's emphasis on the will to the Indian ethic of nonviolence. It said that we should respect the lives of all beings, because all beings thirst for life. Drawing on Indian religions, Schweitzer insisted that this ethic extends not only to human life but also to animals and plants. All living things are our neighbors. Each has a will to live. Their lives, too, must be respected as our own.

In November 1917, after fewer than five years in Africa and as World War I was grinding on, Schweitzer and Helene were deported by French authorities and interned as "hostile foreigners." During this physical and mental ordeal, which took them to Bordeaux, a former monastery in the Pyrenees, and a sanitorium in Saint-Rémy-de-Provence that once housed Vincent van Gogh, Helene suffered yet another tuberculosis relapse. Schweitzer contracted dysentery and slipped into a deep depression. After being released in a prisoner exchange in July 1918, they returned to Alsace, where their only child, Rhena, was born on January 14, 1919. To support his wife and newborn daughter, Schweitzer returned to his prior job as an assistant minister at Saint Nicholas. He also worked as a medical doctor. As he endured surgeries for complications from dysentery, he struggled to account for the losses the war had visited on him—of his hospital, his health, and his dream of working on behalf of humanity.

Then came what he regarded as the fourth and final turning point in his life: a letter, received on Christmas Eve 1919, from Nathan Söderblom, a Church of Sweden archbishop, asking him to lecture at the University of Uppsala. "The invitation came as a complete surprise," Schweitzer later explained. "In my isolation at Strasbourg, ever since the war I had felt rather like a coin that has rolled under a piece of furniture and has been forgotten there." Söderblom, who would later win the Nobel Peace Prize, brought light and air into Schweitzer's world once again. In an organ concert in Barcelona he saw "that as an artist I was still appreciated." His Uppsala lectures proved that his thinking was still appreciated, too. Returning to Strasbourg, he made quick work of a book a Swedish woman had urged him to write: an autobiographical account of his time in Lambaréné. Though written in German, it first appeared in 1921 in a Swedish translation. (*On the Edge of the Primeval Forest* was the English title.) Schweitzer resigned from his medical and church jobs, and prepared to return to Africa.

When he made it back in 1924 (without Helene or Rhena), the jungle had reclaimed his hospital. Schweitzer got it up and running, but by 1926 he had moved to a new, larger facility two miles up and across the river. For the next four decades, he propagated and refuted the myth of himself as a modern-day renunciant who went to Africa as Thoreau had gone to Walden Pond (but at greater cost and to greater effect). Schweitzer spent most of the rest of his life at Lambaréné without Helene, whose tuberculosis restricted her travel. But he returned home regularly, shuttling back and forth between Africa and Europe more than a dozen times. While in Europe, he recuperated from the strains of the jungle and spent time with his family. He also raised money for his hospital by lecturing, playing concerts, and accumulating honorary degrees and other awards.

By the start of 1949, Schweitzer had been at Lambaréné uninterrupted for nearly a decade. Helene had been able to join him from 1941 to 1946, riding out much of World War II by his side. Harvard, Yale, and Princeton had invited Schweitzer to come to the United States to lecture, but he turned them all down. Then the University of Chicago chancellor Robert Hutchins invited Schweitzer to speak at a festival he was planning in Aspen, Colorado, for July 1949. The occasion was the two-hundredth anniversary of the German polymath Johann Wolfgang von Goethe, who had captured Schweitzer's attention during his academic years. To sweeten the pot, Hutchins offered Schweitzer an honorary degree at the University of Chicago. Now well into his seventies, Schweitzer wanted to decline the offer, but after he realized that he could turn the fee (over $6,000) into a leper hospital he had been wanting to build, he reluctantly agreed to make his first and only trip to the United States.

One biographer has argued that Schweitzer was "barely known" to Americans before that visit, only to become "a media star in the USA overnight." That is not quite right. Though he was more celebrated in Europe, his fame had been building gradually across the Atlantic. As early as 1925, the ethicist and theologian Reinhold Niebuhr had said of Schweitzer that history might "set him down as one of the greatest men of the twentieth century." But Schweitzer did not begin to gather a significant American audience until the 1940s. Exman published a handful of Schweitzer books early in that decade, and Mel Arnold at Beacon Press, a Boston-based Unitarian effort, contributed a half dozen more. In 1946, *Reader's Digest* celebrated Schweitzer in a story called "God's Eager Fool." In 1947, *Life* magazine featured him. As news of his US visit spread, photographers and journalists knew enough about the man to besiege him when an ocean liner deposited him in Hoboken on June 28, 1949, and to follow his trail to Aspen and Chicago. Exman and Arnold helped drum up publicity for this tour, which led to a *TIME* cover story that anointed Schweitzer "one of the most extraordinary men of modern times."[18]

Schweitzer's guide on his American visit was Dr. Emory Ross, an African missionary and longtime Schweitzer associate. Exman was able to arrange with Ross to join him and Schweitzer on the train to and from Aspen. At the Goethe Festival, Schweitzer spoke on July 8 in French, with Ross interpreting, and again on July 10 in German, with the translation provided by Exman's friend the celebrated playwright Thornton Wilder. Exman was also at the University of Chicago on July 11 when Schweitzer received an honorary doctorate, followed by an impromptu organ concert at the university's Rockefeller Memorial Chapel.

Before departing for Europe on July 22, 1949, Schweitzer invited Exman to Lambaréné, and Exman accepted. When Exman arrived at Schweitzer's compound in October 1950, Schweitzer was a runaway international celebrity: "Christ's thirteenth apostle."[19] In an atomic-bomb world in which Western civilization itself seemed to be imploding, Schweitzer offered some reassurance that perhaps all was not lost, that the good life was still possible, and even race relations might somehow be repaired.

Exman in Africa

In October 1950, Exman spent eight days in Lambaréné. "I was treated royally and allowed to enter the life of the place without reserve," he told Sunny in a letter. He watched at least one operation, visited a nearby leper village, trekked into the forest to watch loggers take down trees, and photographed his adventures. His guide was Emma Haussknecht, a schoolteacher-turned-nurse who spent thirty years at Lambaréné and ran Schweitzer's compound while he was away. Exman sat for at least two interviews with Schweitzer, one (more professional) on books Schweitzer might write for Harper and another (more personal) on ethics, religion, and mysticism. Exman ate with his host and shadowed him as he made his rounds. He kept a diary and wrote to family, friends, and colleagues. In a letter to John Chambers, Exman wrote, "While the emphasis and activity of this place is quite different than with Gerald Heard at Trabuco, one can't help but feel that the 'main heart of the matter' is the same: an effort to give spiritual expression to man's day-by-day existence."[20]

Sensing Exman's desire to see the sacred in the hospital, Schweitzer told him, "Life here is not so romantic as Americans think it is. . . . To be successful in Lambaréné you must be a mechanic, a farmer, a boatman, a trader, as well as a physician and a surgeon." Musician he did not mention, but soon Exman was sitting next to Schweitzer on his piano bench, reveling in a private recital alongside Schweitzer's two pet antelopes. "Surely the appeal of the man was his many gifts," Exman thought. "Other humanitarians had given up opportunities for fame, wealth and ordinary comforts, but few had ever given up so much."[21]

Exman did not come just to gaze, however. He came to see whether Schweitzer might write his theological summa for Harper, and to interview Schweitzer for articles he hoped to write himself. During their personal interview, Exman asked Schweitzer about mysticism. He was particularly interested in how intellectual puzzles that have vexed our ordinary minds for years can be answered "in a flash of illumination, after we had ceased to struggle with our thoughts." Schweitzer replied, "All deep thinking ends in mysticism," before arguing that mystical experiences are surprisingly common, by no means confined to "the privilege of a few." Echoing a theme Exman was already developing in his Book of Books, Schweitzer argued that "mysticism is not necessarily religious" and that religion is seldom mystical, because of the tendency in religious institutions to "keep to traditions and forms." However, he believed that we owe a debt to the world's religions for safeguarding and passing on mystical traditions, because "the deepest religion is mystical, as are the deepest religious individuals."[22]

Shifting from mysticism to prayer and meditation, Schweitzer told Exman that "all deep thinking is prayer" and "real prayer is always meditation." Echoing Heard, he said that petitionary prayer—asking God for stuff—is "is a low, naïve form of prayer. . . . Real prayer is finding peace in all that comes to you and not fretting against that which comes. . . . The best prayer is 'Thy will be done.'"[23]

As Schweitzer spoke of the simple words of Jesus in the New Testament, Exman reflected on the simplicity of Schweitzer's office, including his homemade writing desk and its kerosene lamp. What a contrast, he thought, to the "gilded ballroom" of the Stevens Hotel, where Schweitzer addressed Chicago's mayor and other dignitaries after receiving his honorary University of Chicago doctorate. And with the Harper boardroom. And with Exman's comfortable life. Schweitzer's life exemplified both the Buddha's "right livelihood" and Jesus's observation that "to find his life a man must first lose it."

Schweitzer "had lost his life in the African forests and the world had beaten a path to his jungle door," Exman later wrote. "Who in our day had more truly found his life?"[24]

Exman left Lambaréné with a promise that Schweitzer would allow Harper to publish his upcoming "big theology book." He also left with a long list of supplies desperately needed at the hospital.[25] On his return trip on the *Queen Elizabeth* he met Ben Friedman, president of the US-based Arlington Steel Corporation. Exman told Friedman about Schweitzer's need for corrugated iron for roofing for his leper hospital. A few months later, a shipment, paid for by Friedman, was on its way to Lambaréné. Back in New York, Exman convinced another man to contribute one hundred yards of muslin cloth for mosquito nets.

The World of Albert Schweitzer

Schweitzer's celebrity skyrocketed after he was awarded the 1952 Nobel Peace Prize, but he and Exman continued to write and to see one another. Although Exman was not in Switzerland when Schweitzer formally accepted his Nobel Peace Prize in 1954, he was in London when Schweitzer received the Order of Merit from Queen Elizabeth II in 1955. He was also in Colmar, just outside Gunsbach, for the premiere of a Schweitzer documentary that went on to win the Academy Award for best documentary in 1957.

In the decade after returning from Lambaréné, Exman wrote and lectured widely on Schweitzer. "I have more requests for speaking than I can take care of (I'm also a publisher)," he told Schweitzer's administrative assistant Emma Haussknecht a few months after he got back home, but he managed to give dozens, perhaps hundreds, of Schweitzer talks, drumming up donations and often giving his honoraria to the cause. He gave talks to church and civic groups in New York, New Jersey, and Massachusetts, and at universities such as Harvard, Columbia, and NYU. He also wrote two long-form magazine pieces. In June 1957, he convinced the *Reader's Digest* editor Charles Ferguson to commission an article on Schweitzer for the astronomical sum of $1,800 (the equivalent of $17,000 today). Schweitzer "is not just another do-gooder, or sentimental sermonizer," he told Ferguson. "He is as practical and down-to-earth as a mechanic or farmer." Exman interviewed Schweitzer for this article in Frankfurt in October 1957, but the article was killed.[26]

Schweitzer's big theology book never materialized either, but Exman published a series of books by and about him in the 1950s and 1960s. There were two books of essays by Schweitzer: *Music in the Life of Albert Schweitzer* (1951) and *The Problem of Peace in the World of Today* (1954). Exman also convinced his friend Norman Cousins, the editor in chief of *Saturday Review*, to write a short book, which Harper published in 1960 as *Dr. Schweitzer of Lambaréné*. Exman also shoehorned articles by Schweitzer into American newspapers and magazines, leading one publisher to joke that Exman had set himself up, "willy-nilly, as Dr. Schweitzer's literary agent."[27]

Exman also contributed to a collaborative book called *The World of Albert Schweitzer* (1955). Erica Anderson, a Viennese-born photographer and filmmaker who spent time with Schweitzer in Europe and Africa, contributed the photographs. Barbara Morgan, also a photographer, designed the book. Exman wrote the captions and the text, which track Schweitzer—as doctor, musician, philosopher, and theologian—from his Lambaréné hospital to lectures and concerts across Europe. Reviews were strong. The *New York Times* called *The World of Albert Schweitzer* "a splendid panorama of a vigorous genius in action." *The Washington Post* called the photographs "superb, technically and artistically" and Exman's text "sensitive" and "inspired." The book sold surprisingly well, hitting the *New York Times* bestseller list on February 6, 1955, and remaining there for at least four weeks.[28]

A few months before *The World of Albert Schweitzer* appeared, Thornton Wilder had warned Exman about Erica Anderson, whom he described as a celebrity hanger-on who seemed to think she made the stars she photographed more than they made her. Exman and Anderson seem to have gotten along well, however, with Exman working behind the scenes to promote her work. But the financial success of the book (and the fact that Exman had published it without a written contract) led to legal maneuvering and ill will with Anderson, who objected to the royalty cut Exman had given Morgan. Harper executives and Schweitzer himself were also drawn into the conflict, which Exman worked hard to mediate, in part by giving up some of his own royalties. "Never during my 28 years as a book publisher have I had more difficulty in consummating a contract for a book," Exman confided to Schweitzer. Perhaps to smooth things over, Harper later published two additional books by Anderson: *Albert Schweitzer's Gift of Friendship* (1964) and *The Schweitzer Album* (1965).[29]

The Myth of Schweitzer

In the late 1940s, Schweitzer's hospital had been on the brink of closure. Then Schweitzer came to the United States and won the Nobel Peace Prize, leaving journalists grasping for ever more superlative superlatives to refer to *le bon doctor*. When Schweitzer joined Exman and Fosdick in calling for nuclear disarmament in the 1950s, popular interest in him spiked again. "Every word he cared to utter was printed and reprinted, translated against the clock, interpreted and reinterpreted," wrote one observer. With this hype came a cult of Schweitzer. Predictably, the chorus of hallelujahs from these "Schweitzerenes" was quickly followed by boos from a cadre of critics determined to recast the good doctor as a very bad man.[30]

Central to the myth of Schweitzer was a series of paradoxes. One was the paradox of a man who gave up fame in academia and the arts to serve humanity, only to win even greater fame in his self-imposed obscurity. Drawing on this paradox, Exman often spoke of Schweitzer as a Christlike saint who gained his life by losing it, winning fame not by telling his followers "how to become popular or prosperous" but by speaking as a prophet about civilizational decay.[31]

Less discussed was the paradox of Schweitzer's humble bragging. Schweitzer was often said to be an uncommonly modest man who swatted away compliments like so many mosquitoes. Exman, for example, called him "one of the most truly humble men I've ever met."[32] Yet Schweitzer was also a savvy self-promoter. To read even a small cross-section of the mountain of books and articles about him is to run headlong into a Schweitzer myth largely of his own making. Like Fosdick and other middlebrow popularizers in Exman's Book of Books, he spoke with ease across religious and denominational boundaries, demonstrating a simplicity of expression that contrasted sharply with the performances of complexity of so many academic theologians. He distilled difficult concepts into easy-to-understand sentences. He told good stories. He stayed on message. He offered up memorable quotes. And he authored autobiographies to broadcast his version of his story to the world.

As has been mentioned, Schweitzer regularly returned in narrating that story to key moments, which reappear through the Schweitzer literature like antelope in his jungle hospital. Four have already been mentioned: when, at the age of twenty-one, he decided to devote himself to humanitarian efforts as soon as he turned thirty; when, at the age of twenty-nine, he opened a French missionary journal and decided to go to Central Africa to help; when his Reverence for Life ideal suddenly came to him on a boat ride during his fortieth year; and when that invitation from Sweden pulled him out of his wartime funk in his mid-forties, steeling him to return to Lambaréné to rebuild his hospital and renew his life.

These formulas were dreamed up by a man who disdained theological formulas (Schweitzer) and spread by another man equally allergic to them (Exman). To sit with their various retellings is to grow weary of the myth of Schweitzer, whose central narrative depicts its hero as a modern Western renunciant, emphasizing the sacrifices he made along the byways of Alsace, the hallways of wartime internment camps, and the waters of Lambaréné. Observer after observer notes (as this chapter already has) that Schweitzer wore old clothes and never traveled first class. He gave to his hospital virtually all the money he made. True enough. Equally true is the fact that Schweitzer was a savvy storyteller, as expert at shaping the myth of Schweitzer as the PR guru Ivy Lee was at shaping the public images of Fosdick and the Rockefellers.

This mythmaking also had a physical component, depicting Schweitzer as a man of Bunyanesque proportions—a "silver-maned, bushy mustached old lion of a man," in the words of a *TIME* reporter and, according to the *New York Times*, a "barrelbodied" man "with a mustache that you could have swept the street with." This aspect of his mythology was not all Schweitzer's doing, but he did cultivate his look nearly as carefully as Lady Gaga cultivated hers at the height of her celebrity. In Africa, he wore an all-white outfit as reliably as the novelist Tom Wolfe later wore his trademark white suit. His "walrus mustache" was another sartorial signature, as was the unruly head of gray hair spilling out from under his pith helmet—a long-standing "emblem of imperialism," according to the novelist George Orwell, which survived after World War II largely in Hollywood films (and atop Schweitzer's ample head).[33]

To be clear, Schweitzer did refuse accolades. He didn't want his name plastered on anything. And he was forever trying to sidestep the showers of superlatives. Moreover, his myth of himself doubtless served the interests of his African patients, as it paid, directly and indirectly, for buildings and drugs and medical supplies. But the Schweitzer mythology also served its hero's interests, just as the unending cycle of accolades/refusals/more accolades burnished his public image as a self-sacrificing village doctor.

Tastes vary, but this myth of Schweitzer sold extraordinarily well in Europe and the United States from the late 1940s into the 1950s. Civilizations have long demonstrated a lack of civilization, but the dropping of atomic bombs broadcast that lack to the world. One response to the shock was a postwar "search for meaning" that preoccupied virtually everyone in Exman's network and many of his readers. What to think of a world in which a nation-state not only dropped nuclear weapons but also justified its actions as morally sound? How to find a path through such a world, other than by despairing over the impossibility of purpose and the impotence of God?

Such questions had driven the founding of Trabuco College and the Catholic Worker, which like Lambaréné aimed to put mysticism in motion. Trabuco had tried (and failed) to produce a spiritual vanguard of seekers and saints expert in the ways and means of prayer and meditation. The Catholic Worker had produced at least one saint and had a better track record when it came to acts of mercy. The ambitions of Schweitzer's hospital were modest, but it largely met them by providing for decades both local medical care and a global model for the moral life.

Schweitzer said that he went to Africa to atone for the sins White colonizers had visited upon colonized Black people. In the 1950s, however, it was his renunciation of fame and fortune that promised salvation. Is civilization in decline? Absolutely, Schweitzer argued. However, his own life suggested a more upbeat answer, and his emphasis on individual action offered a way forward. Yes, institutions were broken, but individuals were still capable of good and godly work. Individuals could hear and heed that still, small voice within. Fosdick had emphasized psychological healing. Schweitzer focused on healing the body. He wasn't trying to save the world. He didn't preach salvation. He was just offering medical care, one patient at a time, to the multitudes he encountered. Still, European and American writers flocked (imaginatively in most cases) to his riverside hospital in search of therapies for their readers' spiritual ills. Why? Because he had walked into the arid valley of meaninglessness that cracked open during the world wars and somehow emerged with a life drenched in purpose. In this way, he became an example to millions who desperately wanted to believe that God had not withdrawn from the world, that sainthood was still possible.

Exman was drawn to Schweitzer as someone who had reached spiritual heights far beyond his grasp. But the two men also shared much. Both had dedicated their lives to searching for meaning by searching for God. Both were convinced that religious institutions had failed to meet the challenges of the early twentieth century, and in many cases had multiplied its woes. Secure in the knowledge that individual experience lay at the heart of true religion, both took refuge in persons and personality instead. Exman was also sympathetic to Schweitzer's ethical mysticism, in which the search for God was simultaneously a search for "right livelihood." Since his Trabuco days, he had been concerned about the temptation of mystics to slip into egoism and escapism, and Schweitzer offered a living example of a man for whom mystical experience and ethical action were mutually reinforcing. Finally, Exman saw in Schweitzer a popularizer of religion on par in many respects with Fosdick—another preacher who knew how to distill key ideas out of complex subjects and speak to ordinary people in language they could understand.

The Bad Doctor

It is a fact of modern communications as surely as a fact of physics that the higher one goes the farther one can fall, so it should not be surprising that, as the myth of *le bon doctor* spread, critics gathered to confine it. As early as 1949, a *New York Times* piece during Schweitzer's Aspen trip concluded on this foreboding note: "It would be most unfortunate if Albert Schweitzer should become something of a bore to us. There is a danger. Contributing factors are the unrelieved eulogies and unqualified superlatives brought to bear on both Dr. Schweitzer's person and works. Some resistance is bound to set in, some suspicion is bound to be created."[34]

That suspicion set in like sepsis during the 1950s, and by the 1960s Schweitzer was contending with far more than boredom. In a 1963 article called "Albert Schweitzer: An Anachronism," *TIME* complained he "lives in the Africa of 1913, hardly knowing or caring that a continent and a century have passed him by." His operating room is "antiquated," and his hospital is "without telephone, running water or refrigeration." As the 1960s pressed on, similar suspicions came out of the woodwork like termites in Schweitzer's riverfront study. Schweitzer responded with silence. "That has always been my principle, and I have stuck to it loyally," he wrote in a private letter in 1963.[35]

The silence deepened upon Schweitzer's death in 1965 at the age of ninety. But the chorus of critics swelled, and the "greatest soul in Christendom" soon became in many eyes yet another damnable so-called White savior of benighted Black Africans. In its ongoing search for the historical Schweitzer, the world now uncovered "a self-seeking hypocrite, an incompetent doctor," "A White Hat Colonialist," and "An Enemy of the Free World." Then, in the 1970s, he was almost entirely forgotten, erased. Emory Ross, following Schweitzer's triumphant cross-country trip in 1949, had written in the *American Scholar* that "Schweitzer wishes to be understood rather than remembered." In the end, he was neither.[36]

The causes of this reversal were many. Schweitzer had gone to Africa because he wanted to work independently, and he did things his own way and on his own time until the end. He ruled over his hospital like a medieval lord. And he refused to modernize it, even when new medical equipment became available. A nineteenth-century man by birth and inclination, he lived defiantly in the past, his ways as deep set as his eyes. He never learned to drive a car. As if intent on proving he was a living anachronism, he wrote his letters by hand (typewriters were too loud, he said).

Schweitzer was also intellectually anachronistic. During the 1950s, nine African nations gained their independence from European powers. In 1960 alone, seventeen more followed, including Gabon. But Schweitzer continued to hold on to the relics of colonialism and imperialism like fond reminders of old friends. If in the

1960s you were searching for a culture hero with a mystical bent, a renouncer who had tuned out the mythologies of the modern, Gandhi, not Schweitzer, was your man. As the values of cultural and religious pluralism spread, not least through Exman's Book of Books, Schweitzer was increasingly tagged as an intolerant Christian missionary who ranked African religions among the "lower religions" and Christianity as the best.[37]

Though he allowed Muslims to be buried in his cemetery and was kindly disposed toward Muslim mystics, Schweitzer's writing about Islam exhibited none of the sympathetic engagement visible in his writing about Chinese and Indian religions. "It lacks spiritual originality and is not a religion with profound thoughts on God and the world," he wrote of Islam. Therefore, it spreads largely among "the uncivilized and half-civilized peoples of Asia and Africa as the form of monotheism most easily accessible to them."[38]

During the 1950s and 1960s, a series of critics dropped by Lambaréné and left with revelations about how Schweitzer mistreated his staff like "an equatorial King Lear who should have left the stage some time before." The epitome of this genre was *Verdict on Schweitzer* (1964) by Gerald McKnight, who would later pen takedowns of the Warren Commission and the House of Gucci. Having shadowed his quarry in Lambaréné for no more than a few days, McKnight offered his sage verdict: Schweitzer was an autocrat and a hypocrite who went to Africa not for humanitarian but for selfish reasons—to save his own soul.[39]

As the curtain was drawn back and Schweitzer was revealed as a flawed human being, critics attacked even his interpretations of Bach as "dull and stodgy." His scholarship came under attack, too. Philosophers said he arrogantly refused to address secondary sources. New Testament scholars dismissed him as "an intellectual lightweight." Even his big idea of Reverence for Life seemed outdated, impractical. ("I always felt that Dr. Schweitzer owed it to his wife to have got rid of those rats," Bro confided to Exman.) But what ultimately canceled him was his racism.[40]

"Benevolent Racism"

In yet another plot point from his mythology, Schweitzer was said to have been deeply moved whenever he visited a monument in Colmar by Frédéric Auguste Bartholdi, an Alsatian who also designed the Statue of Liberty. As a child, Schweitzer was obsessed with a stone carving of a Black man in that monument. "It is a figure of herculean proportion, but the face wears an expression of thoughtful sadness which I could not forget," Schweitzer wrote. "The countenance spoke to me of the misery of the Dark Continent."[41]

The myth of Schweitzer depicted Schweitzer's decision to answer that call as an act of atonement reminiscent of Christ's sacrificial death on the cross. In a sermon he gave years before moving to Lambaréné, Schweitzer cataloged the sins visited by European colonists on Africans. "Where the white man has come, unhappiness and terror have accompanied him," he wrote. "The book in which the advance of the European nations in the world was to be written would be a book of horror." Later, in *On the Edge of the Primeval Forest* (1922), he evoked the book of life to decry similar sins. "Who can describe the injustice and the cruelties that in the course of centuries they have suffered at the hands of Europeans?" he asked. "If a record could be compiled of all that has happened between the white and coloured races . . . the reader would have to turn [its pages] over unread, because their contents would be too horrible." Schweitzer then characterized his personal sacrifice as a modest payment for those sins. "Anything we give them is not benevolence but atonement," he wrote. "And when we have done all that is in our power, we shall not have atoned for the thousandth part of our guilt."[42]

On such sentiments was built the image of Schweitzer as a reconciler of races—a man born in a French and German borderland who chose to live in the borderlands between Europe and Africa, White and Black. But this image was constructed on a foundation as shifting as the sandbars of the Ogowe.

About Schweitzer and race, there were questions from the start. Howard Thurman, who deeply admired Schweitzer's Reverence for Life ethic, read *On the Edge of the Primeval Forest* in his college dormitory and was "incensed" about how Schweitzer "regarded these Africans as children." Two decades later, the American sociologist and Pan-Africanist W. E. B. Du Bois offered a more sustained critique. In *The Albert Schweitzer Jubilee Book* (1945), an anthology celebrating Schweitzer's seventieth birthday, Du Bois lavished Schweitzer with faint praise. "The little handful of people whom he helped saw in him a vision and a promise; a white man who was interested in them as human beings; who assuaged their bitter pain, who healed their wounds," Du Bois wrote, clearly downplaying the reach of Schweitzer's medical work, which by one estimate eventually extended to some 130,000 patients. What these patients did not see, in Du Bois's telling, was how intimately Schweitzer's project was implicated in the projects of other White people in Africa: merchants and missionaries, businessmen and colonial officials. Regarding Schweitzer's culpability, Du Bois excused him (sort of) on the grounds of ignorance. If he had possessed a "broad grasp" of "what imperial colonialism has done to the world," Du Bois wrote, "he probably would have tried to heal the souls of white Europe rather than the bodies of black Africa." But he had no such grasp, and therefore "he deserves every tribute that we can give him for trying to do his mite, his little pitiful mite, which in a sense was but a passing gesture, but perhaps in the long run will light that fire in Africa which will cleanse that continent and the world."[43]

In December 1945, Schweitzer wrote Du Bois, thanking him for his words. He also responded to Du Bois's criticisms by arguing that Du Bois was viewing the race problem "as a whole" while he was viewing it from the ground up, attending to one "particular case." Citing "old residents" as sources, Schweitzer claimed that French colonization "was felt by all as a great benefit" because it liberated the locals from subjugation "to the will of the cruel chiefs and to fetichisms exerting a terrible power." Should "rapid emancipation" come, Schweitzer feared, the area would likely revert to "the theatre of continuous war between the tribes" that it was before "European occupation put an end" to the violence. In a troubling trope that now pops off the page, Schweitzer concluded, "Here I know many whites who are very good to the natives and who have it at heart to be fair with them and who concern themselves with their well-being."[44]

On July 31, 1946, Du Bois replied with some "plain speaking" that barely masked his anger. After a stern warning against local mythmakers, he offered a history lesson of his own:

> I trust that you will not receive without careful examination the legend that it was white Europe which brought peace and leadership to West Africa and that without the influence of the whites, Africa would retrograde into barbarism.... [C]ivilization in West Africa was not the gift of white folk. . . . It was the American slave-trade carried on by Europeans that degraded and spoiled this civilization. . . . Later white men rationalized their crime by claiming the highest motives first in their man-stealing, then in their missionary work and finally in their system of colonial government. The fact of the matter is that West Africa, just as the rest of Africa, has been organized for the profit of white Europe and America. Until this basic idea of making money out of the stolen toil and material of black folk ceases to be the leading idea, Africa will never recover from her degradation.

Du Bois then urged Schweitzer to visit the United States (his Aspen trip was still a few years off) to see with his own eyes the "the possibilities of black folk." "In one of the greatest, most powerful and most ruthless countries of the earth, we have fought our way forward until today we own property; we share political power;

we make art and literature; we sit in congress and in the legislatures and on the bench," Du Bois wrote, in words that now sound naive. "What we have done, Africa did in earlier ages and can do again if the dead hand of Europe is taken from her throat."[45]

Other critics leaned into interpersonal matters, condemning Schweitzer's patriarchal, condescending, and racist attitudes toward his Black patients, staff, and neighbors. Here the record is replete with what the late Kenyan-born academic (and uneasy holder of the Albert Schweitzer Chair at SUNY, Binghamton) Ali Mazrui rightly described as "benevolent racism." A "racial patriarch," in Mazrui's words, Schweitzer was curiously uncurious about Africa beyond the Ogowe. He never learned an African language. And though he was deeply interested in the bodies of his patients, he showed scant interest in their minds. He didn't train or hire local doctors, importing them from Europe instead. He stereotyped Africans, whom he referred to as lazy "primitives" and untrustworthy "savages." He even segregated his patients, by tribe and by race. Schweitzer's condescension now drips off the pages of his autobiographies, perhaps most cringingly in that infantilizing passage from *On the Edge* that had set Thurman's teeth on edge: "The negro is a child, and with children nothing can be done without the use of authority. We must, therefore, so arrange the circumstances of daily life that my natural authority can find expression. With regard to the negros, then, I have coined the formula: 'I am your brother, it is true, but your elder brother.'"[46]

Exman did not respond directly to these criticisms in print, but he defended Schweitzer in a private letter to his friend the foreign service officer Edward Groth. After listing key allegations, Exman said he could not judge their accuracy. He did say that he "did not observe any attitude of condescension on Schweitzer's part toward the negroes around him" and that locals "respected and revered him." If there was any sinner in this story, Exman told Groth, it was not Schweitzer. "I am the sinner," he confessed, "because I am on the sidelines."[47]

Dismantling Schweitzer

Schweitzer's most influential book, *The Quest of the Historical Jesus*, suggests that myths all fit a time and place. Some are more enduring, some less. Schweitzer's life suggests the same. In the late 1940s and 1950s, demand was strong in Europe and the United States for a peaceable nineteenth-century man with an example to live by in the war-ravaged twentieth century. In the 1950s, this portrait gave millions meaning. It demonstrated that purpose was to be found not in buying stuff but in selfless service. Granted, it was a rare Schweitzerine who went and did likewise. But for many, just knowing there were people like Schweitzer walking the earth was reassuring. His protests against nuclear weapons were part of the appeal. Get rid of them, he said, prompting President John F. Kennedy to laud him in 1962 as "one of the transcendent moral influences of our century."[48]

While Kennedy praised him, "Schweitzer addicts" raced to resurrect his reputation. A few friendly academics gave him the "on the one hand"/"on the other hand" treatment, contending that Schweitzer was "liberal and anticolonial" even if he "shared a number of missionary prejudices and tropes about Africans." But the reputation of the no-longer-so-good doctor was beyond repair.[49] By the early 1960s, criticisms were falling on him like shovelfuls of earth at an internment.

Upon his death in Lambaréné on September 4, 1965, at the age of ninety, local admirers mourned as his body was buried next to Helene's. The world barely stirred. Instead of reinvigorating the myth of Schweitzer, his death nearly extinguished it, as if the last vestiges of respect for the man had been fueled by nothing more than his body temperature. Of all the popular authors featured in this book, only Martin Luther King Jr. (another Nobel Peace Prize winner) was as much of a global celebrity at their height. Schweitzer is now the most obscure.

Looking back on Schweitzer's legacy ten years after his death,

John Russell, an art critic and Schweitzer translator, recalled the years when Schweitzer had been seen as the "conscience of the civilized world" and "a model of unselfishness and devotion to duty and wisdom." His autobiography sold half a million copies, and scholars listed him among the greatest Europeans of all time. As World War II ended and the global economy boomed alongside Schweitzer's reputation, many Europeans and Americans weren't so sure they wanted the plastic delights of consumer capitalism. Then they decided they did, and they threw Schweitzer out with other trash left over from the Victorian era. In the mid-1970s, Russell observed, no one seemed to recall "what all the fuss was about." Schweitzer's outfits looked drab rather than saintly, his hospital unkempt and dangerous, his Reverence for Life impractical, his racism self-evident. "To watch him during those days," lamented Russell, "was to watch a well-meant legend dismantled piece by piece."[50]

There were good reasons for this swift reversal. With the emergence of the civil rights, Black Power, and feminist movements, even his former followers were coming to view Schweitzer as a White patriarch on a power trip. The rise of comparative religion and religious pluralism made many wary of Christian missions. African independence movements made them even warier of colonialism and imperialism. Once again, Schweitzer checked all the boxes, but now those checks were diminishing rather than augmenting his reputation.

Schweitzer's legacy has been reevaluated in recent years in environmental circles. Rachel Carson, whose bestseller *Silent Spring* (1962) is widely credited with launching the environmental movement, kept a photograph in her office of Schweitzer, to whom she dedicated that bestseller. When the Animal Welfare Institute awarded Carson the Albert Schweitzer Medal in 1963, she called Schweitzer "the one truly great individual our modern times have produced" and enlisted his name in protest over how supposedly "civilized" people were "waging war against the natural world."[51] Today, many environmentalists remember Schweitzer as a trailblazer who renounced the Western hierarchy of humans over animals. Philosopher Ara Barsam, who views Schweitzer as "a pioneer in *life-centered ethics*," sees three major contributions he made to environmental ethics: his "ethical mysticism," which views service to others as a pathway to union with God; his repudiation of human-centered creation myths, which privilege human lives over animal and plant life; and his amplification of the Indian commitment to ahimsa, whose global spread was "one of the greatest events in the spiritual history of mankind."[52]

"The Only Thing"

Shortly before his death, Schweitzer wrote Exman to express his gratitude for "all the trouble you have taken on my behalf." He thanked Exman for the assistance he had offered Erica Anderson, praising him especially for *The World of Albert Schweitzer*. "Since I have made your acquaintance I think very often of you," he continued. "I still remember my surprise and my emotion when Mr. Ross told me that you would be our companion on the trip to Aspen because you had wanted to meet me." He thanked Exman "for preparing the way for my books" in the United States, before concluding, "Please remember that I haven't forgotten you and that I am profoundly grateful for everything that you are doing for me."[53]

It is hard to say why Exman fell so hard for Schweitzer. He was not the only American to join Schweitzer's fan club in the 1940s. But he was among Schweitzer's most influential American friends during the last two decades of Schweitzer's life. A few points of contact have already been mentioned. One that merits further exploration concerns that subtle human capacity called the will. This was a major theme in Schweitzer's philosophy, and in his Reverence for Life. "The most immediate fact of man's consciousness is the assertion: 'I am life which wills to live, in the midst of life which wills to live,'" he wrote. "Man has now to decide what his relation to his will to live shall be."[54]

Willpower was also a major theme in Exman's life, but it was Schweitzer's superpower. Schweitzer had what the Yoruba religious tradition of West Africa refers to as *ashe*—the power to make things happen. Exman excelled at making things happen in publishing. He excelled at locating and courting authors and integrating them into his network. He excelled as well at editing and publicizing books, and at making money for Harper and a reputation for himself. Not without reason was he widely known as the dean of religion publishing in the United States. But he lacked *ashe* in the spiritual world. The central contest in Exman's adult life pulled him in opposing directions. One was toward training for the life of the spirit, and perhaps toward sainthood itself. Thus spoke Heard and Bro and Day and King and Schweitzer. This same pull compelled him to try to recapture his teenage experience at the Blanchester graveyard. But then there was the pull of status, money, and the satisfaction born of fulfilling one's duties as a husband, father, and a member of the Harper Board of Directors. Exman and Bro had long planned their escape from the powerful orbit of Harper and New York. But he had remained. He knew Schweitzer would have left. He had willpower, prodigious willpower in Exman's estimation, which Exman could never seem to muster. How did he do it? And was it something Exman could learn?

In his last interview with Schweitzer at Lambaréné, Exman asked, "What can be done to strengthen the will?" What can help us "stick by our highest resolves?" At Trabuco in the early 1940s, Exman had committed himself to becoming the saint Heard and Bro had challenged him to be. But maintaining the required discipline became difficult once he was back on the East Coast. He maintained his Monday evening cell group for many years, but his daily meditation regimen came and went. Exman had far fewer reasons to stay at Harper than to join Bro somewhere in the Midwest to start their own publishing house, but the longer he delayed, the more the accolades and the income piled up. He asked Schweitzer about willpower because he knew Schweitzer possessed it in abundance. He wanted to know why Schweitzer hadn't stayed in Europe. There, he might have inspired millions, through concerts, lectures, and books, to commit themselves to lives of service. But now that he had seen Schweitzer in action, he realized that his questions had been asked and answered. "Is example the main thing in influencing others?" Exman asked. "It is the *only thing*," Schweitzer replied.[55]

Exman included this exchange in almost every article and talk he did on Schweitzer. Why was it so important to him? Why did he keep a photo of Schweitzer and him in his office until his own death? Because he knew he was failing to follow Schweitzer's example, failing to win his life by losing it, failing to make a godly mission of his work. In a draft of a long-form article on Schweitzer, Exman wrote that his pilgrimage to Schweitzer "changed my complete out-look on life."[56] Exman had thought he was a Christian, he explained. Meeting Schweitzer showed him how far he had fallen short.

Exman was a well-to-do businessman who returned from his Africa sojourn on the *Queen Elizabeth*. He was then welcomed back by his wife and children into the comforts of his suburban home. What was the example he was setting for his family, his friends? Where was his willpower? Back in the United States, he would spread Schweitzer's message. He would promote Schweitzer's books. He would raise money for Schweitzer's hospital. He would travel to see Schweitzer in Europe in 1952, 1954, 1955, and 1957. Amid those visits, he would be appointed vice president of Harper & Brothers and a member of its Board of Directors. Such triumphs disappointed Bro and his best self.

Decades before his pilgrimage to Schweitzer, Exman had heard William James's call to sainthood in *Varieties*. "Let us be saints," James had written in concluding his thoughts on "The Value of Saint-liness." Exman heard that call again from Heard, and many times more from Bro. And Exman had tried and tried and tried again. As his aspirations for sainthood foundered, he must have taken solace in James's reassurance that sainthood, like religion itself, came in all sorts of varieties, so "each of us must discover for himself . . . the amount of saintship which best comports with what he believes to be his powers and feels to be his truest mission and vocation."[57]

Exman saw Schweitzer as an exemplary saint. He also saw him as a mystic who glimpsed God nearly every day in Lambaréné. Exman wanted to see God, too, but he was too busy for that, too busy managing the religious book department, too busy pleasing his bosses in the Harper boardroom, too busy making a comfortable life for his wife and kids. Perhaps another author might help him in his ongoing quest for God, someone who had knit a community around him of a very different sort and would win his own Nobel Peace Prize in the process.

CHAPTER SIX

White Liberals and Martin Luther King Jr.'s *Stride Toward Freedom*

A week after Martin Luther King Jr. was assassinated in Memphis, Tennessee, on April 4, 1968, Exman sat down with pen and paper to express his condolences to King's widow, Coretta Scott King. He reminisced about the day in 1960 that he and Sunny hosted her husband for dinner in their Scarsdale home, and about working as King's editor. "Of the many books I was privileged to publish during my thirty-seven years with Harpers, 'Stride Toward Freedom' is one I put on my private 'top shelf,'" he wrote, adding that King was, alongside Fosdick, Schweitzer, and the civil rights pioneer Howard Thurman, "one of the authors whose association has meant most to me." Exman then turned to the day he first met the Kings. "That was the day that I came to Montgomery to convince him that he should write a book on the bus strike that ended in a Supreme Court decision," Exman wrote. "He was spending the day in bed because of a slight bout with the flu. I left your home with his promise to undertake the book."[1]

Exman was drawn to King because of his role in the Montgomery bus boycott, which began one year after the US Supreme Court ruled in *Brown v. Board of Education* (1954) that racial segregation in public schools was unconstitutional. More precisely, the boycott began on Tuesday, December 5, 1955, four days after Rosa Parks, a Black seamstress and local NAACP secretary, was arrested for refusing to give up her bus seat to a White man. The Women's Political Council, a local group of Black women, called for a boycott of Montgomery's buses. Black preachers urged their parishioners to respect it. And all across Montgomery, that citadel of the south where the Confederate flag first flew and Jefferson Davis was sworn in as the president of the Confederacy, Black people and their White supporters walked to work, no matter the distance.

Five thousand of those souls gathered that Tuesday evening at the Holt Street Baptist Church. The speaker was Dexter Avenue Baptist Church's new twenty-six-year-old minister, who, earlier that day, had been elected president of a hastily formed Black ministers group called the Montgomery Improvement Association (MIA). King gave the sort of speech for which he is now remembered:

And you know, my friends, there comes a time when people get tired of being trampled over by the iron feet of oppression. There comes a time, my friends, when people get tired of being plunged across the abyss of humiliation, where they experience the bleakness of nagging despair. There comes a time when people get tired of being pushed out of the glittering sunlight of life's July and left standing amid the piercing chill of an alpine November. There comes a time.

He ended his remarks—on justice and nonviolence and the love of Jesus and the tattered glory of American democracy—by reflecting how his listeners could make history, in that city, on that day. Should they unite, walking when they preferred to ride, and choosing love over violence while insisting on justice, then future historians would doubtless say, "There lived a race of people, a *black* people, 'fleecy locks and black complexion,' a people who had the moral courage to stand up for their rights. And thereby they injected a new meaning into the veins of history and civilization."² The book Exman went to Montgomery to sign would transform King into one of those historians, setting down a freedom story of a thirteen-month civil rights action that, as of that night, was just hours old.

Exman was not the only editor trying to secure a King book, however. He wasn't even the only editor at Harper. On January 23, 1957, days after the Supreme Court had ordered an end to segregation on Montgomery's buses, Marion S. Wyeth Jr., a young trade book editor who would go on to become Harper's editor in chief, wrote to ask King about a rumor he had heard. Was King writing a book about the Montgomery protests? If so, Wyeth very much wanted to see it. King wrote right back. Yes, he had been considering such a book, but "tremendous pressure" on his time had forced him to set it aside. He did have another idea, however, which would be easier to complete: "a book of sermons, most of which have been preached to my own congregation during our struggle here in Montgomery."³

If King had agreed to write the Montgomery story for Wyeth, it would have gone to Harper's trade department, but because King suggested a book of sermons, it was passed along to Exman, who tasked his new right-hand man Mel Arnold to reply. On February 5, 1957, Arnold told King that the religious book department would be happy to see his sermon collection. Two weeks later King appeared on the *TIME* cover, prompting a Knopf editor to ask him for a book on the Montgomery story. Nonetheless, he wrote back to Arnold, indicating that he was "delighted" by Harper's interest but discussions would have to wait until he got back from an upcoming trip to Africa and Europe.⁴

During the first week of April, right after King returned from that trip, two more book requests hit King's mailbox: one from Little, Brown and another from Houghton Mifflin. In May, a Farrar, Straus & Cudahy editor reached out, too.⁵

Amid this flurry of letters, Exman showed up at King's doorstep in Montgomery. Today historians still debate whether the civil rights movement was a religious movement, but Exman instinctively understood that it was. King and other ministers played leadership roles. Key meetings were held in churches. And the rhetoric was shot through with references to the Exodus story of God leading his people out of bondage and marching toward freedom. Exman also understood that history was being made in Montgomery as surely as Gandhi had made history in India. Yes, sermon collections sold well for Exman. But the King collection could wait. The urgent task was to get into print King's account of the historic struggle to integrate Montgomery's buses.

Writing *Stride Toward Freedom*

King told Exman he would write that book for him, and he chose the New York literary agency of Marie Rodell and Joan Daves to represent him in the negotiations. On October 17, 1957, he signed a contract with Harper for "A Moment in History: The Montgomery Story." The due date, January 15, 1958, was less than three months away.

King was twenty-eight years old. He had never written a book. His days were overflowing with responsibilities to family, church, and a growing civil rights movement. And he was besieged by death threats. Exman and Marie Rodell agreed that the book would be done quicker and would read (and sell) better if he had help. Rodell floated two seasoned New York City ghostwriters as possibilities, but King insisted on writing it himself, with the help of Lawrence Reddick, a history professor at Alabama State College who would go on to become the author of the first King biography (also published by Exman). Exman asked Bro to do the Harper editing, but she was too busy. He then approached Hermine Popper, who had been an assistant editor at Harper and was now doing freelance book editing.

On February 4, 1958, a few weeks after the January book

deadline had come and gone, Exman returned to Montgomery. In a letter to Bro narrating that visit, Exman said he met with King and Reddick to take Reddick's measure and to iron out the roles everyone would play in finishing the book. Again, King refused outside help. "He said it would take two weeks for him to bring a ghostwriter up to date; also, he thought a ghostwriter might write the book as he wanted it and not as King wanted it," Exman told Bro. "Furthermore, King was concerned that a ghostwriter walking the streets of Montgomery would advertise the fact that King was not able to write his own book; King wants to write his own book and he wants people to know that he's writing his own book."[6]

Exman played the role of a skilled editor, coaxing the writer along while informing him that it takes many hands to bring a book into the world. He told King that the manuscript would require editing and that parts might require "complete rewriting." King replied, "That's exactly the kind of help I expected." Exman suggested Popper as an excellent editor who was eager to work with King. Again King agreed. As for Reddick, Exman was a fan. "I was convinced that he would be an able man to work with King," he told Bro. "We're going to need a lot more meat on the bones of the book—data of various sorts, plus many anecdotes and stories, and Reddick has the best file of anyone living on what transpired in Montgomery." Exman also invited Rodell, who had previously represented the environmental writer Rachel Carson, to join an editorial team that Exman would convene weekly at Harper to work up the manuscript. Exman ended his letter to Bro by sharing his suspicion that one more entity was working on this project behind the scenes: "I think the Lord has a hand in shaping up the book as it should be."[7]

Regarding the humans involved, the making of *Stride Toward Freedom* is unusually well documented. In the Boston University archives, there are chapter drafts written in King's hand, sometimes in pencil, sometimes in red pen. There are multiple typed drafts marked up by Exman, Popper, and others. There are letters about the book exchanged between King and his lawyers, and between

King and his literary agents. There is also extensive correspondence between King and various Harper employees and freelancers.

The plan, as Exman rehearsed it in a follow-up letter to King two days after his second Montgomery visit, was for King to write chapter drafts himself. Exman, Popper, and others at Harper would then prepare a second draft, which would go back with questions to King and Reddick, who would work on it together.

Exman had long prized what Bill Wilson called anonymity and Gerald Heard called egolessness. As has been noted, the way Exman enacted these values brought a certain passivity to his life. When it came to big decisions, he tended to wait on God's leading. In a letter to King written as their project was ramping up, Exman called God the book's "Source." Exman's fervent hope was that all involved would allow themselves to serve as "clear, clean channels" for that "Source." Time spent on the project could be the most important of their lives, he added, "for the proper telling of this story—all of us being used, not for our ends but for that of the book—will of itself make history."[8]

Two weeks later, King sent Exman draft pages from two chapters. Popper edited them. On February 25, Exman convened his "editorial council," which included himself, Popper, Rodell, Mel Arnold, and Elizabeth Lawrence, an editor in Harper's trade department and a friend of Rodell. The following day, Exman and Rodell wrote King independently, telling him they intended to push the book ahead quickly with weekly meetings of this editorial team. Sensitive to King's concerns about a ghostwriter, Rodell stressed that all involved were committed to producing a book that expressed King's thinking "as clearly and faithfully and movingly, and on as broad a base of appeal to many people, as possible." Exman similarly reassured King that Popper "will not be working as a ghostwriter, but as an editorial associate."[9]

In her own letter, Popper offered King additional reassurances, describing her work as an effort "to convert, as it were, an expert orator's style into a writer's style—so that your truly great story will speak for itself." She told King that she had "added less than a dozen sentences" to the current pages, and none would be included without his approval. She also asked King for "additional materials, specific facts or scenes that will make the story more vivid." She ended by expressing her "pleasure in having a share in this enterprise."[10]

Howard Thurman

Stride Toward Freedom was a departure for Exman and his Book of Books, which had not lived up to the pluralistic promises of the mission statement that first appeared in his department's catalogs in 1952. Though Exman had crossed religious barriers by moving aggressively into books by and about Hindus and Buddhists, his list had slighted Black writers. But it hadn't entirely ignored them.

In the late 1930s, Exman had written to Howard Thurman, who was working at the time as a theology professor and dean of Rankin Chapel at Howard University in Washington, DC. Thurman would go on to become a mentor to many in the civil rights movement, King included. *Life* magazine would tap him as one of the greatest preachers in the United States, and *Ebony*, mindful of his mystical bent, would call him a "twentieth-century holy man."[11]

Exman asked in the letter for a meeting to discuss the possibility of a book. When they met, they talked for hours. Thurman later wrote of this first meeting, "There began a friendship that lasted to the end of his life."[12]

Both men were Baptists indifferent (or hostile) to denominational distinctions. Both were Christians wary of organized Christianity. Both were internationalists and pacifists who would go on to support the United Nations and to play leadership roles in the interfaith peace group the Fellowship of Reconciliation. Born a year apart, Exman and Thurman were also members of the Lost Generation, which lived through one world war as teenagers and would endure another in middle age. Both men responded to modern militarism and materialism by searching for meaning alongside fellow seekers. That search prompted a shared interest in uncanny experiences such as spiritual healing, clairvoyance, and communication with the spirits of the dead. (Thurman, too, would take a keen interest in things psychic, and he, too, would become fascinated by the medium Edgar Cayce.)

Finally, both were eager practitioners of the religion of experience who had been blessed with epiphanies that became blueprints for their lives. Thurman's "experience of vision" came during a "pilgrimage of friendship" to India in 1936. As he stood in the Khyber Pass at the border between Afghanistan and what was then India, Thurman felt the powerful presence of God. He also felt called to "test whether a religious fellowship could be developed in America that was capable of cutting across all racial barriers"—to see "if experiences of spiritual unity among people could be more compelling than the experiences/doctrines which divide them."[13]

No book was immediately forthcoming, but roughly a decade after Exman first contacted him, Thurman authored a short volume, *The Negro Spiritual Speaks of Life and Death* (1947), which would turn out to be the first of fifteen Thurman books published by the Harper religious book department. In the catalog copy for this book, Exman introduced Thurman as "one of the best-loved and popular speakers and preachers of his race" and the spiritual as a poignant expression of "eternal truth about death and life." Drawing unconsciously on colonialist themes, the catalog also indulged in a species of Orientalism that reduced African Americans to their religiosity—by overpraising the spiritual as "the greatest contribution of the American Negro." Also announced in that catalog was *The Christian Way in Race Relations* (1948), an edited volume gestated at Howard's Institute of Religion. It included chapters by two men from Morehouse College in Atlanta who would go on to become close advisers to King: its president (and Thurman's former psychology professor) Benjamin Mays and George Kelsey, a Bible professor who had taught King as an undergraduate. A chapter by Thurman drew on Schweitzer to argue for "a profoundly revolutionary ethic" hiding in plain sight in Christian churches. Because all human beings are "children of a common Father," all human beings are kin, Thurman argued. Therefore, there can be no Christian basis for either racial segregation or race-based hatred.[14]

Thurman was at the time best known as a pastor and preacher. From 1932 to 1944, he had served as dean of Howard University's Rankin Chapel. In 1944 in San Francisco, in an effort to make good on the promise of his Khyber Pass epiphany, he had founded and led an ambitious experiment in interracial and interreligious community known as the Church for the Fellowship of All Peoples. Later, he would move back to the East Coast to serve from 1953 to 1965 as dean of Boston University's Marsh Chapel, which he worked to transform into "a non-creedal, non-sectarian, interracial, interfaith and intercultural religious fellowship."[15]

Thurman also wrote and spoke on race, though he did so reluctantly. "I'm not a movement man. It's not my way," he explained.[16] He was shy and private, an intellectual wary of the vulgarities of politics, allergic to the easy platitudes of partisan rhetoric, and therefore more apt to want to inspire activists than to be one himself. His spirituality called him to the inner journey rather than the march across Selma's Edmund Pettus Bridge. And though he would later attend the March on Washington, where King delivered his famous "I Have a Dream" speech, he would do so inconspicuously, as a man in the crowd rather than a dignitary on the platform. If King was a "drum major for justice," out in front of the marching band, Thurman sat in the back of the orchestra quietly playing his flute.

Like others in Exman's mystics club, Thurman was a Quaker-friendly mystic who excelled at writing and speaking in the meditative mode. Titles of a few of the books he authored for Exman—*Deep Is the Hunger, Meditations of the Heart, The Inward Journey, Disciplines of the Spirit*—hint at the devotional interests he shared with his editor. His sermons, delivered deliberately, included long pauses, as if inviting parishioners to sit with him in the spaces his deep voice was carving out of time. For Thurman, that dialogue with the divine often took place out of doors, while walking along the seashore or sitting back against a tree. In an article he wrote for BU's *Bostonia* magazine, he referred to a favorite oak tree of his youth as "a trysting place where I met and communed with God."[17]

As a Black man in a country with a history of lynching, Thurman knew that trees carried other meanings. And though attracted temperamentally to efforts to transcend race by White liberals such as his mentor, the Quaker mystic and pacifist Rufus Jones, he knew from experience that such luxuries would not be afforded to him. As a result, he wanted nothing to do with mysticism of the escapist variety. In keeping with the religious traditions of enslaved people (and their spirituals), he affirmed the interdependence of body and soul, this world and the next. Following William James, he was convinced that the truth of any mystical experience should be judged by its fruits, the first of which was making justice and peace. To be graced with "a sense of Presence" was in Thurman's view to be confronted by the grim realities of racism, colonialism, and the military-industrial complex. This confrontation led Thurman to argue for the Equal Rights Amendment and to edit a book about a radical feminist named Olive Schreiner. It turned him into an environmentalist who prophesied, "One day nature will revolt and man will discover that he cannot destroy and plunder without being destroyed himself and all his kind." It also led him to echo Frederick Douglass in supporting the original religion of Jesus while opposing the organized religion about Jesus. "Why is it," he asked in his spiritual and social classic *Jesus and the Disinherited* (1949), "that Christianity seems impotent to deal radically, and therefore effectively, with the issues of discrimination and injustice on the basis of race, religion and national origin?" Any true religion must stand with those "who stand with their backs against the wall." And on that score, American Christianity had failed.[18]

Today Thurman is widely described as the forgotten man of the civil rights movement. In fact, this claim has been made so often that it is now difficult to take it seriously. During the "pilgrimage of friendship" trip to the Khyber Pass in 1936, he, his wife, Sue Bailey Thurman, and two colleagues became the first African American delegation to meet with Gandhi. In a wide-ranging three-hour conversation on slavery, lynching, discrimination, Christianity, and colonialism, Gandhi praised the Indian doctrine of ahimsa—noninjury or nonviolence—as a powerful force for political change. According to Thurman's autobiography, at the end of the meeting Thurman asked Gandhi, "What . . . is the greatest handicap to Jesus Christ in India?" Gandhi answered that it was Christianity itself, "as it is practiced, as it has been identified . . . with Western civilization and colonialism." An earlier and competing account, written in 1936 by Gandhi's personal secretary, offers a different ending. Thurman told Gandhi that African Americans were ready to embrace Gandhi's message. If so, Gandhi replied, "it may be through the Negroes that the unadulterated message of non-violence will be delivered to the world."[19]

Six years after that trip, in 1942, the *Pittsburgh Courier* tried to tap Thurman as that deliverer, calling him "one of the few black men in the country around whom a great, conscious movement of Negroes could be built." But Thurman did not want to be America's Gandhi. Once, when Reinhold Niebuhr praised him during a talk at Howard, a student interrupted to criticize Thurman for betraying the movement: "We were sure that he had the makings of a Moses and then he turned the mystic on us." But few activists who knew Thurman were disappointed. Congressman John Lewis called him "the saint of the movement." And Thurman did influence the civil rights struggle, by connecting the dots between freedom fighters in India and the United States, by bringing ideas of nonviolent resistance to public consciousness, and by serving as a source of spiritual renewal for many movement activists, including the one who would come to be known as America's Gandhi.[20]

Thurman and King exchanged warm letters but were never close friends. Thurman was to King more of a mentor and father figure. He was almost exactly the age of King's father, Martin Luther King Sr., who had been a Morehouse undergraduate alongside Thurman. Before Martin Luther King Jr. came into the world on January 15, 1929, Thurman had already graduated first in his class from high school (Florida Baptist Academy in Jacksonville, Florida), college (Morehouse), and divinity school (Rochester Theological Seminary in Rochester, New York). He had also been ordained as a Baptist minister and had returned to Morehouse to teach.

King quoted from Thurman's *Jesus and the Disinherited* in a divinity school paper at Crozer. After arriving at Boston University in the fall of 1951 as a doctoral student in philosophy, he heard Thurman preach at Marsh Chapel. Later he drew on Thurman's sermons in delivering his own. King is said to have carried a well-worn copy of *Jesus and the Disinherited* on his travels, and Thurman's spirit was surely there in his speech on the opening night of the Montgomery bus boycott, when he referred to Blacks being sent to the backs of buses as "the disinherited of this land."[21]

As King was rising to national prominence in Montgomery, Thurman reached out in March 1956 to see if they might sit down and talk privately. King wasn't able to make that work, but he invited Thurman to come preach at his church. Thurman wasn't able to make that work. In their letters, both men seemed keen to meet, however. King kept offering new dates for Thurman's sermon, and Thurman kept saying he was eager for "a long, unhurried, probing conversation" with "several hours in uninterrupted talk."[22]

Age aside, there was a temperament gap between these two men. Thurman was a "contemplative" and King an "active," though King does seem to have had a mystical experience akin to Thurman's Khyber Pass experience. On January 27, 1956, not quite two months into the Montgomery bus boycott, he came home late at night. The phone rang. "Listen, n****r, we've taken all we want from you; before next week you'll be sorry you ever came to Montgomery," a voice said. This was not unusual. King and his wife had received threats before, sometimes dozens a day. But as the threats had piled up, King had become increasingly afraid. "I was ready to give up," he later wrote, and so he prayed. "I am afraid," he said out loud. "I am at the end of my powers. I have nothing left. I've come to the point where I can't face it alone."[23]

"At that moment," King continued, "I experienced the presence of the Divine as I had never experienced Him before. It seemed as though I could hear the quiet assurance of an inner voice saying: 'Stand up for righteousness, stand up for truth; and God will be at your side forever.'" His fears fell away. His resolve hardened. "I was ready to face anything," he said. Three days later his house was bombed, but King, convinced that God was with him, pressed on toward the "beloved community" he and his fellow marchers were struggling to build.[24]

Bro Row

During the late 1950s, Exman moved aggressively into books on race. When Exman signed King's Montgomery book in October 1957, Bro was already working on two other race-and-religion books that Exman would publish around the same time, one by Thurman and another by Bro's sister Harriet Harmon Dexter.

Dexter's *What's Right with Race Relations* (1958) offered an upbeat assessment of racial injustice overcome through "goodwill and mutual appreciation." Her "under-publicized record of what is right" examined transportation, housing, education, labor, religion, sports, electoral politics, the press, and the military, with upbeat case studies of integrated churches in Chicago, President Truman's integration of the armed forces, and the end of segregated dormitories at Michigan State University.

Thurman's *Footprints of a Dream: The Story of the Church for the Fellowship of All Peoples* (1959) was less cheery. It read like a hard-to-write report on a tricky lab experiment, with the experiment being the church he started in San Francisco. The hypothesis, as Thurman put it, was that "people of great ideological and religious diversity" could be united if they focused on shared experiences rather than different beliefs.[25] His findings were mixed.

King's *Stride Toward Freedom* (1958) was simultaneously uplifting and sobering. It documented how tens of thousands of ordinary citizens of Montgomery were willing to risk their lives to make justice. It also documented how little White integrationists were doing to support them, and how determined White segregationists were in opposition. "It is becoming clear that the Negro is in for a season of suffering," King wrote.[26] Whereas Dexter and Thurman presented churches as a force for good in interracial relations, King saw three kinds of churches: Black churches working to relieve suffering, White segregationist churches continuing to inflict it, and White liberal churches sitting on their hands.

As these African American religion books moved toward publication, Exman and Bro clashed as never before. In January 1958, Exman told Bro that he was pushing back the publication date for Dexter's book in order to publish King in his upcoming fall list, when the back-to-school season would make integration front-page news. "I was really shocked," Bro told him, and she detailed her objections—moral, financial, and otherwise—in half a dozen letters in January and February. "We scheduled this Dexter book first and we have a responsibility to the author," she argued. Besides, the book is "one of the best books I have ever had a hand in."[27]

Bro suggested that Exman publish the Dexter and King books together in the fall as "companion pieces." King's book "is a specialized account of a particular advance in a particular place and . . . the Dexter book is the over-all account of progress," she wrote. Moreover, "King is a Negro; Dexter is white. King is famous; Dexter speaks as . . . one of the thousands who has worked for a lifetime to make possible the climate in which the Montgomery advance could be made."[28]

Bro also suggested that Dexter might go to another publisher if her book was pushed back, adding that it was shortsighted to lose "a good solid on-going author for the sake of one popular book from a big name." Yes, King might outsell Dexter. "But he is likely to be a one-book author, since this present book is having to be ghost-written, while she will go on with good books." Bro also called Exman's decision to prioritize King unfair and unprofitable. "If the King book comes out with a whoopla and our salesmen put every-thing behind it, it will skim the cream off the Harper market for a race relations book," she wrote.[29]

Exman's compromise plan was to prepare for both books to fill a two-page feature in the fall catalog. If King's book wasn't ready, they would publish Dexter's. "I know that you feel badly," Exman wrote. "However, if you can look at the thing not as Harriet's sister, but as the head of the publishing department, you can see that in the case of King we are dealing with an author who has been highly pub-licized, who is not only himself involved but with him has brought in a literary agent, who is expecting to sell some of his story to *Look* or the *Post* or *Life*."[30]

Bro's rejoinder began on a conciliatory note. "If we are going ahead in this field of race relations, I am perfectly delighted that we shall be not only writing about the position of the Negro at the present time, but doing some publishing by Negroes," she wrote, adding, "I am terrifically interested in the King book also and I hope it packs a wallop, especially on the non-violent angle." However, she continued to press Exman to publish Dexter's book immediately. "It seems completely necessary to me to put this book out with dispatch, while it is fresh and right up-to-date," she wrote. "I am NOT speaking as Harriet's sister but as an editor who would say the same thing of this book no matter who had written it."[31]

In late March, Exman, clearly annoyed by all the back-and-forthing, sent Bro an unusually stern letter, detailing her own history of missing delivery dates and noting that the Dexter manuscript, whose delivery had itself been repeatedly postponed, still was not submitted. He also wrote that he had just met with King in New York and was able to report that his manuscript was on schedule and would be published in September. After saying nice things about

Dexter's book and its strong sales prospects, he told Bro that, if she was still "rankled," she and Dexter should feel free to take the book elsewhere.[32]

Bro responded by saying more nice things about the King book, which she had just read in part. She reminded Exman that she had sent money to support the Montgomery action long before it was national news. She was "elated that his book is being written and that Harpers will be publishing it," adding, "This is the kind of publishing we should be eternally proud of." But Bro then redirected the conversation from sisterly solidarity to bookman ethics. "You know I have raised questions before about procedures which seem to me a bit less than ethical and the persons concerned were not my relatives," she wrote. "In this case, I feel we had an agreement with an inconspicuous author who had done a workmanlike job, into which she had put at least five thousand dollars in travel and reduced teaching load while writing, and that we had accepted the book for a definite date."[33]

She then told Exman it was time for her to step down from her Harper job:

It is not profitable for either Harpers or for me to continue my work there for the small amount of money involved. I use up too much creative energy on editing. From your point of view, my part is so very small compared with all the books which the department publishes that I am sure the House won't be handicapped without me! I've really had a whale of a good time in much of the Harper work and have enjoyed the association tremendously. I shall be quite lost without it.[34]

Resignation

For years, Bro had expressed her disappointment in Exman, though always in an effort to nudge him to be his best self, and perhaps even to become the sort of saint Gerald Heard had challenged him to be. As they fought over the Dexter and Bro books, the slights and embarrassments piled up and spilled over.

On Easter Day 1958, two days after she gave her notice, she wrote a hard-hitting five-page, single-spaced personal letter to Exman addressing the broader issues. "I know you are disappointed in yourself because I am disappointed in you, too, and one always has higher aspirations for oneself than anyone else has for one," she began. "I feel that for you growth is stymied. . . . Once you felt that no price was too great for a constant sense of God's leading." But now Exman was succumbing to "the pressure of practicalities." He was increasingly distracted by unimportant things. He had "no time nor energy for inner probing." He worried too much "about the esteem [of] certain people 'upstairs.'" In the office he avoided conflict, refusing to face down ethical dilemmas. His "poor memory" was causing "financial hardship" on the people around him (including Bro). His lack of attention to detail was hurting his coworkers.[35]

God is seeking you out, Bro told her friend. It is time to refocus spiritually, to heed "your High Self," to "get back into the clear" via "disciplined meditation," to "go into the Presence." "You can never come to anything like full stature in any other way. Life will pass you by. In fact, relatively speaking, it is passing you by. You could be a great editor, an influence on public life, if you had a clearer mind and more invincible integrity."[36]

In an effort to exonerate himself, Exman drafted eleven handwritten pages of notes toward a point-by-point reply that got deep into the weeds of the economics of publishing. In those notes, he described "balancing author needs and house policy and practice" as an impossible task, likening himself to "a guy balancing two big rubber balls on long sticks, one stick resting in his right palm and the other in his left." Mindful of the fact that Bro was particularly disappointed in him for letting their cooperative venture pass them by, he included a justification for his choice. He admitted that money was a factor—"years of work and sacrifice, now being recompensed"—but presented his decision almost entirely in altruistic terms: "Should I have given up Harpers and started a coop? I seriously considered it. Chose to stay by Harper—prestige of name important for authors; friendships; associates to whom I felt loyalty." He added that he could have made the move if he had only himself to consider but he had responsibilities to Sunny and three children to educate.[37]

After reviewing this draft, Exman smartly opted to send a more contrite letter of apology for his "sins of commission and omission" and most especially for hurting Bro. "Fundamental, as you point out, is my failure to make spiritual progress. Partly, this lack of progress is due to wrong choices made; partly it is lack of time given to meditation; partly it is too much busy-ness," Exman wrote. He agreed he needed to devote more time and energy to cultivating a "clearer mind and more invincible integrity." He then observed that one reason Bro was disappointed in him was that "I am not the five-star person you have sometimes thought (or hoped) that I was. My gifts are offset by limitations." Exman ended this already intimate letter by referring to "dear Margueritte" as "one of the closest" of his friends. "You have given me more than I have given you and I hope that in the years ahead I may be able to restore the balance of trade."[38]

This was the most fraught exchange of their long relationship, but it was also tender on both sides. Bro began her five-page letter by thanking her friend for sending her a basket of a dozen red tulips. "That's sweetly nuts," she said. After sharing with him her conviction that the vast force seeking him out was "inexorably stern but profoundly compassionate" (not unlike the letter writer herself), she signed off, "with love." Exman's short reply was a model apology, both gracious and grateful. He signed his letter, "Your friend forever." And he followed it up with a contrite phone call.

Bro did walk away from her Harper job, but her exit was gradual, as she stayed on to finish projects that were on her desk. There was some tension over a Bible book of hers that Exman turned down that summer, but the letters they exchanged continued to be friendly.

Exman said he was sad to see her go but knew the decision was best for her because she had told him many times that all the editing she did left little creative energy for her own writing. He said he hoped she would continue to do some freelance work for him from time to time. When she got her last Harper paycheck in October 1958, she thanked Exman for "all of the happy associations through the years" but said, "It was right to get off on my own. . . . I'm sure this was the right course."[39]

It was an amiable parting, but it was a parting nonetheless. The late 1950s had been tumultuous for both of them. John Chambers had died in 1955, and Albin Bro the following year. Bro had gone to work for Exman and continued to try to convince him to pick up and start a new publishing cooperative with her in the Midwest. Exman had followed the path of least resistance and remained. Bro had followed a more courageous path and left. After her exit, their correspondence fell off to a few letters a year, often pegged to major life events, such as Wally's marriage and the death of Bro's brother.

Selling the Montgomery Story

Harper planned a huge publicity blitz for *Stride Toward Freedom* just before and after its publication date on September 17, 1958. King solicited reviews from friends. Exman and his Harper colleagues landed blurbs from Blacks and Whites and Protestants and Catholics, featuring them prominently in ads that cost close to $5,000 in religious magazines, Black newspapers and magazines, and city newspapers from New York to Atlanta to Chicago to Dallas to Los Angeles. The *New York Post* ran excerpts. An ad in the African American newspaper the *Amsterdam News* promised "an exciting book crammed with ugly facts that will make your blood boil."[40] Exman himself spoke on the book (in more measured tones) at Riverside Church.

As for King, he spoke at the National Baptist Convention in

Chicago and signed copies of the book at a shopping center there. In New York City, he appeared on NBC television and CBS radio and signed books at a Harlem bookstore. As Exman told Bro, "There has been a busy, almost breathless schedule of radio and TV appearances, lectures, bookstore appearances and conferences. If the poor man survives this New York lionizing, it will be because of his strong constitution and the Providence which watches over him."[41]

He almost didn't. On September 20, 1958, at a Harlem department store book signing, a mentally disturbed Black woman stabbed King in the chest. He was raced to Harlem Hospital, where doctors operated for two hours. As King was recuperating, Exman sent flowers. On September 28, Thurman had a "strange visitation" in which "Martin emerged in my awareness and would not leave." The next day, he took the train to New York to see King, with Exman accompanying him to the hospital. There Thurman counseled King to use this rare time of stillness and quiet to look inside to see, as King put it in a thank-you letter to Thurman, "where do I go from here."[42]

Dozens, perhaps hundreds, of daily newspapers reviewed *Stride Toward Freedom*. So did leading magazines such as the *New Republic*, *The Economist*, and *Saturday Review*, as well as a few academic journals. In the religious press, reviews came in from Catholics in *Commonweal*, White liberal Protestants in *Christian Century*, and White evangelical Protestants in *Christianity Today*. Lutheran, Episcopal, and Mennonite periodicals also reviewed it. A curious review in Dorothy Day's *Catholic Worker* called the book a bracing antidote to the sleepless nights and depression that can overwhelm activists working and living among the poor, even as it praised the nonviolent action in Montgomery as an eminently practical way of love that gives the lie to stereotypes of nonviolence as "an effeminate appeasement with and toward evil." Representing the irreligious press, Perry Miller, a Harvard professor and atheist who devoted his life to understanding the intricacies of Puritan thought in colonial New England, praised King as "the most self-effacing of men" and likening the "restraint" of his prose to the "serenity" of the writing of the eighteenth-century Quaker abolitionist John Woolman.[43]

There were a few negative reviews. In *Christianity Today*, E. Earle Ellis, a Bible professor at Southwestern Baptist Theological Seminary in Fort Worth, Texas, criticized King-style integration as "racial socialism"—a "radical" ideology that, in ignorantly proclaiming "one race," refuses to recognize "the moral right of each race to separate institutions." A reviewer in the *Chattanooga News–Free Press* blasted King as an uneducated "malcontent" who "prates" on for "many tedious pages" about "imaginary" ills. This reviewer also said he was thankful that King was stabbed "in the North by a Negress" because if he had been stabbed in the South by a White man "headlines would have screamed 'racial abuse.'"[44]

Almost every other review was positive. These reviews typically followed the structure of the book by narrating King's life and the Montgomery protest before zooming out to broader matters. Gandhi was often mentioned alongside King's own strategy of nonviolent resistance. Many authors marveled at the discipline of the protesters, who refused to strike back or even express anger. Another common observation was that this was a Christian book by a Christian preacher of Christian love. Father George H. Dunne wrote in *Commonweal* that the true goal of racial segregation was not to denigrate Blacks but to elevate Whites: "White supremacy is the end. It is the idol, and the deepest malice of racial segregation lies in this terrible and idolatrous pride of race which it preserves." Hardly anyone failed to mention King's prophetic voice. In the *New Republic*, the MIT political scientist Harold Isaacs wrote, "Dr. King throws down a rigorous challenge to American white society and to Negroes. He calls on his fellow Christians to be Christians, his fellow democrats to be democrats, and he asks right-thinking whites and his fellow Negroes to join him in refusing to cooperate with evil."[45]

Many reviewers described King as a modest man who made "no effort to steal the show." But few could resist the temptation to ratchet up his significance, preparing the way for his later entry into the pantheon of national and international heroes. One reviewer began by comparing King with Gandhi and Schweitzer. Another concluded that "King's name will be added to those of Nat Turner, Harriet Tubman, Sojourner Truth, Frederick Douglass, W. E. B. Du Bois, and Paul Robeson when the final chapter of the fight of the Negro for full citizenship is written." Harold E. Fey, who as editor in chief of the *Christian Century* had carefully covered the Montgomery story, ended his review with his own prophecy: "Many books record history; a few books make history. *Stride Toward Freedom* will, I believe, do both."[46]

King solicited reviews from many friends and acquaintances, including Lillian Smith, a White Southern novelist and civil rights advocate who spent time as a missionary in China while Bro was there and left committed to fighting colonialism and White supremacy. "This is the most interesting book that has come out of the current racial situation in the South," she wrote in an insightful assessment in the *Saturday Review*. The book is "important as documentary, full of accurate facts that historians will value; exciting as one dramatic scene after another unfolds; wise and compassionate in its point of view." As it layered "a group's story" with "a personal story" and built both on top of "a solid rock of values," Smith wrote, *Stride Toward Freedom* reached and stretched for larger truths, transforming Montgomery itself into "a symbol of man's capacity to meet ordeal not with violence but with creative love and imagination—and in the doing of it, to transcend his limitations."[47]

Why We Can't Wait

King's creative love and imagination would result in two more books with Exman, and he would work with Hermine Popper on both. The first was that collection of sermons he first proposed in January 1957. Exman discussed the idea with him again in 1960, and

King finally began it while jailed in Albany, New York, for fifteen days in July 1962 with his close friend and adviser Ralph Abernathy. This book included sermons preached at Martin Luther King Sr.'s Ebenezer Baptist Church in Atlanta and Dexter Avenue Baptist Church in Montgomery. It appeared in 1963 as *Strength to Love*.

In his sermons and in this book, King drew extensively on Fosdick's first sermon collection, *Hope of the World* (1933), which he had requested many years earlier from Harper. Fosdick had expressed "some misgiving" in his foreword about publishing those sermons, because "the essential nature of the sermon as an intimate, conversational message from soul to soul makes it impossible for printing to reproduce preaching." In the preface to his own sermon collection, King expressed a similar sentiment: "I have been rather reluctant to have a volume of sermons printed. My misgivings have grown out of the fact that a sermon is not an essay to be read but a discourse to be heard. It . . . is directed to the listening ear rather than the reading eye."[48]

Why We Can't Wait (1964), the third and final book King authored while Exman was at Harper, came next. Following in the footsteps of Dorothy Day, who produced two autobiographical books for Exman, this was in some respects a sequel to *Stride Toward Freedom*. It told the story of a campaign in Birmingham, Alabama, that included a boycott of downtown businesses in the spring of 1963 and a stint in jail, where King set his now iconic "Letter from Birmingham Jail." The book also covered the March on Washington for Jobs and Freedom of August 28, 1963, when an estimated quarter of a million people arrived in the nation's capital demanding civil rights. It was there that King delivered his "I Have a Dream" speech, which he drafted with the help of the Black author Alfred Duckett, who worked with King and Popper on *Why We Can't Wait*.

Exman continued to correspond with King until his retirement from Harper in 1965. In 1962, he wrote to inform King about the recent addition of five hundred books to President Kennedy's White House library: "Your book, *Stride Toward Freedom*, was one of the titles selected. Isn't that fine?" King went on to receive far more important accolades. *TIME* named him "Man of the Year" for 1963. In October 1964 he won the Nobel Peace Prize for his work in nuclear nonproliferation, making him Exman's second author (after Schweitzer) to become a Nobel laureate.

Toward the end of his life, King more explicitly integrated his civil rights work into antiwar and antipoverty activism—by publicly opposing the Vietnam War, including at a speech in Riverside Church in April 1967, and by organizing a Poor People's Campaign that would be held in May and June of 1968. He also continued to march—across the Edmund Pettus Bridge in Selma, Alabama, and into Memphis, Tennessee, where he delivered his "I've Been to the Mountaintop" speech one day before he was shot and killed on April 4, 1968.

Eulogizing King

Among the most insightful words that followed the silencing of King's voice were remarks Howard Thurman hastily prepared for the radio the night King was assassinated. Stepping into the space between meaning and meaninglessness that cracks open in such moments, Thurman cycled back to themes of the religion of experience of Exman's mystics club, casting King first and foremost as a human being who marched with the disinherited and walked with God.

"There are no words with which to eulogize this man," Thurman began, but the moment demanded something, so he said:

> Perhaps his greatest contribution to our times and to the creative
> process of American society is not to be found in his amazing
> charismatic power over masses of people, nor is it to be found
> in his peculiar and challenging courage with its power to trans-
> form the fear-ridden black men and women with a strange new
> valor, nor is it to be found in the gauntlet which he threw down

to challenge the inequities and brutalities of a not quite human people—but rather in something else. Always he spoke from within the context of his religious experience, giving voice to an ethical insight which sprang out of his profound brooding over the meaning of his Judeo-Christian heritage. And this indeed is his great contribution to our times. He was able to put at the center of his own personal religious experience a searching, ethical awareness. Thus organized religion as we know it in our society found itself with its back against the wall. To condemn him, to reject him, was to reject the ethical insight of the faith it proclaimed. And this was new. Racial prejudice, segregation, discrimination were not regarded by him as merely un-American, undemocratic, but as a mortal sin against God. For those who are religious it awakens guilt; for those who are merely superstitious it inspires fear. And it was this fear that pulled the trigger of the assassin's gun that took his life.[49]

It is important to remember that King's reputation then was nothing like it is today. In a recent study, researchers asked high school students in all fifty states to name the most famous Americans, presidents excepted. The leading answer was King. That is not surprising. Today Martin Luther King Jr. Day is an official US holiday. Atlanta's Ebenezer Baptist Church, where King was baptized and where his funeral was held, is part of a national historic park. In Washington, DC, King stands, literally larger than life, in a granite-carved statue at the Martin Luther King Jr. Memorial. Revelations of King's plagiarism at Boston University and evidence of his marital infidelities, captured over years of FBI surveillance, do not seem to have tarnished that reputation.

At the time of his assassination, however, King was far from a revered man. A poll conducted days after his death found that one-third of Americans blamed King for his own assassination. Later in 1968, a survey found that three-quarters of Whites disapproved of him, but Black Americans were also divided, with some lauding him and others dismissing him as a sellout. He was caught, as James Baldwin had observed years earlier, "in the center of an extremely complex crossfire." Only years after his death did he become an American icon. In this respect, King's afterlife charted a very different path from that of Schweitzer, who died a saint and was then forgotten. King died largely unloved and became a blessed martyr.[50]

Observers have long debated the meaning of Martin Luther King Jr. Was he the leader of the civil rights movement? Or was he a relatively small player whose importance has been exaggerated by editors at *TIME* and Harper? Was he the liberal nemesis of the radical Malcolm X? Or was he a radical himself? And where and how was he formed?

In his books and essays, King credits Thoreau and Gandhi for his understanding of nonviolent civil disobedience. He also pays his debts to European and American thinkers such as the social gospel theologian Walter Rauschenbusch, the social ethicist Reinhold Niebuhr, and various personalist philosophers and theologians he read and studied under at Boston University.

Some have argued that this genealogy of King's influences underplays the crucial influences exerted on King by his family, his church, and broader African American culture. According to this point of view, King contributed little to his books and essays, which were constructed to satisfy northern White editors and readers, and were ghostwritten by advisers such as his friend Bayard Rustin, his lawyer Stanley Levison, and the civil rights advocate Harris Wofford. Therefore, they are not reliable primary sources for understanding King's faith and thought. According to the Black liberation theologian James Cone, the real King is to be found in the "preached word" of his unpublished sermons and the "practiced word" of his nonviolent direct actions.[51] There one hears the unmistakable echoes of the slave spirituals, the Black folk tradition, the Black church tradition, and King's father, "Daddy King."

Cone and others are right to correct misunderstandings that King was somehow unaffected by his upbringing in his family, the Black church, and Black culture, as if he sprang full-born from the mind of Walter Rauschenbusch or Reinhold Niebuhr. They are also right to observe that King's writings do not present some pure, pristine King. His Harper books were certainly collaborations. However, his spoken words were collaborations, too. King had help with many of his speeches, and drew extensively in his sermons from other preachers, both Black and White. Neither were the influences of the White theologians and philosophers he read in college and graduate school absent from his preached and practiced word.

Among those influences, King was indebted to Harry Emerson Fosdick, who may have shaped King more than any academic theologian or philosopher. Unlike some of his more optimistic liberal Protestant colleagues, Fosdick carried forward from the depths of his depression an awareness of the tragic sense of life. He was a pacifist. He denounced racial segregation as early as 1933. And he spoke and wrote from the perspective that the world was in crisis. It is no accident that King delivered his most powerful speech against the Vietnam War in Fosdick's Riverside Church.

Aware of these debts, King sent Fosdick an inscribed copy of *Stride Toward Freedom*. "If I were called upon to select the foremost prophets of our generation, I would choose you to head the list," wrote King, who would himself be anointed with that mantle. Fosdick replied graciously, thanking him for the book and the kind inscription:

> We are all unpayably in your debt, not only for what you did but for putting the story down where thousands of people can read it.
>
> As for that inscription, my dear friend, I never possibly could deserve it. . . . I am sure that I never faced the kind of problem that you face with anything like the courage that you have so magnificently displayed. I am sure you know without my saying so with what intimate care and sympathy we here in the North share with you the struggle you are carrying on in the South.[52]

What emerges from this evidence is a picture of King as an adept in cultural and religious combination, creatively mixing into a new practice of nonviolent protest the insights of social gospel theologians and personalist philosophers, the examples of Gandhi and Thoreau, and the things he learned in Sunday school and in the pew at Ebenezer Baptist. Like Bill Wilson and AA's Big Book, King was by no means the sole author of *Stride Toward Freedom*. But he orchestrated its making as dexterously as Wilson did. He rejected the ghostwriters Rodell auditioned in New York City, bringing on Reddick instead. He accepted Popper because Exman recommended her, but he chose to work with her on future books because she did an excellent job setting down what King was thinking, doing, and feeling. Readers are right to find at least as much Alex Haley as Malcolm X in the "as told to" *Autobiography of Malcolm X*, which Haley completed after Malcolm X was himself assassinated. But King was alive and well when *Stride Toward Freedom*, *Strength to Love*, and *Why We Can't Wait* appeared, and in their making he was neither passive nor disempowered. Still, debates about authorship linger to this day.

Some claims about the ghostwriting of *Stride Toward Freedom* are based on misunderstandings about the different roles ghostwriters play in writing books. There are cases where authors not only fail to write a single word but also never read one. The former NBA star Charles Barkley said he was misquoted in his own autobiography, and President Ronald Reagan said of his memoir, "I hear it's a terrific book. One of these days I'm going to read it myself."[53] There are cases where authors meet a few times with a ghostwriter, tell their stories, and then leave the rest to the ghostwriter. There are also cases of closer collaboration, where the author produces drafts for a ghostwriter to polish. And there are cases where the hired hand acts more like a copyeditor. Bro worked for Exman on books that fell all along this spectrum. *Stride Toward Freedom*, which was produced from King's handwritten chapter drafts, then amended by others with King's approval and input, clearly fell on the active-author side of the ghostwriting spectrum.

The argument that King's books are somehow not his own also seems to neglect that good ghostwriters work hard to stay in the background. Their job is to suppress their own voices in order to channel those of their authors. If ghostwriters are writing their own books in their own styles, they aren't doing their jobs. As Bayard Rustin said of his work with King, "I don't want to write something for somebody where I know he is acting like a puppet. I want to be a real ghost and write what the person wants to say. And that is what I always knew was true in the case of Martin. I would never write anything that wasn't what he wanted to say."[54]

White Liberals

This is not to suggest that King's collaborators did not influence *Stride Toward Freedom*. There were tensions between the desires of the White liberals (Exman included) who worked on King's books and the political and theological commitments of King himself. And there were ways that Exman and his staff bent books on race by King and Thurman alike in the direction of their desires.

In the late 1950s, many White liberals were in thrall to *An American Dilemma: The Negro Problem and Modern Democracy* (1944) by the Swedish economist and sociologist Gunnar Myrdal. The dilemma in the title pointed to the yawning gap between the lofty ideals of justice and equality enshrined in what Myrdal called the "American Creed" and the refusal of many Whites to grant civil rights to Blacks, or simply to recognize their humanity. Why such a gap between ideals and realities?

Though widely credited with influencing the Supreme Court to reject "separate but equal" public schools in *Brown v. Board of Education* (1954), Myrdal has been criticized for presenting an overly rosy assessment of the march toward a postracist society. Seduced by Myrdal's report, and by their shared belief in the goodness of human nature, the power of reason, the efficacy of education, and the inevitability of social progress, many White liberals became convinced that civil rights would come gradually, without coercion and with little conflict. The key to resolving the dilemma was attitudinal rather than legal and political: to get Blacks and Whites to love and respect one another as citizens of one nation.

Exman, Bro, and other White liberals at Harper were with Myrdal here. They saw themselves as allies in the civil rights struggle. They wanted to improve "race relations" in the United States, but they wanted to do so without posing any real threat to their White privilege, their own ways of living and thinking. Dexter's *What's Right with Race Relations* was a model of the naïveté that led so many White liberals to sit on the sidelines of the civil rights struggle. As Dexter moved in the book from one feel-good story to another, she offered a wildly premature celebration of the arrival of a postracial society. In the debate about whether integration should proceed quickly or slowly, she refused to take sides. In a chapter called "Search for a Culprit," she refused to find one. "No one today is to blame!" she insisted. Critics saw through this wishy-washy Pollyannaism, which with the benefit of more than six decades of hindsight now seems cruelly credulous. Working "the bright side of the street," Dexter "thinks that the present momentum generated by good race relations will carry us shortly into a widely desegregated society," wrote one reviewer. "The author does not see, however, that we may just now have come to the hardest part of the road."[55]

Bro and Exman didn't see the hard stuff either, despite their anti-war radicalism. Neither did Exman's staff. Perhaps that is because they sided with Fosdick and other liberal Protestants on sin, preferring to see human nature as basically good rather than basically evil, and rejecting Reinhold Niebuhr's argument, accepted by King, that Christian love sometimes demands coercion. Perhaps it was because they were assimilationists rather than antiracists, to borrow from the Boston University professor Ibram X. Kendi.

One recurring request in the notes Harper's White liberals gave to King's group in Montgomery was that King should appeal to both White and Black readers by writing about both Whites and Blacks in Montgomery—a request, in other words, to integrate *Stride Toward Freedom* itself. Underlying this request was a related desire for quick and easy racial harmony that would prove elusive.

When it came to race, Exman's perennialist belief in the unity of religions did not serve him well. Perennialism is rooted, among other things, in a desire to see commonality over difference. There can be good reasons to feed this understandable desire—to prevent religious warfare, for example, or to foster interreligious harmony. But when the perennialist desire for religious unity shaded over in Harper's offices into a desire for racial unity, it often reproduced a desire to leap prematurely to racial repair and reconciliation, as if centuries of slavery, lynching, and Jim Crow could be overcome with one wave of a magic wand (or one bestselling book).

Bro was waving this wand when she glibly told Thurman that segregation was "done away with," and when she described *Footprints of a Dream* in Harper's catalog copy as "the dramatic story of the first American church which actually achieved full interracial unity." Exman and other members of King's editorial team were waving it when they asked King to end *Stride Toward Freedom* with "an eloquent plea for love and the brotherhood of man."[56]

White Supremacy and Antiracism

In late March 1965, about a year and a half after King's "I Have a Dream" speech and while King and other civil rights activists were in the news for leading marchers from Selma to Montgomery, Exman dreamed about King. "I dreamed a dream; a dream within a dream," he wrote in his dream diary:

I had just heard Martin Luther King preach.

Gave him bear hug.

I said that I had a great respect for him ever since we first met and valued his friendship highly; that I loved him as a brother.

He replied that he felt that way and we agreed that the color line did not exist for us in regard to each other.

There was a strong feeling of affection.[57]

This was more dream than reality. King surely perceived a "color line" operating at Harper, and King and Exman, while friendly, were never close.

Exman and Thurman, who worked together on eleven books, did share "a strong feeling of affection." Thurman was close to two of Exman's best friends: Margueritte Bro and John Chambers (at whose funeral Thurman officiated). Thurman deeply admired Albert Schweitzer, as did Exman. Thanks to his Khyber Pass epiphany, Thurman was also a member of Exman's mystics club and a partisan of socially conscious "affirmative mysticism." After being invited to Exman's retirement party in 1965, Thurman wrote a warm letter of congratulations and regret: "Gene, you have been an abiding [source] of strength and renewal to so many of us in whom you believed with such integrity," he wrote. "I wish I could join your friends at dinner; instead I greet you with my heart."[58]

There are many reasons why King and Exman never became as close as Exman and Thurman. The most obvious is that King was too busy. Another is that he often worked with Exman through a veil of advisers and lawyers. Yet another is that Exman, as a well-to-do White liberal, never really understood King's struggle. Thurman's life, which combined interracial and interreligious activism, was more legible to Exman. He and Thurman both had mystical experiences and paranormal interests. They were both pacifists who had served in the Student Army Training Corps at the end of World War I. They both liked hanging around academics and engaging in long, lingering conversations. Exman joined King in denouncing the Vietnam War, but he never called for the radical restructuring of American life that King demanded as he took on poverty and capitalism more forcefully over the course of the 1960s.

Exman must be credited with actively seeking out both Thurman and King as authors, traveling to Washington, DC, to meet Thurman in the late thirties and to Montgomery to meet King in the late fifties. His resulting collaborations with these men produced more than twenty enduring books on religion and race in the United States. Together King and Thurman made major contributions to Exman's Book of Books. But their experiences at Harper also demonstrate the depths of racial injustice in American life. Exman was able to cross over to a form of religious pluralism that saw Christianity as but one vessel in which mystical experiences of the divine might be contained. He argued for absolute pacifism over the course of his entire adult life. But he was unable to see the power of the White supremacy that confronted King and Thurman daily.

Back when Marie Rodell was working to find a New York City ghostwriter to work with King on *Stride Toward Freedom*, she and King's lawyer Stanley Levison had interviewed two White candidates. Rodell prepared for the meeting by going to the library and reading a couple of articles by Reddick. Afterward, Levison, who was White, wrote to King about a disconnect he felt in the meeting:

> This is the old story that too many white liberals consider themselves free of stereotypes, rarely recognizing that the roots of prejudice are deep and are tenaciously driven into the soil of their whole life. I know I did not resolve this for myself by reading a few articles and pronouncing myself a person of good will. The acid test I have always used is deeds involving significant sacrifice based on the acceptance of the painful truth that we share responsibility for the crimes and gain release from complicity only by fighting to end them. On this score the two men we met fell short.

Exman and Bro fell short, too, though Bro did better than Exman. For all her naïveté about the future of race relations in the United States, Bro was out in front of most liberal Protestants in her early support for civil rights. In 1936, in *Christian Century*, she endorsed experimental Black cooperatives in Gary, Indiana. She leaned on her brother Henry Harmon to hire more Black faculty while he was the president at Drake. She also arranged for many Black speakers and musicians to come to Shimer while her husband was the president there. When musicians of the Chicago Symphony rejected a Black man who had won a job alongside them as a violinist after auditioning from behind a screen, she hired him to come to Shimer to perform and to talk with students. After encountering many Blacks, including the civil rights activist James Farmer, on a speaking trip in 1943, she told Exman, "Our race problem is real and mounting."[59]

Exman doubtless saw the books he published by Thurman and King as contributions to the civil rights struggle. And they were. Exman also integrated his mystics club and his Harper list, but there is no evidence that he leaned on anyone to make Harper's workplace more racially equitable or racially just. Dozens of his letters communicate a sense of urgency about opposing war and eliminating nuclear weapons, and he devoted hundreds of hours to helping conscientious objectors get out of jail, enroll in conscientious objector camps, and get jobs. He communicated no similar urgency about opposing racial segregation or White supremacy.

Exman's diary of his pilgrimage to Schweitzer in 1950 reveals a man eager to oppose stereotypes about Black people but unable to avoid those stereotypes himself. About his thirty-two-hour train trip across what is now the Democratic Republic of the Congo, Exman, "the only white aboard," pronounced himself delighted by his experience. "I had more trip for the money than at any other time in my life," he wrote, thanks to "much vivacious talking," much singing, and "much laughter," including by a "handsome black" who was by his sights an "ideal type for a Hollywood producer." Levison was annoyed when he learned that Rodell believed that reading a few articles by Reddick could give her a measure of the man. He would have been more annoyed to know that Exman thought he came away from one train ride with "a pretty good conception of natives." Among other things, he supposedly learned that "black people are a friendly, generous and fun-loving folk."[60]

To be fair, Exman learned a lot more about race as the civil rights movement captured national headlines during the rest of the 1950s, but even in 1959 he wouldn't have passed Levison's test. Shortly after *Stride Toward Freedom* was published, and while King was still recuperating from his bookstore stabbing, Exman corresponded with the *Harper's Magazine* editor John Fischer about an article Fischer wanted King to write. According to a Fischer memo to Exman, which Exman forwarded to King, the article would be "an epistle directed primarily to Negroes, reminding them that their present struggle for equality places certain special burdens and responsibilities on each of them." Instead of calling on Whites to acknowledge the human and constitutional rights of Blacks, the article Fischer envisioned would call on Blacks "to demonstrate to hostile, skeptical, and indifferent white people that they not only have a moral right to full civic equality, but are capable of handling it." Fischer noted that he could get a White writer to say this stuff, but that "might be misinterpreted by both whites and Negroes." Ignorant of how distasteful it would be for King to receive a request to act as a ventriloquist dummy for a White man's desire for peace without justice, Exman forwarded Fischer's memo. In a cover letter he urged King to write the article, which he described as a "step toward bringing Negroes and Whites closer together." King did not comply.[61]

In his book *A Stone of Hope*, the historian David Chappell asked why Black activists were able to put an end to legally enforced segregation while White liberals were not. What set King and other Black activists apart, he argued, was their prophetic religion. Schooled in the rhetoric of the Hebrew prophets and the neo-orthodox theology of Reinhold Niebuhr, they took for granted the sinfulness of individuals and institutions. They knew that power corrupts, that the powerful do not give it up without a fight, and that in such fights religious enthusiasm is more potent than rational argument. Black activists overthrew Jim Crow not because they had a dream but because they had a strategy—a workable campaign rooted not in pieties about human goodness and global progress but in a realistic awareness of the intractability of sin. It was White liberals who were asleep. Lulled by Gunnar Myrdal's writing on race, they came to believe that civil rights would come gradually, without coercion. They were unduly optimistic about human nature, the power of reason, the efficacy of education, and the inevitability of social progress. And because they had no common faith, they could not instill in their followers either solidarity or discipline.

Exman was not naive about human nature. And he had faith. But he relied too much on the power of providence when it came to the civil rights struggle. His "beloved community" was a group of like-minded mystics committed to searching for God and doing some good along the way. There was a passivity about him that irritated Bro. He was allergic to conflict, and often he did little more to resolve it than to wait for it to resolve itself. He justified this hands-off policy by telling himself (and others) that God was in charge. Humans did not pray; God prayed through them; it was God who inspired *Stride Toward Freedom*; the "Source" was King's ghostwriter. King believed in providence. But he believed this, too: the only hands on earth to do the hard work of mercy and justice are human hands.

After his New York City editorial team urged King to end *Stride Toward Freedom* with a paean to love and a plea for human brotherhood, King did the opposite. He concluded with a prophetic warning worthy of Amos, Isaiah, and other Hebrew Bible prophets:

In a day when Sputniks and Explorers dash through outer space and guided ballistic missiles are carving highways of death through the stratosphere, nobody can win a war. Today the choice is no longer between violence and non-violence. It is either nonviolence or nonexistence. The Negro may be God's appeal to this age—an age drifting rapidly to its doom. The eternal appeal takes the form of a warning: "All who take the sword will perish by the sword."

To his credit, Exman let that prophecy stand.[62]

CHAPTER SEVEN

Bill Wilson, LSD, and the Book
That Changed Everything

One of the most important episodes in Exman's life, and one of his biggest contributions to modern American religion, began with a book that got away.

Exman was not quite a decade into his Harper job when a friend named Frank Amos called in the fall of 1938 to ask for a meeting. Amos was an ad man with lots of international experience and lots of experience with alcoholism. Though he was not an alcoholic himself, two of his brothers were, and earlier in the 1930s he had worked to consolidate temperance groups across the United States into one national organization. He was now working with a not-yet-named group of recovering alcoholics who had taken a novel peer-to-peer approach to treating alcoholism. In fact, the *New York Times* would later credit him as one of the nonalcoholic cofounders of Alcoholics Anonymous (AA).[1]

Because of its commitment to anonymity and the reluctance of AA's real founders to violate it, the list of AA's cofounders has fluctuated over time. Even William James has been nominated, for lending AA his signature commitments to pluralism and pragmatism. However, historians of the movement typically trace its genesis to two guiding lights, Bill Wilson and Bob Smith, known in AA circles as Bill W. and Dr. Bob. Wilson was a Wall Street guy from New

York City. Smith was a surgeon from Akron, Ohio. Together they helped keep each other sober and spread their movement world-wide.

In May 1935, with the national unemployment rate hovering around 20 percent, Wilson found himself in Ohio on a failed business trip and desperate for a drink. Equally desperate not to land in a hospital for yet another round of detox, he decided to track down a drunk who could talk him out of his next drink. After a series of fruitless phone calls to numbers listed in a church directory, someone referred him to a woman named Henrietta Seiberling. Wilson called her, and she introduced him to an alcoholic she was trying to rescue: Bob Smith. Wilson and Smith talked for hours over dinner at Seiberling's house, and Wilson never had another drink. Roughly a month later, on June 10, 1935, Smith had his own last drink. That day is now remembered as the founding date for Alcoholics Anonymous, underscoring its core contention that alcoholics move from drunkenness to sobriety not through the prohibitions of the federal government or the volunteerism of nonprofit temperance groups but through the mysterious power of person-to-person encounters. That day also commenced AA's "flying blind period"—a span of four years before AA was known as AA, when Wilson and Smith and their collaborators were struggling to define their mission, including how religious, or spiritual, it should be.[2]

Smith was a Bible-believing Christian who did his daily devotions with his Bible at hand. Wilson was a spiritual seeker and a fan of James's *Varieties of Religious Experience*. Both were active in the Oxford Group, a loose, nonsectarian, yet clearly Christian organization that prided itself on not being a religion. It stressed surrender to God's authority, daily prayer, quiet time for contemplation, and observance of strict standards of personal morality. However, according to its "holy Crusaders in modern dress," the Oxford Group had "no membership list, . . . no hierarchy, no temples, . . . no plans but God's Plan."[3]

As Wilson and Smith planted what was originally known as the

Fellowship in New York and Akron, respectively, they borrowed key practices from the Oxford Group, including "self-examination, acknowledgement of character defects, restitution for harm done, and working with others." Over time, however, the Oxford Group began to rub Wilson the wrong way, especially when it came to theology and social class. According to one biographer, Wilson saw the Oxford Group as "a bunch of Christers, rich folks mostly, all very chic and high-minded." And so the Fellowship gradually distanced itself from the Oxford Group's moral absolutism and Christian doctrines, presenting itself as "religious" rather than "Christian," pragmatic rather than dogmatic, broad rather than narrow, and nonjudgmental rather than moralistic. In this transformation, one of the most influential spiritual leaders of his day (and an Exman author), Emmet Fox, was a crucial influence, charting a path that AA would later follow, away from the militaristic God of laws and punishments many recovering alcoholics associated with Christianity to the kinder, friendlier "Divine Intelligence" preached in Fox's books and sermons.[4]

During the Fellowship's first five years, Wilson struggled to raise money to support its work and those (himself included) who were laboring on it full-time, or more, and going broke in the process. Tall and handsome, Wilson was a natural salesman as addicted to grandiosity as he was to alcohol. Convinced that he and his Fellowship were embarking on "one of the greatest medical, religious and social developments of all time," he decided to shoot for the moon. John D. Rockefeller Jr. was at the time the richest man in the world. Why not try him? Wilson found a way to approach Rockefeller through intermediaries, who set up a meeting at 30 Rockefeller Plaza on December 13, 1937. Smith and Amos and others from the Fellowship were there, as were various Rockefeller men. One of those men, Albert Scott, chaired Riverside's Board of Trustees and had led the Laymen's Foreign Mission Inquiry that had produced the groundbreaking, Exman-published study of foreign missions, *Rethinking Missions*. Scott, who ran the meeting, flattered the Fellowship's small-group work as "nothing less than first-century Christianity in its most beautiful form," only to say it would be foolish "to spoil this great work of yours with money." In the end, Rockefeller agreed to provide $5,000 and nothing more, on the theory that the movement needed to support itself and should not professionalize.[5]

What to do? Plan B was to write a book, which would produce revenue to support the work Wilson and Smith and others were doing. A book would also spread the Fellowship's story to alcoholics far beyond Akron and New York. Much debate ensued. The Akron folks opposed it on oddly originalist grounds, arguing that "Jesus didn't have any pamphlets or books when He started out."[6] (Presumably, he didn't have any alcoholics either.) They also worried that a book explaining their person-to-person approach to recovery might hit them with a barrage of requests for help they could never provide. But Wilson pressed on, beginning writing in the spring of 1938. That decision would lead to another candidate for AA's founding moment: the publication on April 10, 1939, of *Alcoholics Anonymous*, which because of its heavy paper and four-hundred-plus pages came to be known as the Big Book.

"The Book of Experience"

Stories of the founding of religious movements and the compiling of scriptures are always encrusted in myth and legend. Any narrative of the origins of AA and the making of the Big Book must navigate Bill Wilson's tendency to reshape narratives to fit changing circumstances. One of the tall tales told by AA's mythmaker par excellence was that the Big Book was the joint work product of a legion of recovered drunks. One virtue of this tale is that it exemplifies AA's emphasis on anonymity. Another is that it is partly true. As Wilson was gestating the book, he worked closely with Henry Parkhurst (a former Standard Oil executive fired for his drinking) and Ruth Hock (a secretary who did far more for the book than type). Others looked over his shoulder as Wilson was writing, offering suggestions along the way. But it was *his* book. He wrote its famous Twelve Steps. He picked the title. He coordinated the printing, publicity, and distribution. And though the eleven general chapters that begin the book are often presented as distillations of the twenty-nine personal stories that end it, they are better understood as distillations of Wilson's own story, his own ideas.

As they worked on the book, Wilson and Parkhurst did not always agree, but their disagreements were productive, especially when informed by disagreements between the Akron and New York centers. Wilson was, like Exman, a Christian with a mystical bent. Parkhurst began his recovery as either an atheist or an agnostic but morphed into something of a deist, who believed in a distant divinity but rejected any notion of a personal God who answered individual prayers. As Hock recalled it, she and Parkhurst were for "very little" religion in the Big Book. Others, including many in Akron, were "for going all the way with God." Wilson saw himself as going "pretty much down the middle," pushing for lots of religion but happy to leave it as vague as possible.[7]

One reason Wilson insisted on God talk was that he himself had seen God. In the winter of 1934, while in his late thirties, he went on a bender and was admitted for the fourth time to Towns Hospital on Manhattan's Upper West Side. There he wrestled with his demons under the empathetic treatment of the hospital's director, Dr. William Silkworth, and the watchful eye of his friend Ebby Thacher, who all but begged Wilson to beg God for help. Wilson was also treated with a mixture of drugs that included belladonna, a known hallucinogen. What came next was a "white light experience" that exhibited many of the classic features of mystical experiences as described by William James in *Varieties*: personal darkness, a blinding light, a sense of something revealed, and an inability to fully capture that revelation in words. Accounts of this mystical experience are legion in AA lore, but this is how Wilson first described it in public, at an AA convention in 1955:

My depression deepened unbearably and finally it seemed to me as though I were at the bottom of the pit. . . . All at once I found myself crying out, "If there is a God, let Him show Himself! I am ready to do anything, anything!"

Suddenly the room lit up with a great white light. I was caught up into an ecstasy which there are no words to describe. It seemed to me, in the mind's eye, that I was on a mountain and that a wind not of air but of spirit was blowing. And then it burst upon me that I was a free man. Slowly the ecstasy subsided. I lay on the bed, but now for a time I was in another world, a new world of consciousness. All about me and through me there was a wonderful feeling of Presence, and I thought to myself, "So this is the God of the preachers!" A great peace stole over me and I thought, "No matter how wrong things seem to be, they are still all right. Things are all right with God and His world."[8]

After Wilson shared this experience with Silkworth, his doctor responded, "Something has happened to you I don't understand. But you had better hang on to it."[9] Wilson did just that, presenting AA's cure in the book he was writing as a religious and spiritual solution—a conversion from drunkenness to sobriety powered by the mysterious energy of the divine.

As Wilson, Parkhurst, and Hock discussed and debated what they were now referring to as "The Book of Experience," two types of chapters emerged. The bulk of the book would comprise personal testimonies of recovery akin to the conversion stories in James's *Varieties*. The remainder would be devoted to more programmatic chapters detailing key beliefs and practices of their person-to-person approach to recovery, including what are now known as the Twelve Steps.

Wilson wrote one personal testimony chapter (his) and one overarching "general chapter" (diagnosing the alcoholic's problem and outlining the cure). Amos, who supported this book project, urged him to take what he had to Exman—to see if he might offer an advance that could pay the bills for a few months. "Perhaps he would be interested in your new book," Amos told Wilson. "Why don't you go down there and show him the few chapters you have done. I'll fix it up for you."[10]

How Exman and Amos knew each other is unknown. Exman's unpublished account of his role in the making of *Alcoholics Anonymous* refers to Amos as a friend and fellow Denison alumnus, so they might have met through Denison, where they would later serve together on the Board of Trustees. It is also possible they met through Baptist connections, which would later lead both to attend Scarsdale Community Baptist Church in Scarsdale, New York. Another possibility is that they met, directly or indirectly, through John D. Rockefeller Jr. (also a Baptist). Exman knew Rockefeller through Riverside Church and Fosdick. Amos was one of Rockefeller's senior advisers.

Wilson brought Parkhurst to Exman's office in late September or early October of 1938. They gave Exman their best pitch and then handed over Wilson's drafts of the two chapters that would later open the book: a programmatic chapter called "There Is a Solution" and "Bill's Story," a first-person account of Wilson's recovery.[11]

In "There Is a Solution," Wilson shared the "great news" of the Fellowship's alleged one hundred recovering drunks. After defining alcoholism in medical and psychological terms—as a combination of addiction and insanity—he promised that the cure to follow would not include the usual nonsense of churches and temperance societies. "There are no fees to pay, no axes to grind," Wilson pledged, "nor people to please, nor sermons to be listened to, nor moralizing to be endured, nor any attitude of holier than thou, nor anything whatever except the sincere desire to be helpful, and to lay at the feet of another the same simple kit of tools which has enabled us to literally take up our beds and walk." As that last biblical image suggests, however, Wilson's "great news" was religious, or spiritual, or both. In other words, it was a gospel, which like the Four Gospels of the Christian New Testament augured miracle stories to come: the sick would be healed, and drunks delivered to "a heaven right here on this good old earth."[12]

Parkhurst, who had never experienced anything like Wilson's "white light experience" or Exman's Blanchester graveyard epiphany, had been pushing Wilson to write an "irreligious" book resting on a foundation of medicine and psychology alone. Keeping religion out of it was the best way to attract more drunks and more readers, he insisted, and in "To Employers," the chapter he contributed to the Big Book, God is never mentioned. Wilson couldn't set aside God talk, however. God was part and parcel of the cure he was so desperate to preach. "The GREAT FACT" at the center of AA's story, he wrote in "There Is a Solution," is "just this and no less; that all of us have had deep and effective religious experiences which in every case revolutionized our whole attitude toward life, toward our fellows and toward God's great universe."[13]

All this proceeded logically from a binary choice Wilson forced on his readers. Once you have dug your hole and burrowed into it, you have just two alternatives, he argued. One is to proceed on your own. This path will lead only to destruction and death. But there is another possibility, the path of devotion to a personal God of one's choosing. This path alone offers the "vital religious experiences" Carl Jung (another honorary AA cofounder) referred to in a celebrated letter to Wilson.[14] This alone is the road to recovery.

"There Is a Solution" then turned to James's *Varieties* in an effort to reassure agnostics and other religion-allergic readers that, while divine energy is necessary to fuel the conversion from drunkenness to sobriety, no particular conception of the divine is required. As Wilson described it, the Fellowship exhibited James's personal approach as well as his pluralism and pragmatism—his tendencies to understand religion as personal rather than social, to praise religious difference, and to judge religious and philosophical claims by their external results rather than their internal logic. James "indicates a multitude of ways in which men have found God," Wilson wrote. "As a group, or as individuals, we have no desire to convince anyone

that the true God can only be discovered in some particular way."
The Fellowship included "nearly every conceivable political, economic,
social and religious background and shade of belief." Its program
was grounded in whatever would save alcoholics from ruin. "It really
works," Wilson promised.[15]

As Exman scanned the second chapter, now called "Bill's Story,"
he encountered a mystic like himself. While a soldier in his twenties in England during World War II, Wilson "stood in Winchester
Cathedral with head bowed," asking why God seemed to be absent
as thousands of soldiers died that day in Europe. "Suddenly in that
moment of darkness—He was there!" Wilson wrote. "I felt an envel-
oping comforting Presence. Tears stood in my eyes. I had glimpsed
the great reality."[16]

"Bill's Story" also transported Exman to Lower Manhattan and
those desperate times when the stock market crash of October 1929
sank so many on Wall Street. During one of Bill's Depression-era
binges, his friend Ebby Thacher called him up and invited him over.
As they sat at Ebby's kitchen table, Bill's friend told him his own
great news of recovery along the lines of the "Solution" chapter.
Wilson at the time was no atheist—"In a power greater than myself I had always believed," he confessed—but he associated religion
with violence and had no use for the hypocritical professions of a
not-so-loving God. However, as he listened to Ebby, whose "will
had failed," whose doctors "had pronounced him incurable," who
"had admitted complete defeat," he realized it was possible to be
"raised from the dead," not through self-effort but through other-
power. "Never mind the musty past," Wilson testified. "Here sat a
miracle directly across the kitchen table." Inspired by his friend, "I
quit playing God," Wilson continued. "I humbly offered myself to
God, as I then understood him, to do with me as He would." What
happened next was "electric," reminiscent of Wilson's Winchester
Cathedral experience and Exman's Blanchester graveyard event:
"There was a sense of victory, followed by such a peace and serenity
as I had never known. There was utter confidence. I felt lifted up,

as though the great clean wind of a mountain top blew through and through. God comes to most men gradually, but His impact on me was sudden and profound."[17]

After scanning these two chapters, Exman was intrigued. His wariness of alcohol certainly helped. Neither Wilson nor Parkhurst had any reason to know this, but Exman was a teetotaler, as were his parents and his wife. In fact, there was no liquor in the Exman household until after he and Sunny retired to Cape Cod in 1965.[18] Both Exman and Wilson were from the war generation—Exman was in his late thirties when they met, and Wilson in his early forties— whose utopian dreams of modern life in their youth yielded to the nightmares of adulthood during World War I and World War II. Both had responded to wartime by searching for meaning, and both had experienced mystical encounters with God. But Exman was also drawn to Wilson the man, to his sharp awareness of his shortcomings, his openness to God, and his undeniable personal charisma. Their meeting sparked a lifelong friendship.

The possibility of strong revenues also caught Exman's attention. "I recognized at once that the book had a big potential sale if it were at least reasonably well organized and written," he later recalled. "I was soon satisfied on those points." He was also satisfied with the book's emphasis on religion and spirituality, which made it a perfect fit for his department, as did the promised recovery stories (including Wilson's own), which echoed classic conversion narratives. "Could you do a whole book like this?" Exman asked. "Of course," Wilson said with his trademark confidence. "How soon?" Exman continued. "Nine or ten months," Wilson answered. Exman said he would check with Harper president, Cass Canfield, and report back.

During a second meeting with Wilson, Exman offered to publish the book with a generous $1,500 advance. This story is well known in AA circles, because Wilson's response would play a major role in charting the movement's future. But Exman's own account, written by hand in pencil in a draft chapter of his autobiography called "Deans in My Life," provides new details. Wilson, who stood six-feet-two-inches tall, "was always having trouble as to how to manage his long legs and I remember how he twisted them around each other and the legs of his chair," Exman wrote. "He rumpled his hair and tried to wipe the disappointment off his face" after Exman set down the royalty terms he was offering. "You mean," Wilson asked, "that I would only be getting 15%, or forty-five cents, on a three dollar book?" Exman then dove into Economics of Publishing 101—overhead, printing costs, wholesale and retail pricing—before concluding that Harper would likely show a profit of just 10 percent.[19]

Though disappointed by these numbers, Wilson was delighted to learn "that a firm like Harper wanted the book and that an editor of Gene's caliber believed that it was going to be good." However, after consulting with Parkhurst, he began to question the wisdom of signing with Harper. If the book "should prove to be the main text-book of A.A., why would we want our main means of propagation in the hands of someone else? Shouldn't we control this thing?" he asked. Also, why settle for a 15 percent royalty when they could get the whole retail price by publishing it themselves?[20]

Wilson set up a third meeting with Exman to discuss the merits of self-publishing. "To my utter amazement, he agreed, quite contrary to his own interest, that a society like ours ought to control and publish its own literature," Wilson later wrote. "Moreover, he felt that very possibly we could do this with success." Exman's recollection was similar: "I said I thought that AA should publish the book. Their own publicity, much of it by word of mouth, would keep the book circulating. He would forfeit having a publisher's advertising and promotion as well as bookstore display and sale, but he would get a full three dollars for every copy sold and have only the printer's bill to pay." Exman also offered to help Wilson out by convincing his friend Edward Blackwell at Cornwall Press in Cornwall, New York, to "have the book professionally designed and give A.A. the benefit of the Harper schedule of manufacturing costs."[21]

In the end, this is how the Big Book came to be, and Exman took pride in his role: "And so it was and so it should have been, for income from sales of the book—now more than a half million copies—soon was carrying most of AA's financial burden and making it possible for them to spread their gospel further and further afield."[22]

Making the Big Book

AA members and scholars have researched the prepublication history of this book nearly as exhaustively as New Testament scholars have studied the mutual borrowings of Matthew, Mark, Luke, and John. In fact, a book called *Writing the Big Book: The Creation of A.A.* is longer and fatter than the Big Book itself.

Two discoveries from those investigations merit attention. The first concerns race, class, and gender. Though Wilson worked hard in the Big Book to make AA open to people of different religions (and none), he did almost nothing to make it otherwise inclusive or diverse. There isn't a single chapter in the first edition by a person of color. The book's assumed readers are well-to-do (or formerly well-to-do) alcoholics, business executives whose benders had lost them jobs and fortunes. These assumed readers are also male, as if only men drink to distraction and the only spouses hurt by alcohol are wives. There is just one chapter, "A Feminine Victory," written by a "'lady' alcoholic." The only other chapter written by a woman, "An Alcoholic's Wife," casts light on a man's alcoholism from the perspective of his spouse. Another chapter, "To Wives," offers advice to the wives of alcoholics. Lois Wilson wanted to write it, but Bill Wilson said no. He ended up writing it himself.[23]

A second observation regarding the making of the Big Book concerns religion. As Wilson and his collaborators worked on the book, they anticipated and encouraged beliefs and attitudes that would emerge decades later as hallmarks of popular religion in the United States. These features included a mistrust of religious elites, hostility toward organized religion, acceptance of religious diversity, rejection of fundamentalism, and strategically vague definitions of

God. Most important, as the Big Book moved through various drafts, it also charted a trajectory of desire from "religion" (which increasingly connoted coercion, hidebound dogma, and rote ritual) to "spirituality" (which increasingly connoted personal choice, experimentation, and hybridity).

Channeling his inner Humpty Dumpty—"When I use a word, it means just what I choose it to mean"—Wilson had initially insisted on redefining the word *religion* instead of rejecting it, as atheist and agnostic AAs had urged him to do. True religion wasn't about church, Wilson argued. Or dogma. Or clerics. Or rituals. True religion was open rather than closed, broad rather than narrow, pluralistic rather than exclusive, empathetic rather than judgmental. Or so Wilson hoped it would be. In the end, Wilson's collaborators convinced him that the word just couldn't bend that far without breaking. In the final edits, made just before (and in some cases, after) its heavily marked up galleys were sent to Cornwall Press, the words *religious* and *religion* were repeatedly replaced with the words *spiritual* and *spirituality*, so much so that in the first edition *religious* (36) and *religion* (10) appeared 46 times, while the terms *spiritual* (124) and *spirituality* (7) appeared 131 times. In one telling change, a reference by the religion-friendly psychologist Carl Jung to combating alcoholism with a "vital religious experience" was changed to read "vital spiritual experience."[24] In this way, Wilson and AA charted a path Exman's Book of Books and American culture would follow.

Other prepublication changes to the Big Book were similarly revealing of the direction religion was heading in the United States. As has been noted, Wilson fiercely resisted attempts to eliminate the term "God." In fact, in the first edition "God" was used over one hundred times. However, in a series of last-minute edits, Wilson agreed to substitute a series of terms that readers would not be so quick to identify with organized religion. Those terms included "Spirit of the Universe," "Creative Intelligence," and two phrases that have become calling cards for AA and other Twelve-Step programs: "Higher Power" and "God as we understood Him." In the Twelve Steps as they appear in the first edition, the term "God" was used on its own twice, but the phrases "God as we understood Him" and "Power greater than ourselves" were each used three times. Wilson made these changes reluctantly but came to regard them as ingenious. The phrase "as we understood Him" became "perhaps the most important expression to be found in our whole AA vocabulary," Wilson later wrote. It "made a hoop big enough so that the whole world of alcoholics can walk through."[25]

Neither Wilson nor Exman could quite see this yet, but together they were pursuing parallel efforts to sell religion more widely by redefining and rebranding it. They wanted to convince others to embrace religious experience as a practical solution to life's problems, but many people in their target audiences saw *religion* as a bad word that signaled authoritarianism, hierarchy, empty rituals, and hidebound dogma. Wilson believed an encounter with God was a necessary prerequisite for recovery from alcoholism. But he wanted Catholic alcoholics to feel free to come to AA meetings, and he knew that if his movement was seen as a new religious movement, then the Roman Catholic Church would forbid them from doing so. So he learned to speak of "Higher Power" rather than "God," and "spiritual experiences" rather than "religious experiences."

Exman found himself in a similar bind. He believed that religion was a solution to the problems brought on by modern materialism and militarism. Without it, human life on earth could come to an end. So he wanted readers of all religions (and none) to buy, read, and discuss his religion books. However, almost all of those books were by religious people with specific religious identities. How to edit and market them so that readers did not feel they needed to share the author's religious identity to say amen to the message? Exman's solution was to offer something like religion in general. Early in his Harper career, he had thought of his work as a translation project of sorts—reworking the thoughts of Protestant preachers and theologians into language non-Protestants could understand

and embrace. This is evident in his work in the early 1930s on Fosdick's *On Being a Real Person*, which, as the title signaled, aimed to
tell readers how to become real people rather than real Christians,
real Protestants, or real Baptists. The Big Book was pursuing a similar
objective: the erasure of specific religiosity and its replacement by
something more generic. That generic something did not concern
the distinctive doctrines or specific rituals of a particular religious
tradition. What Wilson was offering was more personal than that.
The gateway to recovery was an experience of a Higher Power—
what you as an alcoholic or a reader (or both) understood to be the
divine.

In this way, James, Wilson, and Exman helped introduce to
American culture a "spiritual but not religious" sensibility that
would grow in influence over the next century.

Wilson and his collaborators discussed many titles for their book.
"The Way Out" was popular, as was "One Hundred Men" (after an
inflated number of those who had been saved by their strategies).
Wilson insisted on *Alcoholics Anonymous*, and so the book became
one of those rare titles where the name of the author and the name
of the book are one and the same.[26]

*Alcoholics Anonymous: The Story of How More Than One Hundred
Men Have Recovered from Alcoholism* appeared on April 10, 1939,
which served as a second founding of sorts for the AA movement.
"The book changed EVERYTHING," according to William Schaberg,
author of *Writing the Big Book*: "Suddenly there was a definite program of recovery to follow, one with twelve clearly articulated steps
to be taken if you wanted to move from drunkenness to sobriety,
along with three central chapters explaining in detail exactly what
had to be done to put those Twelve Steps into practice. *None* of that
had been offered to the world or clearly explained prior to April 10,
1939."[27]

The Big Book was a step-by-step guidebook for recovering alcoholics, but, as Exman instantly recognized, it was more than that. Its
thesis seemed to be that spirituality, or religion, or some combination

thereof, could make you sober. It made the case for that thesis by presenting a series of personal stories about born-again drunks—alcoholics who dove deep into the wellsprings of human misery, recognized their inability to cure themselves, turned to a Higher Power for help, experienced a "spiritual awakening," and found themselves by some combination of luck and grace able to live without alcohol. Not without reason is it regarded today as the bible of Alcoholics Anonymous.

But what sort of religion (or spirituality) did this bible preach?

As has been noted, the Big Book channeled pluralism and pragmatism by welcoming virtually any conception of God and by refusing to judge those conceptions against any standard other than whether they worked for some particular individual. It preached a form of ecstatic spirituality in which mystical experiences were to be expected and the path from drunkenness to recovery followed the examples of converts from sin to salvation.

The Big Book also preached what came to be known as perennialism, thanks to Aldous Huxley's use of that term in the Harper bestseller *The Perennial Philosophy* (1945). This view that the world's religions are different paths to one mountaintop was further popularized in another Harper religion book, *The Religions of Man* (1958) by Wilson's friend Huston Smith, and in a series of additional books on Exman's list authored in the 1960s by the Romanian scholar of religion Mircea Eliade. But years before Huxley's *Perennial Philosophy*, Wilson was arguing in the Big Book that there were "spiritual principles and rules of practice . . . common to all of the worthwhile religions and philosophies of mankind."[28]

A "Religious Exhortation"

Wilson and Parkhurst worked hard to muster free publicity for their upcoming book. Approaches to editors at *Good Housekeeping* and *Reader's Digest* got their hopes up only to dash them. But they scraped up $200 for a small ad in the *New York Times* on April 11, 1939, and a long and appreciative *New York Times* review of "this extraordinary book" followed two months later. There, the poet Percy Hutchison called the book's thesis "more soundly based psychologically than any other treatment of the subject I have ever come upon," rightly observing that both the case studies and the programmatic chapters kept cycling back to one central observation: "That the patient is unable to master the situation solely through what is termed 'will power' or volition." Like many reviewers to come, Hutchison saw *Alcoholics Anonymous* as a religious book offering a religious solution to the alcohol problem, which had stubbornly resisted solving through either the persuasive powers of temperance reformers or the coercive national apparatus of Prohibition. Following Wilson's breadcrumbs, Hutchison turned to James's *Varieties* for expert help in describing religion as a plurality, not a unity, and a vague plurality at that. "There is no suggestion advanced in the book that an addict should embrace one faith rather than another," he wrote. "He may fall back upon an 'absolute,' or upon 'A Power which makes for righteousness' if he choose." What mattered was giving up on self-power and relying instead on "a force outside himself."[29]

In addition to soliciting free publicity in magazines and newspapers, Wilson and his collaborators sent out drafts of the book to leading figures in religion, medicine, psychology, and the law. This effort produced more than half a dozen reviews in medical journals. In July 1939, Dr. Silkworth of Towns Hospital published a long article in *Journal-Lancet* that outlined AA's distinctive approach to treating alcoholics and predicted its rapid growth. The venerable *New England Journal of Medicine* also published an appreciative review, concluding that "the authors have presented their case well, in fact, in such good style that it may be of considerable influence when read by alcoholic patients."[30]

Other medical journals couldn't stomach the stink of religion in the book. The *Journal of Nervous and Mental Disease* called it "a rambling sort of camp meeting," likening its preachy voice to that of the baseball evangelist Billy Sunday. The *Journal of the American Medical Association* similarly dismissed AA's approach as a "quack treatment" and the book as "religious exhortation" possessing "no scientific merit or interest."[31]

Of all the professionals solicited for endorsements, the most influential was Harry Emerson Fosdick, who shared with Wilson an awareness of the tragic side of life. After reading a prepublication copy of the Big Book, Fosdick wrote to Rockefeller's associate A. LeRoy Chipman, describing it as "a stirring document" that "would do a great deal of good." Fosdick then produced his own stirring review, which appeared in Protestant periodicals and was reprinted in AA pamphlets. "This extraordinary book deserves the careful attention of anyone interested in the problem of alcoholism," Fosdick began. "It is a sober, careful, tolerant, sympathetic treatment of the alcoholic's problem and of the successful techniques by which its co-authors have won their freedom."[32]

During the year after the publication of the Big Book, AA benefited from attention in popular magazines such as *TIME*, *Newsweek*, and *Liberty*. Catholic and Protestant magazines also took notice. A series of articles in October 1939 in Cleveland's *Plain Dealer* helped that city leapfrog New York and Akron as the number one AA center in the United States. A Rockefeller-sponsored dinner in February 1940 also promoted the book.

Alcoholics Anonymous was no quick fix for AA's finances, or for those of Bill and Lois Wilson. Less than a month after the book appeared, the Wilsons' bank, which had foreclosed on the mortgage on their Brooklyn home, forced them out. For the next few years, they lived as exiles, wandering through a series of homes of AA friends. The Wilsons finally turned a corner, as did AA and the Big Book, with the appearance of a long and fawning article in the *Saturday Evening Post* on March 1, 1941. Thanks in part to its nostalgic Norman Rockwell covers, the *Post* was at the time the most widely circulating weekly in the United States. The Rockwell cover for this issue depicted a reader on a bench reading a copy of the *Post* whose cover (also by Rockwell) bragged about its 3,300,000+ paid subscribers.

As has been noted, a huge issue at the time for AAs (as members called themselves) was how much and what sort of religion was needed for the alcoholic to recover. The reporter assigned to the *Post* story, Jack Alexander, put the best possible spin on this potentially divisive situation. Religiously, all that was required in AA was "a dose of religion in its broadest sense," he wrote. As he explained how big a dose might be for any individual alcoholic, he pushed AA's inclusivism well beyond where Wilson was willing to go in the Big Book or, for that matter, where James had gone in *Varieties*: "Any concept of the higher Power is acceptable. A skeptic or agnostic may choose to think of his Inner Self, the miracle of growth, a tree, man's wonderment at the physical universe, the structure of the atom or mere mathematical infinity."[33]

Here we see AA pluralism starting to take off on its own and fly. When Wilson referred to God as he understood Him, he was thinking of a personal God who intervened in human history and individual lives. Wilson believed it was possible to encounter this God, because he had been blessed with that experience himself. Wilson also believed that this God answered prayers, because his prayers had been answered. However, as the Big Book was bought, read, and discussed, "God as we understand Him" began to follow its own radical logic. Taking cues from the AAs he interviewed, Alexander pushed AA pluralism to include nature religion, even mathematical religion. Soon many AAs would be drawing their inspiration from the French sociologist Émile Durkheim rather than the psychologist William James, taking the term "GOD" to mean the AA community itself—the "Group Of Drunks."

In some ways, the publication of this *Saturday Evening Post* article served as AA's third founding. Ruth Hock reported that the article produced 918 inquiries at AA's New York office in just twelve days. The *Post* fielded (and forwarded) close to a thousand more. At the beginning of 1941, before that article appeared, there were just two thousand AAs nationwide. At the end of 1941, that figure had jumped to eight thousand.

The Writing Life

In the 1940s and 1950s, from World War II into the Cold War, AA moved out of its founding era and entered a period of adolescence and growth. The successes of 1941, as well as royalties on the Big Book, allowed Bill and Lois Wilson to buy a house in Bedford Hills, New York, called Stepping Stones, now the home of the Stepping Stones Foundation. By 1945, AA had expanded to an estimated 15,000 AAs in 560 groups, and by 1950 those numbers stood at nearly 100,000 AAs in 3,500 groups.[34]

During this same period, Wilson cultivated a friendship with Exman and became an integral part of Exman's mystics club. Exman introduced him to the books of Gerald Heard. In the winter of 1943–44, Wilson traveled with Lois to Southern California. There Wilson met Heard on January 1, 1944. Heard took Wilson to the Trabuco community, where Wilson learned firsthand about the spiritual regimen of silence, prayer, and meditation outlined in the two *Training for the Life of the Spirit* pamphlets. Heard also introduced Wilson to Aldous Huxley, who would later flatter Wilson as "the greatest social architect of the twentieth century." According to a Trabuco resident who saw him there, Wilson asked Heard for advice about how to run AA. "Where do we go from here?" he asked. Heard told him to think small. "Don't build a big organization," he said. "Keep it in discrete, small units that are independent of each other and that are centered around the 12 Steps."[35]

Wilson's focus shifted during these years of growth from alcoholics to AA—from helping individual drunks recover to helping AA grow and mature. As AA found legitimacy, Wilson found himself addressing annual meetings of medical organizations, including the

American Psychiatric Association, and collaborating with researchers at Yale. He also struggled with crippling bouts of depression. "The depressions kept me off the road and from making speeches," Wilson recalled in a letter to a friend. "In fact, I was forced to sit home and ask what would become of A.A. and what would become of me."[36]

As AA expanded into every state and took root beyond US borders, Wilson became increasingly concerned about the possibility that its thousands of small groups might splinter. To address that problem, he began working on a series of essays defining what came to be known as AA's Twelve Traditions. This accompaniment to the now famous Twelve Steps initially appeared as "Twelve Points to Assure Our Future" in April 1946 in the *AA Grapevine*, a journal that had itself debuted two years earlier.[37] The Twelve Traditions were then unanimously approved at AA's first international convention, held in July 1950 in Cleveland, Ohio.

With Dr. Bob's health failing—he would die on November 16, 1950—Wilson decided he needed to face the problem of succession. He had tired of playing the role of AA's "headquarters handyman," and had other things he wanted to do.[38] At the 1950 AA convention he introduced a resolution that set up on a trial basis a system of AA governance headed no longer by its founders but by an elected General Service Conference. At AA's second international convention, in Saint Louis in 1955, that democratic system became permanent.

As he spent more time at home in Stepping Stones, Wilson had more time for writing. He also had a place devoted to it—a concrete-block writing shack he had built with a friend. Concerned that the Big Book, which had already attained the status of holy writ, had become "frozen" in time, he worked during the mid-1950s on his second and third books, published in 1953 and 1957, plus a new edition of the Big Book, which appeared in 1955.[39] The success of these projects led to a second golden age in AA publishing.

The two new books were Wilson-Exman collaborations, jointly published by AA's publishing wing and Harper, with the AA-published books marketed directly to AAs and the Harper books

sold in religious bookstores. In keeping with AA's anonymity principle, both were published anonymously. Both were also legacy
projects—efforts to sum up what AA was all about, where it had
been, and where it was going.

Twelve Steps and Twelve Traditions (1953) came first. Following
the pattern of the Big Book, Wilson wrote this modest book with
the help of his friends. Tom Powers, an advertising man who had
sobered up under Wilson's sponsorship in 1946, would split with
Wilson in 1958 and go on to establish an alternative twelve-step
group called All Addicts Anonymous (AAA). But while Wilson was
working on *Twelve and Twelve*, as it is referred to in AA, Powers
was a close confidant and a valued editor. Others who read and
commented on drafts of this book included Father Ed Dowling, a
Jesuit priest who had served as a spiritual adviser to Wilson since
1940, and two journalists, Betty Love and the *Saturday Evening
Post* writer Jack Alexander.

In *Twelve and Twelve*, Wilson offered glosses on the Twelve
Steps. For example, in his discussion of Step 3, he observed that
many AAs who found faith hard to come by had resolved that roadblock to recovery by deciding to "make A.A. itself [their] 'higher
power.'" Wilson also discussed the Serenity Prayer that had become
popular in AA groups worldwide: "God grant me the serenity to
accept the things I cannot change, courage to change the things I can,
and wisdom to know the difference." In this book, Wilson referred
to the Higher Power far more often than he had in the Big Book, and
he continued to stress spirituality over religion.[40]

In response to observations that the Big Book lacked diversity,
Wilson admitted that early efforts to keep AA "respectable" had led
some groups to accept only "pure alcoholics" who would bring no
ancillary complications into meetings. "So beggars, tramps, asylum
inmates, prisoners, queers, plain crackpots, and fallen women were
definitely out," he wrote. In his discussion of Tradition 3—"The only
requirement for an A.A. member is a desire to stop drinking"—
Wilson rejected prejudice and intolerance of any kind, portraying

AA as a society that "cut across every barrier of race, creed, politics, and language." While interpreting Tradition 4—"Each group should be autonomous except in matters affecting other groups or A.A. as a whole"—he rejected efforts to segregate groups by politics ("'Republican' or 'Communist'") or by religion ("'Catholic' or 'Protestant'").[41]

Twelve and Twelve fell short when it came to gender equality. Wilson did refer in passing to "businesswomen in A.A." and to "the alcoholic housewife," but the married, heterosexual, White male alcoholic remained the assumed reader, as he had been in the Big Book. ("After the husband joins A.A., the wife may become discontented," Wilson wrote, while also noting that the founders of a particular AA group "entreat[ed] their wives to brew gallons of coffee.")[42]

In recent years, as AA has expanded its footprint both globally and demographically, some AAs have pushed to weed out of this text its cringe-worthy passages. But *Twelve and Twelve* has itself become part of the AA canon—"A.A.'s New Testament." It, too, has become "frozen" in time, nearly as resistant to revision as the Big Book itself.[43]

Alcoholics Anonymous Comes of Age: A Brief History of A.A. (1957), Wilson's third book and the second he published with Exman, featured his reflections on AA's development, with a special emphasis on its twentieth-anniversary convention, held in Saint Louis in 1955. As always with Wilson's writing, this book oozes personal religion. Clergy such as Father Ed Dowling and the Episcopal priest Dr. Sam Shoemaker are featured. Saint Francis of Assisi is lauded as an impoverished spiritual innovator who established a "lay movement" of "one man carrying the good news to the next." Fosdick is thanked for his early support of AA. Meanwhile, Wilson describes as "providential" the decision to refer to the divine in the Big Book as a "Power greater than ourselves" and "God as we understood Him."[44]

As with so much in AA (and in Exman's Book of Books), the friendly ghost of William James haunted *AA Comes of Age*, not least in the biographical approach Wilson had employed earlier in the Big Book. As Wilson narrated AA's development over time, he returned throughout to personal stories—of alcoholic founders and nonalcoholic trustees and journalist supporters and others. Wilson told his personal story, too, including his sinking to "the very bottom of the pit," his revelatory experience at Towns Hospital, and his reading of James's *Varieties* (a gift from Ebby Thacher), which convinced him that he wanted to devote his life to working with alcoholics. Wilson also told his own version of the making of the Big Book, including his meetings with "Gene Exman, another wonderful friend-to-be of our society" and the debates and negotiations that led him to adopt a "spirituality, yes. But religion, no" approach in the final version of the Big Book.[45]

Picking up on a key theme in *Twelve and Twelve*, Wilson emphasized diversity and inclusion, describing the "folks of every description and persuasion" he encountered at AA's 1955 convention as "plainsmen and mountain people, city dwellers and townsmen, workmen and businessmen, schoolteachers and professors, clergymen and doctors, ad men and journalists, artists and builders, clerks and bankers, socialites and skid-rowers, career girls and housewives, people from other lands speaking in strange accents and tongues, Catholics and Protestants and Jews and men and women of no religion."[46]

Between these two book projects, Wilson also produced the second edition of the Big Book, which appeared in July 1955. AAs remained reluctant to rewrite even a word of what was becoming scripture, but modest changes had been made in various printings of the first edition, and Wilson inserted a few more here. His most obvious change was adding new personal stories and deleting old ones, which had the cumulative effect of making the book more up-to-date and diverse. The second edition included a case history, "Jim's Story," by Dr. Jim Scott, a Black physician who started the first Black AA group. It also featured eleven new stories by women, including "Women Suffer Too" by Margaret Mann, a lesbian and

AA pioneer who went to her first AA meeting at the Wilson home in Brooklyn in 1939.

In a copy of this second edition that Exman saved among the most cherished books in his home library, Wilson wrote, "For Gene—treasured friend, whose good works mean so much to me, and to so many. Gratefully, Bill." Wilson's inscription in Exman's copy of *Alcoholics Anonymous Comes of Age* also testifies to their friendship and to Exman's contributions to AA: "Dear Gene, With this, all my affection—and my gratitude for all that you have done to make AA what it is. Ever, Bill."[47]

As these inscriptions suggest, Exman got more than two books out of the advice he gave to Wilson back in 1938. He also got a friend. Exman and Sunny exchanged Christmas cards with Bill and Lois Wilson, who welcomed the Exmans into their home in Bedford Hills in Westchester County, New York.

Wilson and Exman shared a history of mystical encounters with the divine. They also shared a long-standing interest in Asian religions, particularly Hindu and Buddhist mysticism, which went back to their conversations in California with Huxley and Heard in the early 1940s. Again like Exman, Wilson tended to interpret those religious traditions as essentially one. Wilson and Exman were drawn as well to the spiritual practices of medieval Roman Catholic mystics. Wilson cultivated this interest in conversations with Heard and Father Dowling, who served as Wilson's informal cosponsors and spiritual directors.

An additional convergence point for Exman and Wilson was their participation in the metaphysical tradition. Psychic phenomena and parapsychology are among the concerns of this tradition, which includes a lineage of investigators and authors that run back to James and the Exman author Emmet Fox, whose books became beloved to so many in AA. Like Exman, who saved a Ouija board in his personal archives, Wilson believed that human beings survived bodily death and that it was possible for the dead to communicate with the living. Bill and Lois, who were married in a Swedenborgian church (named after the Swedish mystic and scientist Emanuel Swedenborg), invited guests to try out their Ouija board in the "spook room" in their basement at Stepping Stones. In a letter to Dowling that included chapter drafts for *Twelve and Twelve*, Wilson said he felt the spirit of a fifteenth-century monk helping him write that book from "over there."[48]

After describing the "psychic phenomena" reported by many alcoholics, Wilson told his friend the Episcopal priest Sam Shoemaker in a letter, "I've had a lot of such phenomenalism myself." Wilson also expressed his fervent hope that scientific proof of the afterlife would be forthcoming. "Full proof of survival would be one of the greatest events that could take place in the Western world today," he wrote. "Easter would become a fact; people could then live in a universe that would make sense."[49]

The God Trip

One of the curiouser episodes in the friendship of Exman and Wilson was their experimentation with LSD in the 1950s. Exman, then a fifty-something White man sitting on the Board of Trustees at Harper and enjoying power luncheons at the Century Club, was by all outward appearances the sort of professional to whom the sixties would soon attach the label "square." He didn't even drink alcohol. Wilson was Mr. AA. What was he doing dropping acid? Why was Exman along for the trip? And how did all this happen years before Timothy Leary made LSD hip in the early 1960s?

To answer these questions, it is important to return to Heard and Huxley, who became attracted in the early 1950s to the possibility of attaining mystical union with the divine through chemicals rather than contemplation. The *Training for the Life of the Spirit* pamphlets had offered a step-by-step path to growing closer to the divine through prayer, meditation, and action in the world. But that path was arduous, and as the demise of Trabuco demonstrated, it did not always bear fruit. LSD offered the promise of a quicker and easier route to God.

This was not a novel idea. First Nations had been using peyote for ritual purposes for centuries. James, after experimenting with nitrous oxide, concluded that it called forth "mystical consciousness in an extraordinary degree." And Huxley himself, in "A Treatise on Drugs," published in 1931, had called attention to shamans in Mexico and Siberia, Persia and Greece, using drugs to produce "religious ecstasy."[50]

Huxley first took mescaline in May 1953 with Humphry Osmond, a British-born psychiatrist who had been studying the psychological effects of that drug, which is derived from the cactus peyote. (Osmond would later coin the term *psychedelic* to refer to similar mind-altering drugs.) Huxley and Heard took mescaline together in November 1953 and again, under Osmond's direction, in December 1954.

Following in the footsteps of James, who wrote about his experiments with nitrous oxide in *Varieties*, Huxley wrote about his first mescaline experience in *Doors of Perception* (1954) and reflected on it further in *Heaven and Hell* (1956). Both were published as Harper trade books also sold through Exman's department. Whereas Osmond studied the psychological effects of mescaline, Huxley explored its spiritual and religious effects—as a stimulant of "the beatific vision" and other mystical states. Echoing Huxley, Heard described his mescaline experience in a letter to Exman as "a profoundly religious one, in keeping with that of mystics."[51]

In 1955, Heard pitched Exman a book on mescaline, asking, "Do you think that there would be any interest in such an account from the mystical and devotional point of view?"[52] Suspicious that Heard was attempting to get through drugs what he had been unable to achieve through spiritual discipline, Exman turned him down. In the fall of 1956, Heard collaborated with Dr. Sidney Cohen of the UCLA School of Medicine on a broader book about psychedelics. Heard supplied the historical background while Cohen focused on contemporary research. This time Heard sent the book to Cass Canfield, who had just finished a decade as Harper's chairman of the board. Canfield sent it to Exman, who sent it to Bro for a reader's report.

Though a huge Heard fan, Bro expressed her standard reservations about his turgid writing style, alongside her concern that Cohen might be a "screwball" rather than a respected medical man. But she worried most about protecting Exman's reputation and the integrity of his list. "We should think twice before we offer to an undiscriminating public a panacea for spiritual ills," she wrote, adding that "it is not likely that the short-cut of insight by drug-taking will effect a permanent change in character." None of the mystics she and Exman read and revered "seems to have achieved his power through drugs," she continued, though drugs were doubtless available to them. "They may tranquilize, inspire, and even offer lasting discernment but they may also, for all we know, paralyze initiative into genuine growth in holiness." Her conclusion was this: "We must be slow to over-claim: perhaps the book needs only to raise questions as to the value of this short-cut to insight and to suggest further experimentation to see whether average people are, after the drug experience, moved to set their lives into a pattern of more satisfactory meaning because of their glimpse of widened consciousness."[53]

Harper turned the book down.

Meanwhile, Huxley and Heard were turning their attention to LSD. They worked with Dr. Cohen and his graduate student Betty Eisner, who were studying the effects of the drug on intellectuals, including Heard, who became, in his words, an early "human guinea pig in the lysergic acid research."[54]

Lysergic acid diethylamide (LSD) was first synthesized by Dr. Albert Hofmann in his lab at the Swiss chemical firm Sandoz (now Novartis) in 1938. Its mind-altering effects were discovered in 1943. It came to the United States in 1949. By the mid-1950s, researchers in Europe, Canada, and the United States (including the US Army and the CIA) were studying how it might produce psychosis, assist in psychotherapy, bolster creativity, compel truth-telling, and cure alcoholism. Heard and Huxley were particularly interested in the promise of LSD as an ego reducer, given their shared conviction that ego was *the* barrier to mystical breakthroughs. Here they had a partner in Dr. Hofmann, whose interest in the spiritual effects of LSD led him to be dubbed "the mystic chemist."[55]

Because LSD is now indelibly associated with youthful rebellion in the 1960s, it is important to remember that Huxley and Heard were at the time *in* their sixties. Huxley was sixty-one and Heard was sixty-six when they took LSD together, under Cohen's direction, just before Christmas 1955. LSD was not illegal then and was widely hailed as a miracle drug. Heard interpreted his LSD experience in spiritual terms. In a letter to the Harvard philosopher Ernest Hocking, another Exman friend and author, Heard wrote that the "shift of consciousness" he experienced while under the influence of LSD was "so clearly similar to the accounts given by the mystics that none of us feels able to deny that this is in fact the experience that we undergo."[56]

According to William Forthman, who went to Trabuco as a teenager and returned for a short stint as it was shutting down in 1949, Heard played the "Pied Piper" of acid to Hollywood stars and business leaders, including the *TIME* and *Life* publisher Henry Luce and his wife, the author, congresswoman, and ambassador Clare Boothe Luce. Margaret Gage, the actress and Trabuco stalwart whose socialist and pacifist leanings would land her on Nixon's enemies list, hosted a series of Heard's gatherings at her home, where the movie director John Huston, the talk show host Steve Allen, and other film and literary icons dropped acid, and not always in the service of spiritual growth. Henry Luce spread what he saw as the good news of LSD through a series of articles in *TIME*, including one called "Mysticism in the Lab," which concluded that LSD was able "to induce something like mystical consciousness in a controlled laboratory environment."[57]

Back East, Wilson was reading Huxley's *Doors of Perception* and devouring research on LSD as a possible cure for alcoholism. His fervent hope was that LSD would help God-resistant drunks experience a Higher Power for themselves. He also hoped that LSD might do something to alleviate his depression, which had been bedeviling him for years. Finally, he joined Huxley and Heard in hoping that LSD might produce enduring states of selflessness, since anonymity and unselfish service were as central to the work of AA as egolessness was to Huxley and Heard.

Wilson took LSD for the first time under Cohen's supervision at the Los Angeles Veterans Administration Hospital on August 29, 1956. Heard guided him through his experience. Tom Powers was there, too. Wilson took it again on February 16, 1957, at the home of Cohen's associate Betty Eisner, in a pioneering session in which medical professionals (Eisner and Cohen) took the drug alongside their patients (Wilson and Powers).

According to Gerald Heard's notes on Wilson's first trip, Wilson interpreted his experience in spiritual terms in real time, turning again and again in prayer to God, whom he addressed as "the Father of Lights," "Great One," "Benefactor," "the Infinite," "Divine Master," and "Lord." Wilson referred twice during this trip to his "conversion" experience at Towns Hospital, characterizing the LSD experience as "identical" to that one. Exman had for all his life been seeking to reproduce his Blanchester graveyard experience, and here Wilson was recapturing his "white light experience" through LSD. "Do you get this kind of reaction with alcohol?" Cohen asked him. "No—different. This is the conversion type of experience," Wilson replied.[58]

As Heard's report suggests, Wilson's initial impressions of LSD were positive. In a letter to Heard shortly after this trip, Wilson wrote, "I do feel a residue of assurance and a feeling of enhanced beauty that seems likely to stay by me." Around that same time, Wilson met up in Kansas City with Heard and Heard's friend (and Exman's author-to-be) the comparative religion scholar Huston Smith. Wilson said he was "blown away by the drug," again calling his first experience "a dead ringer" for his "white light experience." In a December 1956 letter he told Heard his experience had "done a sustained good."[59]

Two years later, in a letter to the Episcopal priest Sam Shoemaker, Wilson rejected criticism of LSD as "a new psychiatric toy of awful dangers." He also spelled out a theory he had learned from Huxley and Heard about the spiritual effects of the drug. According to this theory, the ego operates as a force field of sorts that prevents the individual from seeing God. LSD, by deflating the ego, eliminates that barrier, opening the doors of perception to the divine. Later in 1958, Wilson expressed some reservations about LSD in a letter to Dowling, who himself had soured on psychedelics. LSD was but a "temporary ego-reducer," Wilson wrote. "I don't believe that it has any miraculous property of transforming spiritually and emotionally sick people into healthy ones overnight." By October 1959, he was admitting to Dowling that a controversy within AA over his LSD experimentation had "created some commotion." Wilson down-played the growing controversy, writing that "these recent heresies of mine do have their comic aspects." But sometime in 1959 or 1960 he stopped using the drug.[60]

Back east, Exman had written to Heard as early as 1956, asking about how he might bring LSD research to New York. Heard was too busy raising funds for his own research but promised to investigate.[61] Two years later, likely in the spring of 1958, Wilson worked with a few East Coast friends to organize a group dedicated to investigating LSD and mysticism. One of those friends was Eugene Exman.

The Basic Group, as it came to be called, included a surprising number of authors who either had published or would publish with Exman. There was Tom Powers, who wrote *First Questions on the Life of the Spirit* for Exman in 1959 and led retreats with him as well. Powers invited Exman to join and appears to have been the group's key organizer. Exman was also a master networker, however, with contacts extending far beyond publishing into business and academia, as well as Protestant churches and pacifist organizations. He likely recruited two members who were also his authors: Rachel Davis DuBois, the civil rights activist and author of *Get Together Americans* (1943) whom Exman met in La Verne, California, in 1941; and Garma Chen-Chi Chang, a research fellow at the Bollingen Foundation in New York, an authority on Tibetan Buddhism, and the author of *The Practice of Zen* (1959). Dr. Robert Laidlaw, founder of the psychiatry department at Roosevelt Hospital in Manhattan, administered the drug, and Dr. Helen Yoder assisted. Other group members included Helen Wynn, a former actress with whom Wilson was having a fifteen-year affair.[62]

The Basic Group was funded by the Parapsychological Foundation, established in 1951 by Eileen Garrett and Frances Payne Bolton in an effort to demonstrate scientifically the existence of life after death. The money came from Bolton, who was the first woman from Ohio to be elected to the US House of Representatives and an early follower of the controversial tantric yogi "Oom the Omnipotent" of Nyack, New York. Garrett, also known by her middle name, Jeanette, was a medium, an astrologer, and a friend of Margueritte Bro.

If the Los Angeles LSD group swirled around Huxley and Heard, the gravitational pull in this New York group was exerted by the charismatic actress Lucille Kahn, who ran a salon out of her home on the Upper East Side during the 1950s. Her husband, David Kahn, was a follower and friend of Edgar Cayce, and she read widely in Asian religions and practiced meditation. Lucille was the first person to take LSD with the Basic Group. Bill Wilson was there, as were Helen Wynn, Tom Powers, and Exman. All were in search of what Kahn called "the true meaning of an expanded consciousness." All came with great expectations. "The longing of my soul to experience the Reality of Oneness with the Absolute was my paramount hope and motivation in taking LSD," Kahn wrote.[63]

The Basic Group model seemed to follow Heard's advice to Wilson to keep his AA groups small. It followed even more closely the model of Exman's Monday night cell group meetings. Like both those groups, the Basic Group was small and coed. About ten people were regularly involved, and thirteen different people took the drug on sixteen different occasions. During their experiments, which focused on LSD as a gateway to God, Dr. Laidlaw gave the "subject" the drug and oversaw the proceedings, which members described as "experiments." The dose was typically one hundred micrograms, slightly under the average tab of acid that was to become more widespread a decade later. One person took notes on what they saw and heard. Others were there for support. The note taker later drafted an "objective report." The subject wrote a "subjective report," setting down their own recollections of the experience and their reactions to it. Many of these sessions were recorded on reel-to-reel audio tapes. The group met roughly once a week, on Saturdays, during the summer of 1958. These gatherings, held in private homes outside New York City, typically in Westchester County, were intimate, with subjects often weeping, their friends holding their hands or embracing them while offering reassurance.

A Good Trip

Exman was the second member of the Basic Group to take the drug in this controlled setting. The date was July 5, 1958. The place was Helen Wynn's home in Chappaqua, New York. Sunny drove him there but did not stay. In addition to Wynn, Dr. Laidlaw, and Dr. Yoder, Powers was there to support his friend.[64]

After receiving one hundred micrograms of LSD at 9:17 a.m., Exman began to reflect on his body. One of the first things he noticed was his extraordinary fatigue. "I want to rest," he said, according to the objective report.

"Didn't realize I had been driving the body so."
"Been pushing the body too hard."

Exman wasn't just reckoning with what he had been demanding from his body, however. He was struggling to come to terms with his body itself. A relatively small and plain-looking man, Exman had long wished for a better physique. Now he was seeing this wish clearly, observing the fact that he did not really like his body even as he felt reassured that it was just fine as it was. "I can accept the body," he said, as if shaking off two thousand years of Christian suspicions of the body as an occasion for sin.

> *"Body is not evil; it is good."*
> *"It isn't little and shrivelled—it's wholesome and beautiful."*

Oddly, alongside these admonitions of acceptance came a refrain, with clear echoes from Gerald Heard's teaching, about the necessity of disciplining the body: "The body has to be trained."

These reflections about the body then gave way to expressions of fear. "I'm a little afraid," he told Powers. Wynn held his hand. "Don't let me go too far," Exman said. "You can't go too far," Dr. Laidlaw replied. "I'm afraid I'll take more than I can hold," Exman said. Again Laidlaw comforted him: "No chance of that."

Intertwined with these expressions of fear were feelings of pain and suffering:

> *"Only pain—cold without cold—Shivering inwardly."*
> *"The suffering I've gone through today is indescribable."*

This pain was tempered, however, by paradox.

> *"Alternating experiences of pain and ecstasy."*
> *"This is purgatory. Delightful pain."*

Exman also experienced the cosmic consciousness others in the Basic Group would report—the collapsing of time and space, the sense that "all was one," the inhabiting of an "everlasting now" that he described as "a foretaste of immortality." Alongside this consciousness he sensed that he and his friends were sharing something sacred, their own sort of "beloved community."

Scholars of mysticism have long observed that mystical experiences inevitably take cues, both in the moment and in the retelling, from the worldviews of surrounding cultures and societies. As the philosopher Steven Katz has famously argued, no mystic saw Jesus before Jesus was born. Critics of Huxley have contended that he saw what he had preprogrammed himself to see. Exman, during this trip, seems to be bending his interpretations of his experiences in the direction of his hopes. "I suppose it's New Jerusalem," he said. "I guess this is the Beatific Vision."

As he was coming down from his high around 2 p.m., Exman engaged in a kind of highbrow art appreciation that reads, retrospectively, like a rebuke to the counterculture to come. He listened to classical music on a Hi-Fi record player. He looked at images of paintings by Rembrandt, Seurat, and Van Gogh. He even read some Shakespeare. While Beethoven was playing, Exman wept. "It is like a great river with its tributaries, seen from above. It is the praise of God. Beloved Beethoven," he said. "Joy. Joy. Joy. Joy."

It was, as they say, a good trip, and when Exman was asked to speak later that year at a Conference on Parapsychology and Psychedelics sponsored by the Parapsychology Foundation, he narrated his story in a major key. "We all know that the experience brings with it a heightened sense of reality; a higher sense of unity and a more profound sense of being, a sense of order and beauty," he said.[65] He then compared the ecstasy he had felt at the height of his trip with the ecstasy he felt as a teenager on the road to Blanchester. The body pain and body shame he felt during his trip he now interpreted as a necessary reduction of his ego, its crucifixion even.

What he really wanted to say, however, concerned not himself but the Basic Group. He wanted to describe how his LSD experience gave him "a sense of belonging; a group empathy," likely brought on by that deflation of the ego. "There is such a glad community!" he exclaimed during his experience, and in his subjective report he recalled a "sense of kinship . . . so strong that I thought of ourselves as a true brotherhood, a real church." Pressing beyond James's personalism, Exman argued for an interpretation of psychedelic experiences that took into account communities as much as individuals. "It is easy to say that this experience is a kind of joy ride, a kind of selfish, self-satisfying experience," he told the conference. "It isn't at all," because the experience itself sings of connection.[66]

At the end of his published conference remarks, there appears a fascinating note, which reads as follows: "Later, Mr. Exman had the psychedelic experience a second time. While he still believes that what is revealed is of a super-sensible or spiritual nature, he is convinced that it should not be sought after, either to authenticate the religious experience or as a means of spiritual growth."[67]

What happened to Exman during this second LSD trip? What changed his mind?

Lucifer

Unfortunately, the Exman Archive does not include for Exman's second LSD experience all the documents we have for his first. There is no objective report from an outsider, and no subjective report from Exman. This is odd, given his tendency to save everything. Perhaps the record keeping was less careful in the Basic Group's later life than at the beginning. Perhaps Exman or someone else in his family chose to destroy the records. However, there is evidence of that second trip in the Exman Archive. In addition to a reel-to-reel audio tape of Exman's first trip, there is a reel-to-reel tape of the second, dated December 13, 1958, a little over four months after the first. At least one of these tapes, likely the first, was sent by Lucille Kahn to Exman's children after his death, "I felt you would want this 'moment' in Gene's life," she told them. "For him, as for most of us, it provided a transforming breakthrough."[68]

Like Exman's first LSD tape, the second one is selective. Group members turned their recorder on and off as they saw fit. Exman's disquiet in this tape clearly differs from the ebullience of the first. He doesn't talk as much. In fact, he apologizes for under-communicating. More than once, he calls this second trip a "shattering experience." Toward the end, he says that "when you come out of it you realize you are destroyed." But his voice is calm, and there is no hint in the sound that survives of any sense of demonic visitation. There is evidence elsewhere in the Exman Archive, however.

On the second night after his second trip, Exman went to sleep with paper and a pencil beside his bed and the hope that he might receive insights into his unsettling experience. He woke up from a dream of a fire in his office building that had started in Tom Powers's office. Regarding the significance of this dream, Exman wrote:

1. Fire in the upper stories = damage to the brain.

2. Tom Powers' office and papers = represents L.S.D. since it was T.P. who urged me to be one of the small group (inc. Dr. Laidlaw & Bill Wilson) taking the drug.

A few days later, Exman shared with Margueritte Bro his growing unease with LSD. "While I have not reached a final conclusion, I am more and more tending to the conviction that L.S.D. 25 is not a help in the essential path," he wrote in a letter. "I strongly suspect that it is Luciferian, but more of that when I see you."[69]

A year later, Exman was now certain that LSD had failed the "miracle drug" test, at least for him. When Powers told him in a letter that LSD experimentation was "right and good and Christ-sanctioned," Exman dissented by evoking the uncontestable authority of his own personal experience. Why "are you still debating whether or not LSD is a good thing[?]," he asked. "Perhaps I would share your uncertainty were it not for the fact that I had so clear a revealing . . . experience when I took the stuff. Having had that experience, I need no arguments. To experience is to know, although I grant that what may be true for one person may not necessarily be true for another."[70]

Toward the end of his life, while working on his autobiography, Exman jotted down some notes titled "The Hope of LSD." He concluded these notes by compressing his two trips into eight words: "My experience—saw Christ at Gethsemane; saw Lucifer."

A letter Wilson wrote to Dowling just before Thanksgiving 1959 also refers to Exman's bad trip. Though Dowling tried LSD once at Wilson's urging, he was skeptical about its benefits. Wilson told Dowling that members of the Basic Group had become skeptics, too. "G. had quite a negative reaction the second time he tried the material," Wilson wrote, referring to Exman, whom he called Gene. "He saw devils and had a deep sense of malignancy." But Wilson saw Exman's case as an outlier: "With only one exception, this is the only case I have ever heard of where there was such a development."[71]

Wilson also told his spiritual confidant Father Ed Dowling that the Basic Group had disbanded. Why? Because to continue "would have led to a lot of controversy," because many participants were content with having tried it just once, and because some, Exman included, "didn't care to go on." Wilson was done, too. He stopped taking LSD in 1959 or 1960.[72]

The Religion of Experience

All editors have stories about big books that got away. In a 1953 article for *Harper's Magazine* called "Reading, Writing, and Religion," Exman recalled how the clergyman Lloyd Douglas came to him with a hope and a dream and an idea for a novel. It was 1928 and Exman was in his first year at Harper. Exman encouraged Douglas but turned the book down. That book, *Magnificent Obsession*, became a bestseller and was made into a motion picture starring Jane Wyman and Rock Hudson. Douglas went on to become one of the bestselling authors of the first half of the twentieth century. His biblical epic, *The Robe* (1942), sold two million copies, and Richard Burton starred in the Hollywood adaptation.

The Big Book was another big book that got away, but Exman relinquished it happily and reveled in its success, referring to it in his *Harper's* article as "the best modern testimony I know of the power of religion to save sinners." Like Fosdick, who praised AA meetings for evoking God without causing fistfights, Exman praised AAs for understanding that "God is not primarily a theological concept but a power in time of need." AA itself he characterized as "the most exciting modern movement in religion."[73]

Similar judgments followed from *TIME* magazine, which tried to put Bill Wilson on its cover in 1960 (Wilson declined, even after *TIME* offered to photograph him from behind). In 1999, *TIME* included Wilson among its "100 Persons of the Century," and in 2011 the Big Book found itself among the "100 Best and Most Influential Books" published since *TIME*'s founding in 1923. In another end-of-the-century list, HarperSanFrancisco (now HarperOne), an outgrowth of Exman's religious book department, named the Big Book one of "100 Best Spiritual Books of the 20th Century." More recently, the Library of Congress named it one of the eighty-eight "Books That Shaped America."

By 2019, when *Writing the Big Book* gave the making of that book the sort of attention typically reserved for scriptures, it had sold thirty-seven million copies in seventy languages. It had also spawned a series of other twelve-step programs, including Al-Anon, founded by Lois Wilson, and All Addicts Anonymous, founded by Tom Powers.

Wilson's inventive rhetoric did a lot of work for AA. It gave it Jamesian features, making it personal, pluralistic, pragmatic, and perennialist. It also worked on twentieth-century American culture. It helped to elevate the term *spirituality* and downgrade the term *religion*, setting up a contest between religion and spirituality that continues today. It placed experience at the heart of the religious lives of many Americans, pushing doctrine to the periphery. In this way, it helped introduce a "spiritual but not religious" sensibility that would grow in influence into the next century. But Wilson's influence was not just confined to American religious history. He also contributed to a culture of experience, now vibrant in the United States and worldwide, which prizes experiences over things.

Wilson worked on Exman, too. Early in his career, Exman had thought of his department as a purveyor of books on "religion" rather than "theology," on the theory that "religion" was less restrictive and therefore open to more readers, more sales, and more influence. Wilson and the Big Book modeled for Exman a parallel shift from "religion" to "spirituality."

By the early 1940s, Exman was increasingly seeing himself as a seeker of experiences of the divine, and by the late 1950s he had become an investigator of psychic phenomena and psychedelic drugs, as well as a reader and editor of books on Zen Buddhism and Hindu philosophy. He did all this in conversation with Wilson, who offered Exman a model for how to translate into words and actions a new understanding of what was once called religion, in which experience was valued over dogma, diversity was valued over unity, and practices were judged by their fruits. While Wilson preached the gospel of William James from alcoholic to alcoholic in AA meetings, Exman spread that good news from reader to reader in bookstores across the country and across the world.

At that Conference on Parapsychology and Psychedelics in New York in November 1958, Exman concluded his remarks with some pointed reflections on LSD and organized religion. He acknowledged the legitimacy of concerns many religious folks had about the threat LSD research posed to faith. What if God could be found "in the factories of Parke Davis and Eli Lilly" as easily as God could be found "on the Hill of Calvary?" he asked. But Exman directed his remarks most pointedly to what he saw as a worrying tendency among his churchgoing friends: a deep suspicion of experience itself. Because these religious folks were so heavily invested in verbalizing and intellectualizing, they looked askance at spiritual experimenters like himself. "Biblical theology . . . is suspicious of experience," he wrote. Organized religion classifies spiritual experiences, whether drug induced or otherwise, as untrustworthy. The churches offer salvation not to mystics but to those who "follow the routine of the system."[74]

Here we glimpse most of the hallmarks of Exman's lifelong project, which included, on the professional side, his expansive Book of Books and, on the personal side, his long and winding spiritual journey from mystic to mystic as he tried to return once again to his Blanchester graveyard experience—to feel God's power one last time. Neither Wilson nor Exman initially wanted to give up on the term *religion*. In fact, both wanted to redeem the term. But in the end, they helped to turn it into a dirty word and to elevate *spirituality* as its replacement.

It is tempting to argue that Exman and Wilson had no religion. But to say that is to grant too much to critics of religion who equate organized religion with religion itself, as if the only possible incarnations of "religion" are massive institutions with hidebound dogmas, empty rituals, and holier-than-thou clergy. As an alternative to this erasure, it is tempting to refer to the religion of Exman, Wilson, and other mystics club members as "the religion of no religion," a term coined by the Stanford professor of comparative religion Frederic Spiegelberg.[75] That phrase neatly encapsulates the critique of organized religion visible in the work of James, Exman, and Wilson alike—their shared desire to save religion by going beyond organized religion to something else. However, by reducing the "religion" of Exman and his circle to what they denied, that term also erases too much.

Happily, Exman's talk at the LSD conference suggests another possibility—that Exman and Wilson and other members of Exman's mystics club were adherents of the religion of experience. To assert, as Exman did, that religion is about experience is already to sidestep critiques of religion as big and impersonal, as obsessed with doctrine and intent on violence. It is to make common cause with seekers after the mysteries of the divine rather than dwellers in the comfortable routines of churches, synagogues, and mosques. It is to join hands with James and with legions of readers today who believe that life is about living rather than believing or performing.

Wilson referred to the Big Book as "a book of experience."[76] James's *Varieties* was a book of experience, too. So was Exman's massive Book of Books, which tilted heavily toward biography and autobiography and what James referred to as "the feelings, acts and experiences" of individuals "so far as they apprehend themselves to stand in relation to whatever they may consider the divine." In their personal lives, as in their work, Exman and Wilson joined James in locating the beating heart of religion in personal experiences rather than institutional creeds, and in valorizing ecstatic experiences of rupture—conversion and mystical encounters—over the continuity of everyday religious life. However, Wilson and Exman went beyond James in fashioning a new culture of experience. Instead of being "suspicious of experience" like their churchgoing friends, they exalted it. Instead of viewing experiences as untrustworthy, they sought them out, and not only in "religion" or "spirituality" but in culture writ large. Instead of believing that grace came through routine and repetition, they insisted that it came through the unexpected and the unrepeatable. Then they devoted their lives to trying to experience (and describe) that indescribable something one more time.

Selling the Religion of Experience

In the final years of his career, with his LSD experiments behind him, Exman returned to his search for fellow travelers who might assist in his lifelong quest to recapture something like that mystical moment he had as a teenager on the road to Blanchester. Previously that quest had taken him to Southern California and central Africa. In 1961, now in his seventh decade, it called him to India.

Exman had heard through a friend about a guru named Thakur, who had organized a nonsectarian religious community called Satsang in the holy city of Deoghar in the state of Bihar in eastern India. His followers saw him as one in a line of avatars, or divinities who descend into human bodies. Thakur, in a poem that must have struck Exman as surprisingly AA-like, referred to "God . . . or Existence, Whatever you call Him." Thakur was also a pluralist and an internationalist, instructing his followers neither to "think in terms of Hindu, Christian, Muslim, Buddhist" nor to "think in terms of Pakistan, Hindustan, Russia, China, Europe or America either." Instead of theology, he focused on action, and particularly on ethical action. Exman was keen to meet him—to add to his collection of mystics and, perhaps, to add something by or about Thakur to his Book of Books.[1]

In a letter home to his daughter, Judy, in July 1961, he described Thakur as "a genius somewhat akin to Schweitzer." He said he was planning a trip to India with his typical mix of personal and professional agendas. A biography of Thakur was in the works. There was a possibility of an English translation of some of his writings, and perhaps a magazine profile by Exman as well. "I'm sure he's an important man, maybe more important than Gandhi for our day, and I think it's worth the expenses and time to go find out," Exman told Judy. As with his trip to Africa to see Schweitzer, the plan was to stay in Thakur's community for a week. He also planned to find time to tour New Delhi and to take in the Taj Mahal.[2]

Exman left New York by jet on September 6, 1961. On a stopover in Beirut, he saw his first veiled Muslim woman. Upon his arrival in Calcutta (now Kolkata), Ray Hauserman, an American devotee of Thakur who was writing that biography, led him through the airport. Outside, a group of Thakur's disciples hung garlands around Exman's neck—a moment memorialized in photos he saved in his archives. When he arrived at Thakur's ashram, more garlands awaited. Exman stayed there September 8–16, and met with Thakur roughly twice a day.

Before the trip, a State Department friend had warned Exman "in strictest confidence" that elements of Thakur's group were "out to exploit their members" and that their guru was "fundamentally concerned with advancing his personal power." The friend concluded, "Watch your step."[3]

Exman ignored this warning. In a letter home to family members and coworkers, he gushed about the latest member of his mystics club. "Thakur is genuine no doubt," he wrote. "The most compassionate person I've ever met." And one of the most humble. "The Indian tradition is that the guru is God manifest," Exman explained. "If Thakur considers himself as such, he is the most modest of gods." Like Schweitzer, Thakur refused to define God: "Indefinable he says." Again like Schweitzer, he was "always directing attention away from himself to the individual." Thakur also preached a version of Schweitzer's Reverence for Life ideal that was, in Exman's estimation, "more tinged with emotion" and "more personal" than that of his counterpart in Africa.

When Exman got back to New York, his interest in training for the life of the spirit was rekindled. However, having seen a second Schweitzer, he knew he was not cut out for sainthood himself, and he began to wonder whether he would ever see God again.[4]

In the early 1960s, as he approached the mandatory retirement age of 65, Exman began thinking about transitioning from editor to author. He wanted to write a book, but what sort of book should he write?

Years earlier, during a difficult time in their relationship in the late 1940s, Margueritte Bro had received from Exman what she judged to be "one of the most wonderful letters I ever read." She fantasized about writing a book about Exman called "Letters from an Editor." It would include "some things you wrote while you sat by your father-in-law's bedside, some on book trips, some at home, many from the office," she wrote to her friend. "What a biography they will be, those letters; there we will see the soul in the process of growing."[5]

A decade later, in the late 1950s, Bro tried to convince Exman to write his own life story. Exman was just finishing the most productive decade of his career, which saw him publish books by Dorothy Day, Martin Luther King Jr., Howard Thurman, Bill Wilson, Albert Schweitzer, and Harry Emerson Fosdick. His department had also gestated Harper's first paperback series, Harper Torchbooks, which began in 1956 with "quality paperbacks" in religion and was branching out to include all sorts of nonfiction books. Early offerings in this series read like a who's who in comparative religion. There were books in Jewish studies by the renowned philosopher Martin Buber and Abraham Heschel, the theologian who marched alongside King. There were collections of Hindu and Buddhist scriptures and works on Confucius and Muhammad. There were big-name theorists of religion: the philosopher Ludwig Feuerbach, the anthropologist Edward Burnett Tylor, the sociologist Ernst Troeltsch, and the theologian Paul Tillich. Torchbooks also brought the University of Chicago professor Mircea Eliade into the Harper camp. His signature title, *The Sacred and the Profane* (1959), would become a religious studies classic, and Eliade would become one of the most widely read (and debated) scholars of religion in the late twentieth century.

Now Bro was urging Exman to author a contribution of his own to his influential Book of Books: "What an extraordinary book you could write. A sort of literary and spiritual biography of a publisher with the joys and rewards and problems and exasperations of publishing all spread out. Famous persons, simple persons, dumbbells. The story of your life could come in incidentally with throw-backs. . . . I can see a stunning kind of biography, all the more personal because so impersonal."[6]

Exman did write a book as he moved into retirement. In fact, he wrote two. But they were not about his life. They were about his employer. After he officially retired in 1965, he maintained his Harper office and stayed on the Harper payroll in the newly formed position of archivist. In that capacity, he gathered and organized papers the Harper brothers and their successors had been accumulating since they got into the book business in 1817. He also wrote a history of Harper in two volumes: *The Brothers Harper* (1965) and *The House of Harper* (1967).

Harper & Brothers had merged with Row, Peterson & Company, a textbook publisher, to become Harper & Row in 1962, and Exman wrote *The Brothers Harper* "to keep green the memory of the four brothers and their extraordinary partnership." He also wrote it to make a case for the enduring power of books to change minds and transform lives. For his epigraph, he chose a line from *Publishers Weekly* that referred to the house the Harper brothers built as "such a power in the land as the land has seldom known."[7]

On the opening page of his second Harper book, which he described as "a biography of the intangible entity that can best be described as the House of Harper," he promised that the pages to follow would be devoted to "the countless men and women whose personal careers and loyalties have been subordinated to a loyalty to the House." On the last page of the last chapter, he referred to his employer as "an American institution with its own mystique" rooted in the affection its readers had felt for its authors and books.[8]

Exman was one of those "countless men and women" who fell under the thrall of the Harper "mystique." For years, he feared that his loyalty to "the House" was hindering his spiritual progress. Bro saw that happen. She saw the compromises he made, how he subordinated his search for God to his search for the next bestseller. So it should not be surprising that, after his Harper history books appeared, she continued to urge him to write his autobiography. With that goal in mind, he started archiving his own papers, annotating many of the thousands of letters now in his personal archives, adding dates to undated correspondence, last names to letters signed with a first name only, and other tidbits along the way.

In 1965, the year his first Harper book was published, Bro wrote to Exman after learning of his retirement secondhand. "You can't be getting toward sixty-five can you? And why would that necessitate retirement? Haven't you got another iron in the fire?" She couldn't help but hope that retirement might reinvigorate his life, and perhaps even their relationship. "Let's go live in Europe for a year. I'm completely ready to leave my grown-up offspring," she wrote. A few days later she saw Exman as he was coming through Chicago, but the pace of their correspondence did not pick up.[9]

Bro continued to dream, however. "My mind leaps to your former idea of a small publishing company. We once had it all thought out," she wrote to him in 1965. Two years later, in a letter presenting herself as president of the "Society for Appreciating Exman," she suggested they get the rights to books going out of print and breathe new life into them. "I've got an idea that could work," she told her old friend.[10]

Exman had dreams, too—actual dreams in this case—including one where he encountered Bro at a Quaker meeting where the sexes were separated. The setting then shifted to a religious meeting in a prison. "I realized I had done things that made me deserve imprisonment. I recalled one thing which I had done, not known to authorities, which would have put me in prison. On waking I could not remember what this offense was."[11]

As the 1960s pressed on, Exman continued to resist Bro's pleas to write his life story. Channeling Bill Wilson's insistence on anonymity and Gerald Heard's warnings against egoism, he described writing his own life story as "a very egotistical venture." But he allowed himself to imagine how he might craft it as "a kind of spiritual odyssey." While organizing his own papers, he revisited a magazine piece he wrote on his pilgrimage to Schweitzer, as well as an unpublished piece on his pilgrimage to Thakur, whom he now described as the "Schweitzer of India." In the spring of 1969, Exman told Bro "they both read well and could be incorporated into some things I have done, some people I have observed, and some conclusions I have reached." He mentioned that his friend the Yale church historian Jaroslav Pelikan had urged him "to write a book which would show the influence of publishing on public opinion—covering the effect of books I have published on making widespread the thoughts of such men as Fosdick, Teilhard [de Chardin], King, the Schweitzer Renaissance, the spiritual classics, etc." But Harper also called. Its executives wanted a third volume on their history.[12]

The problem, as always, was time and energy. Exman had stepped down from the Harper board and from the boards of various national and international nonprofits, but he had stepped up to local volunteer work. As a result, he was still "much too involved in 'good deeds'" with the Cape Cod Conservatory of Music and with Sturgis Library, America's oldest public library, positioned just a few houses down the hill from his home. He was busy as well in his garden, where he had transplanted roses from his Scarsdale home and planted rows of corn, beans, lettuce, tomatoes, and carrots. "It's running me and not I it," he confessed to Bro, adding, "I am resolved not to spend my last years as caretaker of a Cape Cod estate."[13]

Bro said she wished she had moved to Barnstable so they could be neighbors and she could cajole him to keep writing, but that was not to be. He spent his last years taking care of Sunny. In the early 1970s, she was beset with neurological difficulties that made it almost impossible for her to process language. For her and her family, who had constructed their collective identity around the spoken and written word, her aphasia was devastating. Exman took her to a spa town in Italy for three weeks. He ferried her to an acupuncturist in nearby New Bedford and to a neurologist on Cape Cod. He promised never to put her into a nursing home, but to care for her at home as she had cared for her parents. Trying to keep that promise wore him down. Meanwhile, her body continued to deteriorate, and he was getting up two or three times a night to care for her. When Judy and her husband, Walter, visited in May 1975, he was beyond exhaustion. They convinced him that Sunny needed professional care, and in June they moved her to a nearby nursing home.

Exman's energy returned. "He was having the time of his life," Walter reported. "He could finally do something for himself."[14] He even started smoking. On Labor Day weekend in 1975, he drove to Boston to take in a concert by his old friend the Riverside organist Virgil Fox. Another old friend accompanied him: an Italian American radio news broadcaster named Lisa Sergio, whose *Prayers of Women* he had published in 1965.

Exman came home on Sunday, and on Labor Day he had a heart attack. He was admitted to Cape Cod Hospital, about ten minutes from his home. Five or six weeks later, he was taken to a hospital in Providence, Rhode Island, for open heart surgery. One of his visitors there was Margueritte Bro, who traveled one last time to see her dear friend. She was eighty-one years old. He was seventy-five. "He's collecting himself. He's preparing himself," she told Wally.[15] He died on the operating table on October 12, 1975. Two years later, on February 21, 1977, Bro died from complications of liver cancer. She is buried at Greenwood Cemetery in the small lakeside town of Cable in northern Wisconsin. He is buried in Lothrop Hill Cemetery, in Barnstable, Massachusetts, just a short walk from his home.

Exman's life begins with an uncanny experience he and his horse had when he was a teenager on a warm evening in rural Ohio—an experience he comes to interpret as a mystical encounter with the divine. This encounter sparks a lifelong search for God and a quest to recapture that moment on the road to Blanchester—to experience God in his bones again, to feel the holy moving like an electric or sexual charge through his body.

But Exman is a social person. He realizes he cannot do this alone. And he knows from reading James's *Varieties* that he doesn't have to. He seeks out other people who have had similar experiences. They might be able to help him make sense of his. They might even be able to help him re-create it.

When he finds these fellow travelers he befriends them. Over the course of his life he creates and sustains a vast network of like-minded seekers after God: his mystics club. Members of this club talk with and write to each other. They meditate together. They read and discuss books together. They experiment, together and alone, with various techniques in the life of the spirit. In many cases, they also attend religious services and are part of religious communities. In this regard they are spiritual *and* religious.

These fellow travelers also write books, which Exman edits and publishes. The collected works of this network of mystics and seekers and would-be saints run into the thousands of volumes: the Book of Books. This is Exman's own Big Book, bigger than his Harper volumes, bigger than the autobiography Bro wanted him to write, bigger than AA's Big Book. Its central subjects are individual persons. Their stories form a repository of religious and spiritual experiences in mid-twentieth-century America. They also serve as a model for American religion to come. The go-to genres in this Book of Books are biographies, autobiographies, and what are now called memoirs: see, here, the tale of one unique individual, like you in many ways, the things they desired, the roadblocks they encountered, the choices they made, whom they loved, what they lost. Reckon with their experiences as you make your own. Because that is what is ultimately significant. That is what makes a life. That is what makes meaning.

Amid and alongside all this networking and publishing, Exman also accumulates a lifetime of extraordinary experiences. He cofounds a commune in Southern California dedicated to experimenting with spiritual practices that might save a world on fire from militarism and materialism. He takes LSD as a possible shortcut to God. He travels to Africa to seek out a saint and to India to seek out a guru. Closer to home, he meets and befriends Margueritte Bro, who becomes over the course of his adult life his closest coworker and most intimate friend.

Exman and the members of his unofficial mystics club disagree with one another, of course. But they tend to converge on a few key commitments:

- *They believe in God.*

- *They believe that their purpose in life is to find God, and they dedicate themselves to that search.*

- *That search leads them to experiment with various techniques for entering into God's Presence.*

All are adamant, however, that this search is not escapist. Instead of pushing them to withdraw from the world, their seeking pushes them to engage with it, to work to stop war, and to make the world more just, more equitable, more tolerant.

The inward searching and outward engagement of members of this network lead them to seek out wisdom far beyond the confines of the religious traditions of their birth. If religion is about personal experience, why restrict your experiences to one religious tradition? Many, Exman included, immerse themselves in the beliefs and practices of Asian religions.

Of course, all of these people live on earth, and they do so during the middle decades of the twentieth century. Their lives are defined by big global events: World War I, the Great Depression, World War II, and the Cold War. As they look at the world around them they see a world in crisis, critically endangered by materialism, militarism, and the atomic bomb. As they analyze this crisis, they come to believe it is rooted in the human heart. In selfishness and egotism.

The solution is, in their view, religion. But what sort of religion? Organized religion will not do. In fact, it is part of the problem. It divides people into us and them. It foments war. What is needed is a religion beyond religion: a religion of personal experience that can change human hearts and thereby change the world. In this regard Exman and his circle are "religious and not religious": religious when it comes to personal religion but not religious when it comes to institutional religion.

Members of Exman's mystics club disagreed about the best term to use to describe their shared project. Early on in his Harper career, Exman had attempted to broaden the mission of his religious book department by redirecting it from the narrow argumentation of "theology" to the more capacious experiences of "religion." James had done something similar when he contended that experiences of the divine came in many varieties, and when he described those experiences as broadly "religious" rather than narrowly "Christian." Bill Wilson, in his early drafts of AA's Big Book, made a similar shift (for similar reasons) from championing "religious experiences" to championing "spiritual experiences."

As early as the mid-1940s, while World War II was still on and he was shuttling back and forth between New York and California, Exman expressed a similar concern about the word *religion*. After the death of an extended family member, he wrote a long letter to Sunny's mother affirming his firm faith in God and in life after death. He also expressed a conviction his son-in-law Walter and granddaughter, Katherine, continue to associate with him: "nothing happens just by chance," because whatever happens "is part of God's plan." While setting down this comforting creed, Exman realized he was starting to sound pompous. "Please don't think that I'm very *religious*," he told his mother-in-law. "The word 'religion' has got very fuzzy and queer looking," he added. "I wish sometimes we had a new and different word for it."[16]

Exman was aware of the ways Wilson had gravitated from the term *religious* to the term *spiritual* in the Big Book and in his later AA work. Exman might have gone and done likewise, by changing the name of his religious books department to the spiritual books department, for example. He did not take such a step, but his successors at Harper did, renaming the imprint that grew out of his department HarperSanFrancisco and, later, HarperOne.

Today people who stand in the lineage of James, Exman, Wilson, and other members of the mystics club often refer to themselves as "spiritual but not religious." Exman himself was spiritual *and* religious. He faithfully went to church. He put his money in the collection plate. He sat on church committees. But he didn't believe the real work of the spirit happened amid stained glass and altars. Real religion, experiential religion, happened while you were meditating alone in your office or gathering with a small group of fellow seekers after the divine.

At the end of his days, Exman had reasons to be content. He had led a good life. He had led a meaningful life. His home life had been challenging, but his family was intact. His adopted son, Frank, a farmer, was a bit removed from the rest of the family but maintained a good relationship with Exman. Wally was bitter that his father had not been around as much as he would have wanted. But Judy "revered him," according to her daughter, Katherine Kaess Christensen.[17] And she showed her devotion by walking in his ways of the spirit, pursuing breadcrumbs he had laid down concerning reincarnation and the paranormal.

When he died Judy remembered him in notes she prepared for his funeral as a man who was devoted to his wife and children. "He was a rare person," she said—a "natural leader" and a "good listener" who radiated "great joy and enthusiasm in being alive." His concern about the world ran deep, and he gave his time and treasure to political and social causes he believed in. "He had tremendous spiritual capacity, his being radiated the love of God," she concluded. "He could inspire and lift others. He had inner peace." He also had an abundance of dear friends, whose letters to Sunny and Judy piled up after his death. He had made and kept friends at college, at work, in Scarsdale, and on Cape Cod. One remembered him as "the most genial, kindliest and modest of men."[18]

Exman also had by all measures an extraordinarily successful professional life. He was, his author and friend Norman Cousins wrote in a letter to Exman's family after his death, "one of the editorial giants in book publishing." However, he had failed to become the saint Bro had challenged him to become. He had not practiced the spiritual discipline Heard had urged upon him. He had not served humanity like Schweitzer. He had not marched like King. He had not been jailed like Day. And he had never recaptured that ecstatic moment in front of the Blanchester graveyard. Back in January 1946, while the Trabuco experiment was underway and Exman and Bro were seeking after God under the influence of Gerald Heard, Bro referred to some people there as "unhappy Mystics and not-quite-hatched saints." At the end of his life, Exman found himself in that unhappy category.[19]

He might have done better. But he got distracted by work. He got distracted by status. He got distracted by money. During a life that led him from Blanchester to Denison to Chicago to New York to Harper to Riverside to Trabuco to Lambaréné to Montgomery to India, he always returned home and to his search. But to seek was not his heart's desire. His most needful thing was to find—to feel again that charge of the holy surging like lightning through his bones. It was a high bar, but he knew he had failed to clear it. His moment never came. He died a company man. He died a good man. He did not die a happy mystic.

Exman may have fallen short because creating and re-creating mystical moments is not in human hands. James argued as much in *Varieties*. Passivity is a core feature in his model of mysticism. Mystical moments emerge out of and return to mystery, not from human will.

But some of the failure was Exman's own.

Exman took a life interrupted by a global pandemic, a global depression, and two world wars and dedicated it to making meaning out of what to many in his generation seemed to be a meaningless morass. He transformed that quest for meaning into a quest for the divine. "A man's job is to grow a soul, a continuum of experience that begins here and extends beyond," he wrote in his midforties, in an essay called "Researchers of the Spirit." If it is true that the universe is "created and sustained by a Power we call God," he reasoned, the "chief concern" of human beings "should be to obtain as much knowledge and experience of God as it is possible to get," and then use it all to make the world a better place.[20] In that effort, he sat in silence in the Trabuco Oratory, met in Manhattan with his Monday night cell group, and meditated in his home office. Meanwhile, he worked hard at Harper, moving from bestseller to bestseller. That success made him crave more success, and gradually all that craving crowded out his search for the divine. You can't serve God and publishing.

The irony is that Exman was a victim of his own success, and a victor after his own failure. His personal failure to become a saint made his professional life more successful and the religion of experience he preached more popular. The distance he experienced from God was doubtless disappointing. But he made out of that disappointment a quest. And he made out of that quest a life. And a living. And hundreds of bestselling books, which preached the religion of experience to millions of readers. By any standard, his career was a massive achievement. When he retired, he was the undisputed standard-bearer for religion publishing in the United States. He was the esteemed editor of some of the biggest names in American religion in the twentieth century. He made millions of dollars for

Harper, and if you consider the backlist profits generated by his many bestsellers, he continues to make millions more annually for HarperOne. Yes, he made compromises to get books out into the world. But when his books did well, more people read them. The market and the mission went hand in hand.

Exman's Book of Books succeeded culturally and commercially. It popularized the Jamesian understanding of religion as personal, pluralistic, pragmatic, and perennial, by translating *Varieties* into words ordinary people could understand. It spread the religion of experience to generations of postwar readers in the US and abroad. It taught millions to hate the word *religion* and love the word *spirituality*, and, in so doing, it helped to empty the pews in twenty-first-century America and swell the rolls of the "spiritual but not religious." It also popularized the idea and practice of consuming religion. In fact, it made the notion of individual choice in religion seem inevitable: each of us now expects to select and purchase our own scriptures, our own practices, and we have so many from which to choose.[21]

Exman's project succeeded because its native habitat is the ecology of consumer capitalism. The religion of experience preaches the habit of the never-ending search. That search produces not finding but longing. And the object of that longing is displaced by degrees—from God to the experience of God to the experience of whatever you understand to be God. Seekers then search for experiences that seem to have nothing at all to do with God or religion or spirituality. They set their hearts (and make their bets) on a lifetime of experiences. Make memories is their mantra.

To see what Exman accomplished it is necessary only to look around you. His Book of Books lives today not only in the hundreds of books he edited that are still in print but also in the millions of books and movies and television shows and tweets and TikToks and advertisements those books have spawned. To see the logic of his Book of Books on display, follow Exman on his pilgrimage to Schweitzer in Africa, but go on a shopping spree at Harrods along the way. Or, move well beyond Exman's life to the lives of today's consumers who tell their friends they want a night out on the town for their birthday present. These consumers of experiences give their spouses a spa day or a day at the ballpark. They buy themselves a yoga pass. They take a hike. They surf the internet. They immerse themselves in a video game. They vape weed. They binge a new television series. They get in a car and set out for an adventure. They read a good book. In today's attention economy, experiences are what we value with our time and attention (and money). "Stuff, we love stuff, and there's some really great stuff out there," the Scottish actor Ewan McGregor says in a 2022 Super Bowl ad for the travel company Expedia. "Do you think any of us will look back on our lives and regret the things we didn't buy?" he asks. No. We will regret "the places we didn't go."[22]

Of course, Exman did not write this ad alone. He had partners—in publishing and advertising, to be sure, but also in film and television and advertising and in any other business where there are profits to be made by selling experiences. But his fingerprints are all over our contemporary religion of experience and our broader culture of experience. He stood at the center of a network of talented authors and editors and salespeople who built and sustained it.

Exman's professional accomplishments did not go unchallenged. There are many millions of traditional religious folks in the United States today who go to church regularly and draw comfort as they make their way over the course of a year through the same rituals, the same hymns, the same Bible passages, and in some cases, the same sermons. These people don't find their rituals to be empty or their pastors' sermons to be shallow. What they look for in religion is solidarity, not excitement. They grew up in their church with their parents and grandparents and expect their children to do the same.

There are also many millions of Americans who reject the religious pluralism of Exman's Book of Books. What matters in religion is not experience but truth, they argue. Their group is in possession of that truth, and they need to fight to defend it against falsehoods, perhaps even with guns. Christianity, *their* Christianity, is the one true religion. And that one true religion must find expression not only in the lives of their congregations but also in the life of the nation.

Back in 1922, Harry Emerson Fosdick asked, "Shall the Fundamentalists Win?" That is still a live question. But there is no denying the ongoing power and resolve of the many millions of Americans, religious and otherwise, whose answer to that question is a resounding "NO!" They do not think that religion is fundamentally about doctrine. They value its many expressions. And they are convinced that true religion (or spirituality) will produce efforts to make the world a better place. Such sentiments are growing in the United States, which is undergoing a decided shift away from organized religion to personal spirituality.

Today, a century after Fosdick's sermon, the percentage of Americans who identify as Christian is plunging from 75 percent a decade ago to 63 percent. And many of them are not really practicing. Only a quarter of American adults say they attend religious services at least once a week (and those who actually attend is much smaller).[23]

Meanwhile the fastest-growing religious demographic in the United States is the religiously unaffiliated, or "nones." Many of these people identify as spiritual. In fact, more than one in every four Americans now describe themselves as "spiritual but not religious." And seven in ten say they are "proud to be part of a nation that is becoming more religiously diverse."[24]

All this is to say that the religion of experience remains popular. Obviously, it can be found among meditators and yoga devotees and people who go on retreats and readers of spiritual literature. But it can also be found among many people in the pews, including the spiritual *and* religious, who, as Exman once did, faithfully attend worship services yet find their real sustenance in personal contemplative practices, in small groups of seekers after the divine, and in agitating for a more just and equitable world.

At the height of Exman's influence in publishing, just a month before King's *Stride Toward Freedom* appeared in the fall of 1958,

Bro wrote Exman to ask him about the end game. For years she had been his muse, inspiring much of his best work. But she had also become his conscience, and it was in that role that she observed how his calling had become a job, how his missionizing had devolved into selling. She asked him where it was all going. "What is it you are merchandising?" she asked him. "And what will you be doing besides merchandise?"[25]

He never did answer that crucial question. But there is an answer to be found in the course of his life. His legacy, his contribution, was to refashion American religious and cultural life. What was he selling? He was selling guidebooks to the never-ending search for God. These guidebooks shifted the gaze of their readers from religious institutions and their traditions to individuals and their experiences. They were never as pluralistic or as broadminded as Exman imagined. They never shook their Protestant biases. They were at times anti-Catholic. And they were persistently naïve about the strength and breadth of racism in the United States, and the ways in which White supremacy and religious fundamentalism are mutually reinforcing. But they cracked open a space for religious variety, for spiritual pluralism, for hallelujahs to a vast songbook of hymns in what had been for too long a one-note country.

Exman was a missionary for experience and a merchandiser in the attention economy. And while he never found what he was looking for, he found his calling and his voice. He channeled that voice through his authors, into their books, and out into the wider world. Exman's Book of Books was a song of experience itself. And its rhythms and harmonies could be heard far beyond whatever barriers might spring up to restrict the free range of "religion" or "spirituality." Life is meant to be lived. That's the message he sold. That's the song he sang. That's the story he lived.

Exman wasn't just selling experience, however. He was connecting the dots between spiritual experiences and social and political action, challenging seekers after the divine to work not only to see God but also to make justice and peace. In his life, he opposed war in all its forms. He championed internationalism over nationalism and cosmopolitanism over parochialism. He understood that the dangers of nuclear weapons were magnified by the sins and misdemeanors of human beings. Today the progressive values of his Book of Books are under attack. But in this time when populist strongmen around the globe are threatening nuclear attacks, accelerating climate change, weakening democracy, and persecuting racial and religious minorities, those values have never been more relevant, or more urgent.

Happily, those values endure, in hundreds of bestsellers that remain in print, and in the communities that read and value them. Books are sacred things, Exman once said. As much as the reading of them, the making of them is worthy of a human life.

Acknowledgments

All books are group efforts, and in this one I have collaborated with a particularly large and talented group. My gratitude goes out first and foremost to the Exman family for entrusting to me the Exman Archive: to the late Judy Kaess, who first invited me to her home to see her father's books; to her husband, Walter Kaess, for so warmly welcoming me into that home after Judy's death; to Exman's son, the late Wally Exman, for sitting for so many interviews with me; and to Katherine Kaess Christensen, for representing the next generation in our conversations. I am also grateful to my religious studies colleague Laurie Patton, who graciously agreed to provide a permanent home for Exman's books and papers at Middlebury College, where she serves as president.

Margueritte Bro's family has also been generous with their time. I was lucky to be able to interview Bro's daughter-in-law June Bro and her son Andy Bro before they died. Pamela Bro and Peter Racher told me what they remembered of "Granny," and Peter shared copies of letters she sent home from overseas.

Many thanks as well to Professors Matthew Hedstrom and Leigh Eric Schmidt, who discovered Exman before I did and helpfully placed him in broader traditions of liberal religion and seeker spirituality. Matthew was my most valued academic conversation partner as I worked through the archives. He also read and commented on the whole manuscript.

Early conversations with my friend and former editor Paul Elie helped shape the book in the direction it took as a conversation triangulated between an editor, his authors, and the books they made together. The enthusiasm of my former student Maria Smilios for Exman as a character searching for something he would never find jump-started my early work on the book and kept me going through the final edits.

Fellowships from the National Endowment for the Humanities Public Scholars program and Boston University's Center for the Humanities (BUCH) allowed me to take time off from teaching to complete this book. I am grateful to my wonderful colleagues who set aside their own work to write letters on my behalf for this funding. They include Julie Byrne, Jeff Kripal, Peter Manseau, Eboo Patel, Ann Taves, and Grant Wacker.

Other BUCH fellows—Erin Murphy, Rob Weller, and Jennifer Cazenave—offered insightful readings of one draft chapter, as did the BUCH director (and Marlon Brando expert) Susan Mizruchi. The book was also shaped by participants at a "Spiritual But Not Religious" conference originally scheduled for Esalen and later held (with a slightly different dress code) at Harvard Divinity School. I learned so much there from Andrea Jain, Mark Jordan, Jeff Kripal, Sarabinh Levy-Brightman, William Parsons, Charles Stang, and others. Fellow members of Boston University's Department of Religion also commented on a draft chapter at a departmental colloquium and, later, in emails and hallway conversations. I am especially grateful for my colleagues in American religions, Anthony Petro and Margarita Guillory, and for graduate students who took a seminar I taught on William James and liberal Protestantism in the United States. Three of those students went on to do research for me on this book: Kira Ganga Kieffer, Chad Moore, and Maxwell Pingeon. Kira did a terrific job reading and cataloging Exman's family correspondence. Maxwell was my expert on all things LSD. The folks at Boston University's interlibrary loan office also did their usually expert job tracking down documents for me.

Conversation is the soul of teaching and research, and I learned so much from many other friends and colleagues willing to discuss this project. They include Catherine Albanese, Eva Barbarossa, David Chappell, Linda Exman, Marie Griffith, Robert Jones, John Kaag, Steven Katz, Don Lattin, Martin Marty, Michael Murphy, Robert Orsi, Stacy Spaulding, Carole Stabile, Tom Tweed, Edie Vonnegut, Mark Vonnegut, David Harrington Watt, Lauren Winner, Onaje X. Woodbine, and James Wood.

Experts who agreed to read chapters pushed me to refine my arguments and saved me from putting some howlers into print. They include Robert Ellsberg, Alison Falby, Paul Harvey, J. N. Carleton Paget, Jake Poller, Bill Schaberg, Jay Stinnett, and Ann Taves. A deep bow to the incomparable Kathryn Lofton, who read the whole manuscript just days before it was due and offered her characteristically brilliant and blunt suggestions.

Though I relied in my research largely on an archive sitting in my own home, I also benefited from the hard work of archivists around the country. The in-house HarperCollins archivist Tzofit Goldfarb and her assistant Nina Matti were extraordinarily gracious, welcoming me into their New York City offices on two occasions, digging up old contracts, catalogs, and correspondence, and sending me scans. J. C. Johnson and other archivists in Boston University's Howard Gotlieb Archival Research Center assisted me with locating letters and manuscripts in their extensive Martin Luther King Jr. and Howard Thurman collections. Archivists at Marquette University, Riverside Church, Stepping Stones, Syracuse University, and my local Sturgis Library, where Exman served as president many years ago, tracked down key documents for me. The Reverend Steve Sabin of Blanchester, Ohio, provided information about Exman's controversial minister at Blanchester's First Baptist Church.

Lucy Prothero and Holden Ramage helped me catalog the Exman books, including inscriptions and the ephemera secreted inside them. Lucy also read and expertly fact-checked the whole book.

I owe another big debt to my editor Gideon Weil, who took over from a series of HarperOne editors who preceded him in this project. Margueritte Bro, in one of hundreds of humorous (and insightful) passages in her letters, wrote that "asking a feller to swap editors is like asking him to take on a different home and mother and use somebody else's false teeth." True enough, as a general principle. In this case, the swap was all for the good, as Gideon offered sage advice as he worked and reworked the manuscript. My thanks go out as well to my prior HarperOne editors: Miles Doyle, Mickey Maudlin, and especially Roger Freet, who is now a good friend. Mark Tauber, HarperOne's former publisher, has also been a cheerleader for this project from start to finish. Hugh Van Dusen, who worked with Exman and recently retired after a six-decade Harper career, sat with me for hours of interviews and taught me a lot about publishing along the way. Others at HarperOne who helped to turn this manuscript into a book include assistant editor Maya Alpert, copyeditor Elizabeth Berg, and the talented arts and production team.

And where would my writing life be without my amazing academic-turned-agent, Sandy Dijkstra, and her team at Sandra Dijkstra Literary Agency, especially Elise Capron and Andrea Cavallaro? Sandy has been a steady hand at the helm of my writing career for two decades, and I'm delighted to have been along for the ride.

I also want to express my gratitude to the late William R. Hutchison, my graduate school mentor and a pioneer in the intellectual history of Protestant modernism and religious pluralism. While others looked at religion in the United States and saw mainline Protestant denominations in decline, he looked at American culture and saw the persistence of mainline Protestant ideas, values, and sensibilities. And while others looked at my writing and called it good, he pushed me to write better and think harder. He also encouraged me to follow what the Quakers call the Inner Light, which I continue to try to do. Whatever is good in this book I owe to his mentoring.

Finally, thanks to my family: to Molly and Lucy Prothero, for continuing to put up with a father who spends more time than he should at his laptop; to my mother, Helen Anderson Prothero, for a lifetime of love and support; to my late father, S. Richard Prothero, to whose memory this book is gratefully dedicated; and to my siblings, Laurie, Eric, Dan, and David, who kindly pretend to be interested in what I do. One final deep bow goes out to my partner, cheerleader, fellow author, editor, co-PI, and lifetime collaborator, Meera Subramanian. Words fail.

Notes

Prologue: A Graveyard Epiphany

1. This account of the defining moment in Exman's life is largely based on five key sources. The first four are manuscripts by Eugene Exman in the Eugene Exman Archive, located at Middlebury College in Middlebury, Vermont: "An Experimental College," handwritten autobiographical fragment; untitled, single-page, handwritten account of his Blanchester graveyard experience; untitled autobiographical typescript sent to Gerald Heard, August 1942; and "Week-End Retreat, Rye, New York, May, 1967," transcript. The fifth source is Eugene Exman, "Individual and Group Experiences," in *Proceedings of Two Conferences on Parapsychology and Pharmacology* (New York: Parapsychology Foundation, 1961), 10–13. There are additional scattered references to this experience in Exman's correspondence.

2. Exman baptismal certificate, Exman Archive.

3. Exman, "An Experimental College," Exman Archive.

Preface

1. Patricia Holt, "Harper's Spiritual Quest," *San Francisco Chronicle*, June 2, 1991, Sunday Review, 1, quoted in Matthew S. Hedstrom, "The Commodification of William James: The Book Business and the Rise of Liberal Spirituality in the Twentieth-Century United States," in *Religion and the Marketplace in the United States*, eds. Jan

Stievermann, Philip Goff, and Detlef Junker (New York: Oxford University Press, 2015), 128; Clayton Carlson, "In the Beginning: A Note from Our Founding Publisher," *News and Pews from HarperOne*, September 27, 2017, https://newsandpews.com/in-the-beginning-a-note-from-our-founding-publisher/.

2. Matthew S. Hedstrom, *The Rise of Liberal Religion: Book Culture and American Spirituality in the Twentieth Century* (New York: Oxford University Press, 2013), 128, 92. See also Leigh Eric Schmidt, *Restless Souls: The Making of American Spirituality* (New York: HarperOne, 2005), 260–61.

3. Exman, untitled, handwritten autobiographical fragment, Exman Archive.

4. Exman to Harry Emerson Fosdick, February 16, 1951, Exman Archive.

Introduction: Where God Walks

1. Exman notes in "Permanent Memoranda and Addresses" folder, Exman Archive.

2. Untitled autobiographical typescript regarding Exman's early life, Exman Archive.

3. "Denison Almost Free from Influenza," *The Denisonian*, October 18, 1918, 1; Editor's note, *The Denisonian*, October 25, 1918, 1.

4. Exman, "The Most Unforgettable Character I've Met," draft of unpublished *Reader's Digest* article on Fosdick, circa 1959, Exman Archive.

5. Leola Davis to Exman, September 24, 1921, Exman Archive.

6. Denison College, *The Adytum* (Granville, OH: 1922), 49; J. W. Decker to Exman, November 15, 1921, Exman Archive.

7. Leslie B. Moss to Exman, April 7, 1923, Exman Archive.

8. Harold Exman to Eugene Exman, April 16, 1923, and Mary Etta Exman to Eugene Exman, April 23, 1923, both in Exman Archive. Exman's mother was not a standard speller. In this letter she spelled *maybe* "maby" and *interfere* "interfear." Throughout this book, unorthodox spellings have been silently corrected.

9. Kenneth Latourette to Exman, May 29, 1923, Exman Archive.

10. Johnnie Lechner to Exman, February 23, 1922, Exman Archive.

11. John Calvin Siler, "Modernism," in *The Union Seminary Review* 36, no. 4 (July 1925): 351; Shailer Mathews, *The Faith of Modernism* (New York: Macmillan, 1924), 35.

12. William R. Hutchison, *The Modernist Impulse in American Protestantism* (Cambridge, MA: Harvard University Press, 1976); John Horsch, *Modern Religious Liberalism: The Destructiveness and Irrationality of the New Theology* (Scottsdale, PA: Fundamental Truth Depot, 1921), 266; Mathews, *The Faith of Modernism*, 103, 68.

13. Eugene Exman to Sunny Exman, March 17, 1929, Exman Archive.

14. Exman, "Getting Underway at Harpers," autobiographical fragment, Exman Archive.

15. Exman, "Getting Underway at Harpers," autobiographical fragment, Exman Archive.

16. Exman, "Getting Underway at Harpers," autobiographical fragment, Exman Archive.

17. Mary Rose Himler, "Religious Books as Best Sellers," *Publishers' Weekly*, February 19, 1927, 691; "The Religious Renaissance," *Publishers' Weekly*, February 19, 1927, 684, both quoted in Matthew S. Hedstrom, *The Rise of Liberal Religion: Book Culture and American Spirituality in the Twentieth Century* (New York: Oxford University Press, 2013), 80.

18. David A. Hollinger, "After Cloven Tongues of Fire: Ecumenical Protestantism and the Modern American Encounter with Diversity," *Journal of American History* 98, no. 1 (June 2011): 21–48.

19. *Harper Religious Books & Bibles, Summer–Fall 1948*, HarperCollins Archive, New York, New York. The book was Margueritte Harmon Bro's *More Than We Are* (New York: Harper, 1948); William James, *The Varieties of Religious Experience: A Study in Human Nature* (New York: Longmans, Green, 1902), 31.

20. Mathews, *The Faith of Modernism*, 270.

21. See Robert T. Handy, "The American Religious Depression, 1925–1935," *Church History* 29, no. 1 (March 1960): 3–16; Harper religious book department account pages, Exman Archive. On book sales declines, see Matthew Hedstrom, "The Commodification of William James: The Book Business and the Rise of Liberal

Spirituality in the Twentieth-Century United States," in *Religion and the Marketplace in the United States*, ed. Jan Stievermann, Philip Goff, and Detlef Junker (New York: Oxford University Press, 2015), 130–33.

22. Judy Exman to Sunny Exman, February 2, 1958, Exman Archive; Martin Gardner, *Fads and Fallacies in the Name of Science* (New York: Dover, 1986), front cover, 204, 186.

23. Judy Exman to Sunny Exman, February 2, 1959, Exman Archive.

24. Eugene Exman to Judy Exman, February 16, 1959, Exman Archive.

25. Eugene Exman to Judy Exman, February 16, 1959, Exman Archive.

26. Eugene Exman to Judy Exman, February 16, 1959, Exman Archive. Exman attached to this letter a clipping from Aldous Huxley, whose *The Perennial Philosophy* had popularized mystical experiences as the common foundation on which all the world's religions were built. In that article, Huxley quoted William James approvingly.

27. William James to Miss Frances R. Morse, in William James, *The Letters of William James, Volume II*, ed. Henry James (Boston: Atlantic Monthly Press, 1920), 127; James, *Varieties*, 31.

28. William James to Henry W. Rankin, June 16, 1901, quoted in Robert D. Richardson, *William James: In the Maelstrom of American Modernism* (Boston: Houghton Mifflin, 2006), 406.

29. James, *Varieties*, 419.

30. Hedstrom, "The Commodification of William James"; "Digest of Mr. Exman's Speech at the ATLA Conference," Union Seminary, June 16, 1955, Exman Archive.

31. "Wives of College Presidents Agree Life Has Its Thorns and Theirs Is No Easy Job," *New York Times*, January 12, 1949, 25.

32. Catherine L. Albanese, *A Republic of Mind and Spirit: A Cultural History of American Metaphysical Religion* (New Haven, CT: Yale University Press, 2007); William James, "The Pragmatic Method," *The Journal of Philosophy* 1, no. 25 (December 8, 1904): 682.

33. Margueritte Bro to Exman, December 17, 1949, Exman Archive.

34. Wallace Exman interview, April 2, 2016; Exman to Bro, November 13, 1946, Exman Archive.

35. On this history, see Leigh Eric Schmidt, *Restless Souls: The Making of American Spirituality* (New York: HarperOne, 2005).

36. For the sources of this account of Exman's road to Blanchester experience, see Endnote 1 under "Prologue: A Graveyard Epiphany."

37. Regarding this and other "revelatory events," I have learned much from Ann Taves, whose investigations into these uncanny experiences are deeply informed by wide reading in both religious history and the cognitive science of religion. See, especially, her *Religious Experience Reconsidered: A Building-Block Approach to the Study of Religion and Other Special Things* (Princeton, NJ: Princeton University Press, 2009); and *Revelatory Events: Three Case Studies of the Emergence of New Spiritual Paths* (Princeton, NJ: Princeton University Press, 2016).

38. Both Leigh Eric Schmidt and Matthew Hedstrom take on these stereotypes by taking seekers seriously, and by noting their many contributions to American religion and culture. Schmidt argues that seekers have typically been socially and politically engaged, and as such offer an important antidote to the religious right. Hedstrom observes how liberal Protestants, while seemingly in decline, have scored a "cultural victory" by spreading "spiritual cosmopolitan" well beyond the church pews of liberal Protestant denominations, not least through the publishing of books. See Schmidt, *Restless Souls*; Hedstrom, *The Rise of Liberal Religion*.

39. Exman, "Week-End Retreat, Rye, New York, May, 1967," transcript, Exman Archive.

40. Exman, "Week-End Retreat, Rye, New York, May, 1967," transcript, Exman Archive.

41. Exman, autobiographical fragment on Thakur, Exman Archive.

Chapter 1: America's Pastor Harry Emerson Fosdick and the Religion of Experience

1. "Religion: At Geneva," *TIME*, September 21, 1925, https://content
.time.com/time/subscriber/article/0,33009,721121,00.html; Martin
Luther King Jr. to Harry Emerson Fosdick, November 17, 1958,
Martin Luther King Jr. Research and Education Institute, Stanford
University, https://kinginstitute.stanford.edu/king-papers/documents
/harry-emerson-fosdick. The *TIME* quote is from Rabbi Stephen Wise.

2. Fosdick to Exman, February 10, 1953; Exman, "My Experience with H.E.F.," autobiographical fragment; Exman, "The Most Unforgettable Character I've Met," article draft, all in Exman Archive. Also in Exman Archive, see "Books by Harry Emerson Fosdick Published by Harper & Brothers under EE's Editorship—since 1928," which lists these sixteen books: *As I See Religion* (1932); *The Hope of the World* (1933); *The Secret of Victorious Living* (1934); *The Power to See It Through* (1935); *Successful Christian Living* (1937); *A Guide to Understanding the Bible* (1938); *Living Under Tension* (1941); *On Being a Real Person* (1943); *A Great Time to Be Alive* (1944); *On Being Fit to Live With* (1946); *The Man From Nazareth* (1949); *A Faith for Tough Times* (1952); *What Is Vital in Religion* (1955); *The Living of These Days* (1956); *Riverside Sermons* (1958); and *A Book of Public Prayers* (1959). A seventeenth followed: *Dear Dr. Brown: Letters to a Person Perplexed About Religion* (1961). Fosdick also contributed to many other books on Exman's list. For example, he wrote a chapter in Louis Finkelstein, ed., *American Spiritual Autobiographies: Fifteen Self-Portraits* (New York: Harper, 1948), and the introduction to Benson Y. Landis, *A Rauschenbusch Reader* (New York: Harper, 1957).

3. Exman to Sunny, January 31, 1929; Exman to Sunny, January 30, 1929; Exman to Sunny, February 2, 1929, all in Exman Archive.

4. Exman to Sunny, February 28, 1929; Exman to Sunny, February 12, 1929, both in Exman Archive.

5. Mrs. Miller to Sunny, October 12, 1930, Exman Archive.

6. Harry Emerson Fosdick, *The Living of These Days* (New York: Harper, 1956), 36.

7. Transcript of Exman/Fosdick interview, *Wisdom*, NBC television, May 1959, Exman Archive; Fosdick, *Living of These Days*, 52; Fosdick, "Harry Emerson Fosdick," in Finkelstein, ed., *American Spiritual Autobiographies*, 108; Robert Moats Miller, *Harry Emerson Fosdick: Preacher, Pastor, Prophet* (New York: Oxford University Press, 1985), 40; Gary Dorrien, *The Making of American Liberal Theology: Idealism, Realism, & Modernity, 1900–1950* (Louisville, KY: Westminster John Knox Press, 2003), 359.

8. Fosdick, *Living of These Days*, 213–14, 73.

9. Exman, "The Most Unforgettable Character I've Met," Exman Archive.

10. George M. Marsden, *Understanding Fundamentalism and Evangelicalism* (Grand Rapids, MI: Eerdmans, 1991), 1.

11. James Hudnut-Beumler, "Riverside Church and the Development of Twentieth-Century American Protestantism," in Peter J. Paris et al., *The History of the Riverside Church in the City of New York* (New York: New York University Press, 2004), 14.

12. Harry Emerson Fosdick, "Shall the Fundamentalists Win?," http://historymatters.gmu.edu/d/5070/. In *The Making of American Liberal Theology: Imagining Progressive Religion, 1805–1900* (Louisville, KY: Westminster John Knox Press, 2001), Gary Dorrien observes that nineteenth-century liberal Protestant theologians sought a "third way between regnant orthodoxy and an ascending infidelism" (xiv).

13. Miller, *Harry Emerson Fosdick*, 116; Fosdick, "Shall the Fundamentalists Win?"; Fosdick, *Living of These Days*, 145.

14. Darren Dochuk, *Anointed with Oil: How Christianity and Crude Made Modern America* (New York: Basic, 2019), 12, 269; Miller, *Harry Emerson Fosdick*, 159.

15. Fosdick, "Harry Emerson Fosdick," in Finkelstein, ed., *American Spiritual Autobiographies*, 117.

16. Miller, *Harry Emerson Fosdick*, 162–63.

17. "Fosdick Outlines His Liberal Church in Opening Sermon," *New York Times*, June 1, 1925, 1–2.

18. "1,500 Hear Fosdick at Park Av. Church," *New York Times*, October 4, 1926, 18.

19. Robert T. Handy, "The American Religious Depression, 1925–1935," 3–16.

20. Matthew Arnold, *Culture and Anarchy: An Essay in Political and Social Criticism* (London: Smith, Elder, 1869), viii; Janice A. Radway, *A Feeling for Books: The Book-of-the-Month Club, Literary Taste, and Middle-Class Desire* (Chapel Hill: University of North Carolina Press, 1997), 283. On middlebrow literature, see also Joan Shelley Rubin, *The Making of Middlebrow Culture* (Chapel Hill: University of North Carolina Press, 1992). On middlebrow religious books, see Erin A. Smith, *What Would Jesus Read?: Popular Religious Books and Everyday Life in Twentieth-Century America* (Chapel Hill: University of

North Carolina Press, 2015); and Matthew S. Hedstrom, *The Rise of Liberal Religion: Book Culture and American Spirituality in the Twentieth Century* (New York: Oxford University Press, 2013).

21. Radway, *A Feeling for Books*, 286, 283.

22. Exman, "Deans in My Life," autobiographical fragment, Exman Archive.

23. Exman, "Fosdick as Author," *Christian Century*, May 21, 1958, 619; Exman, "Experience with H.E.F.," autobiographical fragment, Exman Archive.

24. Wallace Exman interview, November 7, 2018.

25. Exman, "Experience with H.E.F.," Exman Archive. In explaining this impasse to *Christian Century* readers, Exman recalled receiving a similar rebuff after asking Albert Schweitzer if he might allow a book of his sermons to go out into the world. "No, sermons are to be preached, not read," Schweitzer replied. "A printed sermon is like a beautiful, embalmed child; it is no longer alive" (Exman, "Fosdick as Author," *Christian Century*, May 21, 1958, 617).

26. Fosdick, *As I See Religion* (New York: Harper, 1932), 1, 4, 32, 33, 40.

27. Fosdick, *As I See Religion*, 148, 6, 16.

28. Harry Emerson Fosdick, *The Hope of the World: Twenty-Five Sermons on Christianity Today* (New York, Harper & Brothers, 1933), vii; Joel Carpenter, "Oral Roberts, Harry Emerson Fosdick, and the Divergent Unities of American Protestantism," *Fides et Historia* 18, no. 3 (January 1, 1986): 75. The other sermon collections written by Fosdick for Exman are *The Secret of Victorious Living: Sermons on Christianity Today* (1934); *The Power to See It Through: Sermons on Christianity Today* (1935); *Successful Christian Living: Sermons on Christianity Today* (1937); *Living Under Tension: Sermons on Christianity Today* (1941); *A Great Time to Be Alive: Sermons on Christianity in Wartime* (1944); *On Being Fit to Live With: Sermons on Post-war Christianity* (1946); *What Is Vital in Religion: Sermons on Contemporary Christian Problems* (1955); and *Riverside Sermons* (1958).

29. Miller, *Harry Emerson Fosdick*, 76; Fosdick, "Then Our Men Came!" *American Magazine* 86, no. 6 (December 1918): 30.

30. Miller, *Harry Emerson Fosdick*, 497, 499; "Fosdick Summons Church to End War in Geneva Sermon," *New York Times*, September 14, 1925, 1, 4.

31. Fosdick, "My Account with the Unknown Soldier," *Christian Century*, June 6, 1934, 754–56.

32. Fosdick, "Harry Emerson Fosdick," in Finkelstein, ed., *American Spiritual Autobiographies*, 109; Matthew Bowman, *The Urban Pulpit: New York City and the Fate of Liberal Evangelicalism* (New York: Oxford University Press, 2014), 258. In his wide-ranging survey of liberal Protestant theology in the United States, Dorrien divides early twentieth-century liberal Protestants into four categories: evangelical liberals, naturalistic-empiricist liberals, personalist liberals, and mystical liberals. See his *The Making of American Liberal Theology: Idealism, Realism, & Modernity, 1900–1950*, 3–9, and throughout.

33. Fosdick, *The Manhood of the Master* (New York: Association Press, 1913), 171.

34. Martin E. Marty, review of Miller, *Harry Emerson Fosdick*, in *Journal of the American Academy of Religion* 54, no. 2 (Summer 1986): 356.

35. Miller, *Harry Emerson Fosdick*, 4, 36.

36. Fosdick, *Living of These Days*, 72, 74–75.

37. Fosdick, *Living of These Days*, 73; William James, *The Varieties of Religious Experience: A Study in Human Nature* (New York: Longmans, Green, 1902), 135. Another key influence was James's student Edwin Starbuck, who is mentioned forty-six times by name in *Varieties*. Starbuck's studies of evangelical conversion convinced him that the world of religion was shifting decisively from old-fashioned dogmas to vital experiences. "A multitude of superstitions and crudities are doomed to fold their tents," Starbuck wrote in a letter to James in 1902. "People will be living in a new era of religious experience before they know it." See Christopher White, "A Measured Faith: Edwin Starbuck, William James, and the Scientific Reform of Religious Experience," *Harvard Theological Review* 101, nos. 3–4 (2008): 432–33.

38. Fosdick, *On Being a Real Person* (New York: Harper, 1943), viii; Fosdick, "Harry Emerson Fosdick," in Finkelstein, ed., *American Spiritual Autobiographies*, 111.

39. Exman, "Experience with H.E.F.," Exman Archive.

40. *Harper Religious Books Spring 1943,* in HarperCollins Archive.

41. Exman, "Books and Authors I've Known," *Christian Herald,* November 1949, 89.

42. Fosdick, *On Being a Real Person,* 3.

43. Fosdick, *On Being a Real Person,* x, 183; Heather Rachelle White, *Reforming Sodom: Protestants and the Rise of Gay Rights* (Chapel Hill: University of North Carolina Press, 2015), 15.

44. Fosdick, *On Being a Real Person,* 33, 52.

45. Fosdick, *On Being a Real Person,* 11.

46. Fosdick, *On Being a Real Person,* 252.

47. Transcript of Exman/Fosdick interview, *Wisdom,* NBC television, May 1959, Exman Archive. It is unclear whether Fosdick got the phrase "divine invasion" from Exman or whether Exman got it from Fosdick, but in accounts of his mystical moment at the Blanchester graveyard, Exman wrote of experiencing a "divine invasion." Exman, untitled, single-page, handwritten account of his Blanchester graveyard experience, Exman Archive.

48. W. B. Yeats, "The Second Coming," in his *The Poems: A New Edition,* ed. Richard J. Finneran (New York: Macmillan, 1983), 187. Data on the phrase "search for meaning" comes from the Google Ngram Viewer, https://books.google.com/ngrams.

49. Exman, "Search for Meaning," *Hibbert Journal* 62, no. 239 (July 1962): 275–83. This essay is also published in Exman, Thomas E. Powers, and Douglas V. Steere, *Search for Meaning* (Rye, NY: Wainwright House, 1961).

50. Ralph Waldo Emerson, "An Address," in *Nature: Addresses and Lectures* (Boston: Houghton Mifflin, 1904), 146; Frederick Douglass, *Narrative of the Life of Frederick Douglass, an American Slave, Written by Himself* (Boston: Anti-Slavery Office, 1845), 118, http://utc.iath.virginia.edu/abolitn/abaufda14t.html. The observation that Fosdick's personal notebooks contained forty pages of Emerson quotes is from Dorrien, *The Making of American Liberal Theology: Idealism, Realism, & Modernity, 1900–1950,* 382.

51. Exman, "Search for Meaning," 279–80.

52. See Robert Wuthnow's useful distinction between "seek-oriented spirituality" and "dweller-oriented spirituality" in his *After Heaven: Spirituality in America Since the 1950s* (Berkeley: University of California Press, 1998), 15.

53. Exman, "Search for Meaning," 276, 278, 279, 283.

Chapter 2: Collecting Mystics in a California Commune

1. Exman to Thomas Kelly, January 4, 1941, Quaker Collection, Haverford College Library, Haverford, PA. This letter is quoted in Leigh Eric Schmidt, *Restless Souls: The Making of American Spirituality* (New York: HarperOne, 2005), 260; and Matthew S. Hedstrom, *The Rise of Liberal Religion: Book Culture and American Spirituality in the Twentieth Century* (New York: Oxford University Press, 2013), 108.

2. Official participants are listed in "Seminar Personnel at La Verne," Exman Archive. This typed and mimeographed sheet of names and addresses is annotated in Exman's hand with some additional names and addresses. The twenty-five typed names also appear in a roster for "LaVerne, CA," in American Friends Service Committee, *Annual Report* (1941), 51. They are Edna Acheson, Donald Booz, Margaret Calbeck, Harold Chance, Rachel Davis DuBois, Eugene Exman, Harry Farash, Denny Fouts, H. Rodney Gale, Marian B. Gale, Felix Greene, Gerald Heard, Allan Hunter, Cora Belle Hunter, Elizabeth Hunter, Christopher Isherwood, Denver Lindley, George Little, Patrick Lloyd, Theodore McCrea, Lucille Nixon, William Rahill, Etta Mae Wallace, David White, and Harold Winchester.

3. Exman, "An Experimental College," Exman Archive; Arthur Vanderbilt, *The Best-Kept Boy in the World: The Life and Loves of Denny Fouts* (Bronx, NY: Magnus Books, 2014), 136; Christopher Isherwood, *Diaries: Volume One: 1939–1960*, ed. Katherine Bucknell (New York: HarperFlamingo, 1998), 162–63.

4. "About Gerald Heard," GeraldHeard.com; Alison Falby, *Between the Pigeonholes: Gerald Heard, 1889–1971* (Newcastle, UK: Cambridge Scholars Publishing, 2008), 1.

5. Jake Poller, *Aldous Huxley and Alternative Spirituality* (Boston: Brill, 2019), 28, 151.

6. Gerald Heard, "Religion and the Problems of a Modern Society," *Time and Tide* 12, no. 6 (February 6, 1932): 145–46.

7. Exman, "An Experimental College," Exman Archive; Jeffrey J. Kripal, *Esalen: America and the Religion of No Religion* (Chicago: University of Chicago Press, 2007), 94.

8. Walter Truett Anderson, *The Upstart Spring: Esalen and the Human Potential Movement* (Reading, MA: Addison-Wesley, 1983), 12; Isherwood, *Diaries*, 21–22.

9. Jules Evans, "Michael Murphy on Esalen, Huxley and Alan Watts," *Medium*, December 4, 2019, https://medium.com/@julesevans/michael-murphy-on-esalen-and-the-mystical-expats-b36a07636913; Exman, untitled, handwritten notes from Trabuco visit, March 8, 1945, Exman Archive.

10. Don Lattin, *Distilled Spirits: Getting High, Then Sober, with a Famous Writer, a Forgotten Philosopher, and a Hopeless Drunk* (Berkeley: University of California Press, 2012), 6.

11. Jiddu Krishnamurti, "Truth Is a Pathless Land," August 3, 1929, https://jkrishnamurti.org/about-dissolution-speech.

12. Alan Watts, *In My Own Way: An Autobiography, 1915–1965* (New York: Pantheon, 1972), 180; Isherwood, *Diaries*, 143; Jake Poller, email to author, April 5, 2022; Isherwood, *Diaries*, 50.

13. Exman, "An Experimental College," Exman Archive. References to this conversation in subsequent paragraphs are from this same source.

14. Heard to Exman, November 26, 1940, and December 18, 1940, both in Exman Archive. Heard continued to write about this "new syncretism" in Heard to Exman, January 2, 1941, Exman Archive; and Heard to E. M. Forster, April 10, 1942, quoted in Falby, *Between the Pigeonholes*, 106.

15. Isherwood, *Diaries*, 169; "Laverne Seminar Report," Exman Archive. This report was written by David White, a young pacifist who attended the seminar. White refers to writing this report in a series of letters to Exman, beginning on August 6, 1941, Exman Archive. For example, in a September 28, 1941, letter, he told Exman that he was in Norman, Oklahoma, "writing our report of the Seminar. Gerald wants

it short, and I am having the very devil of a time shortening the six hundred pages of notes I took to fit the mere five thousand to seventy-five hundred words which he insists on." On December 4, 1941, White wrote to Exman, "I'm glad you find the report usable."

16. Christopher Isherwood, "The Day at La Verne," *The Penguin New Writing* 14 (July–September 1942): 13.

17. Isherwood, *Diaries*, 164.

18. Isherwood, *Diaries*, 162.

19. Isherwood, *Diaries*, 163.

20. Heard, *Training for the Life of the Spirit, Pamphlet No. 1* (New York: Harper, 1941); and Heard, *Training for the Life of the Spirit, Pamphlet No. 2* (New York: Harper, 1942). The quotes are from the second pamphlet, 18, 55, 56. Heard pushed for the first pamphlet to be published anonymously. "It is a joint work of all of us and it is in praise of and emphasis on Anonymity," he wrote to Exman on November 27, 1940 (Exman Archive), but Exman published the pamphlets under Heard's name alone. In a later letter to Exman, Heard referred to "You Denver & I" having "le style collective" "when we amalgamate in anonymity." A marginal note on the letter, written in Exman's hand, refers to "our pamphlet" (Heard to Exman, March 3, 1941, Exman Archive).

21. "Laverne Seminar Report," 6.

22. "Laverne Seminar Report," 6.

23. Sunny to Exman, July 26, 1941, Exman Archive; Isherwood, *Diaries*, 163; Heard, *Training for the Life of the Spirit, Pamphlet No. 2*, 50.

24. Heard to Exman, January 18, 1941; and Exman to Willard Sperry, May 4, 1946, both in Exman Archive.

25. Heard to Exman, February 2, 1942; April 19, 1943; March 3, 1941; June 11, 1941, all in Exman Archive.

26. Heard to Exman, July 9, 1940, and December 18, 1940, both in Exman Archive. See also Falby, *Between the Pigeonholes*, 104–5.

27. Isherwood, *Diaries*, 234.

28. Heard to Exman, March 1, 1942, Exman Archive.

29. Aldous Huxley, typed draft of contribution to leaflet, Exman Archive; Isherwood, *Diaries*, 247.

30. Christopher Isherwood, *My Guru and His Disciple* (New York: Farrar, Straus & Giroux, 1980), 96.

31. Exman, "An Experimental College," and Exman to Sunny, July 20, 1942, both in Exman Archive.

32. Exman, "An Experimental College," Exman Archive.

33. Untitled pocketbook-size ring binder, Exman Archive. See also "Notebook on First Seminar Held at Trabuco with Gerald Heard" (Exman Archive), which includes references on its first page to the Upanishads and the Bhagavad Gita and defines yoga as "the path to Realization of God."

34. "Trabuco Seminar 1942," Exman Archive.

35. Heard to Exman, August 25, 1942, Exman Archive.

36. Exman to Heard, undated autobiographical typescript, Exman Archive.

37. Exman to Heard, untitled autobiographical typescript, August 1942, Exman Archive.

38. *Trabuco* (Trabuco Canyon, CA: Trabuco College, 1942), Exman Archive. This copy is accompanied in the Exman Archive by a September 21, 1941, letter from Felix Greene to Exman. According to Greene, this document was prompted by a mandate of the trustees to "issue a leaflet as soon as we could for the people who keep asking 'what Trabuco is all about.'" "Isherwood was a great help with it," said Greene, who ran off 450 copies and was planning on sending two or three to each of the "seminarists."

39. Isherwood, *Diaries*, 217.

40. "Some First Steps in Meditation," Exman Archive.

41. Untitled Trabuco pamphlet, Exman Archive.

42. "Trabuco Pamphlet #2, Mss. By G.H. (Heard), C.I (Isherwood), A.H. (Huxley)," Exman Archive. See also Isherwood, *My Guru and His Disciple*, 96.

43. Lucille Nixon to Trabuco Trustees, July 14, 1943, Exman Archive; Heard, *Training for the Life of the Spirit, Pamphlet No. 2*, 37; Allan Hunter to Exman, February 14, 1945, Exman Archive.

44. Bro to Exman, February 16, 1945, and February 23, 1945, both in Exman Archive; Swami Yogeshananda, "Trabuco College Tryout," https://www.geraldheard.com/writings-and-recollections/2017/8/2 /trabuco-college-tryout.

45. Bro to Exman, February 23, 1945, Exman Archive; Gerald Heard, *The Eternal Gospel* (New York: Harper, 1946), 168.

46. Exman to Heard, March 28, 1947; and Exman to Malcolm Dana, September 9, 1947, both in Exman Archive.

47. Albert Day to Exman, June 9, 1949, Exman Archive.

48. Swami Yogeshananda, "Trabuco College Tryout," https://www .geraldheard.com/writings-and-recollections/2017/8/2/trabuco -college-tryout.

49. Laurence Veysey, *The Communal Experience: Anarchist and Mystical Communities in Twentieth-Century America* (Chicago: University of Chicago Press, 1978), 272.

50. Sybille Bedford, *Aldous Huxley: A Biography* (New York: Knopf, 1974), 463.

51. Margaret Gage to Exman, April 3, 1947, Exman Archive; Rachel Davis DuBois, quoted in Jan Rosenberg, *Intercultural Education, Folklore, and the Pedagogical Thought of Rachel Davis Dubois* (Cham, Switzerland: Palgrave Macmillan, 2019), 96; Franklin Zahn, "Temporary Monk," https://www.geraldheard.com/writings-and -recollections/2017/8/2/temporary-monk.

52. Bro to Exman, June 15, 1947, Exman Archive. See also Bro to Exman, Labor Day, 1947, Exman Archive: "He [Heard] is always a main factor in my life."

53. Harold Winchester to Exman, June 8, 1949, Exman Archive.

54. Timothy Miller, "Notes on the Prehistory of the Human Potential Movement: The Vedanta Society and Gerald Heard's Trabuco College," in *On the Edge of the Future: Esalen and the Evolution of American Culture*, eds. Jeffrey J. Kripal and Glenn W. Shuck (Bloomington: University of Indiana Press, 2005), 93.

55. Gerald Heard, *Prayers and Meditations* (New York: Harper, 1949), 9; note from John Chambers to Exman, undated [summer of 1947], Exman Archive. Although Heard is credited as the sole author of

Prayers and Meditations, it was a collaborative project; Huxley wrote seven of the meditations.

56. Exman to Bro, March 30, 1945; Exman to Bro, March 28, 1947; Bro to Exman, June 15, 1947, all in Exman Archive.

57. Gerald Heard, "The Philosophia Perennis," *Vedanta and the West* 6, no. 5 (September–October 1943): 149.

58. Heard, *The Eternal Gospel*, 16, 5, 6. The original title for his book, announced in Exman's Spring 1945 religion catalog, had been *Christianity's Contribution to the Eternal Gospel*. The second half of *The Eternal Gospel* is devoted to that topic.

59. Huxley, *The Perennial Philosophy* (New York: Harper, 1945), vii, 23, 200–211. For a useful discussion of Huxley's perennialism, see Poller, *Aldous Huxley and Alternative Spirituality*, 122.

60. Huxley, *Perennial Philosophy*, 270, 242.

61. Huxley, *Perennial Philosophy*, 269.

62. Mark Greif, *The Age of the Crisis of Man: Thought and Fiction in America, 1933–1973* (Princeton, NJ: Princeton University Press, 2015); Huxley, *Perennial Philosophy*, 95, 257, 99.

63. Huxley, *Perennial Philosophy*, 96, 93, 94.

64. Huxley, *Perennial Philosophy*, vii, 242

65. Harold Rosenberg, "The Yogi and the Englishmen," *Commentary*, January 1, 1946, 397; W. E. Garrison, "God's Greatest Mistake," *Christian Century*, December 12, 1945, 1384–85; Bro to Exman, January 8, 1946, Exman Archive.

66. Alfred Kazin, "Shortest Way to Nirvana," *New Republic*, November 5, 1945, 610–613.

67. Signe Toksvig, "Aldous Huxley's Prescriptions for Spiritual Myopia," *New York Times Book Review*, September 30, 1945, 117.

68. See Charles B. Schmitt, "Perennial Philosophy: From Agostino Steuco to Leibniz," *Journal of the History of Ideas* 27, no. 4 (1966), 505–32.

69. Exman to Fred Becker, January 10, 1950, Exman Archive.

Chapter 3: Margueritte Bro, Strange Spirituality, and the Ethics of Publishing

1. Bro, "Psychic Servant: The Other Side of Edgar Cayce," *The Disciple*, November 2, 1975, reprinted in Edgar Cayce, *My Life as a Seer: The Lost Memoirs*, ed. Arthur Robert Smith (New York: St. Martin's Press, 2014), 398.

2. Margueritte Harmon Bro, "Explain It as You Will," *Christian Century*, June 2, 1943, 664–65.

3. Margueritte Harmon Bro, "Miracle Man of Virginia Beach," *Coronet Magazine*, September 1943, https://cayce.com/news/miracle-man -virginia-beach.

4. Bro, "Psychic Servant," 398.

5. Heard to Exman, June 16, 1943, Exman Archive. Bro quotes from the Exman letter in Bro, "Psychic Servant." Almost all of the surviving Bro/ Exman correspondence is now in the Exman Archive. Unfortunately, most of it is from Bro to Exman. Copies of many letters he sent to her also survive, but they are in the distinct minority. Bro's family members also have some of her correspondence, and they shared with the author a few of her letters to them.

6. Bro to Exman, August 27, 1943, Exman Archive.

7. Heard to Exman, October 5, 1943, Exman Archive.

8. Bro to Exman, October 9, 1943, Exman Archive.

9. Bro to Exman, October 22, 1943, Exman Archive.

10. Bro to Exman, October 22, 1943; Bro to Exman, December 27, 1943, both in Exman Archive.

11. Bro to Exman, December 25, 1943, Exman Archive.

12. Bro to Exman, December 25, 1943, Exman Archive.

13. Bro to Exman, December 25, 1943, Exman Archive.

14. Andy Bro interview, February 3, 2017.

15. Andy Bro interview, February 3, 2017.

16. Bro to Exman, November 1, 1955, Exman Archive.

17. Bro to Exman, December 4, 1943, Exman Archive.

18. Bro to Exman, June 21, 1949, Exman Archive.

19. Peter Racher interview, May 24, 2019; Pamela Bro interview, January 19, 2017; Linda Cohen interview, May 4, 2020.

20. Wally Exman interview, November 7, 2018.

21. Exman, "Some Pleasures of Publishing," mimeograph; "Digest of Mr. Exman's Speech at the ATLA Conference," Union Seminary, June 16, 1955; Bro to Exman, October 16, 1949; Exman to Bro and Glenn [Clark], June 17, 1949; Bro to Exman, January 21, 1953; Bro to Exman, April 16, 1958, all in Exman Archive.

22. Andy Bro interview, February 3, 2017.

23. Andy Bro interview, February 3, 2017.

24. Bro to Exman, August 1, 1949, and September 9, 1950, both in Exman Archive.

25. Bro, "Religion and Social Action," in Winfred Ernest Garrison, ed., *Faith of the Free* (Chicago: Willett, Clark, 1940), 80, 79.

26. Bro to Exman, November 24, 1950, Exman Archive.

27. Bro to Exman, October 16, 1949, Exman Archive.

28. Bro to Exman, November 29, 1961, September 12, 1969, April 14, 1944, and November 1, 1953, all in Exman Archive.

29. Bro to Exman, November 25, 1949, and September 14, 1962, both in Exman Archive.

30. Bro to Exman, April 25, 1944; Bro to Exman and John Chambers, January 8, 1954; Exman to Bro, January 14, 1954; Bro to Exman, January 21, 1954, all in Exman Archive.

31. June Bro interview, January 19, 2017.

32. William James, "Address of the President," in *Essays in Psychical Research* (Cambridge, MA: Harvard University Press, 1986), 131, xix. See also Ermine L. Algaier, "Epistemic Sensitivity and the Alogical: William James, Psychical Research, and the Radical Empiricist Attitude," *The Pluralist* 9, no. 3 (Fall 2014): 95–109. The list of James's ASPR committees comes from Algaier.

33. Marcus Ford, "William James's Psychical Research and Its

Philosophical Implications," *Transactions of the Charles S. Peirce Society* 34, no. 3 (Summer 1998): 612–13.

34. Bro to Exman, November 2, 1956, Exman Archive.

35. June Bro interview, January 19, 2017; Pamela Bro interview, January 19, 2017.

36. Bro to Exman, November 21, 1950, Exman Archive.

37. Pamela Bro interview, January 19, 2017.

38. Harrie Vernette Rhodes, *In the One Spirit* (New York: Harper, 1951), 65–66.

39. Bro to Exman, January 21, 1973, Exman Archive.

40. Bro to Exman, October 2, 1959, and December 16, 1955, both in Exman Archive.

41. Bro to Exman, October 21, 1967, and November 2, 1956, both in Exman Archive.

42. *Harper Religion Books Summer/Fall 1957*, HarperCollins Archive; Arthur Ford, *Nothing So Strange: The Autobiography of Arthur Ford* (New York: Harper, 1958), 47; *Nothing So Strange* advertisement, *Los Angeles Times*, June 15, 1958, E7; W. E. Hocking to Exman, May 11, 1959, Exman Archive.

43. Norma Lee Browning, "He Talks with Ghosts," *Chicago Daily Tribune*, July 6, 1958, B3; Paul Lambourne Higgins, letter to the editor, *Chicago Daily Tribune*, August 3, 1958, B6; Martha Hejda, letter to the editor, *Chicago Daily Tribune*, August 31, 1958, B7. Hejda also defended Bro, praising her "warm and down to earth open mindedness."

44. Ford, *Nothing So Strange*, 104, 220, 171.

45. Ford, *Nothing So Strange*, 191.

46. Ford, *Nothing So Strange*, 157, 110. In keeping with AA's anonymity principle, Bro did not describe Ford as an alcoholic. Neither did she refer to Wilson by name. She called AA a "healing group" (215). She also asked Exman to delete references to AA from the catalog copy for *Nothing So Strange*, which he did. See Bro to Exman, January 22, 1958, Exman Archive.

47. Ford, *Nothing So Strange*, 7, 27.

48. Ford, *Nothing So Strange*, 213.

49. June Bro interview, January 19, 2017; Andy Bro interview, February 3, 2017.

50. Exman to Heard, untitled autobiographical transcript, August 1942, Exman Archive.

51. Exman to Blanche [no surname given], October 25, 1946; and Exman to Bro, November 22, 1946, both in Exman Archive.

52. Exman to Alfred [no surname given], November 12, 1945, Exman Archive.

53. Bro to Exman, October 9, 1947, Exman Archive.

54. Bro to Exman, February 4, 1948, Exman Archive.

55. Bro to Exman, October 28, 1949, Exman Archive.

56. Exman, untitled scrap paper with Bro annotations, Exman Archive. These notes are undated, but they refer to Exman's upcoming twentieth Harper anniversary on April 1, 1947, so the list is earlier.

57. Bro to Exman, March 15, 1954; Exman, untitled scrap paper, both in Exman Archive.

58. Bro to Exman, February 26, 1956, Exman Archive.

59. John Chambers to Exman, dated "Tuesday in K.C." and likely November 1946, Exman Archive. For Thurman's eulogy at the First Community Church of New York on August 20, 1955, see *John B. Chambers 1910–1955*, pamphlet, Exman Archive.

60. Bro to Exman, November 10, 1955, Exman Archive.

61. Christopher Isherwood, *Diaries: Volume One: 1939–1960*, ed. Katherine Bucknell (New York: HarperFlamingo, 1998), 164.

62. Wally Exman interviews, April 2, 2016, July 19, 2016, and November 7, 2018; and Bro to Exman, July 29, 1956, Exman Archive.

63. Bro to Exman, October 14, 1955; and Exman to Bro, November 13, 1947, both in Exman Archive.

64. Bro to Exman, February 10, 1947, Exman Archive.

Chapter 4: Catholic Activism, Anti-Catholicism, and *The Long Loneliness* of Dorothy Day

1. Harper books by Solomon Goldman included *A Rabbi Takes Stock* (1931), *The Jew and the Universe* (1936), and *Crisis and Decision* (1938). See also Gaius Glenn Atkins, *Life of Cardinal Newman* (1931); and Bede Frost, *Saint John of the Cross, 1542–1591* (1937).

2. Sholem Asch, *One Destiny: An Epistle to the Christians,* trans. Milton Hindus (New York: G. P. Putnam's Sons, 1945), 70–88.

3. John Cournos, *An Open Letter to Jews and Christians* (New York: Oxford University Press, 1938), 29; Asch, *One Destiny,* 83. On the origins of the Judeo-Christian tradition, see Stephen Prothero, *American Jesus: How the Son of God Became a National Icon* (New York: Farrar, Straus & Giroux, 2003), 258–59.

4. See *Amen, Amen* (New York: Harper, 1942) by Exman's friend (and frequent correspondent) the Catholic layman Sam Constantino; and *Who Crucified Jesus?* (New York: Harper, 1942) by the Philadelphia-based Jewish historian Solomon Zeitlin, who argued that "neither the Pharisees nor the Sadducees, i.e. the Jewish people, were responsible for the crucifixion of Jesus" (*Harper Religious Books and Bibles Fall 1942,* HarperCollins Archive).

5. *Harper Religious Books Summer & Fall 1946*; *Harper Religious Books & Bibles Winter 1949–50,* both in HarperCollins Archive.

6. Reinhold Niebuhr, "Martin Buber: 1878–1965," *Christianity and Crisis* 25, no. 2 (1965): 146–47.

7. Louis Finkelstein, ed., *American Spiritual Autobiographies: Fifteen Self-Portraits* (New York: Harper, 1948), xi, viii, 14, 19. Exman also published Finkelstein's *The Jews: Their History, Culture, and Religion* (New York: Harper, 1949).

8. This mission statement appeared in many Harper religion catalogs from 1952 forward, but none before. See also Eugene Exman, *The House of Harper: One Hundred and Fifty Years of Publishing* (New York: Harper, 1967), 287–88. Many thanks to Tzofit Goldfarb at the Harper-Collins Archive for tracking down dozens of Harper religion catalogs.

9. Eugene Exman, "Reading, Writing, and Religion," 86, 85, 87. In a letter to Exman, Bro praised a draft of this article as "a fine workmanlike job" yet inattentive to Exman's inner life. "Your article sounds as if the new interest in religion were philosophic," she wrote. "It is more than that. People want to participate. They are trying out God for themselves." She urged Exman to connect the dots between what he was observing in society and what he himself was experiencing. Bro to Exman, February 11, 1953, Exman Archive.

10. Exman, "Reading, Writing, and Religion," 89–90.

11. Exman, "Reading, Writing, and Religion," 88.

12. "Pendle Hill Mid-Winter Institute," list of attendees (Exman Archive) includes Exman, Day, and Fritz Eichenberg, an artist who first met Day at this conference and would go on to provide illustrations for the *Catholic Worker* and *The Long Loneliness*. Day, in a December 1978 diary entry referencing Pendle Hill, writes, "That was where I met Eugene Exman, then religious editor of Harper's Pub." Dorothy Day, *The Duty of Delight: The Diaries of Dorothy Day*, ed. Robert Ellsberg (Milwaukee, WI: Marquette University Press, 2008), 596.

13. Daniel Berrigan, "The Long Loneliness of Dorothy Day," in Leroy S. Rouner, ed., *Loneliness* (Notre Dame, IN: University of Notre Dame Press, 1998), 163; David Allen, "'Down Here Near the End of Staten Island': Dorothy Day on the Beach and on the Page," Gotham Center for New York History blog, August 6, 2020, https://www.gothamcenter .org/blog/down-here-near-the-end-of-staten-island-dorothy-day-on -the-beach-and-on-the-page.

14. Berrigan, "The Long Loneliness of Dorothy Day," 161–62.

15. William Miller, *All Is Grace: The Spirituality of Dorothy Day* (Garden City, NY: Doubleday, 1987), 3. In material Day gave him in 1975, Miller found a book-length "collection of retreat notes and spiritual reflections which she had entitled 'All Is Grace'" (2). According to Miller, "she fretted about this intended book for nearly forty years," but never published it (3). In an October, 15, 1964, letter to Day (Exman Archive), Exman referred to a book in progress by the same title. "I hope you will find time to do some work on the new book, All Is Grace," he wrote, noting that, although December 1 was the delivery date, what was most important was writing "a book that satisfies you." Day also refers to a book called *All Is Grace* in three letters published

in *All the Way to Heaven: The Selected Letters of Dorothy Day*, ed. Robert Ellsberg (New York: Image Books, 2020): to Emily Coleman, Tuesday in Holy Week, 1967, 431; to Judith Gregory, April 1967, 433; and to Della Spier, August 26, 1968, 447–448. Drafts of this unpublished book, which was also called *Spiritual Adventure*, are in the Dorothy Day Papers, Marquette University.

16. Exman, "Books and Authors I've Known," 75. William Ruggles, manager of the Oxford University Press religious department, also calls Exman the "Dean of religious publishing" in a letter to Exman, May 19, 1953, Exman Archive.

17. Pope Francis, "Address of the Holy Father," https://w2.vatican.va /content/francesco/en/speeches/2015/ september/documents/papa -francesco_20150924_usa-us-congress.html; Dorothy Day FBI file, https://archive.org/details/DorothyDay/page/n423/mode/2up? _ga=2.206121491.108179348.1623421338–1218422392.1623421338.

18. Day, "From Union Square to Rome," https://www.catholicworker .org/dorothyday/articles/202.html.

19. Alden Whitman, "Dorothy Day, Catholic Activist, 83, Dies," *New York Times*, December 1, 1980, D12; Malcolm Cowley, *Exile's Return: A Narrative of Ideas* (New York: Viking Press, 1934), 69.

20. Day, *The Long Loneliness* (New York: Harper, 1952), 85.

21. Day, *From Union Square to Rome* (Silver Spring, MD: Preservation of the Faith Press, 1938), 26–27; Day, *Long Loneliness*, 41.

22. John Loughery and Blythe Randolph, *Dorothy Day: Dissenting Voice of the American Century* (New York: Simon & Schuster, 2021), 54; Robert M. Dowling, "'Told in Context': Dorothy Day's Previously Unpublished Reminiscence of Eugene O'Neill," *Eugene O'Neill Review* 38, nos. 1–2 (2017): 9, 8.

23. "'Eleventh Virgin,' by Dorothy Day," *Oakland Tribune*, April 20, 1924, 74, https://www.newspapers.com/clip/15168131/oakland-tribune/; Day, *From Union Square to Rome*, 123.

24. Day, "On Pilgrimage," *Catholic Worker*, October–November 1976, 4; Day, *Long Loneliness*, 141.

25. Day, *Long Loneliness*, 144.

26. Day, *Long Loneliness*, 140.

27. John Loughery, "The Best Books on Religion in an Age of Doubt," *Shepherd*, https://shepherd.com/best-books/religion-in-an-age-of-doubt.

28. William James, *The Varieties of Religious Experience: A Study in Human Nature* (New York: Longmans, Green, 1902), 464, 326, 466.

29. James, *Varieties*, 31, 29–30.

30. William James to Mrs. Henry Whitman, June 6, 1899, in *The Letters of William James, Volume II*, ed. Henry James (Boston: Atlantic Monthly Press, 1920), 90.

31. James, *Varieties*, 408, 346, 326. Teresa of Ávila, James continued, "wrote admirable descriptive psychology, possessed a will equal to any emergency, great talent for politics and business, a buoyant disposition, and a first-rate literary style" (346). She would lend Day her confirmation name, her daughter's middle name, and her lifelong devotion to the twentieth-century Saint Thérèse of Lisieux (often described as the second Theresa).

32. James, *Varieties*, 367–68.

33. Day, *Long Loneliness*, 111, 116, 139.

34. Day, *Long Loneliness*, 148.

35. Day, *Long Loneliness*, 144, 148.

36. Dorothy Day, "Pilgrimage to Mexico," *Commonweal*, December 25, 1958, https://www.commonwealmagazine.org/pilgrimage-mexico.

37. Dorothy Day, *Loaves and Fishes* (New York: Harper, 1963), 9.

38. *Catholic Worker*, May 1933, 1, 4, https://merton.bellarmine.edu/files /original/daf15f7742b73d731d7106fb93e137ec1f259e47.pdf.

39. Day, *Loaves and Fishes*, 22.

40. Day, *Loaves and Fishes*, 23.

41. Paul Elie, *The Life You Save May Be Your Own: An American Pilgrimage* (New York: Farrar, Straus & Giroux, 2004), 188.

42. Day diary, May 20, 1951, in her *The Duty of Delight*, 158; John Chambers to Day, February 15, 1951, Dorothy Day Papers, Marquette University.

43. John Chambers to Day, February 17, 1951, Dorothy Day Papers, Marquette University.

44. Day diary, February 1977 and November 1976 diary entries, in her *The Duty of Delight*, 571, 567.

45. Day, *Long Loneliness*, 11, 84.

46. Day, *Long Loneliness*, 51, 120.

47. Day, *Long Loneliness*, 285.

48. Paul Elie, "Why & How Day Wrote It," *Commonweal*, June 14, 2004, https://www.commonwealmagazine.org/why-how-day-wrote-it.

49. *Harper's Religious Books, Winter 1951–52*, HarperCollins Archive.

50. Advertisement, *New York Times*, January 20, 1952, BR21; *Kirkus Reviews*, January 1, 1952, https://www.kirkusreviews.com/book-reviews/a/dorothy-day/the-long-loneliness; "Dorothy Day's Diary," *Newsweek*, January 21, 1952, 85; Marjorie Snyder, *Washington Post*, February 10, 1952, B7; Edward Barry, *Chicago Daily Tribune*, February 10, 1952, 14; *New Yorker*, March 8, 1952, 124. A *New York Times* review hazarded little more than reprising key moments in Day's life. See R. L. Duffus, "Behind the Slogans She Saw the Dream in Men's Hearts," *New York Times*, January 20, 1952, BR12.

51. H. A. Reinhold, "The Long Loneliness of Dorothy Day," *Commonweal*, February 29, 1951, 521–22. A second *Commonweal* review was similarly tepid. See John C. Cort, "The Catholic Worker and the Workers," *Commonweal*, April 4, 1952, 636–37.

52. Day diary, July 1, 1952, in her *The Duty of Delight*, 172.

53. Dwight Macdonald, "The Foolish Things of the World—I," *New Yorker* (October 4, 1952), 37; Dwight Macdonald, "The Foolish Things of the World—II," *New Yorker* (October 44, 1952), 39.

54. Tom Sullivan, "Chrystie Street," *Catholic Worker*, November 1952, 2.

55. Natasha Walter, "Sweetness and Blight," *Guardian*, January 3, 2004, https://www.theguardian.com/books/2004/jan/03/biography; Macdonald, "The Foolish Things of the World—II," 56. Day's hope was to write about the life of Saint Thérèse of Lisieux "from the mother and woman's standpoint" (Day diary, March 15, 1951, in her *The Duty of Delight*, 155).

56. Bro to Mrs. Charles W. Boardman, February 7, 1950, Exman Archive. Aware that she might be overstepping by asking a biographer to rewrite

her subject's prayers, Bro added, "I would not want you to modify your own convictions or even your own taste the least little bit, but often there are two ways of saying the same thing and if one makes a basic truth more palatable, we had just as well use it."

57. Bro to Exman, February 26, 1954, and March 3, 1954, both in Exman Archive. Boardman's biographies were *Such Love Is Seldom: A Biography of Mother Mary Walsh* (New York: Harper, 1950); and *Good Shepherd's Fold: A Biography of St. Mary Euphrasia Pelletier, R.G.S.* (New York: Harper, 1955).

58. Exman to Day, April 19, 1956, Dorothy Day Papers, Marquette University. Day was more compliant when it came to writing for a general audience. In a letter to Saint Thérèse's older sister seeking copies of family letters, she wrote, "I am anxious to bring her story of the little way to the non-Catholic readers of our country" (Day to Sister Genevieve of St. Theresa, April 16, 1956, in *All the Way to Heaven*, 307).

59. Jim Shaw to Exman, June 11, 1956, Dorothy Day Papers, Marquette University.

60. Bro to Exman, July 2, 1956, Exman Archive.

61. Bro to Exman, July 2, 1956, Exman Archive.

62. Exman to Day, October 29, 1958, Dorothy Day Papers, Marquette University; Day diary, December 23, 1958, in her *The Duty of Delight*, 240; Day to Donald Powell, April 9, 1959, in her *All the Way to Heaven*, 327.

63. Dorothy Day calls this book *The Last Eleven Years* in "On Pilgrimage," *Catholic Worker*, June 1960, 2, 7, https://www.catholicworker .org/dorothyday/articles/765.html. In her diary for May 18, 1960, she refers to a contract offered by Harper for a book about the "last eleven years" (*The Duty of Delight*, 297).

64. The Merton quote is from the back cover of *Loaves and Fishes*. The Thomas quote appeared in a Harper ad in the *New York Times*, October 13, 1963, 389.

65. Day, *Loaves and Fishes*, 39, 50.

66. Day, *Loaves and Fishes*, 95, 105.

67. "Peter the 'Materialist,'" *Catholic Worker*, September 1945, 6; "What We Are Doing in Town and Country," *Catholic Worker*, September 1936, 2.

68. "What We Are Doing in Town and Country," 2.

69. Day, *Loaves and Fishes*, 200, 137, 144, 149–150.

70. Day, *Loaves and Fishes*, 215.

71. Robert Orsi, "When 2 + 2 = 5," *American Scholar,* Spring 2007, https://theamericanscholar.org/when-2-2-5/.

72. Day to Bill Gauchat, May 26, 1951, in her *All the Way to Heaven*, 254.

73. Day to Ammon Hennacy, January 1952, in her *All the Way to Heaven*, 259–60.

74. Day to Ammon Hennacy, January 1952, in her *All the Way to Heaven*, 259–60.

75. Day to Exman, December 27, 1962, in her *All the Way to Heaven*, 373–74; Exman to Day, December 28, 1962, Dorothy Day Papers, Marquette Archives.

76. Day, *Long Loneliness*, 11; Day to Ammon Hennacy, February 1952, in her *All the Way to Heaven*, 263.

77. Exman, "God's Own Man: Dr. Albert Schweitzer," *United Nations World*, December 1952, 34; Whitman, "Dorothy Day, Catholic Activist, 83, Dies"; David J. O'Brien, "The Pilgrimage of Dorothy Day," *Commonweal*, December 19, 1980, 711–15.

78. Exman to Day, February 28, 1952; Exman to Heard, July 31, 1952, both in Exman Archive.

Chapter 5: African Missions, Colonialism, and *The World of Albert Schweitzer*

1. Exman to family, September 17, 1950; Exman to Sunny, September 13, 1950, both in Exman Archive.

2. Exman Africa diary, Exman Archive.

3. "Reverence for Life," *TIME*, July 11, 1949, 68–74; "The Greatest Man in the World," *Life*, October 6, 1947, 95–98; Heard to Exman, June 29, 1949, Exman Archive. Exman's early Schweitzer books included George Seaver, *Albert Schweitzer: Christian Revolutionary* (1944); George Seaver, *Albert Schweitzer: The Man and His Mind* (1947); Charles R. Joy, ed., *Albert Schweitzer: An Anthology* (1947); and Charles R. Joy and Melvin Arnold, *The Africa of Albert Schweitzer* (1948).

4. Exman to Harper colleagues, October 6, 1950; Exman to family, October 8, 1950, both in Exman Archive.

5. Exman Africa diary, Exman Archive.

6. Exman Africa diary, Exman Archive.

7. Exman Africa diary, Exman Archive.

8. Exman Africa diary, Exman Archive.

9. Nils Ole Oermann, *Albert Schweitzer: A Biography* (New York: Oxford University Press, 2017), 6.

10. Paul Elie, *Reinventing Bach* (New York: Farrar, Straus & Giroux, 2012), 13.

11. Joy, ed., *Albert Schweitzer: An Anthology*, 155, 246, 155.

12. Joy, ed., *Albert Schweitzer: An Anthology*, 157.

13. Albert Schweitzer, *Out of My Life and Thought,* trans. C. T. Campion (New York: Henry Holt, 1933), 126.

14. Schweitzer, *Out of My Life and Thought*, 139; Albert Schweitzer, *On the Edge of the Primeval Forest*, trans. C. T. Campion (London: A & C Black, 1922), 3.

15. Oermann, *Albert Schweitzer: A Biography*, 100.

16. Ara Paul Barsam, *Reverence for Life: Albert Schweitzer's Great Contribution to Ethical Thought* (New York: Oxford University Press, 2008), ix.

17. Oermann, *Albert Schweitzer: A Biography*, 108.

18. Oermann, *Albert Schweitzer: A Biography*, 165, 169; Reinhold Niebuhr, "Can Schweitzer Save Us from Russell?" *Christian Century*, September 3, 1925, 1093; Reverend John A. O'Brien, "God's Eager Fool," *Reader's Digest*, March 1946, reprinted in *Reader's Digest Omnibus* (London: Andre Deutsch, 1952), 115–20; "The Greatest Man in the World," 95–98; "Reference for Life." Early Beacon books on Schweitzer include: Charles R. Joy, ed., *Albert Schweitzer: An Anthology* (1947); Albert Schweitzer, *Selected Works*, ed. Charles R. Joy (1947); Albert Schweitzer, *Goethe: Two Addresses*, ed. Charles R. Joy (1948); Albert Schweitzer, *The Psychiatric Study of Jesus: Exposition and Criticism*, trans. Charles R. Joy (1948); Albert Schweitzer, *Goethe: Four Studies*, trans. Charles

R. Joy (1949); and Charles R. Joy, ed., *The Wit and Wisdom of Albert Schweitzer* (1949). Exman and Arnold also copublished a book coauthored by Joy and Arnold called *The Africa of Albert Schweitzer* (1948).

19. Oermann, *Albert Schweitzer: A Biography*, 169.

20. Exman to Sunny, October 27, 1950; Exman to John Chambers, October 22, 1950, both in Exman Archive.

21. Exman, "The Most Unforgettable Character I've Met," Exman Archive.

22. Exman, "The Most Unforgettable Character I've Met," Exman Archive.

23. Exman, "The Most Unforgettable Character I've Met," Exman Archive.

24. Exman, "The Most Unforgettable Character I've Met," Exman Archive.

25. Exman to Sunny, October 31, 1950, Exman Archive.

26. Exman to Emma Haussknecht, February 1, 1951; Exman, "A Visit with Albert Schweitzer," *Presbyterian Life*, November 24, 1951, 14 ff.; Exman, "God's Own Man: Dr. Albert Schweitzer," *United Nations World*, December 1952, 30–34; Exman to Charles W. Ferguson, June 19, 1957, Exman Archive. Suggesting that there might be "a lesson here for all executives," Exman told Ferguson that Schweitzer reminded him in some respects of John D. Rockefeller Jr., who also had "great competence for handling and mastering detail."

27. William D. Patterson to Exman, April 2, 1953, Exman Archive.

28. Charles Poore, "Books of the Times," *New York Times*, January 15, 1955, 11; Dorothy Green, "Four Great Men Make Up Schweitzer," *Washington Post*, January 30, 1955, E6; "Best Seller List," *New York Times*, February 6, 1955, BR8; "Best Seller List," *New York Times*, February 27, 1955, BR8. Over these four weeks, the book was number 15, 13, 10, and then 9 on the "general" (nonfiction) list.

29. Exman to Schweitzer, undated, Exman Archive. Exman narrates disputes over *The World of Albert Schweitzer* royalties in an untitled, seven-page handwritten memo in the Exman Archive. Barbara Morgan, whose contributions to the book Exman vigorously defended to both Anderson and Schweitzer, offers her own telling in "The Making of a Great Book—'The World of Albert Schweitzer,'" *Publishers' Weekly*, January 1, 1955 (Exman Archive).

30. John Russell, "Schweitzer Centennial Today: A Legacy Eclipsed?" *New York Times*, January 14, 1975, 41; John Gunther, "The Doctor Darkly: Verdict on Schweitzer," *New York Times*, July 26, 1964, BR3.

31. Exman, unpublished draft of *Reader's Digest* feature on Schweitzer, Exman Archive.

32. Exman, transcript of talk at Riverside Guild, January 15, 1950, Exman Archive.

33. "Reverence for Life"; Russell, "Schweitzer Centennial Today: A Legacy Eclipsed?" 41; Emory Ross, "Portrait: Albert Schweitzer," *American Scholar* 19, no. 1 (Winter 1949–50): 87; George Orwell, "As I Please," *Tribune*, October 20, 1944, http://www.telelib.com /authors/O/OrwellGeorge/essay/tribune/AsIPlease19441020.html.

34. Harvey Brett, "Repeat Performances Appraised," *New York Times*, July 10, 1949, BR20. "Of course," Brett added, "none of this is Dr. Schweitzer's doing." Which wasn't exactly true.

35. "Albert Schweitzer: An Anachronism," *TIME*, June 21, 1963, 35; Schweitzer to Dr. Robert Weiss, 1963, in Albert Schweitzer, *Albert Schweitzer: Letters: 1905–1965*, ed. Hans Walter Bähr, trans. Joachim Neugroschel (New York: Macmillan, 1992), 331.

36. *Christian Register* 126 (1947): 324; "Albert Schweitzer: An Anachronism," 35; David Goodin, *The New Rationalism: Albert Schweitzer's Philosophy of Reverence for Life* (Montreal: McGill-Queens University Press, 2013), 8; Predrag Cicovacki, *The Restoration of Albert Schweitzer's Ethical Vision* (New York: Continuum, 2012), 117; Ross, "Portrait: Albert Schweitzer," 88.

37. James Carleton Paget, "Albert Schweitzer and Africa," *Journal of Religion in Africa* 42, no. 3 (2012): 293.

38. Albert Schweitzer, *Christianity and the Religions of the World* (New York: George H. Doran, 1923), 37–38.

39. Russell, "Schweitzer Centennial Today: A Legacy Eclipsed?" 41; Gerald McKnight, *Verdict on Schweitzer: The Man Behind the Legend of Lambaréné* (New York: John Day).

40. David L. Dungan, *Christian Century*, October 8, 1975, 874; Bro to Exman, November 1, 1950, Exman Archive.

41. Albert Schweitzer, *Memoirs of Childhood and Youth*, trans. C. T. Campion (New York: Macmillan, 1949), 45–46.

42. Schweitzer sermon quoted in Paget, "Albert Schweitzer and Africa," 288; Schweitzer, *On the Edge of the Primeval Forest*, 172.

43. Howard Thurman, "The Inward Journey: Albert Schweitzer— Reverence for Life," sermon, January 14, 1962, Boston University, https://thurman.pitts.emory.edu/items/show/1081; W. E. B. Du Bois, "The Blackman and Albert Schweitzer," in A. A. Roback, ed., *The Albert Schweitzer Jubilee Book* (Cambridge, MA: Sci-Art Publishers, 1945), 119–27, reprinted in W. E. B. Du Bois, *Writings by W. E. B. Du Bois in Periodicals Edited by Others*, ed. Herbert Aptheker (New York: Kraus-Thomson, 1982), 295, 255–56. The estimate that Schweitzer treated roughly 130,000 patients is from George N. Marshall and David Poling, *Schweitzer: A Biography* (New York: Doubleday, 1971), 330.

44. Schweitzer to W. E. B. Du Bois, December 5, 1945, https://credo .library.umass.edu/view/pageturn/mums312-b108-i160/#page/1 /mode/1up.

45. W. E. B. Du Bois to Albert Schweitzer, July 31, 1946, https://credo .library.umass.edu/view/pageturn/mums312-b112-i071/#page/1 /mode/1up/. Two decades later, after dozens of African nations had achieved their independence, Du Bois advanced similar arguments in another Schweitzer commemorative volume. After acknowledging how important medical care is in fighting disease in Africa, he insisted that "what is needed more is free, intelligent manhood and the abolition of the exploitation so often carried on by the very persons who contribute to the hospitals." W. E. B. Du Bois, "Whites in Africa after Negro Autonomy," in A. A. Roback, ed., *In Albert Schweitzer's Realms: a Symposium* (Cambridge, MA: Sci-Art Publications, 1962), 256.

46. Ali A. Mazrui, "Dr. Schweitzer's Racism," in *Transition* 53 (1991): 101, 97; Schweitzer, *On the Edge of the Primeval Forest*, 130–131. Mazrui distinguishes between three types of racism: "malignant racism," "benign racism," and "benevolent racism." Others have referred to Schweitzer's "unconscious racism." See David L. Dungan, "Reconsidering Albert Schweitzer," *Christian Century*, October 8, 1975, 875.

47. Exman to Edward Groth, March 9, 1942, Exman Archive.

48. John F. Kennedy, "Response to Albert Schweitzer," June 6, 1962, https://en.wikisource.org/wiki/John_F._Kennedy_response_to _Albert_Schweitzer.

49. Gunther, "The Doctor Darkly: Verdict on Schweitzer," BR3; Paget, "Albert Schweitzer and Africa," 278.

50. Russell, "Schweitzer Centennial Today: A Legacy Eclipsed?" 35, 41.

51. "Rachel Carson Speaks on Reverence for Life, "Animal Welfare Institute, *Information Report* 12, no. 1 (January–February, 1963): 223, http://linyifaguangzi.com/sites/default/files/uploads/documents /AWI-1963-IR.pdf.

52. Barsam, *Reverence for Life*, x, 4, 60; Schweitzer's Lambaréné hospital, Barsam writes, was "a model of ecological responsibility" that refused to trample on nearby flora and fauna and "reused every piece of wood, string, and glass." Ara Paul Barsam, "Schweitzer, Albert," in *The Encyclopedia of Religion and Nature* (2010), in Oxford Reference Online, https://www-oxfordreference-com.ezproxy.bu.edu/view/10.1093 /acref/9780199754670.001.0001/acref-9780199754670-div1–1570).

53. Schweitzer to Exman, undated English translation, Exman Archive.

54. Schweitzer, *Out of My Life and Thought*, 186–87.

55. Exman, typed draft of article later published as "A Visit with Albert Schweitzer," Exman Archive.

56. Exman, unpublished, twenty-eight page typescript of article on Schweitzer, Exman Archive.

57. William James, *The Varieties of Religious Experience: A Study in Human Nature* (New York: Longmans, Green, 1902), 377.

Chapter 6: White Liberals and Martin Luther King Jr.'s *Stride Toward Freedom*

1. Exman to Coretta Scott King, April 11, 1968, Exman Archive. Exman is conflating two different visits to Montgomery. On the date he gives for this first visit, February 4, 1958, he did in fact visit the Kings. That is confirmed in Exman's personal datebook and the Exman family calendar, which describe Exman taking the "night train to Montgomery" (February 3) and "with Martin Luther King till after lunch which was

served by Coretta King. MLK in bed, recovering from flu" (February 4). However, this was actually Exman's *second* trip to Montgomery to see King, who had already signed a book contract with Harper. The first visit came months earlier.

2. Martin Luther King Jr., "Montgomery Bus Boycott" speech, December 5, 1955, https://www.digitalhistory.uh.edu/disp_textbook.cfm?smtid=3& psid=3625.

3. M. S. Wyeth Jr. to King, January 23, 1957; King to M. S. Wyeth Jr., January 30, 1957, both in the Martin Luther King Jr. Collection, Howard Gotlieb Archival Research Center, Boston University, Boston, MA.

4. Mel Arnold to King, February 5, 1957; King to Mel Arnold, February 28, 1957. See also Henry Robbins (Knopf) to King, February 20, 1957. All are in King Collection, Boston University.

5. Ned Bradford (Little, Brown) to King, April 2, 1957; Arthur E. Burgess Jr. (Houghton Mifflin) to King, April 3, 1957; John Peck (FSC) to King, June 27, 1957, all in King Collection, Boston University. See also Clement Alexandre (Doubleday) to King, June 1, 1956; King to Clement Alexandre, June 18, 1956, also in King Collection, Boston University.

6. Exman to Bro, February 27, 1958, Exman Archive. This letter is a response to a letter Bro sent to Exman a few days earlier, asking, "What happened when you got to Luther King? Was his writer adequate? Is there a date line on his book?" She then suggested her sister Harriet Harmon Dexter as a ghostwriter who could "whip out the King" book. Bro to Exman, February 22, 1958, Exman Archive.

7. Exman to Bro, February 2, 1958, Exman Archive.

8. Exman to King, February 6, 1958, King Collection, Boston University.

9. Exman to Bro, February 27, 1958, Exman Archive; Marie Rodell to King, February 26, 1958, King Collection, Boston University; Exman to King, February 26, 1958, King Collection, Boston University.

10. Hermine Popper to King, March 21, 1958, King Collection, Boston University.

11. Mark Kauffmann, "Great Preachers: These 12—and Others—Bring Americans Back to the Churches," *Life*, April 6, 1953, 126–33; Lerone

Bennett Jr., "Howard Thurman: Twentieth Century Holy Man," *Ebony* 33, no. 4 (February 1978): 68–85.

12. Howard Thurman, *With Head and Heart: The Autobiography of Howard Thurman* (New York: Harcourt Brace Jovanovich, 1979), 218.

13. Thurman, *With Head and Heart*, 136; Thurman, *Footprints of a Dream: The Story of the Church for the Fellowship of All Peoples* (New York: Harper, 1959), 24.

14. *Harper Religious Books & Bibles Winter 1947–48*, HarperCollins Archive; Thurman, "Judgment and Hope in the Christian Message," in William Stuart Nelson, ed., *The Christian Way in Race Relations* (New York: Harper, 1948), 229.

15. Peter Eisenstadt, *Against the Hounds of Hell: A Life of Howard Thurman* (Charlottesville: University of Virginia Press, 2021), 280.

16. Gary Dorrien, *Breaking White Supremacy: Martin Luther King Jr. and the Black Social Gospel* (New Haven, CT: Yale University Press, 2018), 162.

17. Thurman, "Windbreak . . . Against Existence," *Bostonia* (Fall 1960), in *The Papers of Howard Washington Thurman, Volume 4*, ed. Walter E. Fluker (Columbia: University of South Carolina Press, 2017), 282.

18. Thurman, *Deep Is the Hunger: Meditations for Apostles of Sensitiveness* (Richmond, IN: Friends United Press, 1973), 144; Eisenstadt, *Against the Hounds of Hell*, 386; Thurman, *Jesus and the Disinherited* (New York: Abingdon-Cokesbury Press, 1949), 7.

19. Thurman, *With Head and Heart*, 134–35; Mahadev Desi, "Two Negro Visitors," *Harijan*, March 14, 1936, reprinted in Mahatma Gandhi, *The Gandhi Reader: A Sourcebook of His Life and Writings*, ed. Homer A. Jack (New York: Grove Press, 1994), 316.

20. Peter Dana, "Dr. Thurman Speaks on Indian Question," *Pittsburgh Courier*, August 29, 1942, 3, https://theconversation.com/how-howard-thurman-met-gandhi-and-brought-nonviolence-to-the-civil-rights-movement-110148; Dorrien, *Breaking White Supremacy*, 162; *Backs Against the Wall: The Howard Thurman Story*, PBS, 2019, https://www.youtube.com/watch?v=wVl_irB59lM.

21. "Chapter 7: Montgomery Movement Begins," Martin Luther King, Jr. Research and Education Institute, https://kinginstitute.stanford.edu

/king-papers/publications/autobiography-martin-luther-king-jr
-contents/chapter-7-montgomery-movement.

22. Thurman to King, July 18, 1958, and November 9, 1958, both in King Collection, Boston University.

23. Martin Luther King Jr., *Stride Toward Freedom: The Montgomery Story* (New York: Harper, 1958), 134.

24. King, *Stride Toward Freedom*, 134–35.

25. Thurman, *Footprints of a Dream*, 28.

26. King, *Stride Toward Freedom*, 220.

27. Bro to Exman, January 14, 1958, January 9, 1958, and February 22, 1958, all in Exman Archive.

28. Bro to Exman, January 9, 1958, Exman Archive.

29. Bro to Exman, January 14, 1958, Exman Archive.

30. Exman to Bro, March 3, 1958, Exman Archive.

31. Bro to Exman, March 7, 1958, and March 21, 1958, both in Exman Archive.

32. Exman to Bro, March 27, 1958, Exman Archive.

33. Bro memo to Exman and Mel Arnold, April 4, 1958, Exman Archive.

34. Bro memo to Exman and Mel Arnold, April 4, 1958, Exman Archive.

35. Bro to Exman, April 6, 1958, Exman Archive.

36. Bro to Exman, April 6, 1958, Exman Archive.

37. Exman, handwritten draft of unsent letter to Bro, April 1958, Exman Archive.

38. Exman to Bro, April 24, 1958, Exman Archive.

39. Bro to Exman, October 14, 1958, Exman Archive.

40. *Amsterdam News*, September 27, 1958, King Collection, Boston University.

41. Exman to Bro, September 19, 1958, Exman Archive.

42. Thurman, *With Head and Heart*, 255; King to Thurman, November 8, 1958, King Collection, Boston University. Exman may have tried to see King at the hospital on the night of the stabbing. An entry for

that day in his 1958 calendar in the Exman Archive reads: "Eve with Dr. King at Harlem Hosp." But this is crossed out in pencil. In an October 1, 1958, letter to Bro (Exman Archive), Exman wrote: "I saw Howard Thurman on Monday. He came from Boston to see Martin King and we went to the hospital together."

43. "Stride Toward Freedom by Martin Luther King Jr.," *Catholic Worker* 25, no. 4 (November 1, 1958): 4, https://thecatholicnewsarchive .org/?a=d&d=CW19581101-01.2.10&srpos=7&e=-------en-20--1--txt -txIN-%22stride+toward+freedom%22-------; Perry Miller, "The Mind and Faith of Martin Luther King," *The Reporter*, October 30, 1958, 40.

44. E. Earle Ellis, "Segregation and Dr. King," *Christianity Today*, January 19, 1959, 34–35; Kinchen Exum, "Rev. Martin Luther King Has Startling Opinion of Negroes," *Chattanooga News-Free Press*, October 8, 1958, both in King Collection, Boston University.

45. George H. Dunne, "The Meaning of Racism," *Commonweal*, February 6, 1959, 494; Harold R. Isaacs, "Civil Disobedience in Montgomery," *New Republic*, October 6, 1958, 19.

46. Ralph C. Abele, "America's Champion of Non-Violence," *St. Louis Post Dispatch*, November 30, 1958; Marvel Cooke, "Montgomery Story," *Mainstream*, December 1958, 31; H. E. Fey, "Stride Toward Freedom: The Montgomery Story, by Martin Luther King, Jr.," *Christian Century*, September 24, 1958, 1071.

47. Lillian Smith, "And Suddenly Something Happened," *Saturday Review*, September 20, 1958, 21. King later wrote to Smith, "Of all the reviews that I have read on *Stride Toward Freedom*, I still consider yours the best." King to Lillian Smith, January 23, 1959, quoted in "Smith, Lillian Eugenia," King Institute, Stanford University, https://kinginstitute.stanford.edu/encyclopedia/smith-lillian -eugenia.

48. Harry Emerson Fosdick, *The Hope of the World: Twenty-Five Sermons on Christianity Today* (New York, Harper & Brothers, 1933), vii; King, *Strength to Love* (New York: Harper, 1963), ix–x. King requested Fosdick's book of sermons in a June 2, 1958, letter to Mel Arnold, King Collection, Boston University.

49. Thurman, *A Strange Freedom: The Best of Howard Thurman on Religious Experience and Public Life* (Boston: Beacon Press, 1998), 186.

50. James Baldwin, "The Dangerous Road Before Martin Luther King," *Harper's Magazine*, February 1961, 33–42. On unfavorability polling from 1968, see Ibram X. Kendi, "The Second Assassination of Martin Luther King Jr.," *The Atlantic*, October 14, 2021, https://www.the atlantic.com/ideas/archive/2021/10/martin-luther-king-critical-race -theory/620367/.

51. James H. Cone, *Martin & Malcolm & America: A Dream or a Nightmare* (Maryknoll, NY: Orbis Books, 1991), 123.

52. King, book inscription to Harry Emerson Fosdick, November 17, 1958, King Institute, Stanford University, https://kinginstitute.stanford.edu /king-papers/documents/harry-emerson-fosdick.

53. Michael Korda, "Prompting the President," *New Yorker*, October 6, 1997, 88.

54. Bayard Rustin to Stanley Levison in FBI-transcribed phone conversation, quoted in David J. Garrow, *Bearing the Cross: Martin Luther King, Jr., and the Southern Christian Leadership Conference* (New York: William Morrow, 1986), 649.

55. Harriett Harmon Dexter, *What's Right with Race Relations* (New York: Harper, 1958), 11; *Presbyterian Life* 12, no. 3 (February 1, 1959): 46. A *Christianity Today* reviewer was similarly troubled by the naïveté of *What's Right with Race Relations*: "Mrs. Dexter's book speaks the language of a sizeable segment of our intellectual world which is convinced that it is best to emphasize the positive and to assume that things are not so bad in the long run; that our culture is endowed with an immanent predilection for better ways and in spite of occasional distractions and disturbances, e.g. our current racial stresses, the general progress is good basis for optimism." Tunis Romein, "Books in Review: In Search of Proper Balance," *Christianity Today*, November 9, 1959, 38.

56. Bro to Thurman, February 6, 1958, in Howard Gotlieb Archival Research Center, Boston University; *Footprints of a Dream* order form, Thurman Collection, Boston University; "Notes on Conference at Harper," March 26, 1958, King Collection, Boston University. Similar efforts to deradicalize King persisted in the editing of his later Harper books. While working on *Stride Toward Freedom*, Mel Arnold had cut or softened King's critiques of colonialism and capitalism, supposedly to insulate his author from allegations of anti-communism by "enemies

of freedom and of liberalism" (Mel Arnold to King, May 5, 1958, King Institute, Stanford University, https://kinginstitute.stanford.edu/king -papers/documents/melvin-arnold). When it came to *Strength to Love*, he and other Harper staff again chipped away at the sharp edges of King's thought, even when it came to antinuke and antiwar sentiments Exman would have wholeheartedly endorsed. In one telling edit to King's sermon on "Love in Action," editors disposed of criticisms of the stupidity of supposedly good White moderates who just happen to believe in segregation. "There is plenty of information available if we consider it as serious a moral obligation to be intelligent as to be sincere," King wrote in these excised lines. "One day we will learn that the heart can never be totally right if the head is totally wrong." "Strength to Love" manuscript drafts, King Collection, Boston University. Thanks here to the historian Paul Harvey, who graciously provided me with six pages of his notes on King's book manuscripts in the King Collection, Boston University. See also Paul Harvey email to the author, March 10, 2022.

57. Exman, "Dreams" folder, March 24, 1965, Exman Archive.

58. Thurman letter, phoned in to deliver to Exman, handwritten by Harper secretary, undated but definitely 1965, in Thurman Collection, Boston University.

59. Bro to Exman, undated but likely November 1943, Exman Archive.

60. Exman, Africa diary, October 12–13, 1950, Exman Archive.

61. John Fischer memo to Exman, October 27, 1958; and Exman to King, October 29, 1958, both in King Archive, Boston University.

62. King, *Stride Toward Freedom*, 224.

Chapter 7: Bill Wilson, LSD, and the Book That Changed Everything

1. "Alumnus Pushes Temperance Plan," *The Denisonian*, October 3, 1933, 2; "Frank Amos, a Co-Founder of Alcoholics Anonymous," *New York Times*, July 20, 1965, 33.

2. *Alcoholics Anonymous*, 4th ed., "Foreword to the Second Edition," xvii, https://www.aa.org/assets/en_US/en_bigbook_forewordsecondedition.pdf.

3. The Layman with a Notebook, *What Is the Oxford Group?* (London: Oxford University Press, 1933), 6, https://web.archive.org/web /20071015070506/http://www.stepstudy.org/downloads/what_is.pdf.

4. *Alcoholics Anonymous Comes of Age: A Brief History of A.A.* (New York: Alcoholics Anonymous World Services, 1957), 39; Robert Thomsen, *Bill W.* (New York: Harper, 1975), 188; Emmet Fox, *Power Through Constructive Thinking* (New York: Harper, 1940), 43.

5. William H. Schaberg, *Writing the Big Book: The Creation of A.A.* (Las Vegas: Central Recovery Press, 2019), 14–15, 58–59.

6. Schaberg, *Writing the Big Book*, 18.

7. Ruth Hock to Bill Wilson, November 10, 1955, http://www.preston group.org/aa_docs/Ruth_Hock_Recollections.pdf; *Alcoholics Anonymous Comes of Age*, 17. In *Writing the Big Book*, Schaberg calls Parkhurst "the forgotten man of early A.A. history," likely because he fell off the wagon (34). He also describes Parkhurst as "something of a Deist" (202).

8. *Alcoholics Anonymous Comes of Age*, 63.

9. *Alcoholics Anonymous*, 14.

10. *Alcoholics Anonymous Comes of Age*, 153. In narrating the story of Exman's role in the making of the Big Book, I draw largely on *Alcoholics Anonymous Comes of Age*. Because it was published by Exman, he likely agreed with, or at least signed off on, its details.

11. As the first chapters written for the Big Book, these two went through multiple versions. According to Schaberg, the version that Exman likely saw was written between May and June of 1938. That version appears in Appendix 3 of Schaberg, *Writing the Big Book*, 615–36.

12. Schaberg, *Writing the Big Book*, 617, 618, 624.

13. Schaberg, *Writing the Big Book*, 164, 624.

14. Schaberg, *Writing the Big Book*, 624. "Vital religious experiences" appears to be Wilson's paraphrase of Jung's understanding of what is needed to treat alcoholism. In a much later letter to Wilson, Jung refers to the "highest religious experience" as an antidote to the "poison" of alcohol. Carl Jung to Bill Wilson, January 30, 1961, reproduced in "The Jung-Wilson Correspondence," http://recoverytable.blogspot. com/2011/05/jung-wilson-correspondence.html.

15. Schaberg, *Writing the Big Book*, 616, 619.

16. Schaberg, *Writing the Big Book*, 627. For an analysis of how Wilson rewrote this Winchester Cathedral story over time, see Schaberg,

Writing the Big Book, 507–8. Ann Taves carefully compares competing accounts of this story in *Revelatory Events: Three Case Studies of the Emergence of New Spiritual Paths* (Princeton, NJ: Princeton University Press, 2016), 324–27.

17. Schaberg, *Writing the Big Book*, 633–35.

18. According to Exman's son-in-law, Walter Kaess, "The Exmans were taken by total surprise being invited after church on Sunday for Cape Codders" (a cranberry juice and vodka cocktail), but within a few years of their arrival on Cape Cod, "Eugene was drinking Harvey's Bristol Crème Sherry, and Sunny a glass of whiskey at cocktail hours." Email from Walter Kaess to the author, August 19, 2021.

19. Exman, "Deans in My Life," Exman Archive.

20. *Alcoholics Anonymous Comes of Age*, 154; Schaberg, *Writing the Big Book*, 292.

21. *Alcoholics Anonymous Comes of Age*, 155; Exman, "Deans in My Life," Exman Archive. As Exman was going through his papers, he wrote in a January 11, 1957, letter from Wilson (Exman Archive): "I told Bill that he should publish privately if he wanted to use the book to forward his movement."

22. Exman, "Deans in My Life," Exman Archive.

23. *Alcoholics Anonymous*, 217. Florence Rankin was the author of "A Feminine Victory," and Marie Bray wrote "An Alcoholic's Wife."

24. Schaberg, *Writing the Big Book*, 152.

25. *Alcoholics Anonymous*, 71, 71–72, 464. Wilson reported first hearing the phrase "God as I understand/understood Him" from Ebby Thacher, whose pluralism extended to "spiritual principles and rules of practice . . . common to all of the worthwhile religions and philosophies of mankind." Schaberg, *Writing the Big Book*, 122.

26. Ruth Hock to Bill Wilson, November 10, 1955, https://aainthedesert .org/wp-content/uploads/2019/01/RUTH-HOCK-LETTER-TO -BILL-WILSON-1955.pdf.

27. Schaberg, *Writing the Big Book*, 584. Schaberg makes a case for April 10, 1939, as the real "Founding Day" for AA—"The day on which the movement known as Alcoholics Anonymous *truly* came into being" (585).

28. This statement of perennialism, attributed by Bill Wilson to his friend Ebby Thacher, comes from Bill Wilson, "Original Story," https://www.aamo.info/bb/billstory/index.htm. See also Schaberg, *Writing the Big Book*, 122.

29. Percy Hutchison, "Alcoholic Experience," *New York Times*, June 25, 1939, BR10.

30. W. D. Silkworth, "A New Approach to Psychotherapy in Chronic Alcoholism," *Journal-Lancet* 59, no. 7 (July 1939): 312–14, https://silkworth.net/alcoholics-anonymous/journal-lancet-vol-46-july-1939/; "Book Review, *Alcoholics Anonymous*," *New England Journal of Medicine* 22, no. 115 (October 12, 1939), https://silkworth.net/alcoholics-anonymous/new-england-journal-of-medicine-vol-22115-october-12–1939/.

31. "Book Review," *Journal of Nervous and Mental Disease* 42, no. 3 (September 1940), https://silkworth.net/alcoholics-anonymous/journal-of-nervous-and-mental-disease-vol-423-september-1940/; "Book Review," *Journal of the American Medical Association* 113, no. 16 (October 14, 1939), https://silkworth.net/alcoholics-anonymous/journal-of-the-american-medical-association-vol-11316-october-14-1939/.

32. Harry Emerson Fosdick to A. LeRoy Chipman, March 9, 1939, quoted in Schaberg, *Writing the Big Book*, 549; Harry Emerson Fosdick book review, in *Alcoholics Anonymous Comes of Age*, 322–23.

33. Jack Alexander, "Alcoholics Anonymous," *Saturday Evening Post*, March 1, 1941, 9–11, 89–92.

34. Francis Hartigan, *Bill W.: A Biography of Alcoholics Anonymous Co-founder Bill Wilson* (New York: St. Martin's Press, 2000), 163, 185.

35. Huxley quoted in Susan Cheever, *My Name is Bill: Bill Wilson—His Life and the Creation of Alcoholics Anonymous* (New York: Simon & Schuster, 2004), 175; Miriam King, "Life at Trabuco," https://www.geraldheard.com/writings-and-recollections/2017/8/2/life-at-trabuco.

36. Bill Wilson to Mel B., July 2, 1956, reprinted in Glenn F. Chesnut, *Father Ed Dowling: Bill Wilson's Sponsor* (New York: iUniverse, 2015), 387.

37. "Twelve Suggested Points of AA Traditions," *AA Grapevine*, April 1946, https://rbee44.com/misc-literature/page-1/12-suggested-points-of-aa-traditions.

38. *Alcoholics Anonymous Comes of Age*, 221.

39. Schaberg, *Writing the Big Book*, 604.

40. *Twelve Steps and Twelve Traditions* (New York: Alcoholics Anonymous World Services, 1953), 27, 41.

41. *Twelve Steps and Twelve Traditions*, 140, 141, 147.

42. *Twelve Steps and Twelve Traditions*, 51, 118, 133.

43. Edward Dowling, "Catholic Asceticism and the Twelve Steps" (1953), https://silkworth.net/alcoholics-anonymous/01-038-catholic -asceticism-and-the-twelve-steps-by-reverend-edward-dowling-s -j-n-c-c-a-blue-book-an-anthology-brooklyn-1953/; Ernest Kurtz, *Not God: A History of Alcoholics Anonymous* (Center City, MN: Hazelden, 1991), 124. *Twelve Steps and Twelve Traditions* sold well through AA networks but not so well through Harper. In an exchange of letters in 1963, Exman told Wilson that *Twelve and Twelve* was going out of print at Harper because it was selling 250 copies a year at best, while, according to Wilson, AA World Services was selling 7,000 annually. See Exman to Bill Wilson, September 10, 1963; Bill Wilson to Exman, September 17, 1963, both in Exman Archive.

44. *Alcoholics Anonymous Comes of Age*, 110, 167.

45. *Alcoholics Anonymous Comes of Age*, 63, 153, 162. James also figured in Wilson's characterization of AA as a remedy for what James referred to as the "sick soul" type. "Truly transforming spiritual experiences are nearly always founded on calamity and collapse," Wilson wrote in a paraphrase of James (13). "Deflation at great depth is the foundation of most spiritual experiences" (68).

46. *Alcoholics Anonymous Comes of Age*, 40–41.

47. On Exman's influence on AA, here is what AA's first archivist, Nell Wing, wrote to Exman just weeks before his death in 1975: "Your particular contributions were crucial to the development and growth of the A.A. movement in its infancy. Of course, I'm thinking of your enthusiastic help and advice to Bill as a textbook for the movement was being contemplated back in 1938." Nell Wing to Exman, September 3, 1975, Exman Archive.

48. *Pass It On: The Story of Bill Wilson and How the A.A. Message Reached the World* (New York: Alcoholics Anonymous World

Services, 1984), 278; Bill Wilson to Ed Dowling, July 17, 1952, quoted in Chesnut, *Father Ed Dowling*, 339.

49. Bill Wilson to Sam Shoemaker, June 1958, quoted in *Pass It On*, 374.

50. James, *Varieties*, 387; Aldous Huxley, "A Treatise on Drugs," in *Moksha: Writings on Psychedelics and the Visionary Experience (1931–1963)*, eds. Michael Horowitz and Cynthia Palmer (New York: Stonehill, 1977), 3–5.

51. Heard to Exman, January 3, 1955, Exman Archive. Some medical researchers criticized *Doors of Perception*—one reduced its recipe to "99 percent Aldous Huxley and only one half gram mescaline" (Louis Cholden, ed., *Lysergic Acid Diethylamide and Mescaline in Experimental Psychiatry* [New York: Grune & Stratton, 1956], 67)—but it became a countercultural hit that gave the rock band the Doors their name and inspired a generation of Huxley's creative misinterpreters to "turn on, tune in, drop out," as Leary famously put it.

52. Heard to Exman, January 3, 1955, Exman Archive.

53. Bro to Exman, December 1956, Exman Archive. See also an anonymous reader's report, "Journey into Consciousness by Heard and Cohen," Exman Archive.

54. Heard to Ernest Hocking, July 1, 1947, Heard Papers, Department of Special Collections, University Research Library, University of California, Los Angeles, quoted in Steven J. Novak, "LSD before Leary: Sidney Cohen's Critique of 1950s Psychedelic Drug Research," *Isis* 88, no. 1 (March 1997): 93.

55. Dieter Hagenbach and Lucius Werthmuller, *Mystic Chemist: The Life of Albert Hofmann and His Discovery of LSD* (Santa Fe, NM: Synergetic Press, 2013).

56. Heard to Ernest Hocking, July 1, 1947, Heard Papers, Department of Special Collections, University Research Library, University of California, Los Angeles, quoted in Steven J. Novak, "LSD before Leary: Sidney Cohen's Critique of 1950s Psychedelic Drug Research," *Isis* 88, no. 1 (March 1997): 93.

57. Don Lattin, *Distilled Spirits: Getting High, Then Sober, with a Famous Writer, a Forgotten Philosopher, and a Hopeless Drunk* (Berkeley: University of California Press, 2012), 205; "Mysticism in the Lab," *TIME*, September 23, 1966, 62, quoted in Stephen Siff, "Henry Luce's

Strange Trip: Coverage of LSD in Time and Life, 1954–68," *Journalism History* 34, no. 3 (Fall 2008): 126. This intriguing chapter in American psychedelic history is the subject of *Flying Over Sunset*, a 2021 Broadway musical featuring an imaginary encounter between Huxley, Clare Boothe Luce, and Cary Grant.

58. Heard, "Bill W.'s Experiences Under L.S.D.," August 29, 1956, Basic Group LSD Experiments, Harvard University. My thanks to Maxwell Pingeon for tracking down these documents.

59. Bill Wilson to Heard, September 1956, quoted in Chesnut, *Father Ed Dowling*, 700; Don Lattin, *The Harvard Psychedelic Club: How Timothy Leary, Ram Dass, Huston Smith, and Andrew Weil Killed the Fifties and Ushered in a New Age for America* (New York: HarperOne, 2010), 67; Bill Wilson to Heard, December 4, 1956, quoted in Lattin, *Distilled Spirits*, 205. In a letter to the Trappist monk Thomas Merton, Huxley also reported that Wilson saw the spiritual effects of LSD as "identical" to the "spontaneous theophany, which changed his life as completely as St. Paul's was changed on the road to Damascus." Huxley to Thomas Merton, January 10, 1959, quoted in Ernest Kurtz, *The Collected Ernie Kurtz* (New York: Authors Choice Press, 1999), 39.

60. Bill Wilson to Sam Shoemaker, June 1958, quoted in *Pass It On*, 375; Bill Wilson to Ed Dowling, December 29, 1958; and Bill Wilson to Ed Dowling, October 26, 1959, both quoted in Lattin, *Distilled Spirits*, 207–8.

61. Heard to Exman, December 31, 1956, Exman Archive.

62. According to "The Basic Group and Early LSD Experimentation," a summary of the Basic Group LSD Experiments archive at Harvard University, there were eight founding members of this group. Laidlaw and Yoder were the medical professionals. The remaining six were Powers, Exman, Lucille Kahn, Helen Wynn, Carlton Sherwood, and Ewing Reilley. Sherwood was an attorney active in Prohibition enforcement who had been on the team of Rockefeller associates attempting to raise money for AA. He also had religious and spiritual interests, serving on the boards of the New York Theological Seminary, Wainwright House, and the American Society for Psychical Research. Ewing Reilley, who previously funded the LSD research of Cohen and Eisner, may have been a partner at McKinsey and Company. Other participants not listed in the Harvard archive included Wilson,

DuBois, David Kahn, Garma Chen-Chi Chang, and a man named Paul Martin. A journalist and Navy veteran, Martin was sponsored in AA by Powers. Although the Basic Group had no formal leadership, Powers was likely the key organizer. Two important founding documents appear to be typed on the same typewriter that produced a letter to Lucille Kahn signed by Powers. Also, given that the Basic Group was an East Coast outgrowth of the Heard/Huxley/Wilson experiments on the West Coast, and given how close Powers was to Wilson, it would make sense that Powers was the organizational man behind it. The inclusion of Sherwood and Martin, both AAs, among the founding members, also seems to point to Powers.

63. L.K. [Lucille Kahn], "Subjective Report" of June 28, 1958 experience, Exman Archive.

64. For the account that follows of Exman's first trip, see: Exman, "Subjective Report" of July 5, 1958 experience; "Objective Report," headlined "LSD Experience 7/5/58 Subject: E.E."; and a reel-to-reel audio tape of this experience, all in Exman Archive.

65. Eugene Exman, "Individual and Group Experiences," in *Proceedings of Two Conferences on Parapsychology and Pharmacology* (New York: Parapsychology Foundation, 1961), 10.

66. Exman, "Individual and Group Experiences," 11.

67. Exman, "Individual and Group Experiences," 12.

68. Lucille Kahn to Exman family, March 11, 1976, Exman Archive.

69. Exman, "Dreams" folder, December 14, 1958; Exman to Bro, December 19, 1958, both in Exman Archive.

70. Tom Powers to Exman, February 7, 1960; and Exman to Tom Powers, February 11, 1960, both in Exman Archive.

71. Bill Wilson to Ed Dowling, November 23, 1959, quoted in Chesnut, *Father Ed Dowling*, 448. The other exception was likely the LSD experience on November 8, 1958, of the Buddhist scholar Garma Chen-Chi Chang, whose trip was so bad he wrote a letter to the group explaining his reaction and apologizing. "Holy hell, this is bad," Chang says on a reel-to-reel tape of his experience, which began with laughing and ended in tears. Other members of the group try to convince him to experience the "joy," but all he reports is discomfort. "Very bad experience, very bad experience indeed," he says. "I need

help. Will you help me?" See reel-to-reel tape of Dr. Garma Chen-Chi Chang LSD experiment, November 8, 1958, and Dr. Garma Chen-Chi Chang to Lucy Kahn and Dr. Robert Laidlaw, November 1958, both in Basic Group LSD Experiments archive, Harvard University. Thanks to Maxwell Pingeon for transcribing this reel-to-reel tape.

72. Bill Wilson to Ed Dowling, November 23, 1959, quoted in Chesnut, *Father Ed Dowling*, 448. Chesnut does not seem to know that "G." here was Exman, whom Wilson referred to as Gene.

73. Eugene Exman, "Reading, Writing, and Religion," *Harper's Magazine*, May 1, 1953, 87.

74. Exman, "Individual and Group Experiences," 12.

75. Frederic Spiegelberg, *The Religion of No Religion* (Stanford, CA: J. L. Delkin, 1953). This term is also ably utilized by Jeffrey J. Kripal in *Esalen: The Religion of No Religion* (Chicago: University of Chicago Press, 2008).

76. *Alcoholics Anonymous Comes of Age*, 144.

Conclusion: Selling the Religion of Experience

1. Sree Sree Thakur Anukulchandra, "What Does Satsang Want," in *Be Ye Peaceful* 14 (September 2018): frontispiece, https://www.satsangamerica .org/sites/default/files/books/Souvenir-US_2018.pdf.

2. Exman to Judy Exman, July 30, 1961, Exman Archive.

3. Edward Groth to Exman, August 9, 1961, Exman Archive. A similar letter arrived from an English journalist who warned Exman not "to get mixed up in the affairs of such a shady character." Gerald Yorke to Exman, undated but received December 6, 1961, Exman Archive.

4. Exman to "Dear Ones," September 13, 1961, Exman Archive.

5. Bro to Exman, June 21, 1949, Exman Archive.

6. Bro to Exman, Easter Day 1958, Exman Archive.

7. Eugene Exman, *The Brothers Harper: A Unique Publishing Partnership and Its Impact upon the Cultural Life of America from 1817 to 1853* (New York: Harper, 1965), ix, ii.

8. Eugene Exman, *The House of Harper: One Hundred and Fifty Years of Publishing* (New York: Harper, 1967), ix, 302.

9. Bro to Exman, February 9, 1965, Exman Archive. Elsewhere, Bro explained her infrequent letter writing like this: "There isn't any one I write as many letters to as I do to you. The only difference is that I write to you on the ceiling at night or against the backdrop of drab houses seen vaguely outside the windows or on the nose of my car as it speeds from errand to errand. And then I can't find the right kind of stamps for that sort of letter." Bro to Exman, November 5, 1962, Exman Archive.

10. Bro to Exman, February 9, 1965, and October 21, 1967, both in Exman Archive.

11. Exman dream journal, September 2, 1968, Exman Archive.

12. Exman to Bro, May 16, 1969, Exman Archive.

13. Exman to Bro, May 16, 1969, Exman Archive.

14. Walter Kaess interview, December 5, 2019.

15. Wallace Exman interview, April 2, 2016.

16. Exman to Mrs. Miller, June 12, 1944, Exman Archive.

17. Katherine Kaess Christensen interview, July 19, 2022.

18. Judith Exman, handwritten notes for Exman eulogy; Alec Allenson to Sunny Exman, November 2, 1975, both in Exman Archive.

19. Norman Cousins to Sunny Exman, December 12, 1975; and Bro to Exman, January 8, 1946, both in Exman Archive.

20. Eugene Exman, "Researchers of the Spirit," in *Laymen Speaking* 6, no. 3 (May 1947): 45, 42.

21. Thanks here to Kathryn Lofton, personal email, May 1, 2022.

22. Thanks to Matt Hedstrom for alerting me to this commercial.

23. Gregory A. Smith, "About Three-In-Ten U.S. Adults Are Now Religiously Unaffiliated," Pew Research Center, December 14, 2021, https://www.pewresearch.org/religion/2021/12/14/about-three-in-ten-u-s-adults-are-now-religiously-unaffiliated/; Evan Stewart, Nazita Lajevardi, Roy Whitaker, and Tarah Williams, "What Does American Identity Mean? A Cultural Legacy of Pluralism and Exclusion," PRRI, July 15, 2022, https://www.prri.org/spotlight/what-does-american-identity-mean-a-cultural-legacy-of-pluralism-and-exclusion/.

24. Michael Lipka and Claire Gecewicz, "More Americans Now Say They're Spiritual but Not Religious," Pew Research Center, September 6, 2017, https://www.pewresearch.org/fact-tank/2017/09/06/more-americans-now-say-theyre-spiritual-but-not-religious/; "The New Religious Paradigm: From Judeo-Christian to Interfaith America," May 3, 2022, https://www.prri.org/spotlight/the-new-religious-paradigm-from-judeo-christian-to-interfaith-america/.

25. Bro to Exman, August 8, 1958, Exman Archive.

About the Author

STEPHEN PROTHERO is the *New York Times* bestselling author of *Religious Literacy* and *God Is Not One* and the C. Allyn and Elizabeth V. Russell Professor of Religion in America at Boston University. He has commented on religion on hundreds of National Public Radio programs, and on CNN and all the major television networks. Oprah Winfrey, Stephen Colbert, and Jon Stewart have all invited him on air to discuss his books. Prothero worked as the chief academic adviser for the critically acclaimed six-hour WGBH-TV series *God in America* and as a Senior Fellow at the Smithsonian Institution's National Museum of American History. His writing has appeared in the *New York Times*, *New York Times Magazine*, *The Wall Street Journal*, *The Washington Post*, *Newsweek*, *USA Today*, and other publications.